Gathering at the Golden Gate:
Mobilizing for War in the Philippines, 1898

Stephen D. Coats
Department of Joint and Multinational Operations
U.S. Army Command and General Staff College

The cover illustration is from *The Examiner*, 21 May 1898, 1.

Published by Books Express Publishing
Copyright © Books Express, 2012
ISBN 978-1-78039-679-8

Books Express publications are available from all good retail and online booksellers. For publishing proposals and direct ordering please contact us at: info@books-express.com

Foreword

As the US Army shifts from being a forward-deployed force to a continental United States (CONUS)-based force, it must concurrently develop new plans and methods for rapidly deploying large numbers of units to contingency areas outside CONUS. Historically, the US Army has often been challenged in trying to rapidly deploy large forces from CONUS to the theater of operations. One need only review the Army's deployments to Cuba in 1898, to France in 1917, to Saudi Arabia in 1990, or most recently to Afghanistan and Iraq since 11 September 2001 and the enormous complexities associated with such operations to see that the Army has not always met its, and the nation's, expectations.

Dr. Stephen D. Coats's study of the Army's efforts to assemble a contingency force at San Francisco for deployment to the Philippines in 1898 is an example of how the Army got it mostly right. One could argue that 1898 was a much simpler time and that the complexity associated with deploying ground forces has grown dramatically since then, and that would be correct. However, the Army of 1898 was not professionally trained to deploy and fight wars overseas. Additionally, the force that assembled at San Francisco was not a professional army. It was largely a volunteer force led by a few Regular Army generals and managed by a handful of Regular Army staff officers, none of whom had any appreciable experience in deployment operations. Yet they succeeded.

As in all facets of military art, there are timeless principles that, if applied correctly, will go a long way toward helping planners achieve success. A careful reading of Dr. Coats's work will illuminate many of those principles. We and the author hope that those principles will increase the likelihood of successful Army deployments in the future. *The Past is Prologue!*

Timothy R. Reese
Colonel, Armor
Director, Combat Studies Institute

Preface

"The Manila expedition was very thoroughly organized. It was a distance of over 7000 miles from our base, and I think that very few mistakes, if any, were made."

> Major General Francis V. Greene, USV
> 7 October 1898
> Testimony before the Dodge Commission*

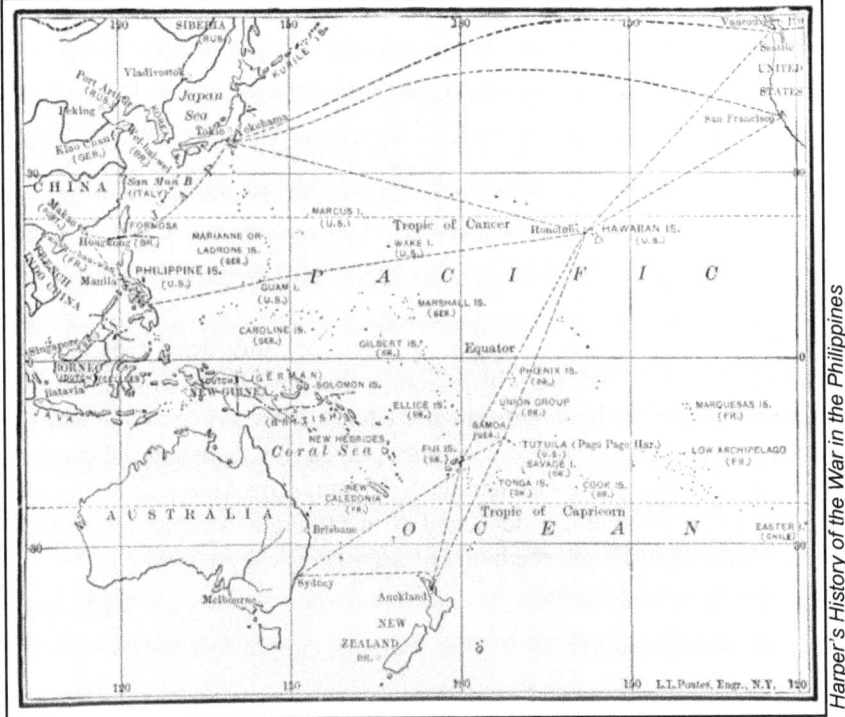

Figure 1. The New Pacific.

Today, as the US military prepares units for conflicts abroad and deploys forces overseas, it is instructive to examine how the Army coped with similar challenges in the late 19th century. This study analyzes efforts during the Spanish-American War to mobilize expeditions in San Francisco for the Army's first major overseas deployment: destination, the Philippines. Not since the Mexican War, fought a half-century earlier, had the American military attempted to prepare a large force to move to a foreign land. No prewar plans existed to provide a blueprint for this endeavor in 1898. To compound deployment challenges on the West Coast, the Army had already moved most of its Regular organizations

v

and logistics support to Southern assembly areas oriented on objectives in the Caribbean.

President William McKinley assigned two general officers, Wesley Merritt and Elwell S. Otis, to quarter, organize, train, and equip designated forces in San Francisco, the port of embarkation. Drawing on available, but limited, logistics resources from military organizations in the area, Merritt's command received thousands of Regulars and Volunteers who poured into the Golden Gate region for duty overseas. Units initially camped on military reservations but eventually spilled over into several locations in the city.

Given the paucity of medical and morale support available to the troops through the military, the San Francisco community rallied behind local relief societies and religious organizations on behalf of the expeditionary forces. Citizens donated money, food, goods, and services through the Red Cross, Young Men's Christian Association, and Catholic Truth Society. Each organization established shelters in the encampments to better assist those in uniform.

This study finds that to mobilize effectively, the Army depended on fundamentals then that are still prized to this day: leadership, initiative, and resourcefulness. It also reveals the vital role that private volunteer organizations and the civilian community played in supporting the military forces assembling at the Golden Gate. Together the American Army and San Francisco community succeeded in sustaining and deploying expeditionary forces that fought the battle of Manila in August 1898.

---

*Observations of Major General Francis V. Greene, USV, to the Commission Appointed by the President to Investigate the Conduct of the War With Spain, 7 October 1898, in US War Department, *Report of the Commission Appointed by the President to Investigate the Conduct of the War Department in the War With Spain*, volume 3, *Testimony* (Washington, DC: US Government Printing Office, 1900), 112.

Acknowledgments

A sincere thanks to those who rendered invaluable assistance in my effort to complete this book. Professor Ted Wilson, University of Kansas, guided my research and writing. He provided superb feedback on the original manuscript.

Colonel (COL) Don Olson, Department of Joint and Multinational Operations (DJMO), U.S. Army Command and General Staff College (CGSC), and COL Rick Swain, Combat Studies Institute (CSI), encouraged the project in their capacity as department directors. COL Jerry Morelock, Dr. Larry Yates, Dr. Chris Gabel, and Dr. Robert Baumann offered suggestions on how to improve the manuscript's presentation.

Lieutenant Colonel (LTC) Steven E. Clay, CSI, supervised the process that brought the book to publication. Patricia Whitten, also of CSI, applied her extensive editing skills to polish the manuscript and lay the book out.

The CGSC Research Fellows Program, established to promote research, publication, and individual professional development among the CGSC faculty, offered a sabbatical to research and write. COL Robert Mackay and Mr. Chuck Zaruba, DJMO, were very supportive in securing this opportunity.

The staff at the Combined Arms Research Library (CARL) provided research resources, gained copyright permission, and secured interlibrary loan references. Susan Fowler, Alice King, Sharon Strein, Karla Norman, and Mary Jo Nelson assisted in these endeavors.

Mary Gentry, Park Archives, Golden Gate National Recreation Area, San Francisco, California, researched maps and photographs that are included in this book.

LTC Jim McLean, US Army Military History Institute, Carlisle Barracks, Pennsylvania, helped to locate Spanish-American War veterans' surveys, letters, and diaries in the institute's archives.

The visual information specialists at the Fort Leavenworth Multimedia/Visual Information Service Center reproduced numerous pictures and newspaper sketches for this volume. Barbara Baeuchle, Robin Hall, Don Middleton, and Glenn McCary brought their considerable skills and talents to this endeavor.

Finally, a very special thanks goes to my family members for their support throughout the duration of this project.

Contents

Chapter	Page

Foreword iii
Preface v
Acknowledgments vii
Figures x

I. Introduction 1
II. Assembly 11
    Creating the Force 11
    Assigning Regular Units 13
    Assigning the State Volunteer Forces 21
    Preparing Volunteer Units: State Musters 25
    Preparing Volunteers Locally: State Camps.................. 28
    Moving to San Francisco 30
III. Getting Organized 43
    Oakland and the Bay 43
    Arrival in San Francisco 46
    The March to Campsites 50
    The City's Military Visitors: A Local Perspective 52
    Into the Camps 55
    Establishing Command and Control 67
IV. Overseeing and Training the Troops 85
    Exercising Command and Control 85
    Drill and Exercise 96
    Discipline and Diversion 108
    Supply and Medical 118
V. The Relief Societies 139
    The Red Cross 139
        Background 139
        Organization 140
        Fundraising 144
        Goods and Services 148
        Arrivals 149
        Departures 154
        In Camp 156
        Fitting Out for the Voyage 161
        Initiatives to Care for Troops Abroad 163
    Patriotic Home Helpers 166
        Organization 166
        Fundraising and Material Donations 168

Chapter	Page
VI. The Religious Organizations	179
Young Men's Christian Association	179
Background	179
Local Organization	180
In the Camps	182
Initiatives to Care for Troops Abroad	185
Fundraising	187
Christian Endeavor Society	189
Background	189
Local Organization	190
In the Camps	192
Fitting Out for the Voyage	194
Initiatives to Care for Troops Abroad	195
Fundraising	196
Goods and Services	197
The Catholic Truth Society	197
Background	197
Local Organization	198
In the Camps	199
Fitting Out for the Voyage	203
Initiatives to Care for Troops Abroad	203
Fundraising, Goods, and Services	204
VII. Deployment Considerations	217
Securing the Transports	217
Selecting the Units	228
Restructuring the Camps and Commands	236
VIII. Epilogue and Conclusions	257
About the Author	265
Glossary	267
Bibliography	269
Appendix A	279
Appendix B	281
References for Figures	283
Index	287

Figures

1. The New Pacific v
2. The Nation's Naval Hero 1
3. The Battle of Manila Bay 2
4. Naval Games at Newport, RI 4

		Page
5.	President McKinley and the War Cabinet	7
6.	MG Nelson A. Miles, USA	11
7.	MG Wesley Merritt, USA	12
8.	Geographical Military Departments, 1898	14
9.	BG Thomas M. Anderson	15
10.	Adjutant General BG Henry Clark Corbin, USA	17
11.	COL Thomas H. Barber and His Officers	25
12.	Physical Examinations for California National Guardsmen	27
13.	Trains From All Over Bearing Soldiers to California	32
14.	Nebraska's Third and Last Battalion of Volunteers Arriving at Oakland Mole	44
15.	Battalions of Kansas Volunteers Landing in San Francisco	45
16.	Ferry Building, Circa 1898	46
17.	California Red Cross Room, Ferry Building, San Francisco	48
18.	Mayor James D. Phelan	48
19.	The Vanguard of the Kansas Troops on the Way to Camp Richmond	51
20.	Iowa Volunteers Unload Their Baggage at Camp Merritt	52
21.	Sturdy Plainsmen Come to Join the Growing Army of the Pacific	53
22.	A Trio of Mascots	54
23.	Fort Mason and North San Francisco, 1896	58
24.	Presidio of San Francisco, 1897-1909	59
25.	How the Troops Are Camped on the Presidio Parade Ground	60
26.	Sunday Sightseers Overran the City of the Soldiers at the Presidio	61
27.	Fontana Warehouse, 1915	62
28.	Northwest San Francisco, 1896	64
29.	Diagram of the Camp at the Bay District	65
30.	The Brigade Hospital at Camp Richmond	66
31.	51st Iowa at Camp Merritt	67
32.	General Merriam at the Presidio Gates	69
33.	Brigadier General Elwell S. Otis	70
34.	The Commander of the Philippine Forces	71
35.	BG Thomas M. Anderson	86
36.	General Francis V. Greene	86
37.	General Charles H. King	87
38.	General MacArthur Here	87
39.	Brigadier General Marcus Miller	88
40.	Brigadier General Harrison G. Otis	88
41.	Headquarters of General Wesley Merritt	90

Page

42. Major General Wesley Merritt, USA 91
43. MG E.S. Otis in his Tent at the Camp Headquarters 93
44. Major General Otis at Work 94
45. Volunteers at the Presidio Are Being Rapidly Drilled Into
    Efficient Form 96
46. The Awkward Squad 97
47. "Close Order at the Colors" 98
48. Utah's Light Artillery Batteries at Their Daily Gun Practice 99
49. Regulars at Camp Merritt in a Skirmish Drill 100
50. Volunteers at Drill Near the Park Conservatory 101
51. Camp Merritt in Foreground; Soldiers Drilling on the
    Presidio at the Upper Right 102
52. Volunteers at Drill on the Grassy Slopes of the
    Presidio Reservation 103
53. Pennsylvania Volunteers at Rifle Practice Prepare for
    Actual Warfare 105
54. Setting Up Exercises 106
55. Calisthenic Drill for the New Recruits at Camp Merritt 106
56. Scenes of Sham Battle Fought in Oakland 107
57. The General Court-Martial in Session at Camp Merritt 110
58. Mild Punishment for Soldier Lawbreakers 111
59. Guard Mount of the Montana Volunteer Infantry—
    Inspection of Arms 112
60. An Artist's Study of Scenes and Happenings at Camp Merritt 114
61. Police Commissioners Call a Halt on Increase of Saloons
    at Camp Merritt 115
62. Writing Home 116
63. 51st Iowa Regiment Football Team 118
64. Major Oscar F. Long 119
65. Bird's-Eye View of Camp Merritt, Looking South 123
66. To Aid the Soldiers is Their Patriotic Aim 141
67. Mrs. Willard B. Harrington 142
68. Mrs. John F. Merrill 142
69. Mrs. Phoebe Hearst 143
70. Enthusiastic Collectors for the Red Cross 145
71. Minnesota Volunteers at Drill 147
72. A Soldier's Comfort Bag 149
73. Ready for Work at the Ferry Building 150
74. Dispensing Hospitality at the Ferry Building 151

	Page
75. A Cup of Coffee at Ferry Red Cross Room	152
76. Good Cheer at the Ferry Building	153
77. Flowers for the Brave	154
78. Lunching Before Sailing From the Transport Dock	155
79. "Regular" Surgeons in Charge	157
80. In the Red Cross Hospital Tent of the Third Brigade at Camp Merritt	158
81. Correct Method of Bandaging for the Red Cross Society	159
82. Mrs. Oscar Fitzallen Long	168
83. Lieutenant Colonel Louis T. Morris, USA	181
84. Will Go to Manila for the Christian Commission	186
85. Scene at the Military Mass at Camp Merritt	199
86. In the Catholic Ladies' Aid Society Tent	200
87. Mrs. Howard Teaching Spanish to Iowa Volunteers	204
88. Big Liner *City of Peking* Chartered by Government	218
89. Assistant Secretary of War Meiklejohn's Room	219
90. Loading the Mules on the *Tacoma* for the Philippines	223
91. The Second Fleet of Troopships for the Expedition to the Philippines	225
92. Fitting Up the *City of Peking* for Duty With the Manila Expedition	227
93. Loading Utah's Light Artillery Onboard the Steamer *China*	228
94. Picture Story of the Transports and Vessels on the Way to Manila	229
95. Regulars and Volunteers Marching Down Post Street	230
96. When the *Peking* Started on Her Voyage to the Philippines	231
97. Newly Uniformed Infantry in Heavy Marching Order	233
98. A Great Jam at Third Street	237
99. Volunteers on Transport *Rio de Janeiro* Leaving San Francisco for Manila	238
100. General Merritt Goes Aboard the *Newport*	239
101. MG Otis Issues His Last Order at Headquarters	240
102. Fontana Barracks Deserted by Artillerymen	241
103. Admiral Dewey and General Meritt in Admiral Dewey's Cabin on the Flagship *Olympia*	258
104. Commodore George Dewey, USN	259

Chapter I
Introduction

On 30 April 1898, Commodore George Dewey's Asiatic Squadron approached Manila Bay under cover of darkness. Steaming with "all lights masked and gun crews at the guns," Dewey's six warships slipped past Spanish shore batteries that guarded the bay's entrance. Aboard his flagship *Olympia*, the commodore ordered his small fleet to reduce speed. Dewey later wrote, "I did not wish to reach our destination before we had sufficient daylight to show us the position of the Spanish ships."[1]

Just after dawn on 1 May, the Asiatic Squadron spotted its objective. Vessels of Admiral Patricio Montojo's Spanish flotilla formed "an irregular crescent in front of Cavite." Led by the *Olympia*, Dewey's squadron eluded the shelling from Spanish gunners and bore down on Montojo's seven warships. At 0540, sailors manning *Olympia's* forward turret opened fire, and the Asiatic Squadron began the first of five passes against Montojo's command. By late afternoon, the opening engagement of the Spanish-American War had ended with a decisive victory for the United States. Dewey could write, "The order to capture or destroy the Spanish squadron had been executed to the letter. Not one of its fighting-vessels remained afloat."[2]

Figure 2.

Dewey's attack was the first engagement of a war, some three years in the making, between the United States and Spain. In February 1895, during President Grover Cleveland's second administration, Cuban rebels began a new quest for independence from Spanish rule. Rebel leaders implemented scorched-earth tactics designed to weaken Spain's resolve to maintain control over the island and its economy. Additionally, Cuban strategists worked to gain American support for their revolution. They knew the war would have some secondary impact on the United States' economy. More important, the rebels believed they could foster the growth of American moral outrage over the ongoing subjugation of Cuba to Spanish colonial rule. The revolutionaries established a junta in New

Figure 3. The battle of Manila Bay.

York City to energize US public opinion against Spain and its efforts to retain control over Cuba.³

Spain's policies toward its Caribbean colony played into the hands of revolutionaries and provided Americans with a reason to focus on the Cuban revolt. Not long after assuming command of Spanish forces in Cuba on 10 February 1896, General Valeriano Weyler y Nicolau instituted his "reconcentration" military policy. The strategy, designed to separate revolutionaries from potential bases of support, moved a half million people from their homes and villages to resettlement camps. Abysmal living conditions at these locations led to the deaths of at least 100,000 Cubans and the suffering of hundreds of thousands more.⁴

The Cleveland administration pressured Spain diplomatically to alter its policy toward the island. At times, Spain seemed willing to make concessions politically and militarily, but the government never suggested that independence was in Cuba's future. William McKinley, who assumed the American presidency in 1897, renewed diplomatic efforts to redefine the relationship between Spain and its colony. By the end of the year, a new Spanish government appeared open to reexamining its Cuban policy and solicited US help in supporting its efforts. Tensions lessened between the United States and Spain.⁵

Hopes for diplomatic solutions to the issues that focused on Cuba changed dramatically in early 1898. On 9 February, the *New York Journal* published a private letter from Enrique Dupuy de Lôme, Spanish minister to the United States, who described McKinley as "weak" and a "would-be politician." The tone of the correspondence called into question Spain's sincerity in restructuring its Cuban policy. Then on 15 February, the USS *Maine*, an American battleship sent to Cuba as a sign of US interest in the island, exploded and sank in Havana harbor. Hundreds of sailors were killed. Some in the United States suspected that Spain was behind the tragedy.[6]

About a month after the *Maine* was destroyed, Senator Redfield Proctor, a friend of the president, reported to colleagues on a fact-finding trip he had made to Cuba. Proctor graphically described the Spanish concentration camps that caused so much suffering among the island's indigenous population. The senator, who was not originally disposed to war, certainly made a case for intervention as he offered passionate descriptions of the abysmal living conditions he observed. On 21 March, four days after Proctor's oration, an American court of inquiry the president appointed to investigate the *Maine* disaster reported its findings. The board "concluded that an external mine of unknown origins had destroyed the vessel." Many Americans believed the board's findings confirmed their suspicion that Spain was to blame for the loss of 266 US naval personnel.[7]

Moved to pursue belligerent diplomacy, the McKinley administration cabled several demands to Madrid on 27 March: an armistice to end hostilities between Spanish troops and Cuban rebels who wanted independence from Spain, Cuban-Spanish negotiations to secure peace, termination of the "reconcentration" policy, and relief aid to the Cubans. On 9 April, Spain offered some concessions but did not address all of the American requirements. Two days later, McKinley, still hoping to avoid war, asked Congress for authority to intervene in the Cuban-Spanish conflict "to stop the misery and death, protect American lives and property in Cuba, curtail the damage to commerce, and end the onerous task of enforcing neutrality."[8]

McKinley's request prompted a surge of decisions and actions on both sides of the Atlantic. On Friday, 15 April, the War Department ordered Regular Army infantry, artillery, and cavalry to four Southern assembly areas oriented on the Caribbean.[9] Military depots across the United States moved ordnance and equipment to the same four locations. The following Tuesday, Congress responded to McKinley's 11 April petition with a joint resolution that exceeded the president's requests. Both houses called for Cuba's independence, Spain's immediate withdrawal from the island, and if necessary, the use of armed force to attain these goals. The Spanish government reacted by breaking diplomatic relations on 21 April. The day before Spain declared war on the United States on 23 April, American warships initiated a blockade of Cuba, an action recommended during prewar naval planning.[10] On 24 April, President McKinley approved another option in those plans. Through the Secretary of the Navy, the president ordered Commodore Dewey into his attack.[11] Twenty-four hours later, Congress passed a formal declaration of war on Spain retroactive to 21 April.

The blockade of Cuba, attack at Manila Bay, and assembly of Army forces in the South corresponded to prewar planning measures articulated by both services. In that capacity, the Navy had taken the lead in preparing for conflict. Dewey's strike was conceived years earlier through evolving naval contingency plans that assumed a war with Spain. First developed in training exercises during 1894 at the Naval War College, students designed these strategies to achieve American supremacy at sea. Subsequent planning revisions called for US Navy squadrons to destroy enemy fleets and merchant vessels "and perhaps bombard or blockade Spanish cities and colonies," wrote historians Allen R. Millett and Peter Maslowski.[12] Between 1896 and 1897, advanced plans outlined several sea operations designed to wrestle Cuba from Spanish rule. One secondary naval effort would secure Spain's Philippine capital, Manila, and gain control over commerce with the archipelago. Naval planners envisioned Manila as a bargaining chip to end the war. According to their hypothesis, once the United States freed Cuba, Spain would be more likely to end hostilities if the Americans agreed to depart Manila Bay.[13]

It was by the close study of the great naval checkerboard that George Dewey was able to blow the Spanish fleet to pieces in the harbor of Manila.

The Examiner, 5 June 1898

Figure 4. Naval games at Newport, RI.

The Navy had created these plans in a political vacuum. Writing 73 years after Dewey's victory, historian Graham Cosmas observed that the services readied for war without political guidance from President McKinley. No one in the War or Navy Departments knew of the president's ultimate goals in a conflict with Spain. Cosmas captured the dilemma of the armed services: "They were to prepare for war, but for what kind of war and for what political objective?"[14]

Devoid of input from the president, planners created their own assumptions. One key premise that both the Navy and Army embraced was that major territorial acquisitions would not be an objective. A war with Spain would be "mainly a naval conflict with little Army activity." The president seemed to accept this supposition when, after Congress dedicated $50 million on 9 March 1898 for national defense, McKinley channeled $29 million to the Navy without giving it guidance on how to spend it.[15]

Army planners, who to that point had little to show for a possible war with Spain, took $19 million apportioned to their service from the 9 March law and poured much of it into coast defense.[16] They also did not ignore the possibility that land forces could be assigned an expeditionary mission in conjunction with naval operations. Should Spain need additional incentive to sue for peace after American warships struck in the Caribbean, the Army intended to send contingents led by its Regular force to secure a Cuban beachhead and attack targets in the region.[17] As Regulars would be pulled from their posts in the United States to constitute the core of ventures into Spanish colonies, National Guardsmen could man the nation's coast defense works. Calling for methodical manpower mobilization that would gradually increase the Regular Army from 28,000 to 104,000, the War Department found a congressional sponsor in Representative John A.T. Hull. The Iowa Republican introduced a bill for an "expansible Army" to the Congress on 17 March 1898.[18]

Influenced in part by inland National Guard advocates who bitterly opposed the Hull Bill, Congress had shelved the War Department's plan to create an "expansible" Regular Army for combat operations against Spain.[19] In lieu of that proposal, a 22 April law, forged out of a compromise between the War Department and National Guard leaders, established an Army of the United States composed of two branches: the Regular Army and Volunteer Army.[20] Unlike the Hull Bill, which looked to increase the Regular contingent, the new law created a separate force dominated by state Volunteers who had served in the National Guard.[21]

Empowered by the act of 22 April, the president made two decisions that surprised the Army. First, one day after Congress gave him the authority, McKinley moved to expand the size of the Army. That initiative was expected; however, War Department officials were flabbergasted to learn that McKinley asked for 125,000 men. Politically, the call was a stroke of brilliance. Estimates placed National Guard enlisted strength at approximately that figure.[22] Essentially, the call would allow all guardsmen a chance to volunteer. State governors would not have to turn away those who wished to participate. Militarily, a call that size caught the Army unprepared. The War Department originally planned a systematic enlistment of 75,000 men for its Regular Army. On 23 April, the Army was directed to accept that number plus 50,000 more as quickly as National Guardsmen could be mustered for federal service.

As the Army arranged to deal with a massive influx of personnel, the president made a second decision that the War Department had not anticipated. In early May, McKinley decided to send Army forces to San Francisco where they would prepare for missions in the Philippines.[23] Lacking political guidance to the contrary, military officers who developed prewar plans had not envisioned the dispatch of Army expeditions against Spain's Pacific holdings. McKinley gave this course of action little to no consideration before Dewey's naval victory at Manila Bay. After all, virtually all of the Regular Army had oriented on the Caribbean, having been ordered to points in Georgia, Louisiana, Alabama, and Florida on 15 April. Those units unaffected by the directive to proceed to Southern assembly areas had remained at inland posts or garrisoned coast defenses.

As the Army positioned for an expedition to Cuba, McKinley pondered the extent to which the United States should gain control of the Philippines. Dewey's victory had opened the door to that line of thinking. However, nearly 20,000 Spanish troops, based predominately in the environs of Manila, threatened to deny American influence beyond the bay. The president therefore ordered an Army contingent to exploit Dewey's success. Still not fully cognizant of the objective he wished to pursue in the islands, McKinley nevertheless intended to establish an American presence around Manila.[24]

Beginning in May 1898, Merritt's Department of the Pacific deployed Regular and Volunteer forces to Luzon. Between May and August 1898, the Army converted from a frontier constabulary that picketed the Great Plains of North America to an expeditionary force stationed 7,000 miles west of San Francisco. By the end of August, American troops defeated the Spanish garrison at Manila and awaited McKinley's decision on the fate of the Philippines.

This study examines how the US Army mobilized expeditions for de-

Figure 5. President McKinley and the War Cabinet.

ployment to the archipelago. Much of Chapter II explores several questions related to mobilizing forces for the mission abroad. Specific questions are Why did the president designate San Francisco as the port of embarkation for the Philippine expeditions? What considerations influenced the War Department's process for specifying which units, Regular and Volunteer, would be sent to San Francisco? How did states gather and prepare their Volunteer organizations for federal duty? How did the Army transport regiments to the West Coast, and what did troops encounter on their way to California?

Chapters III and IV analyze the military experience by the Golden Gate. How did the military in the region receive the troops? What regard did San Francisco citizens have for the military, and how did they assist soldiers upon their arrival? Where and why were units quartered at several municipal locations? Who led within the Department of the Pacific, and how was command and control exercised? What did the troops experience in terms of drill, discipline, exercise, and diversion? How well did the Army sustain its organizations logistically and medically?

Chapters V and VI examine how the Golden Gate community supported Regulars and Volunteers during their stay in San Francisco. What relief societies and religious organizations emerged to care for the troops? Who led these groups, and what were their ties to the community? Who

7

contributed resource support in the form of money, goods, and services? What formal and informal connections were established between civilians and soldiers to support the military encamped about the city?

Chapter VII studies preparations for deploying units to the Philippines. How was oceanic transportation secured? What factors determined which units were selected to sail before others? As expeditions organized to move abroad, what impact did departing units have on the encampments in San Francisco? Why did the camps and commands undergo restructuring?

This study of the military's earliest preparations for missions overseas has relevance for those who seek to understand the challenges that faced America's armed forces of a bygone era. Today's service personnel routinely face deployments over vast distances, commitment to hostile environments, murky political objectives, and military operations short of war. Learning how earlier generations mobilized to meet deployment requirements for duty overseas without the benefit of recent experience and planning systems should prove enlightening to those of a subsequent age.

Notes

1. George Dewey, *Autobiography of George Dewey, Admiral of the Navy* (New York: Charles Scribner's Sons, 1913) 207-211.
2. Ibid., 212-23.
3. Kenneth E. Hendrickson, Jr., *The Spanish-American War* (Westport, CT: Greenwood Press, 2003), 17-18; David F. Trask, *The War With Spain in 1898* (New York: Macmillan Publishing Co., 1981), 1-6.
4. Hendrickson, 18; Trask, 8-9; Thomas G. Paterson, J. Garry Clifford, and Kenneth J. Hagan, *American Foreign Relations: A History Since 1895*, 4th edition (Lexington, MA: D.C. Heath and Co., 1995) 11.
5. Trask, 11-21; Paterson, et al., 11-14; Hendrickson, 18-19.
6. Paterson, et al., 14-16; Hendrickson, 20-21.
7. Trask, xii, 35-36; Paterson, et al., 16.
8. Allan R. Millett and Peter Maslowski, *For the Common Defense: A Military History of the United States of America*, (New York: The Free Press, 1984) 268-69; Paterson, et al., 16-17.
9. H.C. Corbin to Commanding General, Department East, 15 April 1898, in US War Department, *Correspondence Relating to the War With Spain and Conditions Growing Out of the Same, Including the Insurrection in the Philippine Islands and the China Relief Expedition, Between the Adjutant-General of the Army and Military Commander in the United States, Cuba, Porto Rico, China, and the Philippine Islands, From April 15, 1898 to July 30, 1902*, Volume I (Washington, DC: US Government Printing Office [GPO], 1902), hereafter cited as *Correspondence I*, 7.
10. Hendrickson, 20-23; Millett and Maslowski, 268-69; Paterson, et al., 17; Trask, 70-78.
11. Ibid., 92.
12. Millett and Maslowski, 270.
13. Trask, 75; Ronald Spector, *Admiral of the New Empire: The Life and Career of George Dewey* (Baton Rouge: Louisiana State University Press, 1974), 32-35.
14. Graham A. Cosmas, *An Army for Empire: The United States Army in the Spanish-American War* (Columbia, MO: University of Missouri Press, 1971) 74-75.
15. Trask, 78, 82; Cosmas, 73, 75, 83; Millett and Maslowski, 270-71.
16. Cosmas, 83; Millett and Maslowski, 271.
17. Ibid., 271-72.
18. Cosmas, 89-93.
19. Millett and Maslowski, 272; Cosmas, 93-102.
20. US War Department, *Annual Reports of the War Department for the Fiscal Year Ended June 30, 1898. Report of the Major-General Commanding the Army*. Annual report of the adjutant general to the major general commanding the Army (Washington, DC: GPO, 1898), 485; Trask, 151; Cosmas, 100-102.
21. Trask, 151-52.

22. Millett and Maslowski, p. 273; Trask, p. 152; Cosmas, p. 109.

23. W. McK. to the Secretary of War, 4 May 1898, in US War Department, *Correspondence Relating to the War with Spain and Conditions Growing Out of the Same, Including the Insurrection in the Philippine Islands and the China Relief Expedition, Between the Adjutant-General of the Army and Military Commander in the United States, Cuba, Porto Rico, China, and the Philippine Islands, From April 15, 1898, to July 30, 1902*, Volume II (Washington, DC: GPO, 1902), hereafter cited as *Correspondence II*), 635; Nelson A. Miles to the Honorable, the Secretary of War, 3 May 1898, in *Correspondence II*, 635.

24. Cosmas, 119-21.

Chapter II
Assembly

When President William McKinley decided to send US Army forces to Manila, senior political and military officials had to make several critical decisions. Specifically, the War Department needed to settle on the size and composition of the Philippine expedition. Secretary of War Russell A. Alger and ranking general officers collaborated to determine what Regular and Volunteer organizations should be assigned to the Pacific Command. State governors worked to meet their manpower quotas. Where troops assembled to fulfill overseas missions and how they reached their West Coast destination were two other issues that political and military officials had to resolve.

Creating the Force

Between May and August 1898, Philippine expeditionary forces, designated the VIII Corps on 21 June, consisted of troops from the Regular and Volunteer Armies. At the outset of discussions on task organization, the consensus among military officials was that Regular units would form the nucleus of US expeditions for Manila. In terms of their numbers, however, state Volunteer organizations would dominate most of the overseas contingents. Even the numbers of Volunteers would greatly surpass those of active duty troops. Deployed within multiple expeditions, Volunteers would constitute at least 75 percent of the force in the Philippines before the United States and Spain agreed to a peace protocol in August 1898.[1]

First to advocate the approximate force ratio of nearly four Volunteers to one Regular was Major General (MG) Nelson A. Miles, Commanding General of the Army. On 3 May 1898, two days after Dewey's stunning victory, Miles recommended that the United States deploy three state Volunteer infantry regiments and two batteries of heavy artillery to the Philippines, accompanied by

Figure 6. MG Nelson A. Miles, USA.

11

a smaller Regular contingent of two infantry battalions and two cavalry troops.² Miles' proposal nicely complemented Dewey's appeal for 5,000 troops, a request received in Washington on 13 May.³

By that date new considerations called into question the troop numbers Dewey proposed and the force-mix that Miles suggested. The president had named MG Wesley Merritt to command the Philippine expeditionary force.⁴ After conferring with the president about his new assignment, Merritt offered his own appraisal to McKinley on 13 May. The general argued for an Army expedition to Manila nearly three times the size that Dewey requested.⁵ The number of Spanish troops in the archipelago, estimated to be as many as 25,000; the recommended ratio of Regulars to Volunteers; and McKinley's growing interest in the Philippines influenced Merritt's assessment.⁶ The War Department, too, was preparing for a larger presence in the islands. On 13 May, the Adjutant General, Brigadier General (BG) Henry C. Corbin notified MG Henry C. Merriam—commander, Department of California and in whose jurisdiction the force would assemble—that "it is now thought that it [the expedition] will probably consist of about 12,000 men, or one army corps."⁷

Figure 7. MG Wesley Merritt, USA.

In his 13 May correspondence to the president, Merritt also expressed little confidence in the proficiency of the Volunteer force originally suggested for duty in the Philippines. He urged that the expedition consist of a much larger Regular contingent, some 44 percent of the total number, including four active duty infantry regiments. He argued that states could provide a large reserve force oriented on the Caribbean where, by virtue of proximity, objectives would be much more easily supported. Conversely, the force deploying to the Philippines, so distant from its base of operations in the United States, must be capable of handling challenges without assistance. Merritt concluded that this self-sufficiency could be achieved only if a skilled, professional force composed of Regulars formed the expedition's core.⁸

In correspondence dated 16 May, three days after Merritt expressed these views, MG Miles presented a new proposal to the Secretary of War, one that substantially revised the recommendations he had made two weeks earlier. Miles agreed that the expeditionary force should be larger than he originally anticipated to maintain "our possession and our flag on the Philippine Islands, and at the same time relieve our navy as speedily as possible." Addressing the Secretary of War, Miles calculated that, in the main, two Regular infantry regiments; two Regular cavalry squadrons; three Regular artillery batteries; and nearly 13,000 Volunteers should comprise the force.[9] Essentially, he increased the force size but maintained the ratio of Volunteers to Regulars.

When apprised of Miles' recommendation, Merritt considered the proposal unacceptable. On 17 May, Merritt responded, noting that the Regular force Miles had advocated was "a very small proportion of the 42 regular regiments in the Army." As the core of the expedition, such a force would be insufficient to accomplish the tasks of "conquering territory 7000 miles from our base, defended by a regularly trained and acclimated army of from 10,000 to 25,000 men, and inhabited by 14,000,000 of people, the majority of whom will regard us with intense hatred born of race and religion."[10]

In the end, Miles prevailed. He pointed out that, in his view, Merritt's assessment suffered from two shortcomings. First, Miles believed that Merritt overestimated the number of Spanish soldiers and Filipinos in the archipelago. Second, and more important, Miles felt that Merritt had misconstrued the mission. Miles wrote that "the force ordered at this time is not expected to carry on a war to conquer an extensive territory." Miles viewed the expedition's task as one of "establishing a strong garrison to command the harbor of Manila, and to relieve the United States fleet under Admiral Dewey with the least possible delay."[11]

Merritt lost his battle with Miles and the War Department but had little time to grumble. The challenge of assigning, preparing, and moving Army units to a port of embarkation demanded Merritt's and other military officers' attention and energy. Additionally, political officials and Army leaders sought to influence the process of shaping the expeditionary force to the Philippines.

Assigning Regular Units

Despite their disagreement over the ratio between active duty troops and state Volunteers, both of the Army's senior generals were of like minds on one issue: Regulars should constitute the nucleus of the force deploying to the archipelago. The War Department faced a tremendous challenge, however, when deciding which units should be allocated for Pacific missions.

Reaching that decision would not be easy. A month before the commencement of hostilities with Spain, the War Department exercised administration through eight geographical military departments.[12] On 15 April, BG Corbin telegraphed orders to department commanders preparing the Regular Army for war against Spain.[13] In the name of the commanding general, Corbin ordered an impressive array of units from the US Army's artillery, cavalry, and infantry regiments to several national assembly stations in the South.[14]

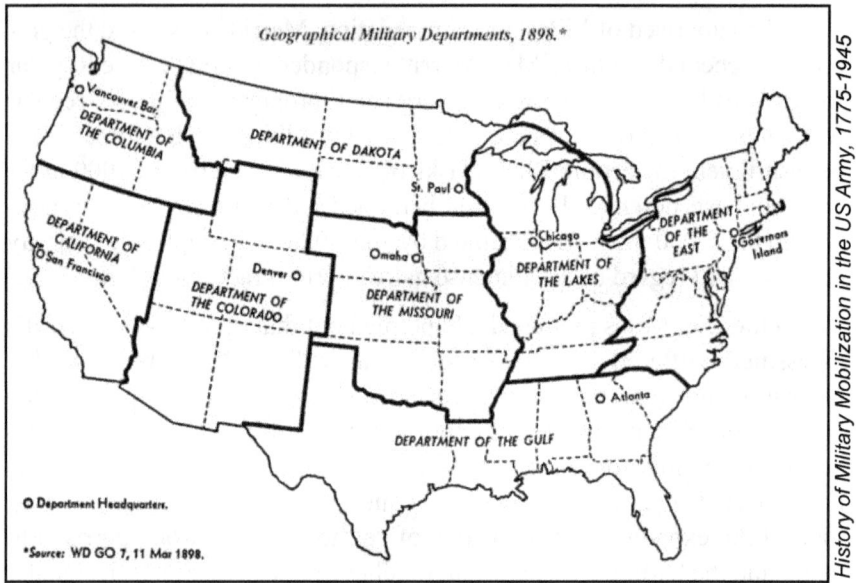

Figure 8.

Essentially, Corbin had stripped seven territorial commands of their combat organizations and had poised them for attacks into the Caribbean. The beneficiary of this directive, the Department of the Gulf—the eighth territorial command—prepared to receive 23 of the Army's 25 infantry regiments, six of 10 cavalry regiments, and the light batteries from all five artillery regiments (two more artillery regiments were organizing to bring the total to seven). Coast defense obligations and constabulary duty responsibilities pursued in other territorial departments simply precluded the Army from reassigning all infantry, cavalry, and artillery units.

The president's decision to dispatch troops to the Philippines required the War Department to reexamine its manpower allocations. Senior Army officials considered their options and elected to retain Regular forces at locations already oriented on possible deployments into the Gulf; they would not be repositioned from Southern assembly areas to West Coast sites. That decision left the War Department with the onerous task of moving Regular units away from coast defense or frontier policing and replacing them with federalized state Volunteers.

On 4 May, President McKinley designated San Francisco as the national assembly station for troops marshaling on the Pacific coast. The city by the Golden Gate at once became the potential port of embarkation for the Philippine expedition.[15] Had this announcement occurred a few weeks earlier, the 1st Infantry Regiment would have been an attractive candidate for any force deploying to the archipelago. Through the first few months of 1898, the regiment had been based at the Presidio of San Francisco performing a variety of missions in the Bay Area. By late April, however, Corbin had sent the regiment to New Orleans, Louisiana, for possible duty in the Caribbean.

Of the Regular infantry regiments subsequently ordered to San Francisco for duty in the Pacific, the War Department initially selected the 14th. Like several other regiments in the decade before the Spanish-American War, the 14th Infantry had been diced into undermanned companies and distributed piecemeal throughout several locations in the West to perform a variety of missions. With their regimental headquarters at Vancouver Barracks in Washington state, several companies took station in northern Idaho during 1892. When mining disputes in that region erupted into violence, members of the regiment served as train guards, protected property, and helped civil authorities make arrests. Between 1893 and 1898, some companies of the regiment protected lands allotted to American Indians near Tacoma and the Indian Territory, and others guarded railroad property in the Northwest during the Pullman and American Railway strike.[16]

When the United States went to war with Spain, elements of the 14th Infantry were two months into duty in Alaska. In February 1898, Colonel (COL) Thomas Anderson, the regiment's commander, and four of its companies took station in Alaska to maintain order during the Klondike gold rush. From the regiment's forward headquarters,

Figure 9. BG Thomas M. Anderson.

COL Anderson also took command of the Lynn Canal District, an area of land that both Great Britain and the United States claimed. Upon his arrival in the territory, Anderson discovered that a Canadian mounted police patrol had established itself in the region, flying a British flag. The colonel ordered the police removed. In March, a British vessel arrived with two companies of armed Canadian Mounted Police. Anderson deployed two companies of the 14th and refused to let the Canadians disembark until they agreed to vacate the disputed land. Anderson's show of force led to the withdrawal of the Canadian police.[17]

When MG Miles recommended two battalions from the 14th Regiment as the core infantry force of the first expedition to the Philippines, he must have taken into account their availability and location. Of the 25 infantry regiments that were active in the Army at the beginning of the war, the 14th and 15th were the only organizations not ordered to assembly points in the South on 15 April 1898. Of the two uncommitted regiments, the 14th Infantry was the closest to San Francisco.

By mid-May, however, the War Department was anticipating a requirement for a larger Pacific force and an attendant increase in the numbers of Regular infantry to deploy. Nevertheless, as Merritt acknowledged in a telegram on 17 May, the 14th Infantry would remain only partially available.[18] Troubles in Alaska among miners and between the United States and Britain could not be ignored. Therefore, the War Department ordered two of the 14th Regiment's eight companies to stay at Dyea and Fort Wrangel. Companies B and H remained in Alaska for the duration of the war. Companies A, C, D, E, F, and G received orders for San Francisco where they were reunited with COL Anderson after he had relinquished command of the regiment in early May.[19]

On 19 May 1898, President McKinley validated the War Department's inclination toward a beefed-up expeditionary force. The president apprised Alger of his intent "to send an army of occupation to the Philippines for the twofold purpose of completing the reduction of the Spanish power in that quarter and of giving order and security to the islands while in the possession of the United States."[20] That same day the War Department reconsidered an earlier decision and began to shift manpower resources away from a Southern assembly area. Corbin informed Merritt that two additional Regular infantry regiments, the 18th and 23d, had been ordered from New Orleans to San Francisco.[21] To provide troops for McKinley's evolving vision for the Philippines, the War Department demonstrated a willingness to reallocate manpower from the Caribbean and a desire to meet Merritt's request to assemble additional Regular infantry troops at San Francisco.

Despite being assigned the 18th and 23d, Merritt held to a conviction that he was still short one Regular infantry regiment. Apparently he viewed as a requirement, rather than a recommendation, his request for four Regular infantry regiments identified in his 13 May message to the president.[22] One of those four regiments he assumed to be the 15th, as had Miles.[23] When informed that the 15th would not be forthcoming, Merritt wrote Corbin that he expected a replacement: "Either the Fourth or the Twentieth would be satisfactory to me, or any other regiment that can better be spared."[24] The War Department did not respond to Merritt's replacement option.

Merritt was undeterred. The general revisited the size of his Regular infantry contingent when, at the end of May, Secretary Alger decided that McKinley's goals in the archipelago required a 20,000-man expeditionary force. In notifying Merritt of the decision, Corbin asked the general to "intimate the States from which you would like to have the additional force sent."[25] From San Francisco, Merritt began his telegraphed response: "the additional force should be sent from States having their troops in best order for immediate shipment." Then he revisited earlier requests for specific Regular units: "The greatest difficulty to contend with here is want of organization. The addition of the Twentieth and Fifteenth regiments of infantry would be of greatest value."[26] Both regiments, however, were in the midst of commitments to other missions. Corbin had ordered the 20th Infantry to Mobile nearly a month and a half earlier. Merritt knew this, but believing that the War Department had stopped fencing the Caribbean force when it reassigned the 18th and 23d to San Francisco, he forwarded the request.

The status of the 15th Infantry was another matter. It and the 14th Infantry were the

Figure 10. Adjutant General BG Henry Clark Corbin, USA.

17

only two infantry regiments not assigned to assembly points in the South a week before the war began.[27] Like part of the 14th Infantry, the 15th continued to perform missions closer to home. Corbin's order of 15 April to department commanders included a directive that the 15th dispatch a company "to proceed to Fort Wingate and take station at that post."[28] Territorial responsibilities in the Southwest required the 15th to maintain a presence at locations in Arizona and New Mexico.[29]

Corbin's response to Merritt's request did not address the status of the 20th Infantry. Nor did he suggest anticipating the dispatch of any other Regular infantry regiment then located in Southern assembly areas. Corbin, however, approached the 15th's assignment in different terms. The AG asked Merritt if there was "a regiment of volunteers now on Pacific coast that you think would be willing to take post of Fifteenth Infantry. . . . Secretary of War desires, far as possible, to ascertain whether this is practicable and report accordingly."[30]

Corbin's proposed solution is illuminating for several reasons. First, in declining to address the 20th Infantry, Corbin tacitly indicated that any further diminution of the Caribbean force's Regular infantry would not be forthcoming in the short term. That resource was now closed to the Philippine expedition. Second, the AG's treatment of the 15th Infantry ostensibly indicated that the War Department would consider assigning another Regular infantry regiment to the Philippine expedition, something Merritt had been pressing to achieve in the past several weeks. While giving a signal that the field commander would have some input into the composition of his command, Corbin also held Merritt responsible for finding a Volunteer unit in lieu of the 15th Infantry.

That solution never developed. On 1 June, Merritt telegraphed Corbin that he had exhausted efforts to find state substitutes for the 15th. The commander wrote, "No regiment will accept this duty voluntarily. I still think it important that one should be ordered for this service."[31] On the East Coast, War Department officials could not find a solution to their own proposal. Corbin wrote Merritt that an effort to secure a Volunteer regiment for the 15th had met with no success "on this side of the continent."[32] He made no reference to ordering any state Volunteer organization to take the 15th Infantry's place. That option was simply politically untenable to McKinley's administration. States were fighting to get their citizen soldiers mustered into the Volunteer Army for duty overseas. Ordering a Manila-bound Volunteer force to remain at home in lieu of a Regular regiment could incur the wrath of voters during an upcoming national election.

The War Department, however, did assign other Regular units to Merritt's command. Although the core of the expeditionary force was composed of Regular infantry units, that nucleus would be augmented with Regular artillery and cavalry organizations. In much the same way that it had decided to pull part of the 14th Infantry from posts in Washington state and Alaska, the War Department took resources from intranational constabulary duties and coast defense, leaving the forces assigned to the Department of the Gulf intact.

Neither leaders within the War Department nor the Philippine expedition ever advocated taking an entire regiment of Regular cavalry troops to the Philippines. Recommendations generally varied between four to eight troops out of a possible 12-troop regiment.[33] As he had done with Regular infantry, Merritt argued for the most cavalry troops. Ultimately, the War Department made Merritt and Merriam responsible for solving this problem, with the caveat that the cavalry troops would come from within Merriam's department commands.[34]

Consensus as to how much cavalry to deploy was relatively forthcoming. Merriam and Merritt agreed to allocate six troops of cavalry to the Philippine expedition.[35] Selecting the regiment that would provide these troops was essentially a foregone conclusion. Like the 14th Infantry Regiment, the 4th Cavalry Regiment had not been assigned to the Department of the Gulf by the diktat of 15 April.[36] Headquartered at Fort Walla Walla, Washington, the regiment took up station at various posts near the West Coast before the war.[37] Also like the 14th Infantry, some troops from the 4th Cavalry would continue to perform constabulary missions near home stations while others marshaled in San Francisco preparatory to going abroad.[38]

Merritt also tried to secure a special detachment of troops from another Regular cavalry regiment. In a note to the Secretary of War on 12 May 1898, Merritt requested 100 noncommissioned officers and men from the 8th Cavalry to man a battery of six Hotchkiss mountain guns pledged to his expedition. The general asked for men from this unit because they "had experience in handling and packing this peculiar weapon."[39]

The commander of the Philippine expeditionary forces got his guns but not his 8th Cavalry men. On 13 May, Corbin instructed MG John R. Brooke, commander, Provisional Army Corps, Chickamauga Park, Georgia, to ship six Hotchkiss guns to Merritt.[40] Corbin's directive, however, did not reassign cavalrymen. When soldiers were not forthcoming, Merritt queried Corbin, stating that the Secretary of War had pledged these specific troops.⁴¹ On 4 June, the expeditionary commander received some unwanted news. The assistant AG informed Merritt that due "to the reported serious condition of the frontier bordering the Sioux Indian reservations and the trouble between the Apaches and reservation Indians in Indian Territory, it is regarded as absolutely necessary to keep the Eighth Cavalry at their present stations."⁴² The response from the AG's office indicated that domestic missions still commanded a priority even when the United States engaged in war outside its borders.

No senior military official suggested deploying a complete Regular artillery regiment to the archipelago. To the contrary, the first proposal MG Miles offered to constitute the Philippine force failed to contain any reference to Regular artillery units.⁴³ Not that the function was ignored; Miles wanted two heavy artillery batteries from the California Volunteers to accompany infantry and cavalry forces sailing for Manila. What Miles' message did reflect, however, was that light artillery batteries—those most appropriate to deal with conditions in the Philippines—were unavailable. The existing light batteries—the 1st through 5th Artillery Regiments—had been concentrated at Chickamauga Park to prepare for operations in the Caribbean.⁴⁴

In subsequent messages, Miles, Merritt, and War Department officials argued repeatedly over the artillery to be designated for Philippine duty. On 13 May, Merritt requested two Regular field batteries; on 15 May, he amended the request to include an additional siege battery.⁴⁵ Miles was first to recommend specific types of field artillery when on 16 May he advocated one heavy and two light batteries from the newly organized 7th Artillery Regiment.⁴⁶ The War Department subsequently settled on a solution similar to the one involving the cavalry. On 1 June, the Secretary of War ordered MG Merriam, who commanded both the California and Columbia Departments, to provide Merritt with four batteries from the 3d Artillery Regiment.⁴⁷

Three days after communicating the secretary's decision to Merriam, Corbin offered Merritt an additional light artillery unit just formed, the Astor Battery.⁴⁸ This unique organization "was presented to the United States by Mr. John Jacob Astor, and was manned by the assignment to it of three officers of the Regular Army, and by a complement of men who were enlisted in the Regular service for a period of three years."⁴⁹ Merritt quickly accepted.⁵⁰

The Astor Battery, authorized at 98 enlisted troops, initially inducted 96 men by 1 June. Captain (CPT) F.A. Whitney, a New York recruiting officer, estimated that "at least 80 per cent of this Battery is made up of educated men, a great many of them graduates of Colleges and professional men. Some of them wealthy."[51] Using resources of the Astor estate, Lieutenant Peyton C. March, the battery commander (and later Chief of Staff, US Army, during World War I), purchased Hotchkiss mountain guns and uniforms for his men.[52] On 11 June, the Secretary of War ordered March and his troops to San Francisco.[53] Later in the month, two light batteries from the newly formed 6th Artillery Regiment joined Merritt to complete his complement of artillery forces.[54] No other Regular artillery unit would be assigned to the VIII Corps before the protocol with Spain.

Assigning the State Volunteer Forces

MG Wesley Merritt never warmed to the reality that Volunteer units, often formed from state National Guard organizations, dominated his command's force structure. As the expeditionary force evolved, the general tried to increase Regular Army strength in his organization. His effort in that regard intensified when, on 13 May, he learned the War Department had tapped the American Northwest for state Volunteers. Merritt believed those mustered from this region were "not as well drilled or disciplined as those from any State in the East or interior."[55]

The general likely formed these impressions from personal experiences. As the former commander, 5th Cavalry, and later, commander, Department of Dakota, Merritt observed militia actions in the trans-Mississippi West. He was not impressed with the National Guard's lackluster attempts to quell violence growing out of labor disputes in 1877 and the 1890s. Some militiamen and their units refused to serve; others joined strikers and contributed to the chaos.[56]

Regulars, including Merritt, had also witnessed the National Guard increase its political clout. The National Guard Association emerged in the late 19th century to lobby Congress successfully for more federal support. The Guard had also worked to kill the Hull Bill in Congress on the eve of the war with Spain. Some active duty officers viewed the Guard's growing influence as a challenge to the Army's status as the nation's primary military force.[57] Friction between the Regulars and militia or National Guard—a tension that could be traced to the Revolutionary era—had only seemed to escalate in the last quarter of the 19th century.[58]

Merritt's low opinion of Guard organizations in general, however, did not apply to all state units in particular. His recollection of the northwestern Guard contrasted sharply with his image of East Coast organizations. Pennsylvania and New York maintained two of the strongest militia programs in America.⁵⁹ The War Department organized military activities of both states in the Department of the East, a command Merritt held from April 1897 to May 1898. The general was obligated to be familiar with National Guard proficiency in his territory. As a department commander, Merritt "was responsible for training militia and volunteer forces called into federal service."⁶⁰

With Merritt's preferences in mind, several explanations account for why a state Volunteer unit received orders to report to San Francisco instead of a federal camp in the South or East. Geography influenced this consideration, particularly during May 1898 in the haste to assemble troops for Pacific duty. Merritt's misgivings notwithstanding, the closer the state was to the western port of embarkation, the more likely that its units would head for that destination. Hence, Volunteers from California, Oregon, and Washington were among the first to be assigned for duty in San Francisco. In a recommendation to the Secretary of War, MG Miles suggested that an infantry battalion from Idaho and a cavalry troop from Nevada be added to the force list as well.⁶¹ Again, proximity to the West Coast may have been a factor in making these suggestions.

Evolving national interests and military concerns combined with geographic considerations to summon additional Volunteer units as the month wore on. By the middle of May, Dewey had issued his formal request for land forces, and President McKinley's intent to establish a presence in the archipelago had begun to solidify.⁶² Miles, Merritt, and the War Department had already articulated their respective arguments, all of which advocated assembling a larger force to send to the Philippines.

Cobbling together additional units meant tapping into extra manpower, and War Department officials looked to the nation's interior for resources. In a memorandum dated 16 May, the Secretary of War assigned more Volunteer organizations to San Francisco. These units came from states deep within the trans-Mississippi West, including Kansas, Minnesota, Montana, Nebraska, Utah, Wyoming, North Dakota, and South Dakota.⁶³ All newly assigned organizations were infantry except those from Utah. That state was directed to provide the first light artillery batteries to the force gathering at the Golden Gate. Merritt needed artillery, especially light artillery, and those kinds of state Volunteer units were at a premium.

Of the states that eventually sent Volunteers to the Bay Area, all but three were located west of the Mississippi River. Geography, evolving national interests, and military needs necessitated gathering units from western states. Other factors, however, contributed to assigning forces from states east of the Mississippi.

Political influence assisted in bringing the first East Coast Volunteer unit to San Francisco. Merritt added a Pennsylvania regiment to his command because the general's need for additional troops coincided with a US congressman's personal request. On 17 May, the 10th Pennsylvania received instructions to proceed to Chickamauga Park to be integrated into the invasion force bound for Cuba.[64] That same day, Pennsylvania Congressman J.B. Showalter, US House of Representatives, sent a message to Secretary Alger. Showalter urged, "Should you decide to send any Eastern troops to Manila, I would respectfully request that the Tenth Pennsylvania Volunteers be taken. They are anxious to go." The following day, the Army's AG changed the unit's destination to San Francisco.[65] Showalter again petitioned the War Department for another Pennsylvania unit to be included in the Pacific force but this time to no avail.[66] The War Department was growing concerned that it should not give the impression of favoritism by assigning multiple units from one state to Merritt's command.

Political and domestic considerations accounted for the assignment of a regiment from another state east of the Mississippi—Tennessee. Providing Merritt with Volunteers out of a former Confederate state could gain Southern support for the McKinley administration and mend sectional wounds that had lingered from the Civil War. The president had already chosen to pursue these aims by supervising Army commissions. For example, former Confederate cavalrymen Joseph Wheeler and Fitzhugh Lee, both strong Southern Democrats, received general officer appointments.[67]

Opportunity afforded the McKinley administration another way to achieve these same goals. In late May, when Secretary Alger decided to increase the Philippine expeditionary force to 2,000 men, Corbin, as a courtesy, asked Merritt for his preferences on the states from which additional forces should be drawn to augment the expedition.[68] The general fired back a reply the same day with one request: those states that had units prepared to make the trip.[69] Merritt essentially gave the War Department carte blanche authority to make assignments, and the Secretary of War acted accordingly.

On 1 June, Alger wrote a confidential note to the governors of Iowa and three Southern states: Virginia, Kentucky, and Tennessee. He inquired of each "if it would be agreeable for a regiment from your State now awaiting assignment to be ordered to report to General Merritt, San Francisco, for duty with expedition to the Philippines."[70] Iowa responded favorably and sent the 51st.[71] Of the three former Confederate states solicited, Tennessee subsequently dispatched an infantry regiment to California.

Administration officials must have delighted in the San Francisco reception accorded Tennessee Volunteers. Surely President McKinley became aware of the enthusiastic coverage the city's print media accorded Southern Volunteers. "Cheered for the 'Boys in Gray'" proclaimed *The Examiner* when the regiment arrived in mid-June.[72] The *San Francisco Call* quoted COL William C. Smith, commander, 1st Tennessee, and a former captain in the Confederacy: "I know now that there is no longer any North, or South, or East, or West. The reception accorded my regiment at every point amply demonstrates that sectional lines are forever obliterated."[73] The colonel proved to be the darling of locals with ties to the Civil War. Local newspapers noted his presence at activities featuring veterans from that war.[74]

Finally, general officer preference brought another Volunteer regiment to San Francisco from a state east of the Mississippi. Although Alger and Corbin did not honor all of Merritt's appeals, the War Department solicited and attempted to act upon many of his manpower requests. One of Merritt's petitions involved a unit from New York. By the middle of June, Merritt had calculated that even with the inclusion of regiments from Pennsylvania, Iowa, and Tennessee, his command warranted additional units to reach the 20,000 men Alger had promised. For the first time, Merritt requested specific Volunteer organizations: the 1st Maine and the 9th New York.[75] Both units hailed from states associated with the general's former command, the Department of the East. These regiments, however, had already been committed to Southern assembly areas. Just as it had done with Regular forces, the War Department was not about to reposition these units when other state forces remained unassigned in state camps.

With both units unavailable, Merritt was not about to leave the choice of regiments to the War Department as he had done on 29 May. That decision inspired the McKinley administration to send the 1st Tennessee, a regiment that Merritt deemed unsuitable for duty overseas. In a 20 June message to Corbin, Merritt faulted Tennessee troops, describing them as "unlikely to be fit for some time to become a part in this expedition."[76] In the same correspondence, he asked the AG to send the 1st New York. Corbin had informed Merritt of the regiment's availability in a telegram transmitted on 19 June.[77]

On 28 June, the AG's office assigned the 1st New York to Merritt's command.[78] Before the regiment departed for the West Coast in July, a newspaper correspondent asked COL Thomas H. Barber an obvious question: Why would the government assign his command to San Francisco and incur the cost of a cross-country move? Barber's answer focused on Merritt. He explained that Merritt, while commanding the Department of the East, "inspected the regiment, saw it drill," and decided to ask that it be assigned to the expeditionary force.[79]

COLONEL THOMAS H. BARBER and His Officers Greeted on Their Arrival at Oakland by Captain Putnam B. Strong.

San Francisco Call, 14 July 1898

Figure 11.

Preparing Volunteer Units: State Musters

To challenge Spain's hold on islands in the Caribbean or the Pacific, the United States needed more troops than the Regular Army could supply. The president, through the War Department, directed state and territorial governments to furnish manpower in the form of Volunteer units that would be mustered into federal service. How these units were assembled and prepared for movement to national camps hinged upon decisions left to governing authorities at the state or territorial level.

Within days of the 23 April 1898 presidential call for 125,000 men, governors moved quickly to meet their allotted manpower quotas. In most instances, the National Guard apparatus worked to concentrate militia units at various state assembly points. These staging areas became the locus for mustering activities that included recruiting, equipping, and organizing Volunteer forces. Often using existing militia as a foundation, numerous states reshaped their National Guard organizations into the specific type and number of units the War Department required. These tasks could be quite challenging.

Oregon, for example, received an allocation of one infantry regiment.[80] Governor William P. Lord immediately confronted a dilemma: how to take the state's Guard (consisting of two regiments, an additional battalion, and three separate companies) and meet the smaller requirement from Washington. One option Lord explored was to increase Oregon's allocation with an offer of one additional light battery.[81] BG Corbin, the Army's AG, immediately rejected that proposal.[82] The governor then decided to assemble the Guard in Portland and consolidate it into one regiment.[83]

Across the Rocky Mountains, Iowa officials faced a similar problem. When the president issued his first call for Volunteers, the state's four National Guard infantry regiments converged on Camp McKinley at the State Fair Grounds in Des Moines. The problem for state officials was that the Secretary of War had levied Iowa for three infantry regiments and two light batteries.[84] Private John Snure, one of Iowa's Volunteers, wrote that "there was much talk of consolidation—much dissatisfaction at the prospect of four regiments merging into three. Such a step would have thrown out many officers of the guard." Governor L.M. Shaw telegraphed Iowa's influential Republican senator in Washington, W.B. Allison, for help in mustering four regiments, explaining, "Any other course now would create such a ruction as we nor you have ever known in Iowa. For God's sake see Sec'y of War at once. . . . You cannot imagine excitement here and in the State." Alger approved the request, and on 30 April, BG Corbin sent the good news to the governor. Senatorial leverage paid dividends.[85]

Elsewhere in the Midwest, another state chief executive chose to gather Volunteers in a manner considerably different from his peers. Governor John W. Leedy distrusted the Republican-dominated National Guard in his state of Kansas. A Populist serving a two-year term when the war began, Leedy opted to mobilize without using the existing Guard organization. To achieve the state's Volunteer quota, the governor determined to form regiments from the state's citizenry at large.[86] Leedy's decision prompted Kansas AG L.E. Walker to seek justice from sources outside the state. As the senior National Guard officer in the state, Walker appealed directly to President McKinley. Claiming guardsmen "ready to answer the call," Walker wrote that "apparently an effort is being made to run politics into this matter by ignoring them and calling for entirely new volunteers."[87]

Walker's petition elicited a response from the Secretary of War. In a telegram to Leedy, Alger wrote "to express the earnest wish that the National Guard of your State, as is done in all other States, shall be first recognized and organized; this because they are drilled, officered and armed, and will be soon ready for active service."[88] Leedy exercised his prerogative as the state's chief executive and refused to change his mobilization plan. Although some Kansas militiamen eventually became Volunteers, Leedy did not allow the Guard to shape muster activity.

Those states that chose to create Volunteer organizations from existing National Guard units faced an additional challenge: manpower shortages. The War Department calculated that, on the average, state Volunteer companies included among their numbers only 30 National Guardsmen or 50 percent of the manpower assigned to the original Guard company. In his annual report for 1899, BG Corbin observed that militia companies usually carried a maximum strength of 60 men. Among those seeking federal service, about 25 percent failed to pass physical examinations before muster.

Figure 12. Physical examinations for California National Guardsmen.

Another 25 percent declined to volunteer or were rejected upon physical examination after muster. Corbin calculated that each Volunteer company required a minimum of 77 troops for induction into federal service, "in many instances about 47 recruits, mostly untrained and without uniform or equipment, were hastily obtained and physically examined."[89] This revelation suggested that even the most proficiently drilled and thoroughly equipped National Guard companies likely absorbed untrained men into their ranks on the way to becoming state Volunteer organizations.

Preparing Volunteers Locally: State Camps

Units tagged for San Francisco mustered, drilled, and to varying degrees equipped in their local camps before boarding trains bound for the Golden Gate. The time each unit spent in its respective state or territory varied. Gaining sufficient manpower to admit the unit into federal service constituted the principal local task. Equipping and drilling began in state camps and continued more vigorously on the West Coast.

The 10th Pennsylvania Infantry concentrated at Pittsburgh and Greensburg before traveling to Mount Gretna, Pennsylvania, on 28 April 1898. For the next two weeks, the organization, along with other Pennsylvania regiments, worked to increase manpower in each company from 60 to 75 men.[90] One of the men, Private William S. Christner, wrote his sister: "There is (sic) over ten thousand eight hundred soldier boys here and we are eating hard tack and drinking black coffee. . . . To day (sic) we enter in to (sic) the United States service providing we can pass the examination. There is (sic) a great many of the boys leaving the ranks for home but as I write there are thousands going cheering past me who have mustered in."[91]

On 13 May, Governor Daniel H. Hastings informed the Secretary of War that the 10th Pennsylvania Regiment, commanded by COL Alexander L. Hawkins, had been mustered into the Volunteer Army. Hawkins' organization consisted of 36 officers and 604 enlisted men spread over eight companies.[92] Although the regiment had not finished equipping, Hawkins reported the 10th en route to San Francisco by 19 May.[93]

Tennessee Volunteers, representing the only Southern state assigned to Merritt for duty in the Pacific, began their assembly into three regiments on 24 April. The state tried to use guardsmen to man Volunteer organizations, but that practice proved difficult. Governor Robert L. Taylor wrote of the medical standards that each prospective serviceman had to meet: "The examination which is being held is more rigid than was expected for our national guards and is materially reducing the number of men in the regiments."[94] Camping at Cherokee Park, 8 miles outside of Nashville, those forming the 1st Tennessee Infantry would not complete their muster into federal service until 26 May. The unit remained in-state another two weeks conducting various drills before boarding trains for San Francisco.[95]

Iowa engaged in a muster that BG Corbin described as "much behind that of other States."[96] Volunteers spent more than a month in their state camp at Des Moines. Private John Snure wrote of the duty routine: "Battalion drills each morning with the afternoons reserved for regimental drills. Training also included numerous marches, skirmish drills and outpost duty." The 3d Regiment, renamed the 51st Iowa at the governor's request to "save existing numbers sacred to Old soldiers," took shelter in old horse barns on the fairgrounds. Cold and rainy weather diminished the comfort of most, but visitors and Sunday excursions into town helped to brighten the troops' spirits.[97] The Volunteer infantry regiment departed for San Francisco on 5 June 1898.[98]

North Dakota's Volunteers assembled at Camp Briggs in Fargo on 2 May where they remained for the better part of the month. Not having had a National Guard encampment in nearly five years, the men drilled in squad and platoon movements, then company and battalion skirmish drills. In summarizing his comrades' logistics readiness, First Sergeant Phil H. Shortt observed that "they were poorly equipped in all military supplies. Arms in sufficient numbers were unobtainable, many men were ununiformed." Nevertheless, they used available resources to conduct the best training possible.[99]

Two factors determined how quickly a unit could leave its home station. The first consideration dealt with getting organized—the time needed to assemble minimum numbers of personnel who met the physical requirements for muster. That process could take days or weeks. Some organizations moved to San Francisco with decidedly fewer troops than others. When the War Department subsequently increased the personnel strength of each Volunteer company, units already in San Francisco dispatched recruiting parties to fetch additional men, some from their home states.

The second factor that affected the timing of an organization's departure from state camps was equipment status. Corbin encouraged each unit to equip itself with the requisite arms, ammunition, clothing, and tentage before moving toward the West Coast. The AG could waive that practice if an organization's stay in its home state threatened to delay departures from San Francisco for the Philippines. In that case, Corbin encouraged immediate deployment to the Golden Gate. Once there, Benicia Arsenal would provide arms, ammunition, and tentage to those Volunteer organizations with shortages.[100]

Moving to San Francisco

Nearly a week before the United States declared war on Spain, War Department officials ordered most of the Regular Army to four assembly points in the South: Chickamauga Park, Georgia; New Orleans, Louisiana; Mobile, Alabama; and Tampa, Florida.[101] There the Army organized commands, received Volunteer forces, and readied seaborne assaults against Cuba and later Puerto Rico.

Tampa, augmented by the other three staging areas, offered ready access to the Gulf of Mexico. In geographic terms, each area presented deployment advantages as long as the McKinley administration focused on Caribbean objectives. Once the president's priorities expanded to include goals in the Pacific, however, the Army needed a western assembly point where forces could be gathered preparatory to movement overseas. Securing a Pacific Coast port for this undertaking became essential if forces were to reach the Philippines in a timely manner.

Boosters from Oregon seized the opportunity to nominate Portland for such a role. On 5 May, H.R. Lewis, secretary of the city's Chamber of Commerce, sent a telegram addressed to Oregon's senator in Washington, George W. McBride. Lewis asked McBride, the Chairman, Committee on Coast Defenses, to "Suggest to the war department the advisability of out fitting and starting one or more Philippine transports from Portland sailing distance same, markets equal to San Francisco, north-western troops easily concentrated at Portland."[102] The following day, McBride attached the telegram to a personal letter to Alger, closing with the sentiment "I trust you will favorably consider Portland as a point of departure for Northwestern troops."[103]

By 5 May, however, arguments favoring Portland were moot. The preceding day, McKinley verified with the Secretary of War that troops "should be assembled at San Francisco, Cal., for such service as may be ordered hereafter."[104] Several factors account for San Francisco's selection as the port of embarkation for troops deploying into the Pacific.

By 1898, San Francisco was the premier city on the West Coast, boasting a population of more than 330,000. It possessed first-rate municipal utilities as well as telephone and telegraph service. As a terminus on the transcontinental railroad, the community offered ready access to Regular and Volunteer forces traveling west for rendezvous. The location featured one of the country's best ports; transportation overseas could be secured through oceanic steamship companies that maintained headquarters or offices in the city.[105]

San Francisco also sported one of only six Army general depots in the United States over which the quartermaster-general had direct control. Depending on available stocks, the military could use this facility and its organization to outfit both Regular and Volunteer forces converging on the West Coast. Additionally, since the 1870s the Subsistence Department maintained a purchasing depot in the city. Through this facility, the commissary acquired fresh beef, flour, and other commodities largely through local sources. Subsistence officers could secure forage, lumber, and other products to establish Bay Area campsites.[106]

San Francisco offered one other feature no community could claim on the West Coast: an entire infantry regiment. CPT Frank de L. Carrington, a Regular Army officer attached to duty with the California National Guard, submitted a very strong evaluation on the state's 1st Infantry Regiment. In his "Statement of the Condition of the National Guard of California in 1897," Carrington noted that the regiment, organized into three battalions composed of four companies each, maintained its headquarters in the city. The organization paralleled that of the Regular infantry in other important ways; its uniforms and equipment generally replicated that of active duty forces.

Carrington rated as "excellent" the National Guard's personnel and discipline. He observed that the 1st California's central location gave it "great advantage" in drill over other state regiments. He emphasized the progress he observed during encampments, writing, "They were all much better than I have ever seen before in the California National Guard."[107] San Francisco therefore offered transport, supply, and manpower resources that the War Department could easily tap.

The task of moving troops, animals, and freight to San Francisco belonged to the Quartermaster Department. Beginning with the order to reposition Regulars in April 1898, chief quartermasters of geographical departments worked with railroad companies to arrange transportation.[108] When apprised by the AG of destinations for Volunteer units, department quartermasters advertised for and contracted with the rail carriers who generally offered the lowest bids.[109] Total costs to the government depended on several variables, including the magnitude of the shipping order, the distance to be traveled, and the railroad companies involved. Several of the more expensive Volunteer rail movements to San Francisco involved the 1st Tennessee for $20,454.90, the 51st Iowa for $15,981.81, and the 1st Nebraska for $15,808.80.[110]

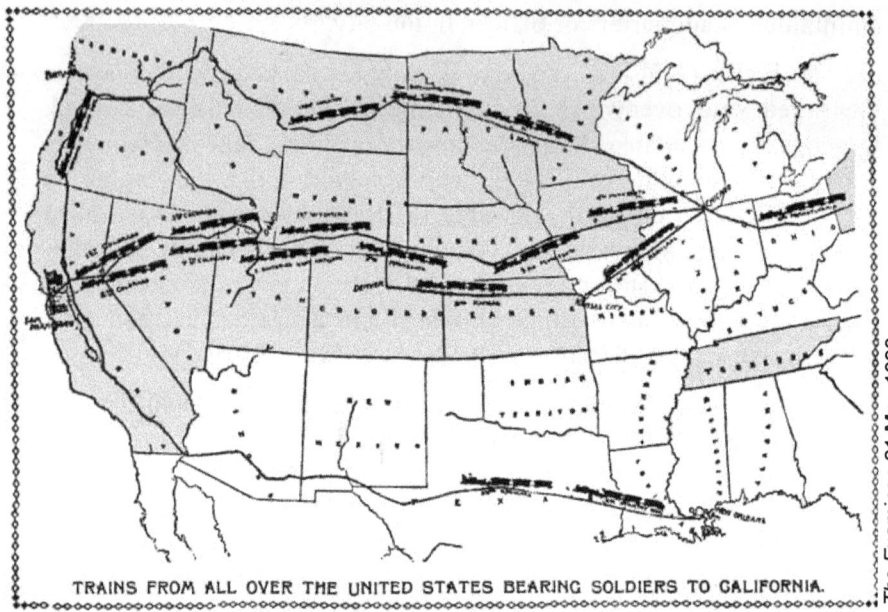

TRAINS FROM ALL OVER THE UNITED STATES BEARING SOLDIERS TO CALIFORNIA.

Figure 13. States shaded, including New York and Pennsylvania, sent Volunteers to San Francisco.

As the troops relocated from state or territorial encampments to rendezvous with expeditionary forces staging out of the Bay Area, virtually all experienced an outpouring of support from local citizens. Most Volunteer organizations broke camp and paraded to train depots surrounded by cheering crowds. Private Madison U. Stoneman of the 1st Wyoming wrote, "We were marched down through thronged streets, amidst men and women, some joyous, others weeping. . . . Here and there squads of citizens fired salutes from double barrelled shot guns." Reaching the depot platform, Stoneman and his comrades were presented with "pies, cakes, fruits and other articles of food; musical instruments, testaments and mementoes."[111]

As they moved through the state of origin, troop trains occasionally stopped in the larger towns or cities where their passengers were treated to foods and speeches of all types. Men of the 51st Iowa, who experienced a 2,200-mile rail journey to San Francisco, remembered the special treatment accorded them during their trip through the state. Private John Snure wrote of traveling through Iowa's towns, "Flowers fairly strewed their path, and the proverbial hunger of the soldier was never forgotten or allowed to go unsatisfied." Citizens at Council Bluffs and Red Oak fed the men.[112] The celebrations did not stop when crossing state boundaries but frequently continued along the routes to California.

For numerous young men, the trip to state assembly camps was their first journey, and adventure, away from home. Revelations followed as newly mustered Volunteers formed into units and then loaded onto trains that made their way across hundreds, even thousands, of miles to the West Coast. Their odyssey, however, was just beginning. The San Francisco community waited, preparing to host the military guests about to converge on the city.

Notes

1. John K. Mahon, *History of the Militia and the National Guard* (New York: Macmillan Publishing Co., 1983), 131-32; US War Department, *Annual Reports of the War Department for the Fiscal Year Ended June 30, 1898. Report of the Secretary of War. Miscellaneous Reports*. Report of the Adjutant-General to the Secretary of War (Washington, DC: US Government Printing Office [GPO], 1898), 268-69.

2. Nelson A. Miles to The Honorable, the Secretary of War, 3 May 1898, in US War Department, *Correspondence Relating to the War with Spain and Conditions Growing Out of the Same, Including the Insurrection in the Philippine Islands and the China Relief Expedition, Between the Adjutant-General of the Army and Military Commander in the United States, Cuba, Porto Rico, China, and the Philippine Islands, From April 15, 1898, to July 30, 1902*, Volume II (Washington, DC: GPO, 1902), hereafter cited as *Correspondence II*), 635.

3. David F. Trask, *The War With Spain in 1898* (New York: Macmillan Publishing Co., 1981), 382-83.

4. H.C. Corbin to MG Wesley Merritt, 12 May 1898, in *Correspondence II*, 637.

5. W. Merritt to His Excellency William McKinley, 13 May 1898, in *Correspondence II*, 643-44.

6. W. Merritt, Respectfully Returned to the Adjutant-General of the Army, 17 May 1898, in US Senate, *Report of the Commission Appointed by the President to Investigate the Conduct of the War Department in the War With Spain*, volume II, *Appendixes* (Washington, DC: GPO, 1900), hereafter cited as *Report II*, 1204.

7. H.C. Corbin to General Merriam, 13 May 1898, in *Correspondence II*, 639; Trask, 383.

8. Merritt to McKinley, 13 May 1898, in *Correspondence II*, 643-44.

9. Miles to the Secretary of War, 16 May 1898, in *Report II*, 1203-1204.

10. Merritt to the Adjutant-General of the Army, 17 May 1898, in *Report II*, 1204.

11. Miles to the Secretary of War, 18 May 1898, in *Report II*, 1204-1205.

12. Marvin A. Kreidberg and Merton G. Henry, *History of Military Mobilization in the United States Army, 1775-1945*, Department of the Army (DA) Pamphlet No. 20-212 (Washington, DC: DA, November 1955), 150-51; US War Department, *Annual Reports of the War Department for the Fiscal Year Ended June 30, 1898*, Report of the Major-General Commanding the Army, Annual Report of the Adjutant-General to the Major-General Commanding the Army (Washington, DC: GPO, 1898) 495-96.

13. Exchange between COL Charles Denby and Corbin during the latter's testimony before the Commission Appointed by the President to Investigate the Conduct of the War with Spain, 22 December 1898, in *Report of the Commission Appointed by the President to Investigate the Conduct of the War Department in the War With Spain*, Volume VII, testimony (Washington, DC: GPO, 1900), hereafter cited as *Report VII*, 3280-83. Through his questions, Denby attempted

to elicit from Corbin why the Regular Army was ordered to assembly points more than a week before the United States declared war. Corbin repeatedly parried the questions, observing at one point, "It is only fair to the Adjutant-General to add that a great many things are often said to him that would be a question of propriety for him to testify before this commission." The committee deferred to BG Corbin's judgment.

14. H.C. Corbin to Commanding General, Department East, 15 April 1898, in US War Department, *Correspondence Relating to the War With Spain and Conditions Growing Out of the Same, Including the Insurrection in the Philippine Islands and the China Relief Expedition, Between the Adjutant-General of the Army and Military Commander in the United States, Cuba, Porto Rico, China, and the Philippine Islands, From April 15, 1898 to July 30, 1902*, Volume I (Washington, DC: GPO, 1902), hereafter cited as *Correspondence I*, 7.

15. W. McK. to the Secretary of War, 4 May 1898, in *Correspondence II*, 635.

16. Captain L.S. Sorley, *History of the Fourteenth United States Infantry* (Chicago: Privately printed, 1909) 7-8.

17. Ibid., 9-10.

18. W. Merritt, Respectively Returned to the Adjutant-General of the Army, 17 May 1898, in *Correspondence II*, 648.

19. Sorley, 11, 25.

20. William McKinley to the Secretary of War, 19 May 1898, in *Correspondence II*, 676.

21. H.C. Corbin to General Merritt, 19 May 1898—11:45 p.m., in *Correspondence II*, 662.

22. Merritt to McKinley, 13 May 1898, in *Correspondence II*, 643-44.

23. Miles to the Secretary of War, 16 May 1898, in *Correspondence II*, 647-48; Merritt to Corbin, 17 May 1898, in *Correspondence II*, 648.

24. Merritt to the Adjutant-General of the Army, 21 May 1898, in *Correspondence II*, 666.

25. Corbin to Merritt, 29 May 1898, in *Correspondence II*, 680.

26. Merritt to the Adjutant-General of the Army, 29 May 1898, in *Correspondence II*, 680.

27. The telegram dated 15 April 1898 from Corbin to territorial department commanders ordering infantry regiments to assembly areas in the South omitted reference to the 25th Infantry. See Corbin to the Commanding General, Department East, 15 April 1898, in *Correspondence I*, 7. One reason for the omission may have been that units of the 25th received orders to converge on Chickamauga as early as 10 April. See Captain John H. Nankivell, *The History of the Twenty-Fifth Regiment, United States Infantry, 1869-1926* (Fort Collins, CO: The Old Army Press, 1972), 65-67.

28. Corbin to Commanding General, Department East, 15 April 1898, in *Correspondence I*, 7.

29. Corbin to Merritt, 30 May 1898—Midnight, in *Correspondence II*, 682.

30. Ibid.

31. Merritt to the Adjutant-General of the Army, 1 June 1898 (Received 5:46 p.m.), in *Correspondence II*, 684.

32. Corbin to Merritt, 3 June 1898, in *Correspondence II*, 687.

33. Miles to the Secretary of War, 3 May 1898, in *Correspondence II*, 635; Merritt to McKinley, 13 May 1898, in *Correspondence II*, 643-44; Miles to the Secretary of War, 16 May 1898, in *Correspondence II*, 647-48; Merritt to the Adjutant-General of the Army, 17 May 1898, in *Correspondence II*, 648.

34. Corbin to Merritt, 31 May 1898—12 midnight, in *Correspondence II*, 683; Corbin to Merriam, 1 June 1898, in Correspondence II, 683-84; Corbin to Merritt, 2 June 1898, in *Correspondence II*, 685.

35. General Merriam to the Adjutant-General of the Army, 2 June 1898 (Received 4:56 p.m.), in *Correspondence II*, 685; Merritt to the Adjutant-General of the Army, 3 June 1898 (Received 3:41 p.m.), in *Correspondence II*, 688.

36. Corbin to the Commanding General, Department East, 15 April 1898, in *Correspondence I*, 7.

37. US War Department, *Annual Reports of the War Department for the Fiscal Year Ended June 30, 1897, Report of the Secretary of War. Miscellaneous Reports*, Report of the Major-General Commanding the Army (Washington, DC: GPO, 1897) 115; US War Department, *Annual Reports of the War Department for the Fiscal Year Ended June 30, 1898, Report of the Major-General Commanding the Army*, Report of MG Henry C. Merriam, Commanding the Department of the Columbia (Washington DC: GPO, 1898), 179-81.

38. US War Department, *Annual Reports of the War Department for the Fiscal Year Ended June 30, 1898, Report of the Major-General Commanding the Army*, Annual Report of the Adjutant-General to the Major-General Commanding the Army (Washington, DC: GPO, 1898), 488.

39. W. Merritt to Mr. Secretary, 12 May 1898, in *Correspondence II*, 638.

40. H.C. Corbin to MG John R. Brooke, 13 May 1898, in *Correspondence II*, 639.

41. Merritt to the Adjutant-General of the Army, 3 June 1898 (Received 7:26 p.m.), in *Correspondence II*, 688.

42. Carter to General Merritt, 4 June 1898, in *Correspondence II*, 689.

43. Miles to the Secretary of War, 3 May 1898, in *Correspondence II*, 635.

44. Corbin to the Commanding General, Department East, 15 April 1898, in *Correspondence I*, 7.

45. Merritt to McKinley, 13 May 1898, in *Correspondence II*, 643-44; Merritt to McKinley, 15 May 1898 (Received 16 May 1898), in *Correspondence II*, 645-46.

46. Miles to the Secretary of War, 16 May 1898, in *Correspondence II*, 647-48.

47. Corbin to Merriam, 1 June 1898—12:15 a.m., in *Correspondence II*, 683-84.

48. H.C. Corbin to Major General Merritt, 4 June 1898, in Record Group 94, Office of the Adjutant General Document File, Document Number 82934, Box 612: 82867-83122 (Washington, DC: National Archives).

49. H.C. Corbin to Hon. John Murray Mitchell, US House of Representatives, Peyton C. March to The Adjutant General, USA, 24 February 1899, in Record Group 94, Office of the Adjutant General Document File, attached to Document Number 286981, Box 612: 82867-83122 (Washington, DC: National Archives).

50. Merritt, Major General, Commanding., to Adjutant General, 4 June 1898, in Record Group 94, Office of the Adjutant General Document File, Document Number 126599, filed with 82934, Box 612: 82867-83122 (Washington, DC: National Archives).

51. F.A. Whitney to Adjutant General, US Army, 1 June 1898, in Record Group 94, Office of the Adjutant General Document File, Document Number 84401, filed with 82934, Box 612: 82867-83122 (Washington, DC: National Archives).

52. March to The Adjutant General, June 1898; Edward M. Coffman, *The Hilt of the Sword: The Career of Peyton C. March* (Madison: University of Wisconsin Press, 1966) 12-13; Peyton C. March to The Adjutant General, USA, 7 June 1898, in Record Group 94, Office of the Adjutant General Document File, Document Number 88160, filed with 82934, Box 612: 82867-83122 (Washington, DC: National Archives).

53. H.C. Corbin to Commanding Officer, Astor Battery, 11 June 1898, in *Correspondence II*, 698.

54. "Camp Miller," *San Francisco Call*, 29 June 1898, 5.

55. Merritt to McKinley, 13 May 1898, in *Report II*, 1199-1200.

56. Donald E. Alberts, *Brandy Station to Manila Bay: A Biography of General Wesley Merritt* (Austin, TX: Presidial Press, 1980), 247, 292, 298.

57. Peter Karsten, "Armed Progressives: The Military Reorganizes for the American Century," in *The Military in America From the Colonial Era to the Present*, Peter Karsten, ed. (New York: The Free Press, 1980) 248; Allen R. Millett and Peter Maslowski, *For the Common Defense: A Military History of the United States of America* (New York: The Free Press, 1984) 248-49.

58. Mahon, 262.

59. US War Department, Adjutant General's Office, *The Organized Militia of the United States: Statement of the Condition and Efficiency for Service of the Organized Militia From Regular Annual Reports and other Sources, Covering the Year 1897* (Washington, DC: GPO, 1898), 226-35, 257-75.

60. William G. Bell, et al., *American Military History*, (Fort McNair, DC: Center of Military History, 1989), 185.

61. General Miles to the Secretary of War, 6 May 1898, Record Group 94, Office of the Adjutant General Document File, Box 601, Documents 80846 to 81158, Document No. 80916 (Washington, DC: National Archives).

62. Graham A. Cosmas, *An Army for Empire: The United States Army in the Spanish-American War* (Columbia: University of Missouri Press, 1971), 119.

63. Memorandum of assignments of volunteers to various camps, no date, in Record Group 94, Office of the Adjutant General Document File, Document No. 80518, filed with Document No. 80916, Box 601: 80846 to 81158 (Washington, DC: National Archives).

64. *Annual Report of the Adjutant General of Pennsylvania for the Year 1898* (PA: State Printer of Pennsylvania, 1900), 232; *History of the 10th Pennsylvania Volunteer Infantry: Its Forebearers and Successors in the Spanish-American War, World War I, World War II, and the Korean Emergency*, n.p., n.d., 65.

65. J.B. Showalter to General Alger, Secretary of War, 17 May 1898 (Received 18 May 1898), in *Report II*, 1214; H.C. Corbin to COL A.S. Hawkins, 18 May 1898, in *Report II*, 1214.

66. Showalter to Alger, 19 May 1898 (Received 20 May 1898), in *Report II*, 1219.

67. Cosmas, 148-49.

68. Corbin to Merritt, 29 May 1898, in *Correspondence II*, 680.

69. Merritt to the Adjutant-General, 29 May 1898 (Received 6:15 p.m.), in *Correspondence II*, 680.

70. R.A. Alger to the Governor of Iowa (and Governors of Tennessee, Kentucky, and Virginia), 1 June 1898, in *Correspondence II*, 684.

71. COL John C. Loper to the Adjutant General, USA, 3 June 1898, in Record Group 94, Office of the Adjutant General Checklist Entry 182, Muster in War With Spain, 1st Call, Document Number 249516, Inclosure 81, filed with Iowa Documents, Box No. 2: Florida through Iowa.

72. "Cheered for the 'Boys in Gray,'" *The Examiner*, 18 June 1898, 8.

73. "Brave Battalions From Tennessee," *San Francisco Call*, 17 June 1898, 5.

74. "Local War Notes," *San Francisco Daily Report*, 11 July 1898, 3; "War Incidents," *San Francisco Call*, 26 June 1898, 7.

75. Merritt to the Adjutant-General of the Army, 13 June 1898 (Received 9:45 p.m.), in *Correspondence II*, 699.

76. Merritt to the Adjutant-General of the Army, 20 June 1898, in *Correspondence II*, 707.

77. Corbin to Merritt, 19 June 1898, in *Correspondence II*, 706.

78. Heistand to the Commanding General, Department of the East, 28 June 1898, in *Correspondence II*, 716.

79. "Colonel and Regiment," *San Francisco Daily Report*, 14 July 1898, 3.

80. "The Following Apportionment Has Been Made for the Several States, and Territories and the Dist. of Columbia" in Record Group 94, Office of the Adjutant General Document File, Document No. 84869, filed with Document No. 74259, Box 534: 74121 to 74321.

81. William P. Lord to the Secretary of War, 26 April 1898, in Record Group 94, Office of the Adjutant General Checklist Entry 182, Muster in War With Spain, 1st Call, Document Number 253366, Inclosure 6, filed with Oregon Documents, Box No. 6: Columbus, Ohio through South Carolina.

82. H.C. Corbin to Governor William P. Lord, 27 April 1898, in Record Group 94, Office of the Adjutant General Checklist Entry 182, Muster in War With Spain, 1st Call, Document Number 253366, Inclosure 6, filed with Oregon Documents, Box No. 6: Columbus, Ohio through South Carolina.

83. BG C.U. Gantenbein, *The Official Records of the Oregon Volunteers in*

the Spanish War and Philippine Insurrection, n.p., n.d., 16-18.

84. "The Following Apportionment Has Been Made For the Several States, and Territories and the Dist. of Columbia" in Record Group 94, Office of the Adjutant General Document File, Document No. 84869, filed with Document No. 74259, Box 534: 74121 to 74321.

85. Private John Snure, *Official History of the Operations of the Fifty-First Iowa Infantry, U.S.V. in the Campaign in the Philippine Islands*, n.p., n.d., 1-3; R.A. Alger, Secretary of War, to the Governor of Iowa, 30 April 1898, in Record Group 94, Office of the Adjutant General Checklist Entry 182, Muster in War With Spain, 1st Call, Document Number 249516, Inclosure 5, filed with Iowa Documents, Box No. 2: Florida through Iowa.

86. Frederick Funston, *Memories of Two Wars: Cuban and Philippine Experiences*, (New York: Charles Scribner's Sons, 1911), 150-51; Thomas W. Crouch, *A Leader of Volunteers: Frederick Funston and the 20th Kansas in the Philippines 1898-1899* (Lawrence, KS: Coronado Press, 1984), 5.

87. L.E. Walker to Hon. Wm. McKinley, 26 April 1898, in Record Group 94, Office of the Adjutant General Checklist Entry 182, Muster in War With Spain, 1st Call, Document Number 247203, Inclosure 13, filed with Kansas Documents, Box No. 3: Kansas through Massachusetts.

88. R.A. Alger to Governor John W. Leedy, 28 April 1898, in Record Group 94, Office of the Adjutant General Checklist Entry 182, Muster in War With Spain, 1st Call, Document Number 247203, Inclosure 20, filed with Kansas Documents, Box No. 3: Kansas through Massachusetts.

89. US War Department, *Annual Reports of the War Department for the Fiscal Year Ended June 30, 1899: Reports of Chiefs of Bureaus*, Report of the Adjutant General to the Secretary of War (Washington, DC: GPO, 1899), 10-11.

90. Annual *Report of the Adjutant General of Pennsylvania for the Year 1898*, 232.

91. William S. Christner, 10th Pennsylvania Infantry Regiment, to "Dear Sister," 3 May 1898 (Carlisle Barracks, PA: US Army Military History Institute).

92. Hastings, Governor of Pennsylvania, to the Secretary of War, 13 May 1898, in Record Group 94, Office of the Adjutant General Checklist Entry 182, Muster in War With Spain, Document Number A31 249946, filed with Pennsylvania Documents, Box No. 6: Columbus, Ohio through South Carolina.

93. COL Hawkins to the Adjutant General, US Army, 19 May 1898, in Record Group 94, Office of the Adjutant General Checklist Entry 182, Muster in War With Spain, Document Number A81 249946, filed with Pennsylvania Documents, Box No. 6: Columbus, Ohio through South Carolina.

94. Robert L. Taylor, Governor, to Hon John A. Moon, 9 May 1898, in Record Group 94 Office of the Adjutant General Checklist Entry 182, Muster in War With Spain, 1st Call, Document Number 261669, filed with Tennessee Documents, Box No. 7: South Dakota through Washington.

95. Allan L. McDonald, *The Historical Record of the First Tennessee Infantry, U.S.V. in the Spanish War and Filipino Insurrection*, n.p., n.d., 2-5.

96. H.C. Corbin to Captain Olmstead, Mustering Officer, 10 May 1898, in

Record Group 94, Office of the Adjutant General Checklist Entry 182, Muster in War With Spain, 1st Call, Document Number 249516, Inclosure 32, filed with Iowa Documents, Box No. 2: Florida through Iowa.

97. Snure, 2; L.M. Shaw, Governor of Iowa, to Honorable W. B. Allison, Senate, 5 May 1898, in Record Group 94, Office of the Adjutant General Checklist Entry 182, Muster in War With Spain, 1st Call, Document Number 249516, Inclosure 19, filed with Iowa Documents, Box No. 2: Florida through Iowa.

98. COL Jno. O. Leoper to the Adjutant General, US Army, 5 June 1898, in Record Group 94, Office of the Adjutant General Checklist Entry 182, Muster in War With Spain, 1st Call, Document Number 249516, Inclosure 82, filed with Iowa Documents, Box No. 2: Florida through Iowa.

99. First Sergeant Phil H. Shortt, *Official History of the Operations of the First North Dakota Infantry, U.S.V. in the Campaign in the Philippine Islands*, n.p., n.d., 1.

100. H.C. Corbin to COL James A. Smith, 14 May 1898, in *Report II*, 1196; H.C. Corbin to Commanding Officer, 14th US Infantry Battalion, 14 May 1898, in *Report II*, 1197; H.C. Corbin to COL L.S. Babbitt, Benicia Arsenal, 14 May 1898, in *Report II*, 1197; H.C. Corbin to COL Hawkins, 18 May 1898, in *Report II*, 1215.

101. Corbin to the Commanding General, Department East, 15 April 1898, in *Correspondence I*, 7.

102. H.R. Lewis to George W. McBride, 5 May 1898, in Record Group 94, Office of the Adjutant General Checklist Entry 182, Muster in War With Spain, 1st Call, Document Number 629918, Inclosure 19, filed with Oregon Documents, Box No. 6: Columbus, Ohio through South Carolina.

103. George W. McBride to Honorable Russell A. Alger, Secretary of War, 6 May 1898, in Record Group 94, Office of the Adjutant General Checklist Entry 182, Muster in War With Spain, 1st Call, Document Number 253366, Inclosure 18, filed with Oregon Documents, Box No. 6: Columbus, Ohio through South Carolina.

104. McKinley to the Secretary of War, 4 May 1898, in *Correspondence II*, 635.

105. William Doxey, *Doxey's Guide to San Francisco and the Pleasure Resorts of California* (San Francisco: Doxey Press, 1897), 17-21, 88-93.

106. Erna Risch, *Quartermaster Support of the Army: A History of the Corps, 1775-1939* (Washington, DC: Office of the Quartermaster General, 1962), 427, 457, 492.

107. US War Department, Adjutant General's Office. *The Organized Militia of the United States. Statement of the Condition and Efficiency for Service of the Organized Militia. Regular Annual Reports, and other Sources, Covering the Year 1897*, (Washington, DC: GPO, 1898) 32-39.

108. US War Department, *Annual Reports of the War Department for the Fiscal Year Ended June 30, 1898. Report of the Secretary of War. Miscellaneous Reports*. Report of the Quartermaster General of the Army (Washington, DC: GPO, 1898), 386-87.

109. Testimony of COL Charles Bird, 2 December 1898 in US Senate, *Report of the Commission Appointed by the President to Investigate the Conduct of the War Department in the War With Spain*, volume VI, *Testimony* (Washington, DC: GPO, 1900), 2608-2609, hereafter cited as *Report VI*.

110. Record Group 92, The Textual Records of the Office of the Quartermaster General. Entry 1496, Register of Transportation of Troops and Their Equipment, 1898-1900 (Washington, DC: National Archives), 110, 135, 173.

111. Madison U. Stoneman, *Official History of the Operations of the First Battalion Wyoming Infantry, U.S.V. in the Campaign in the Philippine Islands*, n.p., n.d., 3.

112. Snure, 4; Joseph I. Markey, *From Iowa to the Philippines: A History of Company M, Fifty-First Iowa Infantry Volunteers* (Red Oak, IA: Thomas D. Murphy Co., 1900), 55-56.

Chapter III
Getting Organized

Army units moved from points around the country to converge on San Francisco between May and August 1898. Their efficient reception at the port city became the next step in a process designed to organize overseas expeditions. Local military and civilian authorities contemplated the appropriate actions that should be taken to receive troops and move them to assigned campsites near the Golden Gate. A routine gradually developed that pooled resources from the San Francisco military and civilian communities.

Trains bearing forces from the east carried organizations into California as far as Oakland. Troops detrained and boarded vessels for a trip across the bay. After disembarking near the Ferry Building, soldiers received a meal or refreshments that volunteers from the state Red Cross Society served. Following Red Cross festivities, military escorts guided Regular and Volunteer organizations through the city to their designated campsites. These areas could be at any of several locations: the Presidio, Bay District Racetrack, Jordan Tract, or Fontana warehouse. Time of arrival in the city and, later, unit mission dictated assignment to a specific location on or near the Presidio.

Preparing the force for wartime missions also required suitable command and control. In early May, the War Department established a new department-level command to preside over the expeditions. Later in the month, a division command structure emerged to organize, train, and equip the units designated for overseas duty.

Oakland and the Bay

Most of the units that gathered at the Golden Gate had traveled by rail to Oakland. Train sections made their way to the city's 16th Street station, not far from the Oakland mole—a terminal where railroad passengers could connect with ferry transportation to San Francisco. Troops could use the ferry service that operated from early morning through late afternoon.[1] The Southern Pacific, a railway company that managed ferry service, agreed not to dispatch units across the bay after 1600.[2] The reason was that soldiers still had to disembark, handle equipment, march to camp, and establish their campsites. Reaching the city late, only to be transported across the bay, meant the deeper into an evening they would take to get settled.

At least one regiment, the 10th Pennsylvania, arrived to be welcomed

NEBRASKA'S THIRD AND LAST BATTALION OF VOLUNTEERS ARRIVING AT OAKLAND MOLE.

Figure 14.

by a group of citizens at the Oakland station. Remarkably, when the train pulled into the mole at 0100, "500 people, the remnants of a much larger crowd, were waiting under the electric lights to cheer and to distribute flowers." However, most of the troops were sound asleep and missed their warm reception.[3]

How quickly organizations embarked for the trip across San Francisco Bay depended principally on the time they reached the Oakland terminus. Part or all of several regiments remained overnight in Oakland because ferry operations had ceased for the day. Troops from Kansas, Pennsylvania, New York, Utah, Montana, Iowa, Tennessee, Minnesota, Wyoming, and the Astor Battery slept in railroad cars on sidetracks and awaited ferry service the next day.[4] At least one unit that stopped in Oakland established security around its train; the 1st Battalion, 13th Minnesota, posted armed guards with ammunition chambered. A reporter for the *San Francisco Call* wrote, "No one was allowed to approach nearer than twenty feet to the train until he had been admitted by a commissioned officer."[5]

When ferry service resumed, most organizations detrained, and the men walked aboard vessels like the *Piedmont*.[6] Each passenger ferry accommodated about 250 men.[7] Troops boarded and could share their 6-mile excursion across San Francisco Bay with civilian passengers.[8] Ferries were not chartered for military use; units took available vessels that made routine runs between Oakland and San Francisco.

Not all troops took passenger ferries. Exceptions included mounted units from Utah and the 4th Cavalry. These organizations arrived fully equipped with horses, saddles, and bridles. Specifically, the Utah Cavalry transported 84 Volunteers and 87 horses on six railway cars.[9] All six cars, including troops and animals, were run aboard the freight boat *Transit*, which took an hour to reach San Francisco's docks. The same procedure occurred with Troop E, 4th Cavalry.[10]

Whether conveyed by passenger or freight vessels, troops formed diverse impressions about their jaunt across the bay. Private James Camp, 1st Idaho, wrote that he and his comrades arrived in Oakland "somewhat cranky" after being cramped in crowded rail cars for three days. Camp observed, "Our trip across the bay did not improve our tempers."[11]

For others, the excursion was another segment of a revealing odyssey that began with assemblies in state camps. The *San Francisco Chronicle* suggested that bay sights must have been particularly spectacular for those coming from origins east of the Rocky Mountains. After 1st Nebraska men docked at the Ferry Building, a *Chronicle* reporter wrote, "Strangers to the far West and to deep water, hundreds of them never having seen a ship or an ocean steamer before in their lives, these newcomers marveled at what they beheld while crossing from the Oakland side." Troops strained to see "the warlike Monterey and the forest of towering masts of merchantmen and the scores of funnels of big passenger liners lying peacefully all along the extensive water-front. It was a novel experience in a new country."[12]

Figure 15.

Arrival in San Francisco

Starting on 7 May 1898, units that had formed outside of San Francisco began to close on the city. By the peace protocol of 12 August, Volunteer organizations from 18 states, Regular troops representing seven active duty units, and the special military force that John Jacob Astor funded had poured into the Bay Area. (See appendix A.) Authorities were busiest receiving troops over the last two weeks of May. During that period, men from 11 infantry regiments, two batteries of artillery, one troop of cavalry, and one company of engineers reached the Golden Gate. Military organizations arrived before and after those hectic 14 days but never at the same pace.

Reception activities for those reaching San Francisco started at the Ferry Building. In this newly constructed, spacious depot funded by California state, troops experienced a special greeting that for many created lasting memories.[13] The men were treated to a lavish spread of refreshments that had been organized, and in some cases prepared, by members of the Red Cross Society. Volunteer histories compiled after the war often regarded the Red Cross welcome as the noteworthy event of their organizations' San Francisco experience.[14]

Figure 16. Ferry Building, circa 1898.

Individual soldiers accorded this Red Cross activity with similar recognition. Private William S. Christner of the 10th Pennsylvania Infantry wrote his parents on 26 May 1898: "When we arrived at Frisco the ladies of the Red Cross Society met us and such a breakfast the boys had not eaten for some time. Then they packed our haversacks with sandwiches, oranges, and bananas. Grapes and apricots were given us in plenty."[15] Private A.G. Baker of the 1st Colorado recalled the event in his personal narrative of the war. As Colorado Volunteers disembarked near the Ferry Building on 21 May, Baker observed, "Our coming had been anticipated by the noble ladies of the Red Cross Society of California, who had provided an excellent dinner for us."[16]

Unlike Pennsylvania and Colorado Volunteers, the first troops to reach San Francisco entered the city and marched to camp on empty stomachs. On 7 May, the 7th Californians crossed the bay after a tiresome 24-hour railway journey. They believed that food awaited them at the Presidio. *The Examiner* reported that "somebody played 'Philippine' with the provisions," and the troops received "nothing at the end of the trip but sea breeze and dirt."[17] Companies of men from the 14th US Infantry and 6th California followed over the next four days and also went into camp without refreshments.

A similar experience befell troops of the 2d Oregon's first battalion who docked at the city's wharf on 13 May. Their neglect elicited criticism from two city newspapers. A *San Francisco Daily Report* article decried the apathy accorded those in uniform. Another publication, the *Call*, observed, "The men were hungry and tired from their long trip from Oregon, and they were obliged to tramp all the way to the Presidio with no one to even offer them a drink of water."[18]

Spurred by this lack of consideration and supported by the Salvation Army, the city's Red Cross Society established a suitable welcome. On 18 May, the society positioned civilian volunteers at the Ferry Building to greet incoming troops shortly after they stepped off vessels from Oakland. Fittingly, the remainder of Oregon's Volunteers were the first to enjoy this reception. Thereafter, Red Cross representatives, surrounded by tables of refreshments, awaited dockside to offer military arrivals "a practical California welcome."[19]

The dockside fiasco of 13 May also energized the mayor and other civic organizations. On 22 May, the Knights Templars conferred with Mayor James D. Phelan on "how to provide for the incoming troops that the Government seems so powerless to provide" for. The Knights asked the mayor "what had been done by the city and by himself toward properly

Figure 17. California Red Cross Room, Ferry Building, San Francisco, September 1898.

receiving the troops." The mayor highlighted several steps he had taken to furnish bands and escorts, and cited the program the Red Cross had undertaken. Phelan urged the Knights to become involved and to support the society, and they did so with alacrity.[20]

The Ferry Building provided a backdrop for some memorable scenes. One highly publicized incident involving the Red Cross Society and an Army captain occurred at the depot in June 1898. When the Astor Battery docked on 20 June, the society's welcome for troops had reached obligatory status. Red Cross volunteers and the city that supported them expected new arrivals to participate in reception activities. Allegedly, Peyton C. March, commander, Astor Battery, and recently promoted to captain of Volunteers, had not been apprised of the expectation that this ritual would be observed. In an article titled "A Discourteous Lieutenant" (the demotion itself a written jab at the Astor captain), the *Call* ac-

Figure 18. Mayor James D. Phelan.

cused March of rendering "a snub so direct and given with such studied discourtesy as to stamp the offender as totally lacking every qualification of a gentleman."

March, it seemed, had the audacity to decline the Red Cross breakfast. Pressured anew to allow his men inside the Ferry Building's dining area, the captain "did unbend enough to march his men into the room, and the ladies offered each a bunch of flowers and an orange, which were gratefully accepted." While hot food was also available to the men, a correspondent wrote that March forbade them to indulge. The Astor's commanding officer felt that the artillerymen, having had their fill of hardtack and coffee before crossing the bay, required no more food. Branding him "an obscure lieutenant of artillery, lifted into momentary conspicuousness by the favor of a millionaire," the *Call* wished the worst for March. "It is to be hoped he will be assigned to the next expedition and given every opportunity to extinguish himself on the field of battle," judged an editorial.[21]

The incident found its way into additional newspapers. Private Joseph I. Markey, 51st Iowa, wrote a state newspaper claiming the Astor Battery "refused to accept lunch proffered by the kind ladies of the Red Cross, on the ground that it was not good enough for them."[22] Other reporters described the incident in less sensational terms than those the *Call* employed. A writer for *The Examiner* quoted one Red Cross volunteer who characterized March as "high-toned" and "curt." The same reporter acknowledged that the captain, despite his perceived aloofness, relented and permitted his men to take refreshment.[23]

Unlike other newspapers, the *Daily Report* came to March's defense. In an article titled "The Ladies not Snubbed," the paper offered observations from another society volunteer, Mrs. Mark Requa. She confirmed that although March at first declined the society's hospitality, he subsequently consented. Mrs. Requa added that the captain "had no intention of acting discourteously" and expressed his appreciation to the Red Cross ladies.[24] The following day, the *Daily Report* went so far as to offer an editorial defense of March and his unit, concluding, "The Astor Battery is all right."[25]

The Ferry Building was also the scene for another incident involving a different unit, the 1st Tennessee. Portending racial incidents to come, the Tennesseans docked in San Francisco with "a prisoner . . . the colored porter" from one of the Pullman cars carrying Southerners to the Golden Gate. The *Call* alleged that troops from one company had coerced the porter to smuggle liquor aboard the train, but guards caught and confined him. Apprised by telegraph of the situation, a Pullman Company superintendent secured his employee's release when the 1st Tennessee arrived in the city.[26]

The last regiment to dock at the ferry depot before the peace protocol was also the only organization of that size to be feted at a special reception. After the 1st New York Regiment reached San Francisco on 15 July, it marched to the Mechanics' Pavilion where the New York Association of San Francisco treated the troops to a breakfast banquet. The event offered the first signs of special treatment that would be accorded New Yorkers during their stay in the city.[27]

The March to Campsites

Led by the Red Cross, the city worked to improve the welcome bestowed upon Volunteers and Regulars. Army officials, too, needed to reassess their reception activities. The 2d Oregon's arrival on 13 May highlighted shortcomings in Army plans to accept units at the Golden Gate. To the embarrassment of the military, the *Daily Report* informed readers that Oregonians "were surprised at not being met at the ferry by an army officer to guide them through the streets out to the Presidio. While the officers knew something about San Francisco, they did not know the best route to reach camp and had to inquire their way."[28]

The 2d Oregon and every Volunteer unit that followed neglected to dispatch anyone to San Francisco who could coordinate their organization's arrival. Perhaps more grievous, no one from the US Army already at the Golden Gate routinely met every force debarking in early May. Instead a "to each his own" philosophy prevailed. Members of the California National Guard tended to California units, and the 4th Cavalry sent a representative to meet companies of the 14th Infantry. That method worked well until Volunteer forces outside of California approached the bay city.[29]

Arguably, the Army should have addressed this oversight in receiving incoming Volunteers no later than 9 May. On that date, MG Henry C. Merriam, commander, Department of California, wired his adjutant general in San Francisco: "Instruct the commanding officer at the Presidio to designate one officer to aid each volunteer regimental commander in drawing and issuing arms, clothing and general outfit, and accounting for same, as these regiments arrive and go into camp, and give all other aid necessary to start administration."[30] Unfortunately, the order was strictly interpreted. Lieutenant Colonel (LTC) Louis T. Morris, commander of the Presidio, appointed CPT James Lockett, 4th Cavalry, to fulfill these tasks. The captain discharged his responsibilities—but only after Volunteers reached their campsites. Between the waterfront and the Presidio, units were on their own.

With some additional prompting, Army officials adjusted their reception procedures. The *Daily Report* article from 13 May, plus Merriam's return to San Francisco on 16 May, provided the incentive to resolve the dockside glitch. By 18 May, Army escorts, assigned to guide units into designated campsites, met organizations as they disembarked near the Ferry Building.[31]

The march to camp constituted the final stage of a unit's welcome to San Francisco. After being presented with food and flowers by Red Cross volunteers, troops vacated the ferry depot sporting blossoms on their uniforms and in gunbarrels.[32] Often a civilian crowd, anxious to catch a glimpse of the city's newest military visitors, gathered just outside the gated docks. Atop the Claus Sprekels Building a cannon fired to announce that another unit had set out for camp.[33] Accompanied by military guides and frequently preceded by bands, units journeyed to bivouac sites.[34] Most marched to the cheers of flag-waving, clapping citizens. Municipal police assisted in crowd control.[35]

The trek was lengthy: 3 to 4 miles along the city's avenues.[36] It had its challenges beginning with Market Street's cobblestones, which some troops quietly cursed.[37] From Market, units traveled along Golden Gate, then Van Ness Avenue and Lombard Street into the Presidio.[38] Others took Golden Gate or Geary into camp if their organization was given a site away from the military reservation.[39]

THE VANGUARD OF THE KANSAS TROOPS ON THE WAY TO CAMP RICHMOND.

Figure 19.

One unit took a circuitous route to camp because its Army escorts became disoriented. On 10 June, Iowa's Volunteers started their march led by two orderlies from Merriam's command. The *Daily Report* claimed that the escorts, who lacked familiarity with the encampment, took the regiment "on a wild goose chase." After the 51st Iowa engaged in considerable marching and endured numerous catcalls from troops in camp, the newspaper reported that "a sergeant was detailed to pilot the Iowans to their proper position."[40]

Even if guided by the most knowledgeable of sergeants, units needed assistance moving unwieldy cargo from docks to camps. Troops used heavy wagons, or trucks, located near the Ferry Building to convey their baggage and weightier items. Sometimes the demand for wagons exceeded the supply. On 21 May, for example, elements from four state Volunteer organizations docked in San Francisco. Soldiers from two organizations, the 13th Minnesota and 1st Colorado, nearly came to blows over who would first use the trucks. The Minnesotans prevailed, filled their wagons with equipment, and got to camp as storms threatened. While hurrying to unpack shelters, troops discovered much to their dismay that the gear belonged to the 1st Colorado Infantry.[41]

Figure 20.

The City's Military Visitors: A Local Perspective

City newspapers offered critiques and colorful descriptions of units during their welcome to the city and their march to camp. The *Call* wrote of the Oregonians: "The men are fine looking soldiers, and are a magnificent body of physical manhood. Tall, strong and brawny with a determined look on their countenances."⁴² On 20 May, *The Examiner* dubbed Nebraskans "brave boys" though "rather smaller than the Oregon volunteers."⁴³ Ten days later, the same newspaper wrote respectfully of the "bronzed troops from the South," the Regulars of the 18th and 23d Infantry Regiments: "their sinewy figures bespoke the health and vigor of men inured to life on the frontier."⁴⁴ "Husky men, all these," proclaimed the *Chronicle* in its assessment of the 1st Montana.⁴⁵ The *Call* in particular employed vivid descriptions to delineate Volunteers: the "hardy miners and mountaineers" of Idaho; "the crack troops of the Keystone State," Pennsylvania; the "fine-looking lot of men, big strapping plainsmen," who hailed from Iowa; and "the Gotham Regiment" from New York.⁴⁶

Sturdy Plainsmen Come to Join the Growing Army of the Pacific.

Figure 21.

Local journalists also delighted in identifying the mascots that accompanied Volunteers and Regulars. Many regiments and a number of smaller organizations sported some type of bird or animal. Company D, 7th California, arrived in early May with an American eagle.⁴⁷ Nebraska's second battalion brought "Nebraska," a huge golden eagle that William Jennings Bryan presented to the regiment.⁴⁸ Company F, 51st Iowa, toted a black eagle.⁴⁹ Two companies from the 1st Idaho brought their eagles,

"Pocatello Joe" and "Admiral Dewey."[50] One company from the 1st New York carried a "bird of a different feather"—a crow named "Hobson."[51]

Figure 22.

Dogs were another favorite mascot among the troops. "Bummer," a great dane, trotted alongside his masters in the 1st Battalion, 2d Oregon.[52] Four dogs came with the troops from Idaho.[53] A fox terrier, "Boojum," accompanied the Astor Battery.[54] Another artillery unit, the Alger (Wyoming) Battery, brought an Irish spaniel, "Jeff," noteworthy for his "long legal history" in Cheyenne courts. The *Chronicle* observed "hord[e]s of other canine company mascots, most of which are named 'Dewey.'"[55] The 10th Pennsylvania had a large black-and-white dog that bore the admiral's name.[56] So, too, did a bulldog accompanying the 1st New York and a mutt with one company from the 51st Iowa.[57]

Other units adopted less domesticated animals. One company from Idaho brought a five-week-old coyote.[58] The 1st Tennessee carried a raccoon.[59] One of the men in Nebraska's second battalion marched to camp with a wolf pup, "Sampson," cradled in his arms.[60]

Perhaps the most novel of these mascots were teenage boys who accompanied three regiments. George Froam, a 64-pound "orphan waif from the streets of New Orleans," connected with the 23d US Infantry during its brief stay in Louisiana. When the regiment departed for the Bay Area, Froam decided to tag along. Acting as willing accomplices, several troops smuggled the boy aboard the train. By the time the 23d Infantry reached the Golden Gate, Froam had earned a reputation for being a "hustler" who could make money singing, dancing, and polishing officers' footwear.[61]

The ability to shine shoes endeared "Boots," a 13-year-old bootblack, to the men of Company D, 10th Pennsylvania. Before leaving the East Coast, each of the troops contributed 25 cents to buy their mascot an outfit, then tried to sneak him onto the trains. Occasionally, the men paid his fare when railway authorities discovered the stowaway. Apparently, troops purchased the cheapest seat, for Boots nearly froze atop railroad cars when riding through snowsheds on the way to California.[62]

The 1st Tennessee was the last regiment to cross the bay with a teenage mascot. Zeke Carsey, 13, began his association with Tennessee units in 1896. A native of Nashville, where he lived with his parents, Zeke endeared himself to the troops by employing "his ready wit and his superior musical abilities." He had a reputation for being adept at playing the piccolo, drums, and banjo. Allegedly, his mother gave her permission for Zeke to go with the 1st Tennessee to the West Coast. Unlike his fellow mascots in the 23d Infantry and 10th Pennsylvania, Zeke traveled in style on the troop train; he rode in "the colonel's car and was a constant source of entertainment to the officers."[63]

Into the Camps

The question of where to locate Volunteers and Regulars upon their arrival in the city had to be answered in relatively short order. Logically, the first places to consider were those military posts that were already established in the Bay Area. Evolving from military plans first conceived in 1850, the Army, by May 1898, possessed a network of installations designed for coast defense.[64]

Two locations sat astride the Golden Gate straits: Fort Winfield Scott and Fort Baker. On the Marin County side north of the straits, Fort Baker occupied part of the Lime Point Military Reservation and its 1,335 acres of rugged, coastal terrain. A battery-size unit of artillery manned the fort's crew-served weapons.[65] MG Miles had dubbed Lime Point "the Gibraltar of the Pacific."[66] To the south, across the waterway, Fort Scott included coast artillery weapons and the old Fort Point fortress. The brick structure could accommodate several companies of infantry or comparable units of artillery.[67]

Deeper into the Bay Area, the Army occupied smaller outposts that had been built to support Forts Baker and Scott during an attack. If enemy ships fought through the crossfire from these two forts and successfully negotiated minefields that protected the straits, US troops on Alcatraz Island could engage the seaborne force. Should a belligerent land force attempt to besiege Fort Scott, the works at Fort Mason protected Fort Scott's vulnerable flank. Mason overlooked the bay about a mile and a half to the east of the

Presidio. Any land force threatening Marin's Fort Baker would have to contend with artillery and the small garrison positioned on Angel Island. Theoretically, troops at Angel Island and Fort Mason could also engage direct threats against the Alcatraz force.[68]

In an emergency, Alcatraz and Angel Islands, as well as Fort Baker across the bay, offered potential bivouac sites for incoming forces. Establishing campgrounds at these locations, however, presented unattractive challenges of accessibility and support. Incapable of logistics self-sufficiency, these positions were sustained by San Francisco Bay watercraft. Each locale would eventually maintain small garrisons during the war, but these existed to man and maintain defense works.[69] In early May, local military officials needed suitable grounds quickly to accommodate the thousands of troops that President William McKinley was about to send to the Golden Gate.[70]

The Presidio of San Francisco, the facility that provided manpower resources for these bay outposts, at once emerged as the most attractive site to locate incoming Volunteers and Regulars. Occupied continuously by American forces since May 1849, the military reservation encompassed 1,479 acres of land northwest of the city's more populous areas. It lay within walking distance of docks that could both receive and dispatch military forces. By May 1898, the Presidio tied into a mass transit system that provided access to parts of the city via cable car. A series of wells kept the post supplied with water. In addition to maintaining a small hospital, the reservation served as home to the US Marine Hospital, Fort Winfield Scott complex, and recently constructed brick barracks that sheltered Regulars assigned to the Bay Area.[71]

The Presidio was also close to MG H.C. Merriam's headquarters. Alerted that troops would stage in his California area of responsibility, Merriam issued a 4 May order to the reservation commander, LTC Louis T. Morris, to select campsites for an estimated 6,000 troops who were expected to converge on the city.[72] That figure included Regulars of the 14th Infantry and Volunteers from California, Oregon, and Washington.

Morris looked over the Presidio for space to accommodate such a large contingent. Grounds located in elevated areas where water would "have to be brought, either by piping or by water carts," appeared most suited for an encampment.[73] The reservation's water wells, however, barely possessed the capacity to provide for the garrison currently assigned. The thousands of troops expected momentarily in the city would simply overwhelm the Presidio's water supply.[74]

Morris's encampment options were not limited just to the Presidio or other Bay Area military outposts such as Angel Island that could take about 500 men.[75] Some citizens in the San Francisco community stepped forward to render assistance by offering shelters or real estate. Fontana and Company, local canners, offered a large brick warehouse on the bay shore near the foot of Van Ness Avenue. Once home to the Mission Woolen Mills, the warehouse had the added advantage of being located close to Fort Mason, part of the Bay Area defense network.[76] (See figure 23.) Other sites tendered included "the old race-track property, a site on the hills dividing the Richmond District from the Presidio and another on the hospital tract."[77] Like the Fontana warehouse, all were within a mile of the Presidio.

By 6 May, Morris had chosen his preferred campsite—along the southern periphery of the Presidio's spacious drill field (labeled "Parade Ground" by the *Call*) that bordered a stretch of road just inside the Presidio's Lombard Street entrance not far from the Union Street cable line terminus.[78] That decision unquestionably received the endorsement of officers affiliated with the California regiments, the first units to go into the designated location. CPT Frank de L. Carrington, the Regular Army officer directed to muster California Volunteers into federal service, preferred that "the new soldiers should at once accustom themselves to camp life," an environment best developed on a military reservation.[79] (See figure 24.)

LTC Victor D. DuBoce of the 1st California Infantry also supported the Presidio option. Indeed, the *Call* reported that Morris' decision turned on DuBoce's plea "to put them at the Presidio, where the military surroundings as well as the presence and example of the regular troops and of the other regiments would help to infuse the military spirit into the organization."[80] In a separate article, the same paper reported: "The camp will be independent of the Presidio proper, but the troops will be compelled to obey the post regulations."[81]

Merriam endorsed Morris's selection and published General Orders Number 8, which specified 120,000 square feet of camping space for a regimental-size force. The order directed First Lieutenant (1LT) John M. Neall, 4th Cavalry, to assign plots to arriving units "keeping in view, first, facilities for water supply, and, second, economy of space."[82] Subsequently, Regulars of the 4th Cavalry "laid out the camp grounds, marked off the company streets and in various ways did all in their power to make officers and men comfortable."[83]

On Saturday, 7 May, the 1st California Infantry commanded by COL James F. Smith marched onto the Presidio and then into camp. 1LT Neall

57

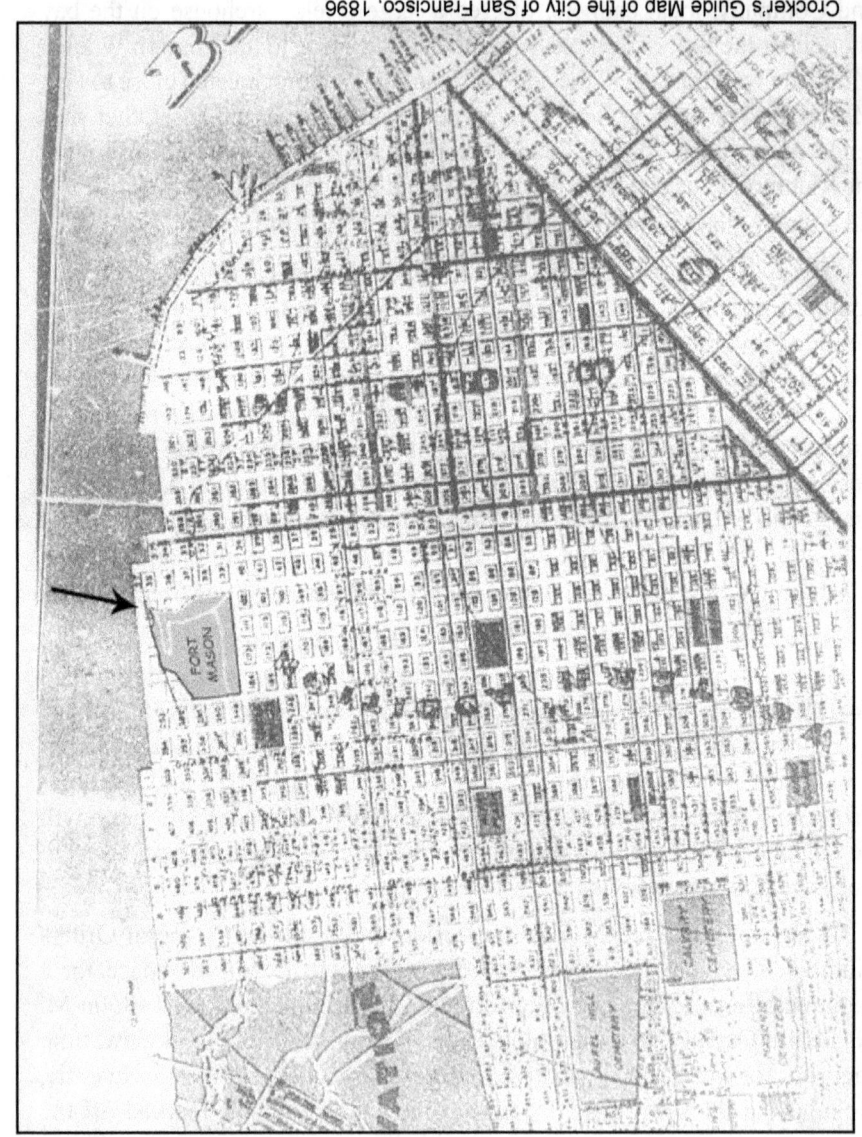

Figure 23. Fort Mason and north San Francisco, 1896. Arrow points to general vicinity of Fontana warehouse.

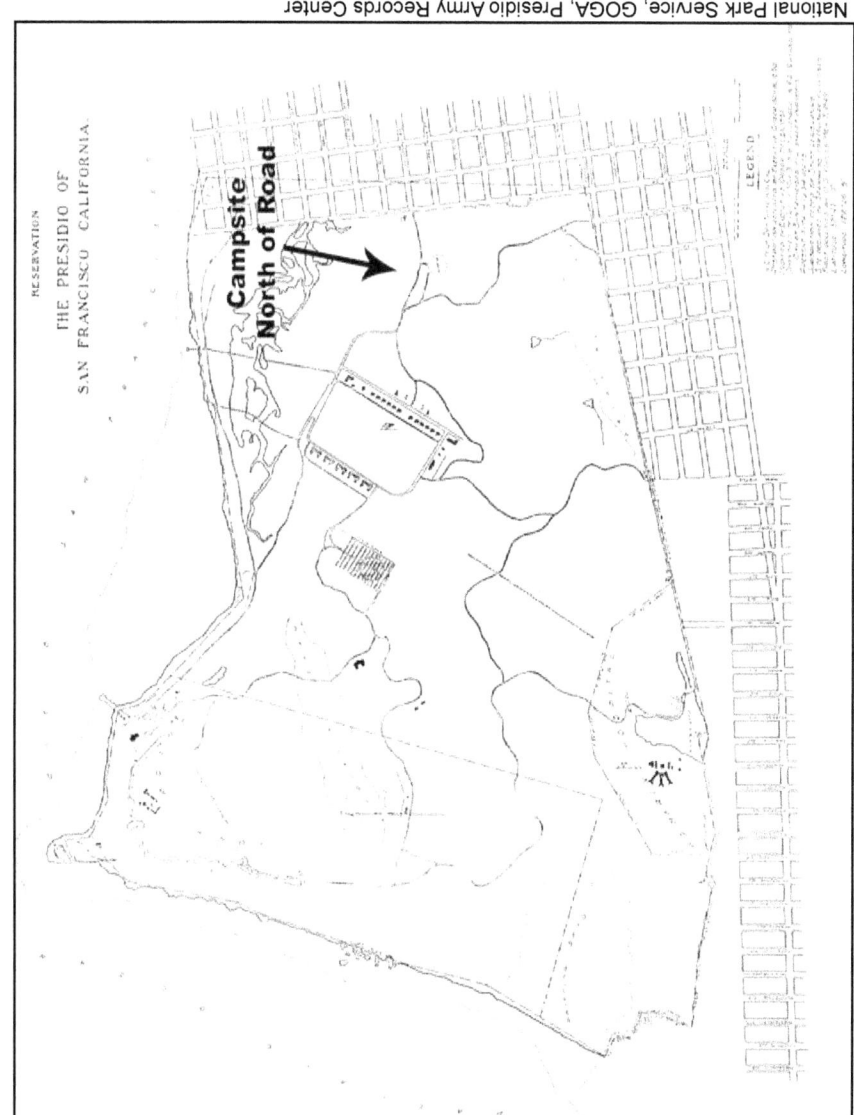

Figure 24. Presidio of San Francisco, 1897-1909 (campsite location added).

showed the colonel his regiment's designated location, just inside the Lombard Street gate.[84] COL John R. Berry's 7th California Infantry arrived later in the day and established its bivouac area to the west of Smith's regiment. Soon units from the 14th Infantry, 6th California, and 2d Oregon, in succession, joined the Presidio encampment. By 13 May, the military reservation boasted a campsite composed of approximately 3,200 Regulars and Volunteers.[85]

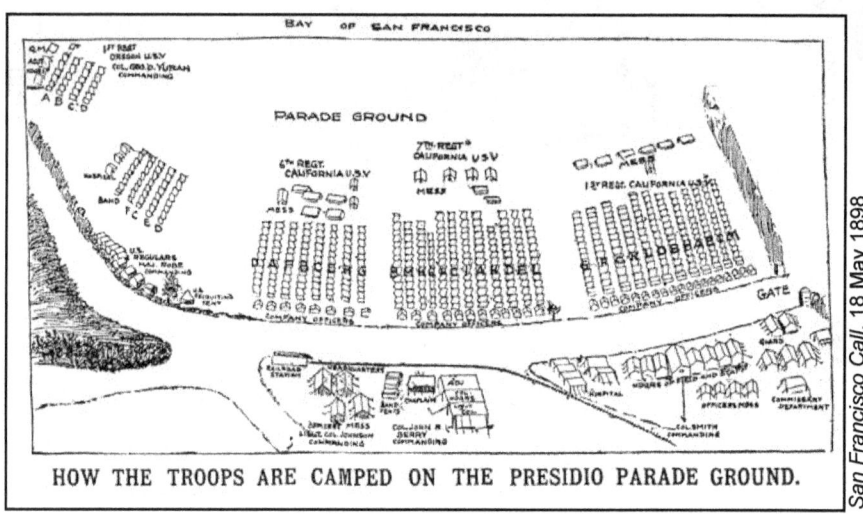

Figure 25.

Starting at the southeast edge of the large, somewhat barren drill field, the camp's bivouac sites sprang up by regiment with approximately 50 feet separating each organization. Company streets ran north and south; tents faced and opened to the east because of strong, westerly winds that prevailed in the afternoon. The *Chronicle* reported that what little vegetation existed on the plain soon disappeared in the wake of "detached groups of men marching and wheeling and squatting and aiming their rifles, according to the manner prescribed for an outlying skirmish line." Clay and sand turned quickly to dust. When San Franciscans flocked to visit the camps during early May, they churned up a dark haze of dust that engulfed the bivouac area.[86]

While other areas of the reservation may have offered greater protection against the elements, access to water effectively dictated the camp's location. When LTC Morris first conducted his reconnaissance for suitable campsites, Hermann Schussler, chief engineer of the Spring Valley Water Works, always seemed near at hand. 1LT Neall's instructions regarding site selection placed a premium on access to water. Ultimately, the

Figure 26.

Presidio's cavalry drill field emerged as the top choice because there the military could tap into water more quickly and cheaply than in other areas. The *Chronicle* quoted a Presidio officer who stated, "There is a large main at the Lombard-street entrance, and to supply any ground below that level nothing but pipes was necessary. To supply the slope above the road every drop of water would have to be pumped. The mains above the hillside are a long way off, and to have chosen them would have involved delay, which was inadmissible, and expense, which was unjustifiable."[87] Beginning 6 May, Presidio officials arranged to have workers from the Spring Valley Water Company lay 6-inch pipe off the Lombard Street main to give the new encampment its source of water.[88]

Spring Valley water could quench the thirst of those soldiers who were equipped to establish their own bivouac sites. That condition distinguished the first regimental organizations that marched onto the Presidio. Each possessed sufficient quartermaster blankets, uniforms, and tentage to establish outdoor dwellings. Such was not the case with all units closing on San Francisco in early May, including one of California's own, the heavy artillery.

Hastily organized, these four batteries of 600 men had no mess equipment, uniforms, or other quartermaster gear. Part of the reason was that when the California National Guard reorganized in 1897, artillery regiments and light batteries disappeared from state rolls.[89] Nevertheless, the War Department directed the state to provide four heavy batteries in addition to its infantry commitment.[90] Assessing the situation, CPT Carrington, the mustering officer, telegraphed BG Corbin from San Francisco on 9 May: "I think it advisable to hold batteries of heavy artillery here for a few days until they are fully equipped to go into camp complete. . . . I have the use without cost to the government of a building for quartering them and can feed them as at present at seventeen cents per meal per man."[91] That building of which he wrote was the warehouse Fontana and Company had offered.

Figure 27. Fontana warehouse, 1915.

On 11 May, the artillerymen, attired in civilian clothes, marched out of their armory looking "more like a column of the unemployed."[92] The Volunteers converged on the old Mission Woolen Mill, which Private Charles R. Detrick of the 1st California described as "under the old smooth-bores of Fort Mason."[93] There the troops took up quarters in the four-story structure. With the cannery still conducting business on the first floor, artillerymen spread over the upper three levels. Mark J. Fontana, one of the owners, offered the facility to the military for as long as needed.[94] Within a week, the Californians were joined in the warehouse by units from the 1st Washington, a regiment that MG Merriam judged to be "half uniformed and half armed."[95]

Merriam likely formed his impression of the 1st Washington before leaving Vancouver Barracks for San Francisco to oversee the assembly of forces. By the time he arrived in the city on 16 May, troops from California, Washington, Oregon, and the 14th Infantry had taken shelter at two locations: the Presidio and the Fontana warehouse. But other troops were coming by the thousands, and Merriam had to decide where to quarter those units that were scheduled to arrive starting 18 May.[96]

After making a quick inspection of the Presidio encampment and conferring with LTC Morris, Merriam chose the site of the old Bay District Racetrack. The location, less than a mile due south of the Presidio, could be accessed easily by foot or streetcar. Bounded by Point Lobos Avenue to the north, Fulton Street to the south, and 1st through 6th Avenues running east to west, the site and its environs promised to accommodate many regiments that were about to arrive in the city.[97] (See figure 28.)

Merriam chose the location for several reasons. The military preferred to keep regimental organizations together at campsites. Smaller posts in the Bay Area could not host organizations that size. Another option, the Fontana warehouse, could be dismissed because of the number of troops already located there. When Merriam reached San Francisco, more than 1,000 men had found shelter in the building.

Expanding the Presidio encampment seemed the most likely choice, but the general was not persuaded that such a step was needed. Merriam wrote, "sufficient ground, suitable in all respects for so large an encampment, could not be made available on the Presidio reservation and supplied with water without considerable time and an expenditure of more than $50,000." Additionally, Merriam conducted his arrival inspection at a time when the Presidio camp did not look its best. Deluged by rain and crowds of visitors during the 48 hours preceding his arrival, the campsite had been transformed into what the *Call* described as a veritable quagmire of mud, sand, and standing water.[98] Sandy soil, water, and thousands of additional troops would likely produce similar results anywhere else on the reservation. That mix of men with elements could have had catastrophic effects on the post forestation project begun nine years earlier. Congress had provided

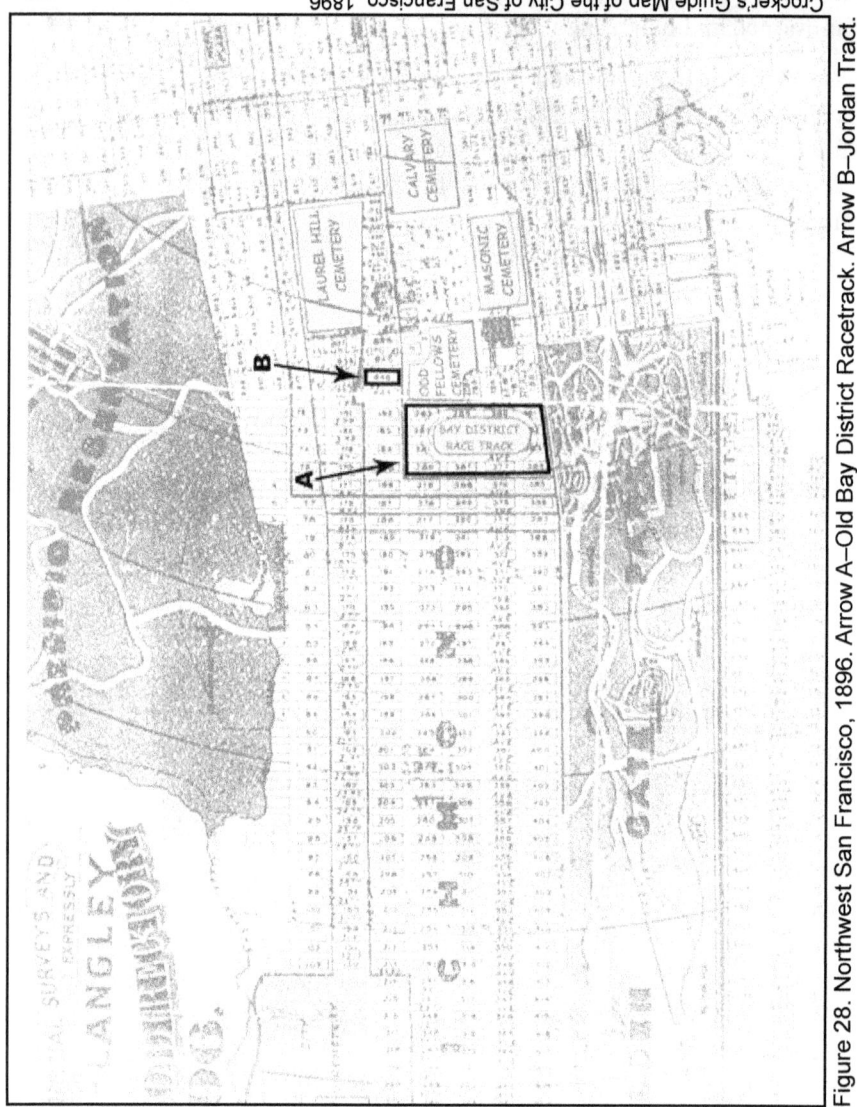

Figure 28. Northwest San Francisco, 1896. Arrow A—Old Bay District Racetrack. Arrow B—Jordan Tract.

some $10,000 for a Bay Area firm to plant 400,000 eucalyptus, cedar, pine, and acacia to reclaim sand dunes and protect the installation's water supply.[99] Preserving the effects of this program provided an additional incentive to finding accommodations elsewhere for incoming troops.

The old Bay District Racetrack site possessed attractive features in its own right. Like the Fontana warehouse, the grounds would come at virtually no cost to the military. The Crocker Estate Company owned the property and required only "that the army authorities shall leave the premises in as good condition as they find them." City mains in the vicinity could readily provide sufficient water for the site, which could hold as many as 10,000 troops.[100]

Beginning 18 May, Volunteers and Regulars poured onto the old Bay District Racetrack, officially dubbed Camp Merritt.[101] Over the next several days, Merritt became the campground for units from Nebraska, Kansas, Colorado, Minnesota, Idaho, Pennsylvania, California, Utah, and Wyoming. Regular engineers and infantrymen from the 14th, 18th, and 23d Regiments joined the campsite. A week after opening, the bivouac absorbed the old Bay District Racetrack and several surrounding city blocks. It boasted a population of more than 7,000 troops.[102]

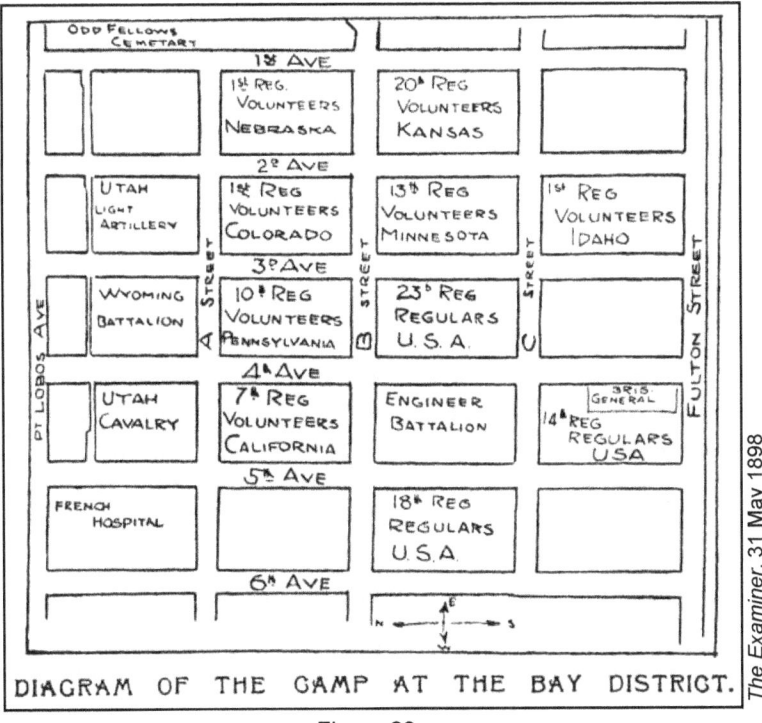

Figure 29.

So great was the influx of forces to the Golden Gate that the military sought additional space to position troops. James Clark Jordan, a San Francisco real estate entrepreneur, owned land just northeast of the old Bay District Racetrack. In late May, Jordan offered the military an area bounded by California Avenue to the north, Point Lobos Avenue to the south, and Maple to Michigan Streets running east to west. On 25 May, MG Elwell S. Otis wrote Jordan, "I am in receipt of your communication tendering the free use of the land known as 'The Jordan Tract' [see figure 28, arrow B] to the government for camping purposes of its troops now being assembled at this point. The tract is most convenient for such purposes and is gladly accepted."[103] On 28 May, the Army spilled across 1st Avenue into this new section of Camp Merritt. Eventually, the Jordan Tract included the division hospital and troops from Montana, North Dakota, South Dakota, Nevada, and Iowa.

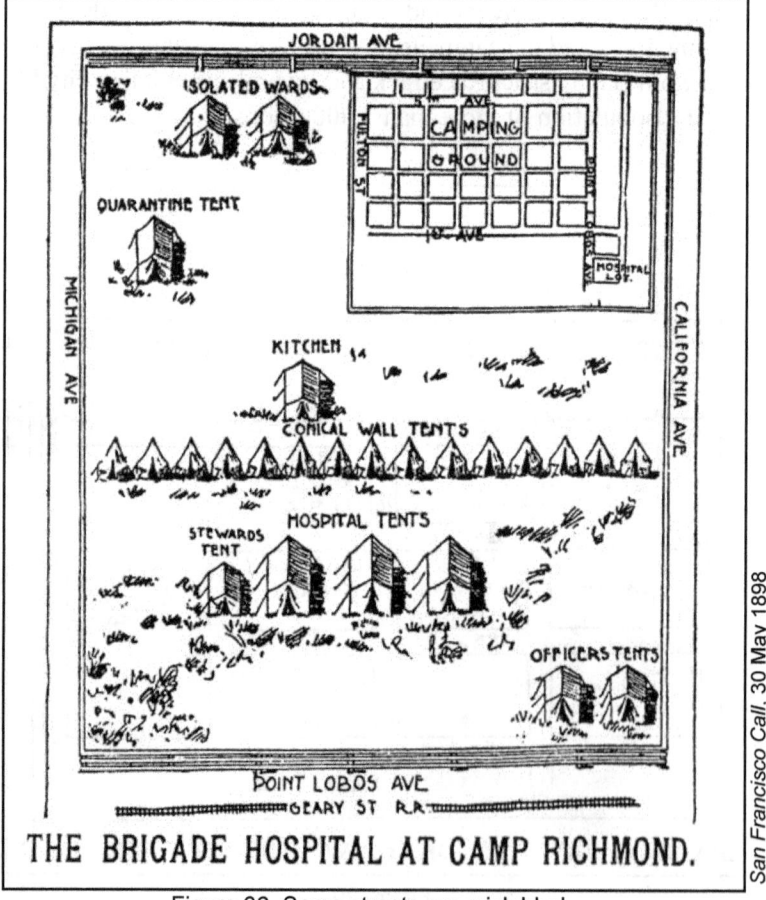

Figure 30. Some streets are mislabled.

By 14 June, nearly 15,000 Regulars and Volunteers were assembled in San Francisco. Military officials spread the troops about four sites: 2,180 soldiers on the Presidio, including the original bivouac area subsequently called Camp Miller; 680 Volunteers at the Fontana warehouse; and just under 12,000 men at the two locations constituting Camp Merritt.[104]

Figure 31. 51st Iowa at Camp Merritt.

Establishing Command and Control

MG Henry C. Merriam would be the first, and several months later the last, senior Army two-star commander to influence the forces assembled in San Francisco for the war against Spain. A career officer who received a bachelor's and master's degree from Colby College in Maine, Merriam entered the service as a captain during the Civil War. In that conflict, he earned several brevet promotions and the Medal of Honor for gallantry on the battlefield. Beginning in 1866, Merriam spent the next 30 years performing various duties on the frontier. He participated in combat operations against Mexican forces during 1876, the Nez Percé in 1877, and the Sioux from 1890 to 1891.[105]

Promoted to brigadier general on 30 June 1897, Merriam took command of the Department of Columbia a month later. In that position, the general assumed responsibility for operations in Idaho, Oregon, Washington, and Alaska. The attendant problems created by a rush of miners into Yukon territory demanded the use of departmental resources. In early 1898, the spat over boundaries between the United States and Canada described in chapter II that involved COL Thomas Anderson's 14th US Infantry occurred within Merriam's command.[106]

Due south of Merriam's Columbia Department, Brigadier General (BG) William Shafter headed the Department of California at the beginning of the war with Spain. Shortly after ordering the 1st US Infantry Regiment from the California territory to an assembly area in the South, the War Department directed Shafter to leave his post at San Francisco and take command of troops assembling at New Orleans.[107]

With Shafter's departure, Merriam assumed responsibility for the Department of California while retaining control of the Department of Columbia.[108] His combined territory encompassed the entire West Coast of the United States, Alaska, Idaho, and Nevada. Merriam was, therefore, at once responsible for the Army's portion of Pacific coast defense. Merriam initially elected to remain at Vancouver Barracks in Washington state where, in addition to coast defense, he was also ordered to "supervise organization of volunteers in Washington, Oregon and California."[109]

Merriam's choice of locations from which to exercise command may have been appropriate through late April. By early May, however, he should have reconsidered his decision. The president's directive to send Army forces to the Philippines through San Francisco had considerable implications regarding the Department of California. A senior officer needed to be present to supervise the reception, quartering, and equipping of forces due into that port of embarkation. Coast defense and state militia mobilization could be monitored just as easily from San Francisco as it could from Vancouver Barracks. Merriam tried to establish a de facto presence by communicating via telegraph with the department's staff, but that action did not allow for a personal assessment of actions.

Merriam's decision did not rest well with the War Department. Between 3 and 16 May, Corbin, Miles, and Alger had no general officer contact at the Golden Gate to render status reports on the assembly of forces. They received information piecemeal and from numerous sources by wire. Finally, on 13 May, Corbin telegraphed Merriam, "The General Commanding the Army would like for you to repair to San Francisco soon as possible and give the organization of these troops your personal attention."[110]

To his credit, Merriam, reacting to Corbin's message, departed for the city within 24 hours.[111] Nevertheless, to ensure that Merriam fully understood his priorities, the AG's office followed up with a message on 16 May:

"Secretary of War directs that until further orders you establish your headquarters at San Francisco, Cal. You will continue to exercise command of both the Departments of the Columbia and of California."[112]

GENERAL MERRIAM AT THE PRESIDIO GATES.

Figure 32.

Merriam's first major decision after his arrival on 16 May would be his most controversial: selecting the Bay District Racetrack as a campsite. Before he made his choice, *Call* accounts looked for the Presidio to absorb additional forces reaching the Golden Gate beginning mid-May.[113] The newspaper even cited 1LT Neall as saying incoming troops would be accommodated at the Presidio "upon the slope south of the Union car line."[114] Given his responsibility to establish campsites, Neall was certainly in a position to know where troops would most likely be quartered.

After moving to establish an additional encampment away from the Presidio, Merriam's influence over all the forces positioned in San Francisco diminished due to the presence of MG E.S. Otis. On 11 May 1898, Secretary of War R.A. Alger offered Otis "second in command" of the Philippine expedition.[115] (See figure 33.) Alger's proposal was not due to happenstance; the War Department knew firsthand of Otis's talents. He was an experienced senior leader, and he held both regimental and brigade command positions during the Civil War. In the 1880s, Otis led the Regular Army's 20th Infantry Regiment. After his promotion to brigadier general in 1893, he took command of the Department of Columbia. In 1897, he left that post to become commander of the Department of Colorado.[116]

BRIGADIER-GENERAL ELWELL S. OTIS.
Figure 33.

Otis also possessed superb organizational and administrative skills. In 1881, MG William T. Sherman directed Otis to develop the new School of Application for Cavalry and Infantry at Fort Leavenworth, Kansas. For four years, he served as the school's first commandant, helping to introduce a formal system of education to officers within the military profession. In 1896, he worked in the War Department revising US Army regulations. When asked to become a part of the Philippine endeavor, Otis was finishing duty as president of a court-martial proceeding, using analytical skills acquired on his way to earning a law degree from Harvard.[117]

After accepting Alger's offer, Otis received a twofold directive from the Secretary of War. First, as a newly promoted major general of Volunteers, he was ordered to take command of forces assembling in San Francisco, assisting "in their organization and equipment as rapidly as possible."[118] Later, Alger instructed Otis to join the first force leaving for the Philippines. He wanted Otis to confer with Admiral Dewey and then occupy "such part of the islands as you may be able to do with this force until the arrival of other troops."[119] The War Department urged Otis to depart for the archipelago as soon as possible.[120]

Otis acted quickly following his arrival at the Golden Gate on Tuesday evening, 17 May. He spent Wednesday making personal inspections and developing a sense of what had been accomplished and what needed to be done.[121] That evening he dashed off a superb report to Washington, the first of its kind to come from the West Coast, highlighting the status of vessels, troops, and supplies designated for the Pacific. He concluded with one recommendation based upon his onsite observation and assessment: Otis requested permission from the War Department to remain in San Francisco, "putting the troops here in condition" for service abroad.[122] He assessed that the Army needed a senior officer to organize the effort at the port of embarkation.

Wisely, after consulting with the president, Secretary Alger directed Otis to remain.[123] On 20 May, the general established Headquarters, US Expeditionary Forces, and assumed command of all troops "for contemplated expeditionary purposes."[124] Over the next several days he prepared the first expedition for departure, readying the troops and their vessels. He apprised the War Department of coordination that should be conducted with the Navy over convoy support and raised concerns about acquiring transports for subsequent deployments. By 24 May, troops of the first expedition were onboard and prepared to steam for the Philippines.[125]

With that accomplished, Otis learned that the Secretary of War had renewed his desire to have the general sail with the next expedition.[126] The secretary's preference would not be fulfilled in the short term. Instead, Otis assumed command of a new organization established on 1 June 1898: the Independent Division, Philippine Islands Expeditionary Forces.[127] More important, he established his headquarters at Camp Merritt on the grounds of the old Bay District Racetrack.[128] From that location, Otis would be in a position to exercise command and control over his newly organized division that was composed of four brigades. The division was created in part to ensure Otis's retention in San Francisco, even after the arrival of the Army's second-highest ranking officer, Wesley Merritt.

Figure 34.

Like Merriam and Otis, Merritt was a career soldier; however, he came into the service under circumstances quite different from those of the other two generals. Born in New York City on 16 June 1836, Merritt entered the Army after graduating from West Point on the eve of the Civil War. During the conflict, he commanded a cavalry division as a brevet major general of Volunteers.

After the war, Merritt reverted in rank to a Regular Army lieutenant colonel but continued to serve in the cavalry. In 1887, he completed a tour as superintendent of his alma mater, then assumed control of the Department of the Missouri as a brigadier general. In 1895, Merritt received a promotion to major general and, subsequently, command of the Department of the East.[129]

Merritt had presided over the East's jurisdiction for about a year when the war began in April 1898. Early in the month, he completed an inspection of the Army's coast installations with a view toward sustaining a possible maritime attack mounted by the Spanish.[130] As had Merriam on the West Coast, Merritt prioritized eastern seaboard defense from Maine through Virginia. For the first 10 days of May, he remained oriented on his responsibilities in the East as that department's commander. Correspondence with the Governor of Pennsylvania indicated that he was concerned with protecting docks and harbors, particularly around Newport News, Virginia.[131]

On 12 May, the War Department abruptly shifted Merritt's focus. The AG, BG H.C. Corbin, informed Merritt that he had been relieved as commander, Department of the East. Acting on directives that filled key command positions, Corbin notified Merritt that "by direction of the President you are assigned to the command of the expedition being sent to the Philippine Islands. You will repair to San Francisco, Cal., and assume command of and organize troops assembling there."[132]

Merritt did not reach the West Coast until 26 May, which is why the locations and actions of Merriam and Otis were so important. At least one of the three general officers needed to be in San Francisco, directing the efforts of those units reaching the city and coordinating troops' departure for the Philippines. Despite Merriam's proximity to these activities, Otis emerged early as the key general officer to shape the Philippine command evolving in San Francisco.

While Otis worked to reach the bay city and establish control, Merritt elected to fight other battles. In the two weeks preceding his arrival at the Golden Gate, Merritt visited Washington, DC on two occasions, conversing with the president and Secretary of War on details related to the Philippine expedition. During these meetings and in subsequent correspondence, Merritt advanced his requests for more Regulars, fewer Volunteers, and specific kinds of equipment for the force.[133] His running debate with the Commanding General of the Army over Regular versus Volunteer force ratios culminated in a partial victory for Merritt.[134] In a sense, his efforts during these two weeks represented his focus for much of the war. Merritt concentrated on squeezing Washington for more manpower resources; Otis received, shaped, and shipped them.

By the time Merritt joined Otis in San Francisco, the Philippine expedition had achieved departmental status.[135] On 30 May 1898, Merritt established in San Francisco the Headquarters, US Expeditionary Forces and Department of the Pacific.[136] With this step the general assumed command of all forces allocated for duty in the Philippines, including the Independent Division at Camp Merritt that MG Otis commanded.

He also established a departmental staff to coordinate actions between Washington and San Francisco. When Merritt received orders to take command, Corbin telegraphed, "You will be accompanied by your authorized aids (sic). General staff officers will be assigned you hereafter."[137] McKinley had the power to appoint staff members when circumstances permitted him to name general officers.

McKinley's authority did not deter Merritt from initiating requests of the president. Just as he had been prone to do for units and equipment, Merritt appealed for specific individuals. In a succinctly written letter to the president prepared on 15 May, Merritt addressed several concerns relating to his command, including the "urgent necessity that the chiefs of the staff departments be appointed at once to assist in organizing and equipping their specialties. They will need time to get information of the conditions and to study their respective problems. We are going too far from our base to permit of any guess work." Merritt then submitted a list of staff officers "being those that I would select, but any capable men, chosen by their respective chiefs, would be agreeable to me."[138]

In this instance, the president honored many of Merritt's requests. The general submitted his preferences for 10 general staff positions; seven of those he asked for joined his department. Equally significant, he urged the commissary general in Washington on 15 May to expedite the assignment of his chief commissary, LTC David L. Brainard, to San Francisco "in order to make every preparation for the subsistence of the command going to the Philippines."[139] Brainard received orders and reached the Golden Gate on 24 May, two days before Merritt arrived.[140]

Two other officers noteworthy for their role in preparing troops to deploy joined Brainard on the Pacific department staff. COL Robert P. Hughes, Inspector General (IG), charged with examining each unit assembled, assessed what Merritt described as "all matters relating to its operations and involving its efficiency."[141] At the outbreak of the war, Hughes served Merritt as the IG for the Department of the East. The *Call* reported that Hughes also acted as a courier between Merritt and Secretary Alger when the two negotiated force mix.[142]

LTC James W. Pope served as the department's chief quartermaster. In writing a description of the supply departments in an 1893 publication, Merritt singled out the quartermaster for its significance. He assessed the department as "second to none in importance. On it depends the supply of the army of clothing, forage, transportation, and everything that is required by the soldier in barracks or in the field connected with these."[143]

Pope and other quartermasters worked closely with one officer who already operated in San Francisco at the beginning of the war, CPT Oscar F. Long. In April 1898, Long served as acting Depot Quartermaster, San Francisco. In this position, he maintained close ties with designated territorial departments while working directly for the Quartermaster-General, US Army. Long managed a general supply depot from which divisions and departments could, on order from the War Department, draw essential clothing and equipment.[144]

By early June, many of the troops destined for service abroad had arrived in the city. They were assigned to one of four quartering sites: a section of the Presidio, the Fontana warehouse, or either of two locations that constituted Camp Merritt. Three major generals interacted to accomplish the major missions pursued on the West Coast. MG Merriam commanded the Department of California and Department of Columbia, facilitating the establishment of coast defense; the mobilization of western Volunteers; and the support of units marshaling in San Francisco for duty in the Philippine archipelago. MG Merritt commanded the Department of the Pacific, gathering resources from Washington, DC and the Department of California to outfit his expedition abroad. MG Otis led the Independent Division, a part of Merritt's command, and coordinated receiving, equipping, training, and shipping the force bound for duty in the Pacific. That process of preparing and deploying the Philippine expeditionary force for war against Spain spanned three and one-half months and drew upon all three commands' resources.

Notes

1. "Troops Pouring Into the City," *San Francisco Daily Report*, 21 May 1898, 2; "Fifty-First Iowa Regiment is Here," *San Francisco Chronicle*, 10 June 1898, 7.

2. "Willing to Help," *San Francisco Call*, 22 May 1898, 14; H.S. Crocker Company, *Crocker-Langley San Francisco Directory for Year Commencing May 1899* (San Francisco: H.S. Crocker Co., 1899), 1611.

3. "Fighting Tenth Here From Pennsylvania," *San Francisco Chronicle*, 25 May 1898, 4.

4. Lieutenant Martin Tew, *Official History of the Operations of the 13th Minnesota Infantry, U.S.V., in the Campaign in the Philippines*, n.p., n.d., 3; "Troops Massing for the Manila Expedition," *San Francisco Chronicle*, 21 May 1898, 9; "Fighting Tenth Here From Pennsylvania," *San Francisco Chronicle*, 25 May 1898, 4; "Astor's Guns on the Mole," *San Francisco Chronicle*, 20 June 1898, 5; "Volunteers All the Way From New York," *San Francisco Chronicle*, 14 July 1898, 12; "Another Utah Battery Here," *San Francisco Chronicle*, 2 August 1898, 7; "Pennsylvania's Crack Regiment is Here," *San Francisco Call*, 25 May 1898, 3; "Stalwart Volunteers," *San Francisco Call*, 29 May 1898, 8; "Iowans at Oakland," *San Francisco Call*, 10 June 1898, 5; "Brave Battalions From Tennessee," *San Francisco Call*, 17 June 1898, 5; "Astor Artillery at Oakland Mole," *San Francisco Call*, 20 June 1898, 5; "Volunteers From the Empire State," *San Francisco Call*, 14 July 1898, 8; "Will Sail This Afternoon," *San Francisco Daily Report*, 25 May 1898, 1; "Tennessee Men Arrive Today," *San Francisco Daily Report*, 17 June 1898, 1; "The First New York," *San Francisco Daily Report*, 14 July 1898, 3; "Penn's Sons at Our Doors," *The Examiner*, 25 May 1898, 3; "Iowa's Men Arrive at the Camp," *The Examiner*, 11 June 1898, 3; "Astor's Battery Pitches Tents," *The Examiner*, 21 June 1898, 3; "Wyoming's Volunteer Artillery Battery," *The Examiner*, 28 June 1898, 14.

5. "Over Night in Oakland," *San Francisco Call*, 21 May 1898, 5.

6. "Troops Gathering in This City," *San Francisco Daily Report*, 9 May 1898, 1.

7. "The Montana Regiment Arrives," *San Francisco Daily Report*, 28 May 1898, 3; "Troops Pouring Into the City," *San Francisco Daily Report*, 21 May 1898, 2.

8. Joseph I. Markey, *From Iowa to the Philippines: A History of Company M, Fifty-First Iowa Infantry Volunteers* (Red Oak, IA: Thos D. Murphy Co., 1900) 57.

9. Record Group 92. The Textual Records of the Office of the Quartermaster General. Entry 1496, Register of Transportation of Troops and Their Equipment, 1898-1900 (Washington, DC: National Archives), 178.

10. "Troopers Came From Far Utah," *The Examiner*, 27 May 1898, 5; "First Cavalrymen of the Volunteer Army Arrive," *San Francisco Chronicle*, 27 May 1898, 7; "Utah Mounted Men," *San Francisco Call*, 27 May 1898, 5; "Utah Troopers Here," *San Francisco Daily Report*, 27 May 1898, 3; "Cavalry Arrive,"

San Francisco Daily Report, 6 June 1898, 3; "New Artillery Camp Formed at the Presidio," *San Francisco Chronicle*, 7 June 1898, 4.

11. Private James Camp, *Official History of the Operations of the First Idaho Infantry, U.S.V. in the Campaign in the Philippine Islands*, n.p., n.d., 3.

12. "All the Way From Nebraska," *San Francisco Chronicle*, 20 May 1898, 12.

13. William Doxey, *Doxey's Guide to San Francisco and the Pleasure Resorts of California* (San Francisco: Doxey Press, 1897), 89-90.

14. Volunteer unit histories from Oregon, Iowa, Nebraska, South Dakota, Wyoming, Minnesota, Montana, Tennessee, and Utah praised the Red Cross reception.

15. William S. Christner, 10th Pennsylvania Regiment, "Dear Dady and Mother," 26 May 1898 (Carlisle Barracks, PA: Military History Institute).

16. A.G. Baker, 1st Colorado Infantry, *The Colorado Volunteers* (Carlisle Barracks, PA: Military History Institute), 10.

17. "From the Presidio to the Philippines," *The Examiner*, 8 May 1898, 15.

18. "Oregonian Volunteers," *San Francisco Daily Report*, 13 May 1898, 2; "Soldiers Will be Welcomed," *San Francisco Call*, 18 May 1898, 7.

19. "Soldiers Will be Welcomed," *San Francisco Call*, 18 May 1898, 7; "Red Cross Work," *San Francisco Daily Report*, 18 May 1898, 3.

20. "Willing to Help," *San Francisco Call*, 22 May 1898, 14.

21. "A Discourteous Lieutenant," *San Francisco Call*, 21 June 1898, 5.

22. Markey, 66.

23. "Astor's Battery Pitches Tents," *The Examiner*, 21 June 1898, 3.

24. "The Ladies not Snubbed," *San Francisco Daily Report*, 21 June 1898, 2.

25. "The Astor Battery," *San Francisco Daily Report*, 22 June 1898, 4.

26. "San Francisco Falls to Tennessee's Troops," *San Francisco Call*, 18 June 1898, 7.

27. "A Great Reception," *San Francisco Call*, 9 July 1898, 5; "The New Yorkers," *San Francisco Call*, 12 July 1898, 5; "Volunteers From the Empire State," *San Francisco Call*, 14 July 1898, 8; "New York Breakfast," *San Francisco Call*, 15 July 1898, 8.

28. "Oregonian Volunteers," *San Francisco Daily Report*, 13 May 1898, 2.

29. "Hail Soldiers From Sunland!" *The Examiner*, 6 May 1898, 3; "From the Presidio to the Philippines," *The Examiner*, 8 May 1898, 15; "Going to the Presidio," *The Examiner*, 9 May 1898, 3; "More Volunteers Arrive," *The Examiner*, 10 May 1898, 3; "Reception to the Boys of the Seventh," *San Francisco Chronicle*, 7 May 1898, 16; "Seventh in Camp," *San Francisco Call*, 8 May 1898, 10; "The Angelenos March In," *San Francisco Daily Report*, 7 May 1898, 3; "Troops Gathering in This City," *San Francisco Daily Report*, 9 May 1898, 1.

30. "Advance Guards of Manila's Invaders Ready for the Front," *San Francisco Call*, 10 May 1898, 7.

31. "Washington Troops," *San Francisco Daily Report*, 17 May 1898, 3; "Troops Pouring Into the City," *San Francisco Daily Report*, 21 May 1898, 2; "At the Presidio Camp," *San Francisco Daily Report*, 23 May 1898, 1; "Arrival of

Pennsylvania's Crack Regiment, the Tenth," *San Francisco Daily Report*, 25 May 1898, 1; "In the Camp," *San Francisco Daily Report*, 10 June 1898, 3; "All the Way From Nebraska," *San Francisco Chronicle*, 20 May 1898, 12; "Volunteers From the Empire State," *San Francisco Call*, 14 July 1898, 8.

32. "Pennsylvania's Regiment in Camp," *San Francisco Call*, 26 May 1898, 2; "A Regiment From Iowa Arrives," *San Francisco Daily Report*, 10 June 1898, 3.

33. "Pennsylvania's Regiment in Camp," *San Francisco Call*, 26 May 1898, 2; "Utah Mounted Men," *San Francisco Call*, 27 May 1898, 5; "Stalwart Volunteers," *San Francisco Call*, 29 May 1898, 8; "San Francisco Falls to Tennessee Troops," *San Francisco Call*, 18 June 1898, 7.

34. "Nebraska Volunteers," *San Francisco Call*, 20 May 1898, 5; "Marching on to Camp Richmond," *San Francisco Call*, 21 May 1898, 5; "Stalwart Volunteers," *San Francisco Call*, 29 May 1898, 8; "Are Not Mendicants," *San Francisco Call*, 1 June 1898, 4; "San Francisco Falls to Tennessee Troops," *San Francisco Call*, 18 June 1898, 7; "Nebraska's Volunteers," *The Examiner*, 20 May 1898, 3; "Merritt Shapes Up His Army," *The Examiner*, 1 June 1898, 4; "Southern Dakota's Soldiers," *The Examiner*, 3 June 1898, 3; "Warm Welcome for Washington Troops," *The Examiner*, 26 July 1898, 7; "Oregon's Levy Now Complete," *San Francisco Chronicle*, 19 May 1898, 3; "Troops Massing for the Manila Expedition," *San Francisco Chronicle*, 21 May 1898, 9; "The South Dakota Troops Arrive," *San Francisco Daily Report*, 2 June 1898, 3; "Astor's Battery Has Arrived," *San Francisco Daily Report*, 20 June 1898, 1; "The First New York," *San Francisco Daily Report*, 14 July 1898, 3.

35. "From the Presidio to the Philippines," *The Examiner*, 8 May 1898, 15; "Troops Pouring Into City," *San Francisco Daily Report*, 21 May 1898, 2.

36. "Oregon's Levy Now Complete," *San Francisco Chronicle*, 19 May 1898, 3; "All the Way From Nebraska," *San Francisco Chronicle*, 20 May 1898, 12.

37. Private James Camp, 3.

38. "Seventh in Camp," *San Francisco Call*, 8 May 1898, 10; "Oregon Volunteers," *San Francisco Call*, 19 May 1898, 5.

39. "Nebraska Volunteers," *San Francisco Call*, 20 May 1898, 5; "Delayed by a Wreck," *San Francisco Call*, 21 May 1898, 5.

40. "In the Camp," *San Francisco Daily Report*, 10 June 1898, 3.

41. "Five States in One Camp, *San Francisco Chronicle*, 22 May 1898, 23.

42. "Troops Arrive From the North," *San Francisco Call*, 14 May 1898, 7.

43. "Nebraska's Volunteers, *The Examiner*, 20 May 1898, 3.

44. "Bronzed Troops From the South," *The Examiner*, 30 May 1898, 3.

45. "Making Soldiers of the Boys at Camp Merritt," *San Francisco Chronicle*, 29 May 1898, 23.

46. "Idaho Volunteers," *San Francisco Call*, 23 May 1898, 5; "Pennsylvania's Regiment in Camp," *San Francisco Call*, 26 May 1898, 2; "Iowans at Oakland," *San Francisco Call*, 10 June 1898, 5; "A Great Reception," *San Francisco Call*, 9 July 1898, 5.

47. "More Volunteers Arrive," *The Examiner*, 10 May 1898, 3.

48. "Nebraska Volunteers," *San Francisco Call*, 20 May 1898, 5; "At Camp Richmond," *San Francisco Call*, 22 May 1898, 14.

49. "Fifty-First Iowa Regiment is Here," *San Francisco Chronicle*, 10 June 1898, 7.

50. "Idaho Volunteers," *San Francisco Call*, 23 May 1898, 5.

51. "Volunteers All the Way From New York," *San Francisco Chronicle*, 14 July 1898, 12.

52. "Making Soldiers Out of the State's Volunteers," *San Francisco Chronicle*, 14 May 1898, 9.

53. "Idaho and Utah Troops Arrive," *San Francisco Chronicle*, 23 May 1898, 7.

54. "Astor Battery in Camp," *San Francisco Chronicle*, 21 June 1898, 7.

55. "Wyoming Battery Joins the Troop," *San Francisco Chronicle*, 29 June 1898, 3.

56. "Pennsylvania's Regiment in Camp," *San Francisco Call*, 26 May 1898, 2.

57. "Volunteers All the Way From New York," *San Francisco Chronicle*, 14 July 1898, 12; "Fifty-First Iowa Regiment is Here," *San Francisco Chronicle*, 10 June 1898, 7.

58. "Idaho and Utah Troops Arrive," *San Francisco Chronicle*, 23 May 1898, 7.

59. "Sons of the Men in Gray," *San Francisco Chronicle*, 18 June 1898, 9.

60. "Nebraska Volunteers, *San Francisco Call*, 20 May 1898, 5; "First Troops From Across the Rockies," *San Francisco Chronicle*, 20 May 1898, 12.

61. "The Mascot of the Twenty-Third," *San Francisco Chronicle*, 3 June 1898, 7; "Re-Enforcement of Regulars," *San Francisco Chronicle*, 30 May 1898, 3.

62. "Six Hundred From Far Pennsylvania," *San Francisco Chronicle*, 26 May 1898, 2.

63. "King's Brigade for the Philippines," *San Francisco Call*, 18 June 1898, 7; "First Regiment From the South," *San Francisco Chronicle*, 17 June 1898, 7.

64. John Phillip Langellier, "Bastion by the Bay: A History of the Presidio of San Francisco, 1776-1906," unpublished dissertation (Manhattan, KS: Kansas State University, 1982), 87-129.

65. Ibid., 228; Workers of the Writers' Program of the Work Projects Administration in Northern California, *The Army at the Golden Gate: A Guide to Army Posts in the San Francisco Bay Area*, n.p., n.d., 85, 109.

66. "The Artillery Camp," *San Francisco Call*, 8 June 1898, 8.

67. John A. Martini, *Fort Point: Sentry at the Golden Gate* (San Francisco: Golden Gate National Park Association, 1991), 22, 27.

68. Ibid., 7-8; Langellier, 97-98, 214-20, 227-31; John A. Martini, *Fortress Alcatraz: Guardian of the Golden Gate* (Kailua, HI: Pacific Monograph, 1990), 16-17, 83-86.

69. Langellier, 168.

70. William McKinley to the Secretary of War, 4 May 1898, in *Correspondence Relating to the War With Spain and Conditions Growing Out of the Same, Including the Insurrection in the Philippine Islands and the China Relief*

Expedition, Between the Adjutant-General of the Army and Military Commander in the United States, Cuba, Porto Rico, China, and the Philippine Islands, From April 15, 1898, to July 30, 1902, volume II (Washington, DC: US Government Printing Office [GPO], 1902), hereafter cited as *Correspondence II*, 635.

71. Map, Reservation, the Presidio of San Francisco, California, 1897-1909, Post Engineer; Langellier, 191-197.

72. "Mobilizing Western Troops in San Francisco," *San Francisco Call*, 5 May 1898, 2.

73. Ibid.

74. "In Camp With the Volunteers," *San Francisco Chronicle*, 11 May 1898, 4.

75. "Mobilizing Western Troops in San Francisco," *San Francisco Call*, 5 May 1898, 2.

76. "Military Taps," *The Examiner*, 10 May 1898, 3; "To-Day the Newly Made Soldiers Will go Into Camp at the Presidio," *San Francisco Chronicle*, 6 May 1898, 9.

77. "The First is Under Orders," *San Francisco Call*, 7 May 1898, 8.

78. Ibid.; "Regular Army," *San Francisco Call*, 6 May 1898, 7; "The First in Camp," *The Examiner*, 8 May 1898, 16; Sketch, "How the Troops are Camped on the Presidio Parade Ground," *San Francisco Call*, 18 May 1898, 7.

79. "To-Day the Newly Made Soldiers Will go Into Camp at the Presidio," *San Francisco Chronicle*, 6 May 1898, 9.

80. "The First is Under Orders," *San Francisco Call*, 7 May 1898, 8.

81. "Orders From General Merriam," *San Francisco Call*, 7 May 1898, 8.

82. General Orders No. 8, Department of California, 6 May 1898, as published in the *Army and Navy Journal*, 21 May 1898, 743 and *San Francisco Call*, 8 May 1898, 10.

83. "Worn and Weary Southern Boys," *San Francisco Call*, 8 May 1898, 11.

84. "Orders From General Merriam," *San Francisco Call*, 7 May 1898, 8; "Worn and Weary Southern Boys," *San Francisco Call*, 8 May 1898, 11.

85. "One Army to Go and One to Wait Orders," *San Francisco Chronicle*, 13 May 1898, 4.

86. "Thousands Visit the Boys in Blue," *San Francisco Call*, 9 May 1898, 5; "Regulars Arrive and Volunteers Drill at the Presidio Growing Camp," *San Francisco Chronicle*, 10 May 1898, 9; "Worn and Weary Southern Boys," *San Francisco Call*, 8 May 1898, 11.

87. "In Camp With the Volunteers," *San Francisco Chronicle*, 11 May 1898, 4; "Mobilizing Western Troops in San Francisco," *San Francisco Call*, 5 May 1898, 2.

88. "The First in Camp," *The Examiner*, 8 May 1898, 16; "Worn and Weary Southern Boys," *San Francisco Call*, 9 May 1898, 10.

89. US War Department, Adjutant-General's Office, Document No. 61, Military Information Division, *The Organized Militia of the United States. Statement of the Condition and Efficiency for Service of the Organized Militia. From Regular Annual Reports, and other Sources, Covering the Year 1897* (Washington, DC: GPO, 1898), 32.

90. "The Following Apportionment Has Been Made For the Several States, and Territories and the Dist. of Columbia," in Record Group 94, Office of the Adjutant General Document File, Document No. 84869, filed with Document No. 74259, Box 534: 74121 to 74321 (Washington, DC: National Archives).

91. Captain Carrington to Adjutant General, USA, Washington, DC, 9 May 1898, in Record Group 94, Office of the Adjutant General, Checklist Entry 182, Muster in War With Spain, 1st Call, Document Number 247387, Inclosure 30, filed with California Documents, Box No. 1: Alabama through District of Columbia (Washington, DC: National Archives).

92. "Uncle Sam in a Hurry," *San Francisco Daily Report*, 11 May 1898, 3.

93. Charles R. Detrick, *History of the Operations of the First Regiment, California U.S. Volunteer Infantry in the Campaign in the Philippine Islands*, n.p., n.d., 96.

94. "The 'Heavies' Now at Work," *San Francisco Call*, 12 May 1898, 7; *Crocker-Langley San Francisco Directory for Year Commencing May 1899*, 656.

95. Merriam, Major General Commanding, to Gen. Corbin, Adjt. Gen., U.S.A., 13 May 1898, in Record Group 94, Office of the Adjutant General, Checklist Entry 182, Muster in War With Spain, 1st Call, Document Number 253960, filed with Washington Documents, Box 7: South Dakota through Washington (Washington, DC: National Archives).

96. US War Department, *Annual Reports of the War Department for the Fiscal Year Ended June 30, 1898. Report of the Major-General Commanding the Army*, Report of Maj. Gen. H.C. Merriam, Commanding, Department of California (Washington, DC: GPO, 1898), 176.

97. "Diagram of the Camp at the Bay District," *The Examiner*, 31 May 1898, 3.

98. US War Department, *Annual Reports of the War Department for the Fiscal Year Ended June 30, 1898. Report of the Major-General Commanding the Army*, Report of Maj. Gen. H.C. Merriam, Commanding, Department of California (Washington, DC: GPO, 1898), 176; "A Moist Camp," *San Francisco Daily Report*, 16 May 1898, 2; "Hurry-Up Orders Have Come," *San Francisco Call*, 15 May 1898, 7; "Anxious to Move on to the Philippines," *San Francisco Call*, 16 May 1898, 5.

99. Langellier, 190.

100. "General Otis is in Command," *San Francisco Call*, 18 May 1898, 5; "Troops to Camp at the Bay District," *San Francisco Chronicle*, 18 May 1898, 3.

101. General Orders, No. 7. Headquarters, U.S. Expeditionary Forces, San Francisco, California, 29 May 1898 in US Army, Department of the Pacific and Eighth Army Corps, Adjutant General's Office, *Index to General Orders and Circulars: Philippine Islands Expeditionary Forces, 1898*.

102. "Seven Thousand Men," *San Francisco Call*, 26 May 1898, 2.

103. *San Francisco: Its Builders Past and Present*, volume I (Chicago-San Francisco: S.J. Clarke Publishing Co., 1913), 161-62.

104. "Quite an Army Here," *San Francisco Daily Report*, 3 June 1898, 2; "Fourteen Thousand," *San Francisco Call*, 3 June 1898, 7; "Iowans at

Oakland," *San Francisco Call*, 10 June 1898, 5.

105. *The National Cyclopaedia of American Biography*, volume XIII (New York and New Jersey: James T. White and Co., 1984), 338; American Council of Learned Societies, *Dictionary of American Biography*, volume XII, (New York: C. Scribner's Sons, 1943), 553-54.

106. US War Department, *Annual Reports of the War Department for the Fiscal Year Ended June 30, 1897. Report of the Secretary of War. Miscellaneous Reports*, Report of Brig. Gen. Henry C. Merriam, Headquarters, Department of the Columbia, Vancouver Barracks, Wash., September 14, 1897, (Washington, DC: GPO, 1897), 197-200; US War Department, *Annual Reports of the War Department for the Fiscal Year Ended June 30, 1898. Report of the Major-General Commanding the Army*, Report of Maj. Gen. Henry C. Merriam, Commanding the Department of the Columbia, Headquarters, Department of the Columbia, Vancouver Barracks, Wash., October 1, 1898 (Washington, DC: GPO, 1898), 179-81.

107. H.C. Corbin, Adjutant General, to Generals Brooke, Shafter, Coppinger, Wade, 15 April 1898, in *Correspondence Relating to the War With Spain and Conditions Growing Out of the Same, Including the Insurrection in the Philippine Islands and the China Relief Expedition, Between the Adjutant-General of the Army and Military Commander in the United States, Cuba, Porto Rico, China, and the Philippine Islands, From April 15, 1898, to July 30, 1902*, volume I (Washington, DC: GPO, 1902), hereafter cited as *Correspondence I*, 7-8.

108. US War Department, *Annual Reports of the War Department for the Fiscal Year Ended June 30, 1898. Report of the Major-General Commanding the Army*, Report of Maj. Gen. H.C. Merriam, Commanding, Department of California. Headquarters, Department of California, San Francisco, California, 10 October 1898 (Washington, DC: GPO, 1898), 174-75, 179.

109. Merriam, Brigadier General, Commanding, Vancouver Barracks, Washington, to Adjutant General, U.S. Army, 30 April 1898, in Record Group 94, Office of the Adjutant General, Checklist Entry 182, Muster in War With Spain, 1st Call, Document Number 253960, filed with Washington Documents, Box No. 7: South Dakota through Washington (Washington, DC: National Archives).

110. H.C. Corbin to General Merriam, 13 May 1898, in *Correspondence II*, 639.

111. Special Orders No. 79, Department of Columbia, 13 May 1898, as published in *Army and Navy Journal*, 28 May 1898, 767.

112. Schwan, Assistant Adjutant-General, to Major-General Merriam, 16 May 1898, in *Correspondence II*, 647.

113. "Hurry-Up Orders Have Come, *San Francisco Call*, 15 May 1898, 7; "Camping in the Rain," *San Francisco Call*, 15 May 1898, 7.

114. "Anxious to Move on the Philippines," *San Francisco Call*, 16 May 1898, 5.

115. H.C. Corbin to General Otis, 11 May 1898, in *Correspondence II*, 636.

116. Thomas F. Burdett, "A New Evaluation of General Otis' Leadership

in the Philippines," *Military Review*, January 1975, 79-80; American Council of Learned Societies, volume XIV, 94-95; *The National Cyclopaedia of American Biography*, 29-31.

117. Burdett, 79-80; American Council of Learned Societies, 94-95; *The National Cyclopaedia of American Biography*, 29-31.

118. H.C. Corbin to General Otis, 12 May 1898, in *Correspondence II*, 637.

119. H.C. Corbin to Major-General Otis, 14 May 1898 (received 4:45 p.m.), in *Correspondence II*, 639-40.

120. Ibid.; H.C. Corbin to Commanding General, Department of California, 14 May 1898, in *Correspondence II*, 641.

121. "Charleston Off for Manila," *San Francisco Call*, 19 May 1898, 5; Otis to Adjutant-General, 18 May 1898 (received 19 May, 1:32 a.m.), in *Correspondence II*, 659.

122. Otis to Adjutant-General, 18 May 1898 (received 19 May, 6:45 a.m.), in *Correspondence II*, 659-60.

123. H.C. Corbin to Gen. E.S. Otis, 19 May 1898, in *Correspondence II*, 661-62.

124. General Orders, No. 1, Headquarters, U.S. Expeditionary Forces, San Francisco, California, 20 May 1898 in US Army, Department of the Pacific and Eighth Army Corps, Adjutant General's Office, *Index to General Orders and Circulars: Philippine Islands Expeditionary Forces, 1898*.

125. Otis to Adjutant-General, 20 May 1898 (received 21 May, 2:11 a.m.), in *Correspondence II*, 664-65; Otis to Adjutant-General, 20 May 1898, 11:20 p.m., in *Correspondence II*, 667-68; Otis to Adjutant-General, 21 May 1898 (received 22 May 1898, 6 a.m.), in *Correspondence II*, 668; Otis to Adjutant-General, 23 May 1898–12 midnight, in *Correspondence II*, 669; Otis to Adjutant-General, 23 May 1898 (received 24 May 1898, 4 a.m.), in *Correspondence II*, 670; Otis to Adjutant-General, 24 May 1898 (received 5:24 p.m.), in *Correspondence II*, 671.

126. H.C. Corbin to Major-General Otis, 27 May 1898–12 midnight, in *Correspondence II*, 675.

127. General Orders, No. 1, Headquarters, Independent Division Philippine Islands Expeditionary Forces, Camp Merritt. San Francisco, California, 1 June 1898 in US Army, Department of the Pacific and Eighth Army Corps, Adjutant General's Office, *Index to General Orders and Circulars: Philippine Islands Expeditionary Forces, 1898*.

128. Ibid.

129. American Council of Learned Societies, volume XII, 572-74; *The National Cyclopaedia of American Biography*, 28-29.

130. Donald E. Alberts, Brandy Station to Manila Bay: A Biography of General Wesley Merritt (Austin, TX: Presidial Press, 1980), 305.

131. Telegram, Merritt, Major General, to Governor Hastings, Mt. Gretna, via Lebanon, Pennsylvania, 6 May 1898, as published in *Annual Report of the Adjutant-General of Pennsylvania for the Year 1898* (PA: State Printer of

Pennsylvania, 1900), 24; Special Orders, No. 101, Headquarters, Department of the East, 9 May 1898, as published in *Annual Report of the Adjutant-General of Pennsylvania for the Year 1898*, 30; Telegram, W. Merritt, Maj. Gen. to His Excellency Gov. Hastings, Mt. Gretna, Pennsylvania, via Lebanon, Pennsylvania, 10 May 1898, as published in *Annual Report of the Adjutant-General of Pennsylvania for the Year 1898*, 34.

132. H.C. Corbin to Maj. Gen. Wesley Merritt, 12 May 1898, in *Correspondence II*, 637.

133. Memorandum, W. Merritt, Major-General, to the Honorable, the Secretary of War, 12 May 1898, in *Correspondence II*, 638; Letter, W. Merritt, Major-General, to His Excellency William McKinley, 13 May 1898, in *Correspondence II*, 643-44; Letter, W. Merritt, Major-General, to His Excellency William McKinley, 15 May 1898 (Received 16 May 1898), in *Correspondence II*, 645-46; Telegram, H.C. Corbin, Adjutant General, to Major General Merritt, 17 May 1898, in Record Group 94, Office of the Adjutant General Document File, Document No. 80950, filed with Document No. 81545, Box 604: 81394-81577 (Washington, DC: National Archives).

134. Second Endorsement, W. Merritt, Major-General, Commanding, to Adjutant General of the Army, 17 May 1898 and Third Endorsement, Nelson A. Miles, Major-General, Commanding, to the Secretary of War, 18 May 1898, in *Correspondence II*, 648-49.

135. Telegram, Schwan, Assistant Adjutant-General, to Maj. Gen. Wesley Merritt, 16 May 1898, in *Correspondence II*, 649.

136. General Orders, No. 1, Headquarters, U.S. Expeditionary Forces and Department of the Pacific, 30 May 1898 in US Army, Department of the Pacific and Eighth Army Corps, Adjutant General's Office, *Index to General Orders and Circulars: Philippine Islands Expeditionary Forces, 1898*.

137. H.C. Corbin to Maj. Gen. Wesley Merritt, 12 May 1898, in *Correspondence II*, 637.

138. Letter, W. Merritt, Major-General, to His Excellency William McKinley, 15 May 1898 (Received 16 May 1898), in *Correspondence II*, 645-46.

139. Merritt to the Commissary-General, 16 May 1898 (Received 4:43 p.m.), in *Correspondence II*, 647.

140. "Brief Military Items," *San Francisco Chronicle*, 26 May 1898, 2.

141. General Orders, No. 1., Headquarters, U.S. Expeditionary Forces and Department of the Pacific, San Francisco, California, 30 May 1898 in US Army, Department of the Pacific and Eighth Army Corps, Adjutant General's Office, *Index to General Orders and Circulars: Philippine Islands Expeditionary Forces, 1898*; Wesley Merritt, et al., "The Army of the United States," in *The Armies of To-Day: A Description of the Armies of the Leading Nations at the Present Time* (London: McIlvaine & Co., 1893), 9-10.

142. "Merritt in Open Rebellion," *San Francisco Call*, 17 May 1898, 1.

143. General Orders, No. 1., Headquarters, U.S. Expeditionary Forces and Department of the Pacific, San Francisco, California, 30 May 1898 in US Army, Department of the Pacific and Eighth Army Corps, Adjutant General's Office,

Index to General Orders and Circulars: Philippine Islands Expeditionary Forces, 1898; Brigadier-General Wesley Merritt, U.S.A., "The Army of the United States," *The Armies of To-Day*, 10.

144. Erna Risch, *Quartermaster Support of the Army: A History of the Corps, 1775-1939* (Washington, DC: Office of the Quartermaster General, 1962), 427-28; 457.

Chapter IV
Overseeing and Training the Troops

Organizing, training, and equipping units for expeditions overseas became a top priority for those in command at San Francisco. The task to prepare and move troops thousands of miles across the Pacific, having no precedent in US Army history, had to be addressed quickly, efficiently, and spontaneously. Military and political officials in Washington were pushing for rapid deployments to the Philippines.

To exercise effective leadership within his department, MG Wesley Merritt needed the services of general officers to lead new brigades and assembled expeditions. He had to establish suitable command and control facilities capable of linking his command to the War Department and various local contacts. He also had to execute several responsibilities that put him in touch with Bay Area political, economic, and social leaders.

As the commander of Camp Merritt, MG Elwell S. Otis faced his own challenges. To Otis fell much of the burden of training the force to achieve proficiency as a military organization. To that end, he and other commanders worked to establish good order and discipline within the Independent Division. They also had to identify those diversions that would be appropriate and suitable for units to maintain their men's morale. Welfare of the troops quickly emerged as a major test for the command. Officers from the ordnance, subsistence, quartermaster, and medical departments grappled with how to equip, feed, and care for Volunteers and Regulars as they prepared to deploy overseas.

Exercising Command and Control

When apprised of his selection as commander of the Philippine expedition, Merritt petitioned the War Department to ensure that his command reflected a greater ratio of Regulars to Volunteers. Along with more Regulars, he solicited additional artillery and cavalry units to augment the sizable infantry forces already committed to his command. To assist in the tasks of receiving, staging, and deploying the force of nearly 20,000 troops, the general recognized the need for ample senior leadership.

Before reaching San Francisco, Merritt initiated a request for additional general officers. On 21 May, during his final trip to the nation's capital before heading west, Merritt submitted to the AG, BG Corbin, a by-name request for one-star officers that would be "necessary to the success of my expedition." Again showing his preference for active duty military, the Pacific department commander began his petition asking for three

The Man Who Will Lead the California Troops to Aid Commodore Dewey in Manila.

San Francisco Call, 5 May 1898

Figure 35. BG Thomas M. Anderson.

Regular Army colonels: George W. Davis, Adna R. Chaffee, and Samuel S. Sumner. Each had recently received a promotion to brigadier general of Volunteers; all had a cavalry connection. Then Merritt added that he would welcome two from civilian life should the president appoint them general officers: COL Francis V. Greene and COL George A. Garretson. Both possessed military experience and were graduates of West Point.[1]

Merritt did not receive his Regular Army preferences. The War Department's assignment of general officers illustrated how the administration emphasized Caribbean over Pacific missions. On 16 May, Alger approved a command list that assigned seven of eight major generals of Volunteers to camps gathering resources for operations against Cuba or Puerto Rico. The only major general named for Philippine duty via San Francisco was MG Otis.[2] Of 19 Regular colonels appointed brigadier generals, including the three that Merritt requested, only one received orders for the Golden Gate: Thomas M. Anderson, former commander of the 14th US Infantry, who was already on the West Coast.[3] Merritt knew at the time of his request that both Otis and Anderson belonged to his command.

MG Merritt fared about the same with regard to his petition for specific civilian appointees. Garretson dodged an assignment to the Philippines, admitting that "I do not care particularly for the detail."[4] Greene was already with Shafter's command in Florida, but the War Department ordered him to San Francisco. Unlike Garretson, Greene welcomed the directive: "Will leave to-night unless otherwise instructed."[5] Greene and Merritt shared a common history. Both had written on military subjects for professional publications.[6] Both had graduated from the US Military Academy. Greene sub-

General Francis V. Greene.

San Francisco Chronicle, 29 May 1898

Figure 36.

sequently taught military engineering at the academy during part of Merritt's tour as superintendent.[7]

Merritt later pursued and secured the services of two other brigadier generals with whom he had served. BG Charles King was adjutant of the 5th US Cavalry when Merritt commanded the regiment in the late 1870s.[8] Upon learning that King had been nominated as brigadier general of Volunteers, Merritt telegraphed his congratulations and asked him to join his command, which the War Department arranged.[9] Another of his by-name requests, BG Arthur MacArthur, had served with Merritt at Fort Leavenworth in the 1880s.[10] MacArthur reached San Francisco in June 1898.[11]

Figure 37.

Two additional general officers joined Merritt. BG Marcus P. Miller, like Anderson a commander on the West Coast at the outbreak of the war, transferred to the Department of the Pacific from the Department of California.[12] BG Harrison Gray Otis reached Merritt's command through a favor of the president. The law to raise a Volunteer Army, passed by Congress on 22 April 1898, empowered McKinley to nominate one- and two-star general officers for each division formed by Regular and Volunteer regiments. The president took a personal interest in filling these billets. He used the law to name Otis, editor of the *Los Angeles Times*, to Merritt's command. Described by one of the Volunteers, Karl Kraemer of the 51st Iowa, as "a tall heavy set man with light hair and a goatee and mustache," Otis had served with the 23d Ohio during the Civil War.[13] The regiment provided Otis with a key connection to the president; McKinley belonged to the 23d Ohio during the same conflict.[14] (See figures 39 and 40.)

Figure 38.

By mid-June, Merritt's department therefore consisted of an additional major general, Elwell S. Otis, and six brigadier generals. Before deploying to the archipelago, Miller, King, H.G. Otis,

BRIGADIER-GENERAL MARCUS MILLER
Figure 39.

BRIGADIER-GENERAL HARRISON G. OTIS
Figure 40.

and MacArthur each commanded one of the Independent Division's four brigades in San Francisco. Anderson and Greene led the first two expeditions into the Pacific shortly after they reached the Golden Gate.

As the commander of the department's Independent Division and Camp Merritt, MG Otis was entitled to a staff. When the Secretary of War ordered Otis to San Francisco to take charge of the expedition pending Merritt's arrival, Alger authorized the general "to take with you such staff officers and clerical assistance as you may desire."[15] Otis quite correctly interpreted that offer to include more than personal aides. He brought with him four officers and seven noncommissioned officers.[16]

Staff members who accompanied MG Otis assumed critical responsibilities. Major Francis Moore performed some quartermaster functions, and CPT John S. Mallory served as acting IG. Two aides attended Otis: CPT John L. Sehon and 1LT Fred W. Sladen. Others who subsequently joined the division staff included CPT George Ruhlen and CPT C.A. Devol, acting quartermasters, and Major W.O. Owen, chief surgeon, who also supervised the division field hospital. Some of these men changed duty positions or held several titles simultaneously during their tours in San Francisco.[17]

After Otis and some of his staff reached the Golden Gate in mid-May, they established the Headquarters, US Expeditionary Forces in downtown San Francisco.[18] The city's Phelan Building at O'Farrell and Market Streets would serve as the command and control center for expeditionary force leadership before deployment. Otis and his staff occupied offices at the site until the end of the month.[19] On 30 May, Merritt's entourage constituting Headquarters, Department of the Pacific, took up residence on the fourth floor.[20] Otis and the staff personnel of the newly created Independent Division relocated to Camp Merritt.[21] When MG Merritt sailed for the Philippines in late June, Otis returned to downtown San Francisco.[22]

The Phelan Building had specific features that appealed to Philippine expeditionary leaders looking to establish a headquarters site. Part of the building already served as the Headquarters, Department of California. The commander and his staff occupied much of the second floor.[23] Officers from the Department of the Pacific occupied office space in rooms adjacent to those of Merriam's organization.[24] Coordination between the two commands became a matter of walking down the hall or tapping into the building's communications system. Officers of both commands could reach national contacts telegraphically and local authorities by using the telegraph or telephone.[25]

The Phelan Building's physical location offered advantages as a command and control center. Less than a mile from the docks, the structure afforded easy access to transports or the steamship companies that leased them.[26] Forces arriving and departing via the bay could be monitored readily. San Francisco's municipal centers were close by, as were offices of the California National Guard. Most important, the headquarters of the depot quartermaster on New Montgomery Street was within easy walking distance.[27]

The headquarters location, however, had some drawbacks. The Phelan Building was located about 5 miles from Camp Merritt. LTC Henry Lippincott, Chief Surgeon, Department of the Pacific, noted that although the headquarters was connected to the camps by "the excellent street railway system of San Francisco, communication with the officers there was somewhat inconvenient."[28]

MG Merritt stayed in San Francisco for 35 days, many of them at work in the Phelan Building. "Surrounded by a cordon of sentries, aides and staff officers," Merritt spent much of his time communicating telegraphically with superiors in Washington. Behind a glass door bearing the inscription "Commander Philippine Expedition," Merritt dictated letters to a stenographer and periodically met with visitors who waited for an opportunity to talk with him.[29] (See figure 41.)

Some visitors included members of the press. Merritt made himself quite accessible to reporters who delighted in quoting the general. Locally, his relationship with correspondents evolved after a slow beginning. When

Figure 41.

Merritt arrived in the city on 26 May, he had little to say.[30] By 5 June, the *San Francisco Chronicle* went so far as to observe: "There is no censorship of news at General Merritt's headquarters, for the reason that no news whatever is given out."[31] M.H. de Young, editor and proprietor of the *Chronicle*, may have regretted the timing of that observation because the same day *Examiner* reporter Alice Rix published her interview with the general. Rix was able to elicit Merritt's views regarding officer leadership and the quality of Volunteer units.[32] Days later, as he prepared to depart for the Philippines, Merritt used an interview to thank the Red Cross, Catholic Truth Society, and citizens of San Francisco for supporting the troops.[33] In another interview with the *Chronicle*, he told of some plans for occupying the Philippines.[34]

For good reason, Merritt shied from Bay Area newspaper reporters at the outset of his stay in San Francisco. Before he reached the Golden Gate, the general voiced concern over the paucity of Regular forces assigned to his command. Those misgivings appeared in New York and California newspapers on 17 May. The next day Merritt telegraphed Secretary Alger,

"I desire you to know that the interviews published in the New York papers this morning are in every way incorrect and unauthorized."[35] Merritt's protestation appeared to be not so much a statement of denial as an effort to avoid trouble with superiors. This instance would not be the last time he felt compelled to address public statements attributed to him with the War Department. Merritt allegedly made some remarks on Philippine policy at an "informal" banquet Mayor James Phelan hosted at the Pacific-Union Club in early June. Later that month, Merritt responded to an inquiry from the Secretary of War and denied that he had made such remarks.[36]

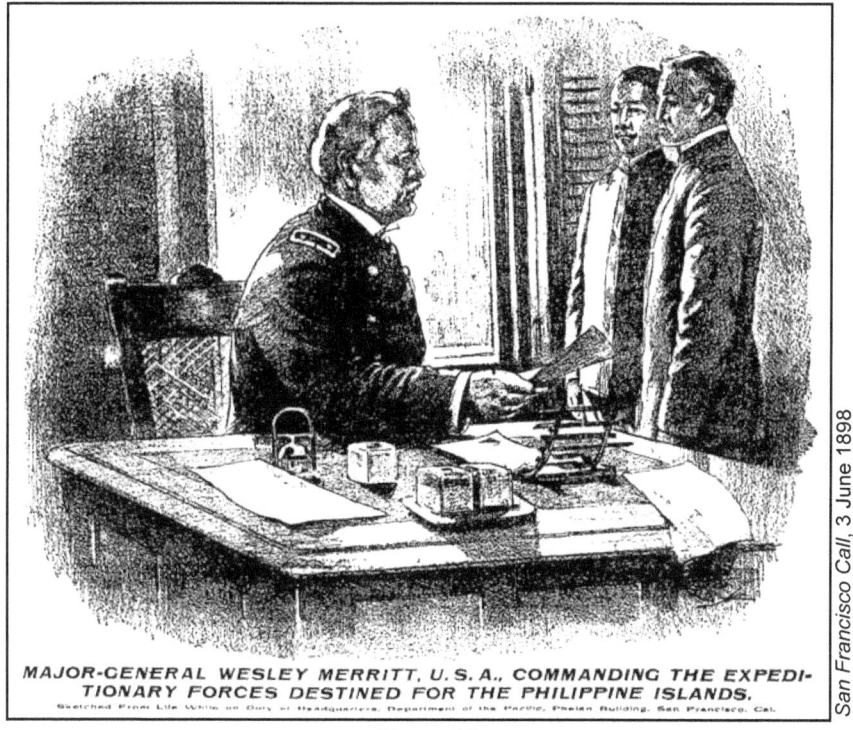

MAJOR-GENERAL WESLEY MERRITT, U. S. A., COMMANDING THE EXPEDITIONARY FORCES DESTINED FOR THE PHILIPPINE ISLANDS.

San Francisco Call, 3 June 1898

Figure 42.

Although Merritt may have entertained reporters, the soldiers of his command did not often see him at Fontana warehouse, Camp Merritt, or the Presidio. Little evidence exists to suggest that Merritt spent much time observing how the troops, be they Regular or Volunteer, trained or lived at these encampments. Local papers reported on four trips that the general made to Camp Merritt, all undertaken principally to confer with MG Otis.[37] Three of the four visits coincided with the departure of the second expedition to the Philippines. Only once did a reporter observe Merritt "informally inspecting the camp."[38] Months later, when queried about Camp

91

Merritt, the general exhibited at best only a vague familiarity with the bivouac site. He said the location used to be "fair grounds." Merritt described the site as "a concentrated camp. The sewerage was good, but it had been established (the Bay District Racetrack area) before I got there, and there was no other place to go except to the other side (the Jordan Tract)."[39]

Merritt may have formed a different opinion of the "sewerage" had he lived there or maintained a headquarters at the campsite, but he did not. He established his residence at the Palace Hotel, not too far away from the Phelan Building. In 1898, the Palace was San Francisco's finest hotel and reputedly the most opulent of any in the West.[40] Merritt must have felt quite at home in such exclusive surroundings, for his biographer, Don E. Alberts, later suggested that the general possessed a "fondness for comfortable urban living."[41]

That affinity manifested itself in other ways. Merritt appeared as the guest of honor at several dinner parties.[42] At one point, city officials planned to host a public banquet in Merritt's honor at the Palace. The general subsequently requested a smaller, more informal affair, which Mayor Phelan and other civic leaders sponsored at the city's Pacific-Union Club on Thursday, 9 June.[43] Eight days later, he appeared at the Mechanics' Pavilion for a Red Cross benefit that featured an exhibition drill by the 13th Minnesota.[44] On 19 June he attended a performance at the Orpheum, a variety theater on O'Farrell Street. As Merritt took his front seat, "the band struck up a patriotic strain and the people arose and cheered the commander to the echo."[45]

The general spent five weekends on the West Coast; parts of two he used to escape the city. On Saturday, 11 June, he departed for the Monterey Bay Area. After spending 24 hours at the beach, he returned to San Francisco late Sunday afternoon.[46] A reporter for *The Examiner* wrote of the general's holiday: "The General has been very closely confined to his headquarters in the Phelan Building and his trip to Monterey is the only recreation he expects to have before his departure for the Philippines."[47]

That expectation may have been accurate at the time, but the following weekend Merritt left town again. On Saturday, he traveled to Burlingame, southeast of San Francisco, where he was the guest of Henry T. Scott. Scott was president and treasurer of the Union Iron Works, "an immense shipbuilding and iron manufacturing corporation capitalized at millions and employing thousands of men—the largest enterprise of the kind on the coast." [48] On Sunday he spent time in Menlo Park, hosted by Major Rathbone, before returning to the Palace Hotel that evening.[49]

While MG Wesley Merritt fulfilled the political, military, and social roles of a department commander, MG Elwell Otis labored to bring organization to the forces assembled in San Francisco. Otis was the perfect complement to Merritt. As Merritt worked out of the Phelan Building engaged in correspondence with authorities in Washington, Otis and the staff of the Independent Division toiled and slept at Camp Merritt, administering to assigned units and preparing to deploy forces abroad incrementally.

Upon establishing Headquarters, US Expeditionary Forces, Otis tackled the challenge of dispatching the command's first expedition to the Philippines on 25 May. After Merritt arrived the following day, Otis shifted his focus to the condition of Regulars and Volunteers that remained. Although expeditionary forces had begun to assemble in San Francisco as early as 7 May, no central command exercised control over those organizations. That situation changed on 1 June when Otis assumed command of the newly created Independent Division and established his headquarters at Camp Merritt.

The staff took several days to prepare the site for operation. Acting IG CPT John S. Mallory and Acting Chief Quartermaster Major Francis Moore supervised site preparation in the southwest section of Camp Merritt.[50] The specific location at Fulton Street and 4th Avenue offered several advantages.[51] At the time of its construction, the headquarters was in a more remote part of camp where noise and dust levels were somewhat diminished. Directly south across Fulton Street lay the "blossoming shrubs and ornamental trees" of Golden Gate Park, one of the more rustic, scenic areas of the city.[52] An additional feature was that the location allowed easy access to the McAllister-Street Line, a cable car service that linked the park to Market Street and the ferries.[53]

MAJOR-GENERAL E. S. OTIS IN HIS TENT AT THE CAMP HEADQUARTERS

The Examiner, 3 June 1898

Figure 43.

While Otis found a somewhat secluded spot for his headquarters, he was by no means removed from the troops in his division. The site rested on slightly elevated ground that permitted him to observe the encampment to the north.[54] He and his staff shared the immediate vicinity of his bivouac with the men of Company G, 14th Infantry. Eventually Regular engineers and infantry from the 18th and 23d Regiments established their campsites in the undeveloped city blocks nearby.[55]

MG Otis was also linked to superiors and subordinates through a comprehensive communications network. A reporter from *The Examiner* observed, "the tents of the Major-General, his lieutenants, adjutants and clerks have been pitched. From them there is telegraphic and telephonic communication with the city and the headquarters of each regiment."[56] Otis's headquarters complex comprised 12 tents, including one for the general's office, another for his sleeping quarters, and a third for storage. At least one tent served as the telegraph center, which likely stood near Otis's headquarters. The others belonged to staff officers and clerks.[57]

The general's staff endured lengthy workdays. That condition was likely a reflection of Otis's penchant for detail as well as the situation encountered upon arriving in the city. One reporter wrote: "There are no men in San Francisco who are harder worked at present than the officers at United States Army headquarters. They are kept busy from early morning until 10 o'clock at night in carrying out the instructions received from Washington in regard to the fitting out of the Manila expedition."[58]

Lengthy workdays focused on outfitting expeditions, and organizing the Independent Division consumed Otis and his staff. Unlike his boss at the Phelan Building, the commander of Camp Merritt neither appeared at social events nor ventured outside of San Francisco. One reporter observed that "only fleeting glimpses may be had of Major-General Otis, as he trudges from his headquarters tent to an adjoining one. An orderly is ever at his door, the tent flaps are closed, and General Otis is alone with his plans, maps and responsibilities."[59]

Major-General Otis at Work.

Figure 44.

94

Absorbed in his tasks, Otis made little time for the press, which journalists did not appreciate. In particular, the *San Francisco Daily Report* took exception to Otis's ostensible indifference toward news personnel. Shortly before the first expedition sailed on 25 May the paper criticized his headquarters for failing to publicize departure information.[60] When Otis established his headquarters at Camp Merritt, the *Daily Report* complained, "This morning a sentry was on duty and allowed no one to come within fifty feet of the General's tent. Even newspapermen were not admitted."[61]

The paper continued to snipe at Otis in early June. At one point, a reporter wrote sarcastically, "There was joy among the newspapermen at Camp Merritt this morning. General Otis braved the persistency of the reporters and walked from his tent to the street cars. He even condescendingly bowed."[62] By this time, another paper had fired a verbal volley at the general. The *San Francisco Call* suggested that if Otis succeeded "in holding off the Spaniards at Manila as he is now doing the press of San Francisco, he can sustain a siege there of indefinite length without any base of supplies."[63]

Otis had reason to distance himself from the press. He knew how Merritt's "incorrect and unauthorized" interviews printed in New York newspapers had generated some unwelcome attention from superiors in Washington.[64] That situation reinforced the value of discretion in dealing with reporters, a lesson Otis grasped from the outset of his arrival in the city. Shortly after detraining on 17 May, the general offered a few observations about receiving orders for the coast and traveling west from Colorado. When asked about the controversy surrounding Merritt, Otis declined to comment. According to a *Call* reporter, the general stated that "military courtesy prevented him from passing any opinion on the subject."[65]

Otis's leadership position relative to Merritt's also accounted for the division commander's reluctance to talk to newspapermen. As a subordinate to Merritt, Otis wisely referred journalists to officials at the Department of the Pacific. On one occasion when the *Daily Report* criticized Otis's inaccessibility, the paper noted, "A 'D.R.' reporter was told that all information would be given out at army headquarters in the Phelan building."[66] The journalist chose to interpret Otis's decision as a rebuff; that notwithstanding, the general exercised his prerogative to defer press inquiries to Merritt's headquarters.

Reporters eventually gained some access to Otis. On 6 June, the *Chronicle* published some remarks he made about the encampment he commanded and the status of BG Greene.⁶⁷ After Merritt sailed aboard the *Newport* on 29 June, Otis became more communicative with the press as the expedition's senior officer in San Francisco. On 8 and 10 July, *The Examiner* cited his views on topics that included Camp Merritt, Hawaii, transports, and California troops.⁶⁸

Drill and Exercise

While MG Otis gave little time to the press, he spent hours tending to the details of preparing expeditionary forces for duty overseas. One dimension of that preparation dealt with drill and exercise. When Otis took command of Camp Merritt and the Independent Division, he defined guidelines that systematized the manner in which units under his command approached these fundamentals. To the credit of those Regular and Volunteer regiments that went into camp before the division command structure evolved, units vigorously pursued drill programs. The *Daily Report* observed on 16 May, "Drill in the manual of arms, drill in signaling, drill in music, the setting up exercises—drill, drill, drill all day long. That is the order of things in the camps at the Presidio—nothing but drill and lots of it."⁶⁹

Figure 45.

Each regimental commander grappled with a most vexing challenge to his training program: inexperience. Not one regiment, Volunteer or Regular, reached the port city with an organization composed entirely of seasoned soldiers. In every case, new recruits who had never donned uniforms populated the ranks. For example, when a guard organization federalized in its home state, new men were added to replace those who were unwilling or unable to volunteer for service. In another case, the president issued his second call for Volunteers on 25 May. Infantry companies, artillery batteries, and cavalry troops increased their authorized manpower. This executive decision meant that units then mobilizing in states, assembling in San Francisco, or deploying to the Philippines would absorb an additional number of raw recruits after they had already begun their drills.

This challenge called upon infantry commanders, for example, to pursue a drill regimen that took into account the varied expertise within each squad, platoon, company, and battalion. That condition called for organizations to plan and execute a variety of drills concurrently, from those that transformed raw recruits into green soldiers to exercises that focused on brigade movements.

Varied drill routines appeared among the first Volunteer and Regular regiments quartered on the Presidio. The 14th US Infantry and two California regiments each trained "awkward squads" of recruits at the battalion or regiment level.[70] These new men received instruction in marching, the manual of arms, and physical exercises. After gaining a certain proficiency, men shed their "awkward" status and moved into the permanent organizational structure.

As these troops worked their way through this rite of passage, others engaged in more advanced activities. On 11 May, seasoned California Volunteers worked at extended

Figure 46.

order movements and skirmisher deployment; Regulars conducted guard mount and company maneuvers.[71] On 13 May, COL Smith took his 1st California through close order and extended order drill at the company and battalion levels.[72]

"CLOSE ORDER AT THE COLORS!"
SCENE AT THE FIRING DRILL ON THE RESERVATION.
Figure 47.

San Francisco Call, 29 May 1898

When Otis brought many of these units under his control, he wisely maintained this decentralized approach to drill while routinizing the training program of units belonging to the Independent Division. On 2 June, he published General Orders No. 2 that stated, "For the present the practical military instruction of the troops of the Division will be of the character which Brigade, Regimental, or Battalion Commanders think most essential." He did, however, add several stipulations that obligated commanders to conduct the following: drill at a minimum of 3 hours per day; daily personnel inspections, including the troops, their arms, clothing, and hygiene, in lieu of formal dress parades; assemblies with arms at reveille and retreat; and guard mount, the only daily ceremony required.[73]

Otis gave his command about one month to work on its priorities in drill. Essentially, that permitted brigade and regimental commanders 34 days to achieve some level of proficiency in close and extended order drill as they accepted new personnel and blended them with veterans to mold a specific unit identity.

Figure 48.

Taking his lead from Otis, BG Marcus Miller, commander of the division's 1st Brigade, looked to his regimental commanders for the drills most needed in their respective commands.[74] Although his was the only command to be composed of Regular infantry, Miller received quite a diverse response from the 14th, 18th, and 23d Regiments because of each command's unique characteristics.

Major Charles Robe, acting commander, 14th Infantry, had just seen five companies of the regiment dispatched with the first expedition to the Philippines. Other companies from the organization had either recently arrived or were converging on the city, and recruits were joining the ranks to reach the 14th's authorized strength. Robe observed, "the instruction most needed is that now being given, viz: the schools of the soldier, and company, in close, and in extended order, 'the squad.' All troops of this command are receiving four hours daily instruction in the above." He anticipated challenging his command to evolve into platoon, company, and extended order.[75]

COL D.D. Van Valzah, 18th Infantry, reported that "heavy guard duty" responsibilities and recruit training had stripped two battalions of "old soldiers." "We have now over two hundred recruits and expect four hundred and twenty-two more, and the instruction of these men will require all the command (the 2d. and 3d. battalions) to assist." He preferred "that all the companies be required to drill all their men three hours a day and recruits four hours a day, and that as the drills and instruction progress the regimental commander advance the instruction from squad drill to company and battalion drill, giving especial attention to extended order exercises."[76]

COL Samuel Ovenshine, 23d Infantry, suggested drill hours that mirrored the 18th Infantry's. He already had four companies of "drilled men" tagged for the next expedition, and he anticipated he would lose their expertise shortly. Ovenshine wrote, "After the arrival of the recruits now en route to the regiment, the eight companies to remain in camp will be virtually recruit companies." Given the circumstances, Ovenshine intended to concentrate on "company or squad drills."[77]

Commanders needed time to get their units into fighting order starting with drill fundamentals. Otis and his brigade commanders understood this reality but expected their organizations to gain proficiency quickly. On 3 July, Miller published a circular with more detailed guidance. He wanted his commanders to submit unit "schemes of instruction" over a 10-day period. While they had the latitude to design their own programs, Miller directed, "The instruction should be progressial (sic), the last three or four days for Cavalry, Infantry and Battalion of Heavy Artillery, California, devoted to marching with advance and rear guards and flank parties establishing pickets and reconnoitering the streets of a city or village."[78] Miller's circular reflected the expectation that units should be engaged in more sophisticated training, particularly along the order of likely missions overseas.

Miller either knew or anticipated his boss's expectations. Two days after distribution of the 1st Brigade circular, MG Otis published new training guidance, challenging his units to tackle more advanced drills. New general orders issued on 5 July formalized drill periods and specified instruction subjects within the Independent Division. Otis expected organizations to engage in three drill periods each day, two scheduled for the morning. In the first session of 45 minutes, infantry, cavalry, and artil-

Regulars at Camp Merritt in Skirmish Drill With Krag-Jorgensens and Sword Bayonets.

Figure 49.

San Francisco Chronicle, 7 July 1898

lery units conducted school of the soldier. During the 90 minute second period, infantry commanders executed school of the company, emphasizing platoon movements and "the preliminary target practice drills in aiming and pointing."[79]

Otis directed that infantry commanders give the single, 2-hour period in the afternoon to "the school of the battalion and evolutions of the regiment, and in the battalion and regimental extended order." The division commander expected cavalry and light artillery to use the second and third drill periods to pursue training that was unique to their arm of service. The cavalry would train in school of the trooper and troop in both close and extended order, and light artillery would train in school of the cannoneer and battery dismounted. Heavy artillery was the only arm directed to train outside of its area of expertise. Men in this branch of service would likely not have siege guns in their possession in an attack against Spanish-held Manila. Not wanting to waste the manpower, Otis directed that they be trained "in the school of the company and battalion for infantry."[80]

Drill at close or extended order required training areas. For those quartered at Camp Merritt, that need presented a challenge. Located near the Richmond District in the northwest part of the city, the campsite offered only limited space for training activities. Regiments used roads within the confines of Camp Merritt for some drills. In late May, the 20th Kansas took to the gravel and pebble streets adjacent to camp for their training.[81]

Figure 50.

Writing after the war, Private James Camp, 1st Idaho, recalled "many drills over sandy or broken rock-covered streets."[82] Commissioners of the Golden Gate Park opened "the main drive of the park up to 9 A.M. each day and the use of the other drives for all day for purposes of drill."[83]

Access to streets assisted in executing close order or guard mount, but larger formations and more complex drills required additional space. The *Call* pointed out on 26 May that "soldiers will have to take a long march before they can secure room enough to maneuver."[84] That "long march" oriented on the Presidio and a few of the reservation's 1,400 acres.[85]

Figure 51. Camp Merritt in foreground; soldiers drilling on the Presidio at the upper right.

On 31 May, *The Examiner* reported that "the Nebraska troops will begin their drills in extended order on the Presidio hills north of the camp at Richmond."[86] On 14 June, the 1st Montana used Presidio terrain to fight a "sham battle," a sort of intramural attack and defense among the regiment's battalions.[87] One member of the regiment, Lieutenant Alexander Haist, recalled that one drill site on the Presidio consisted of "a gently sloping hillside" that overlooked the Pacific Ocean. "When the regiment first marched to it," wrote Haist, "many of its members got their first view of saltwater."[88] CPT Frank W. Medbery, 1st South Dakota, remembered spending 5 hours each day on a Presidio drill site where "the grass was short and slippery" and the terrain uneven.[89]

Collectively, the drills pursued in the space allocated and orders governing their execution were revealing for several reasons. First, beginning

Volunteers at Drill on the Grassy Slopes of the Presidio Reservation.

Figure 52.

in May, commanders challenged their units to gain proficiency. Leaders started with the most fundamental exercises as organizations accepted new men. In relatively short order, however, commanders pursued more complicated company and regimental maneuvers expected of seasoned units even as recruits learned how to march and salute.

Second, regimental commanders worked to attain proficiency at "extended order."[90] These tactical skills reflected the most current doctrinal thinking of the era. In 1891, Fort Leavenworth published references for the infantry, cavalry, and light artillery that "were the United States Army's first true tactical manuals, providing officers with advice on how to fight, on both offense and defense."[91] Both the infantry and cavalry manuals featured instruction on "extended order," which Perry Jamieson, in his 1994 book *Crossing the Deadly Ground*, called "the most important single innovation of the new volumes, basing the battle tactics on loose-ordered squads of eight men each." Extended order "deployed soldiers into loose formations, spreading them out to minimize the targets they would present to the destructive firepower of breech-loading repeaters, Gatling guns, and improved artillery."[92] The infantry manual advised teaching "the mechanism of the movements on the drill ground." Once familiar to troops, extended order would then be "executed on varied ground, making use of the accidents of the surface for cover, etc., and observing the conditions of battle."[93] The instruction had its effect. CPT Medbery wrote of the training, "Men learned to keep step over difficult ground, to execute quickly and accurately all commands and, in a manner that afterward proved most successful, to deploy as skirmishers, take advantage of all accidents of the ground and finally with impetuous charge capture a sand-pit a mile from the starting place."[94]

Finally, drills and orders revealed the Army was at least a generation away from engaging in combined arms training.[95] That is, infantry, cavalry, and artillery did not train with each other to learn how they could support other arms in offensive or defensive operations. As the orders reflected, infantry troops worked to gain infantry skills, cavalry at cavalry, and so forth. The only exception Otis made was to train the heavy artillery as infantry.

The training experience among units in San Francisco exhibited other common features as reflected in newspaper accounts, letters, and regimental histories from the era. Some troops saw drill as one of the dominant occurrences of their encampment. Private Madison U. Stoneman, 1st Wyoming, wrote, "Drill was the order twice each day until it seemed that the most awkward specimen of humanity ought to be quite proficient in tactics."[96] Private James Camp, 1st Idaho, observed that "our stay in 'Frisco had two sides to it; the one made of many drills. . . . The other side was made up of pleasant acquaintances."[97] Writing in his diary several days after Otis issued his 5 July training guidance, Private William H. Barrett noted, "6 hours drill per day."[98] Private Karl Kraemer, 51st Iowa, wrote a letter to his sister on 7 July and observed, "We have not much time anymore." He remarked how a clearly defined schedule featuring drill dominated the routine day for his unit.[99]

In that same letter, Kraemer also referred to sighting, an exercise designed to improve each soldier's marksmanship.[100] Marksmanship training was another common feature in the San Francisco drill experience. The Coloradans were among the first units assembled to engage in "dummy rifle practice" during the latter part of May.[101] On 6 June, several days after assuming command of the Independent Division and Camp Merritt, Otis issued special orders that both encouraged and enabled units to conduct marksmanship training: "All volunteer organizations of the encampment are authorized to expend in target practice from ammunition on hand, ten rounds of the same for each man of their respective organizations" at the Presidio target range.[102]

After Otis published his guidance, units marched to the Presidio to engage targets beginning on 8 June. Volunteer regiments went to ranges most often in the order of their departure for the Philippines. The 1st Colorado and 10th Pennsylvania, regiments chosen for the second expedition, fired first.[103] Organizations composing the third expedition, including the 1st Idaho, 1st North Dakota, and 1st Wyoming, followed between 12 and 22 June.[104] Units that joined subsequent expeditions began to fire in late June. Among those participating were the 1st Tennessee, 51st Iowa, and several companies from the 14th and 18th US Regular Infantry Regiments.[105] The Regular organizations got their turn at the range because recruits dominated the ranks.[106] Most of the experienced men had shipped with the first and second expeditions.

Pennsylvania Volunteers at Rifle Practice Prepare for Actual Warfare.

Figure 53.

Whereas marksmanship drills sharpened the eyes, physical training worked on the body. This activity was another experience the troops commonly shared, especially recruits. Private Kraemer wrote to his grandfather on 9 July 1898, "When we get up before breakfast, we have gymnastic exercises. There are 17 different movements."[107] Kraemer referred to "setting up exercises," so dubbed by the 1891 Leavenworth drill manuals. *Infantry Drill Regulations* described them as arm, hand, trunk, leg, and foot exercises intended "to retain a proper set-up and to keep the muscles supple."[108] (See figure 54.)

Almost from the outset of the San Francisco encampments, newspapers

Figure 54.

commented on physical training. On 9 May, the *Daily Report* observed how recruits in both the 1st and 7th California Regiments received instruction "in the mysteries of setting up and the manual."[109] The following day the *Call* reported on activities at the Presidio: "The new men received special instructions from the sergeants in the setting up exercises and that part of the manual of arms relative to loading and firing."[110] More than a month later, the same paper observed in a paragraph on the 1st South Dakota how "physical exercise drill" had become "a feature of regular camp practice."[111] On 20 June, the *Chronicle* printed a drawing that illustrated "Calisthenic Drill for the New Recruits at Camp Merritt."[112] Nine days later, the *Chronicle* commented on the training received by the new men who filled the ranks of the 14th and 18th Infantry Regiments: "These regulars get daily one hour of calisthenics, two hours of drill without arms and two hours with arms."[113]

Figure 55.

As tedious as the training in drill, marksmanship, and calisthenics may have become for them, soldiers nevertheless shared common incentives to earn a reputation for military proficiency. Unit pride and the competitive spirit inspired some. In a letter to his father on 31 May, Corporal Hugh E. Clapp, 1st Nebraska, surveyed unit rivals in drill at Camp Merritt and wrote, "I say none of them can come up to us, and as a drilled man I will say that while they have companies that can beat some of ours, still we have companies that can beat any of them."[114] Quartermaster Sergeant Louis Hubbard, 1st South Dakota, wrote his mother on 28 June, "Co E is very well at present and they are coming right to the front with their drill. They are considered the best in the regiment at the time."[115] Just before the peace protocol of 12 August, Private Kraemer questioned a "heavy marching order" exercise in a letter to his sister, "I don't know what this drill is for only to see who is the best regiment and then I don't know what they will do with it."[116]

Performing drills for the public provided another incentive to becoming adept at training. Units participated in San Francisco's holiday parades. The 7th California, 1st Colorado, and 13th Minnesota marched in the Memorial Day review on 30 May.[117] MG Otis directed the 7th California, 51st Iowa, 1st South Dakota, 1st Tennessee, and 20th Kansas Volunteer Regiments to join the Independence Day parade on 4 July.[118] That same day, the 1st Montana Regiment ferried to Oakland where it led a holiday procession along the city streets.[119] Later that afternoon while still across the bay, Montana Volunteers fought a sham battle for spectators gathered about the heights near Lake Merritt. Using blank cartridges, troops from six companies attacked comrades reluctantly playing the role of Spaniards.[120] Some participants dropped as if hit by gunfire. *The Examiner* observed that "the drill in which able-bodied Red Cross operatives shouldered supposedly wounded men and carried them to the rear was particularly interesting."[121]

Figure 56. Scenes of sham battle fought in Oakland.

Other regiments performed a variety of training exercises for the public in an enterprising collaboration between the Army and philanthropy. The Red Cross Society and Young Men's Christian Association (YMCA) mounted an impressive volunteer effort to physically and morally care for the soldiers during their stay in the city. To assist in fundraising for both organizations, the military agreed to present exhibition drills for a paying audience at the Mechanics' Pavilion.[122] The structure, measuring 150 feet by 300 feet, could accommodate a crowd of 10,000.[123]

Between the middle of June and the August protocol, five regiments conducted a benefit drill for either the Red Cross or YMCA. The 13th Minnesota performed on 17 June before a "comfortably filled" pavilion. Individual companies demonstrated setting up exercises, a bayonet exercise, physical exercise with arms, company drill, and guard mount.[124] A *Daily Report* editorial called the performance a "great exhibition" and "the finest drill ever seen in San Francisco."[125]

On 28 June, troops from the 51st Iowa Regiment performed drills before 5,000 people on behalf of the Red Cross.[126] The 51st presented a program similar to that of the Minnesotans but added extended order drill to its performance.[127] About two weeks later the 1st Tennessee executed similar, though fewer, drills on behalf of the YMCA.[128] Men of the 7th California and 20th Kansas offered benefit drills on 21 July and 4 August respectively.[129]

Discipline and Diversion

Drill and exercise taught raw recruits fundamental military skills. New men and seasoned veterans learned or relearned tactical procedures that facilitated an organization's maneuver, firepower, and protection against enemies. Drills also contributed to developing another important component of unit proficiency: discipline. Order, conduct, and obedience exhibited by individual soldiers and their regiments influenced how well the Army performed its tasks. As units assembled and encamped near the Golden Gate, leaders worked to establish or reinforce discipline within their organizations.

The first troops to gather in San Francisco marched into a structured routine at their campsite on the Presidio. Both California regiments and elements of the 14th Infantry were obligated to conform to installation regulations.[130] LTC Victor D. DuBoce, 1st California, welcomed locating at the Presidio where he anticipated "the military surroundings" would have a positive effect on his unit.[131] Those "surroundings" were augmented by a prescribed schedule that established three drill periods and several other activities at specified times—0545, first call; 0735, guard mount; 2145, call to quarters; and 2200, taps.[132]

Initially, men from the 1st California who encamped on the Presidio could freely come and go. After two days, however, COL Smith, commander, 1st California, required his men to secure passes to leave post. He allowed up to five men per company to depart at any one time.[133] Getting away from the Presidio became increasingly more difficult, particularly the closer a soldier's unit came to being deployed overseas. The *Chronicle* noted on 17 May that Smith "permitted only five men of the 1000 in his command to leave camp. Theirs were particularly urgent cases."[134]

When more units converged on San Francisco, the encampment expanded, as noted, to include several undeveloped city blocks of an area formerly known as the Bay District Racetrack. Each arriving organization established an autonomous campsite generally contiguous to those belonging to other Volunteers or Regulars. Through May, regiments essentially created their own training schedules. Conducting drills or other activities at times different from one's neighbor was really quite acceptable, except in cases warranting centralized execution. One exception involved flag ceremonies at reveille and retreat. When regiments failed to raise and lower the colors simultaneously, the *Daily Report* commented on the ostensible confusion "about the time of sunrise and sunset." The paper observed, "Each regimental commander has a different time for the ceremonies, as there is no head to the organization as yet."[135]

The observation "no head to the organization" was more correct in inference than fact. A week earlier, on 20 May, Otis had assumed command of all troops tentatively designated to deploy overseas.[136] His headquarters, however, had focused primarily in preparing the first expedition for its departure on 25 May. With that task accomplished and Merritt's arrival, Otis was in a position to turn his attention to the newly established Independent Division's good order and discipline.

On 1 June, Otis assumed command of Camp Merritt and announced in General Orders Number 1 that his headquarters would determine a daily schedule to "prevail throughout the division."[137] The following day he issued an order that outlined his drill guidance and prescribed times for meals, sick call, assemblies, and call to quarters. The second general order specified when units would observe reveille and retreat, noting that the Utah Light Artillery would fire "a morning and evening gun" to coincide with both ceremonies. Sunday duties would be "confined to those necessary in and about the several camps, and to the ceremonies of guardmounting and inspection."[138]

109

Whereas a centralized schedule contributed to the camp's "good order," courts-martial worked to establish a properly disciplined division. On the first day of his command, Otis directed brigade commanders to appoint "the necessary Field Officer's Court for the trial of offenders." Otis referred his subordinates to the 1895 courts-martial manual when reviewing awarded sentences. He also directed that cases outside brigade jurisdiction come to his headquarters for action.[139]

During June and July, several brigade courts-martial boards sat to adjudicate specific allegations.[140] On 28 June, MG Otis ordered a board convened, specifying, "It being necessary for the sake of immediate example the court is authorized to sit without regard to hours."[141] Several cases brought to trial involved insubordination.[142] One board found a 1st Tennessee private guilty of disregarding orders and sentenced him "to three days hard at labor, a $5 fine and forfeiture of the privilege of leaving camp for a period of twenty days."[143] Another board dishonorably discharged a 23d Infantry private for insubordination.[144]

THE GENERAL COURT-MARTIAL IN SESSION AT CAMP MERRITT.

Figure 57.

Some soldiers accused of desertion or drunkenness appeared before boards. A private from the California Heavy Artillery received a two-year sentence in the military prison at Alcatraz for an unauthorized absence from his unit. One 14th Infantry Regular got a year for committing a similar offense. For being drunk and disorderly, a 1st Montana soldier had to forfeit $20 of his pay and spend two months in prison at hard labor. Another trooper from the 1st California received a $10 fine and 10 days confined at hard labor for his drunkenness.[145]

Not all disciplinary matters warranted trial by courts-martial. Lesser infractions could be addressed within units, and Otis did nothing to discourage this alternative. Major Frank White, 1st North Dakota, presided over a field court that tried his regiment's "petty offenders."[146] Lieutenant Alexander Laist wrote of the 1st Montana field officer's court convened by a major in the regiment. Laist observed, "The minor offenses were followed by a few days' work in the kitchen, and some had employment there so steadily that by the time they were mustered out, they had learned the worthy trade of cooking."[147]

COL Alexander L. Hawkins, 10th Pennsylvania Regiment, dealt with recalcitrant men in imaginative ways. On 30 May, the regimental guardhouse held 23 men "for extending the limit of their leaves from camp." While the rest of his unit drilled, Hawkins ensured that his prisoners received special training. The men "were compelled to march for two hours in double-quick time through the six-inch-deep sand of one of the company streets."[148] On 1 June, the eight to 10 men still under guard "were compelled to march up and down one of the company streets shouldering a log of wood." At the end of the street "they deposited the log on the ground, about faced and picked it up again and continued the walk."[149] Hawkins' attention to prisoners inspired others to gainfully employ those who were serving sentences. By late July, military authorities used prisoners to police Camp Merritt.[150]

Prisoners required guards, as did encampments, pay officers, and transports preparing to depart for the Philippines. Private Kraemer, 51st Iowa, discovered that his regiment found another task for sentries. On 11 August, one day before the peace protocol, he wrote his sister, "The next morning

Mild Punishment for Soldier Lawbreakers.

Figure 58.

San Francisco Chronicle, 14 June 1898

111

after you are on guard we have to go around the ground and pick up the paper that is laying around."[151]

Guard duties emerged as an integral component of a program to instill and preserve discipline in the ranks. By 9 May, COL Smith, 1st California, ensured guard mount routinely occurred in his regiment each day at the Presidio.[152] Just to the west of Smith's regiment, 14th Infantry Regulars practiced guard mount as a part of their training.[153] When Otis assumed command of the division and Camp Merritt on 1 June, he ensured that subordinate units conducted guard mount ceremonies each day, including Sundays.[154] LTC Edward C. Little, acting commander, 20th Kansas, ordered the ceremony conducted twice each day to give the men "experience."[155]

Guard Mount of the Montana Volunteer Infantry---Inspection of Arms.

Figure 59.

Some units used the guard mount ceremony to exhibit their military proficiency. Men from the 4th US Cavalry executed a "mounted guard mount" on the Presidio for the benefit of a "large crowd of spectators."[156] The *Call* announced a "crack company of the 13th Minnesotas" would give an exhibition ceremony.[157] When the 13th Minnesota and 51st Iowa performed benefit drills in the Mechanics' Pavilion, both regiments included guard mount as a part of their programs.

Other indicators offered evidence as to the emphasis given guard duties by military units at the Golden Gate. Private Kraemer again wrote his sister on 7 July 1898, observing, "We can't get off as easy now as we could, but we can get off at nights if we know General Orders for Sentinels."[158] COL Frederick Funston, commander, 20th Kansas, "provided all of his men with copies of general instructions to the sentries" and required each man "to commit the instructions to memory" before leaving camp.[159] Commanders of the 1st Colorado and 1st South Dakota Regiments each appointed a major as an "instructor of the guard" who would apprise "the men as to the formalities expected of them."[160]

Some "formalities" and instructions issued to guards addressed those civilians to be barred from camp to preserve the good order of bivouacs. The *Chronicle* noted on 15 May that the Presidio camp was closed to visitors five days a week. The newspaper reported that a visitor could "not go a rod without being stopped by a bayoneted young person." Only a pass from headquarters could guarantee passage through the posted sentinels.[161]

After encampments sprang up in the city, banning undesirables became even more of a challenge. Public roads and streetcars ran throughout Camp Merritt, giving what the *Daily Report* called "loose women" unwanted access to the troops.[162] COL Harry C. Kessler, 1st Montana, was also concerned with other miscreants. According to the *Call*, Kessler observed that "bakers and venders were making themselves a nuisance, and that a number of soldiers had become ill by the unwholesome fruit purchased from peddlers. Disreputable persons of both sexes" should be barred from camp.[163]

Commanders and city officials empowered sentinels to preserve discipline within the camps. Sentries continued to admit only those with passes. 1st Wyoming guards permitted ladies in their camp only if properly escorted. Private Stoneman endorsed the provision, writing, the "rule, while it may have seemed a peculiar one, was certainly commendatory and worthy to be enforced."[164] The *Daily Report* noted that "in a great many of the camps ladies are not permitted after sundown."[165] In late June, the city's street committee acted on COL Kessler's concerns and allowed the military to restrict traffic along public avenues in the northeast section of camp.[166] On 29 June, Kessler's brigade commander, BG Harrison Gray Otis, published general orders for sentries that outlined who could or could not enter regimental campsites.[167]

Through sentinels, commanders excluded undesirables from camp and just as frequently prevented troops from leaving the Presidio or Camp Merritt. Stoneman wrote, "Guards were put to pacing up and down on the four sides of our camp and only those who obtained passes were allowed

Figure 60.

out."[168] Sometimes passes were difficult to acquire. About two weeks after the 1st Nebraska arrived in the Bay Area, Corporal Clapp wrote his father, "Have seen but little of Frisco as it is very hard to get a pass." Clapp hypothesized, perhaps sarcastically, that the situation may have had something to do with the enemy: "We are under pretty strong guard now as they seem to be afraid of Spain here."[169]

Any perceived Spanish threat notwithstanding, military authorities were most likely concerned with the actions of some troops in the city. Saloons or "groggeries" quickly popped up around Camp Merritt after it was established. These popular enterprises rankled citizens, including members of the Point Lobos Avenue Improvement Club, who registered complaints with the Police Commission and MG Merritt.[170] Sometimes soldiers, having had too much to drink, created trouble for themselves and others. The *Daily Report* observed on 8 June that "as might naturally be expected, some of the soldiers who patronize the saloons are getting a little too lively for the peace and comfort of quiet and orderly citizens. Therefore the Richmond folks have asked or are about to ask General Otis to establish a provost guard in order to gather in the boys in blue who are out for a lark."[171]

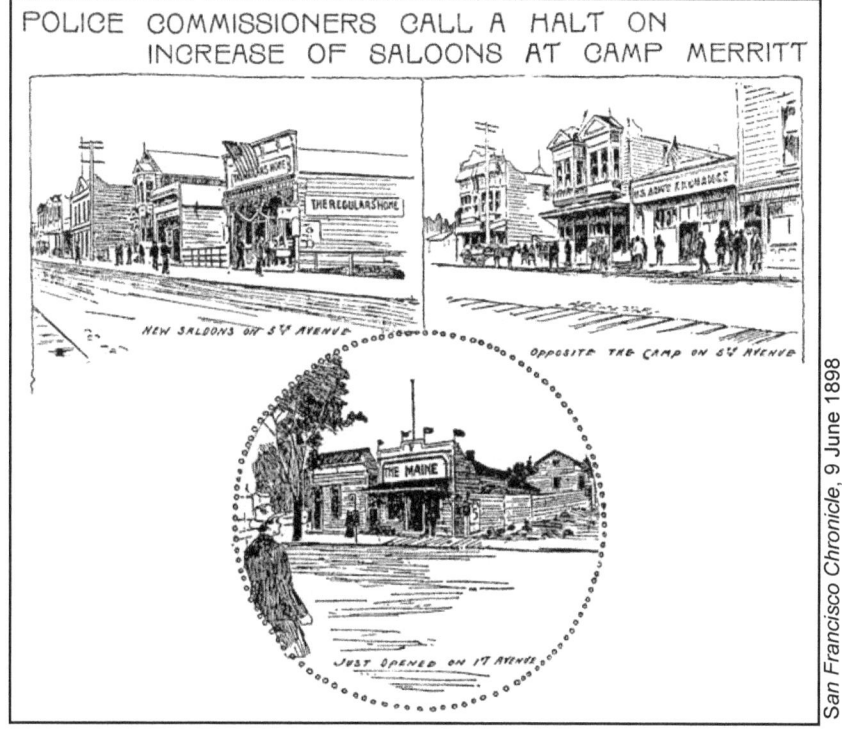

Figure 61.

Provost guards became a disciplinary tool for commanders. The *Chronicle* reported on 10 June that a provost guard patrolled "business streets" the preceding day looking for troops who had stayed out all night.[172] COL Funston employed such a guard later in June to "free" some of his men. Funston dispatched an officer and eight troops "to a saloon on Grant avenue where three of his men were held captive." The proprietor willingly released his prisoners.[173] When COL John R. Berry, commander, 7th California Infantry, learned the whereabouts of one of his troops who was absent without leave, he sent an armed provost guard into the city to get him.[174]

Confronted by so many guards and so few passes, some of the troops found diversion at the expense of sentries. Private Stoneman wrote, "The boys did not take kindly to being kept in, and frequently took the desperate chances of 'running the guard line.'"[175] Soldiers willingly took the risk, particularly before shipping out to the Philippines. An article in the *Daily Report* observed on the eve of the second expedition's departure, "Many of the soldiers, knowing it to be their last night in the city for many months perhaps, ran the guard lines and spent the time down town."[176] Not all were successful at eluding the sentinels. On 25 June, Private S.F. Pepper, 20th Kansas, was wounded "in the back by a bayonet . . . while attempting to run the guard lines."[177]

Other more organized and authorized diversions existed to help troops find relief from the constant grind of drill and discipline. Within the major encampments, civilian volunteers established reading and writing tents, libraries, and assembly shelters where soldiers could relax and enjoy the company of others. A number of regiments stationed at the Presidio or Camp Merritt brought bands that offered camp concerts in the evening.[178] On weekends, those permitted to leave encampments could take the street cars to various points in the city to enjoy the sights of San Francisco. That could amount to quite a number of soldiers. The 1st Nebraska camp, for example, allowed most of its men to leave camp on Sundays between 0900 and 1900.[179]

Figure 62. Writing home.

Several points of interest in San Francisco captured many troops' attention. Just south of Camp Merritt, Golden Gate Park provided a kind of oasis from the sand and grime of encampment life. Once in the park, soldiers could climb Strawberry Hill or enjoy the conservatory, playgrounds, lawns, shrubberies, statuary, avery, and other attractions.[180] The *Chronicle* reported on Sunday, 22 May, that attendance at the park museum exceeded 4,000, "the greater part of this number being volunteers from the interior states."[181] Troops from the 1st Wyoming, 51st Iowa, and 1st Nebraska wrote affectionately of visits to the park.[182]

The Sutro Baths, a facility less than 3 miles from Camp Merritt, was another favorite troop spot.[183] *Doxey's Guide* called it "the finest and most extensive inclosed baths and winter-garden in the world." The L-shaped structure, made from 600 tons of iron and 100,000 "superficial feet" of glass, measured 500 feet long by 100 to 175 feet wide. An amphitheater inside contained 3,700 seats; the building could hold as many as 25,000 visitors. Palms, shrubs, and flowering plants adorned the entrance. Although the bath structure housed both a museum and picture gallery, troops most commonly frequented the six swimming tanks, one of which was 300 feet long.[184]

During their stay at the Golden Gate, many regiments organized trips to the Sutro Baths. The 20th Kansas, 1st Montana, 1st New York, 1st Tennessee, 14th Infantry, 1st Washington, 51st Iowa, Nevada Cavalry, and both Dakota regiments conducted unit visits.[185] By early July, Sutro hosted weekly swimming contests that pitted soldiers against each other and "some of the local professionals."[186] Several of the regiments held their own meets and awarded medals for top performances.[187] At least one trooper found his visit a little overwhelming; he slipped and put his arm through one of the many glass windows that adorned the baths.[188]

Although the Sutro Baths proved to be the most popular swimming facility among the troops, soldiers enjoyed taking a dip elsewhere around the city. On 23 May, the Lurline Salt Water Baths at Bush and Larkin Streets opened its doors to uniformed visitors. The *Call* reported, "They marched in, a half dozen companies at a time, from Camp Richmond, and enjoyed themselves in the large swimming tank."[189] The bay provided yet another alternative for some. Volunteers encamped at the Presidio took the plunge as early as 16 May.[190] Sometimes the troops did not use their best judgment when swimming there. In early August, the proprietor of the Harbor View Gardens registered a complaint "against soldiers bathing in the bay in front of the gardens without any bathing suits on." The *Call* reported, "The necessary orders to prevent this were immediately issued by General Miller."[191]

Besides swimming, the troops enjoyed other sports, either as spectators or participants. On 28 May, the president of the Pacific Coast Baseball League invited Merritt's command to attend all games held in San Francisco. Eugene F. Bert, the league president, wrote to MG Merritt, "Our gate-keepers have been instructed to admit all uniformed soldiers free."[192] To raise money for the Red Cross, the league's San Francisco Baseball Club challenged a Volunteer team from the 13th Minnesota to a game at Recreation Park. The city team soundly thrashed the Minnesotans, 26 to 5, but the game attracted considerable attention, reported the *Chronicle*, "for sweet charity's sake."[193] On 6 August, the 51st Iowa and 6th California dueled at the Presidio Athletic Grounds in the first inter-Volunteer baseball game.[194] A number of regiments also formed basketball and football teams that played either local organizations or other military units.[195]

Figure 63. 51st Iowa Regiment football team.

Supply and Medical

If regiments were to drill effectively or engage in organized diversions, commanders first had to address fundamental troop necessities. Regular and Volunteer organizations, hastily dispatched to the West Coast, frequently reached San Francisco with soldiers lacking essential equipment. MG Merritt observed, "The regiments that reported at San Francisco were of various characters. They all contained good material, but quite a number of them were poorly prepared for service—some came there without uniforms, some without arms; but everything was supplied as quickly as possible."[196] Thousands of men, quartered in tent communities on the Presidio and its environs, required daily rations and adequate medical care. The Golden Gate area possessed the military facilities and civilian infrastructure capable of meeting many units' needs. The challenge for the military leadership was to tap into those sources of aid that would provide for their men's welfare.

The US Army Ordnance Department supported Benicia Arsenal, a major depot on the Pacific Coast, stocked with large quantities of ammunition and .45-caliber Springfield rifles.[197] Located about 43 miles northeast of San Francisco, Benicia afforded easy access to military organizations in need of weapons or munitions.[198] For example, the arsenal's commander, COL L.S. Babbitt, received orders on 14 May to assist two units belonging to the first expedition. Adjutant General BG Corbin directed Babbitt to provide the 1st California and 14th Infantry Battalions with "400 rounds per man" and "such arms as necessary to fully arm" the Californians.[199] Four days later, Corbin hastened a partially armed 10th Pennsylvania to San Francisco, knowing that ordnance shortfalls could be made up on the coast.[200] While in camp by the bay, the 7th California, 1st Tennessee, 8th

California, 2d Oregon recruits, 1st Nebraska, and 1st Montana received Springfield rifles.[201] The arsenal also served as a receiving facility for ordnance and ordnance stores that organizations would not take when they were deployed to the Philippines.[202]

The Army's Subsistence Department operated a purchasing depot in San Francisco.[203] Through this facility, the commissary could obtain and dispense fresh beef, flour, and other commodities that were often produced locally.[204] By 1 June, the department's commissary planned to store a three-month supply of subsistence for 20,000 men.[205] COL William H. Baldwin, the purchasing commissary colocated with the depot quartermaster, ordered "immense quantities of supplies in San Francisco."[206] The chief commissary for Camp Merritt estimated that during July "an average of 9366 men were fed at a cost to the Government for the food materials of $43,416." The *Chronicle* speculated that much of that sum went to city suppliers.[207] Drawing rations every 10 days, unit commissaries provided their men with an assortment of items, including beef, bacon, salmon, flour, potatoes, vegetables, coffee, sugar, and baking powder.[208]

Figure 64. Major Oscar F. Long.

The Quartermaster Department maintained one of only six Army general depots in San Francisco. The depot quartermaster, Major Oscar F. Long, was charged with a twofold responsibility. He had to arrange oceanic transportation for expeditionary forces and provide assembled organizations with military stores and supplies, including clothing, tents, blankets, and "all materials for camp and for shelter for troops and stores."[209] The second task seemed formidable because by 1 May, "nearly all war material available had been sent from San Francisco to the East."[210] When the Army ordered Regular forces to Southern camps for possible operations in the Caribbean, the Quartermaster General also moved tons of stores for their support. Long wrote that repositioning these goods left "this depot almost wholly without any stock to speak of, except tents, on hand, with which to meet the emergency."[211]

To compound Major Long's problem, in early May the McKinley administration urged governors to dispatch Volunteer organizations with all speed. If regiments were not fully equipped but able to travel, War Department officials suggested "that it is best they go ahead and complete their equipment at San Francisco."[212] Additionally, before May ended, the depot quartermaster learned that the projected force to gather by the bay had increased from 6,000 to 20,000.[213] As a result, Long reported, "Regiments, battalions and detachments arrived from 20 States and Territories of the Union, some even without shoes and wearing bandannas in lieu of hats—without tentage, with nothing for comfort and even without the few necessities which suffice for the simple needs of the soldier."[214]

Long specifically cited several regiments that were in dire need of help. He wrote, "The troops from Montana, Kansas and Tennessee were almost entirely unequipped." Even those from Colorado, Iowa, and Pennsylvania who had telegraphed that they had their basic gear "were found, when their requisitions were filled, to be deficient in the most essential requirements of equipment."[215] A reporter for *The Examiner* wrote about the 1st Idaho Regiment's clothing deficiencies when the unit reached San Francisco: "Many of the men had no uniforms, some of them were poorly dressed, but all of them looked well. The fact is that but two companies of the eight, that is to say 168 men out of 672, are fully equipped."[216]

To address these equipment shortfalls, Long acted quickly to replenish stocks in his depot, and San Francisco reaped the dividend. He flooded the Golden Gate and other West Coast cities with quartermaster requests. On 16 May, Long told a *Chronicle* correspondent:

> Our orders for clothing and supplies for the expedition are keeping busy every factory that makes them in this city and on the Pacific Coast. We have reached out to Portland and other cities, wherever there are mills. The government is spending a vast amount of money in this affair. At least 10,000 workingmen and women in San Francisco are today occupied on Government contracts. We have ordered 8000 uniforms, identical in color with the ordinary fatigue uniforms but lighter in weight. We have also ordered 1200 canvas uniforms for wear in Manila, all to be delivered in a few days.[217]

In addition to uniforms, the depot quartermaster let contracts for the manufacture of shoes, overcoats, overalls, and drawers.[218] To expedite procurement, Long acquired "all other supplies which were obtainable ready made in the market."[219] Articles obtained in this manner included blankets, shoes, stockings, suspenders, undershirts, axes, and bedsheets.[220]

The depot quartermaster issued supplies as quickly as they could be purchased or "as promptly as 6000 workmen employed in this City night and day in manufacturing could furnish them."[221] Men from the 1st California Regiment received shoes on 17 May. The 7th California acquired more than 900 complete uniforms on 27 May. Volunteers from Kansas obtained uniforms, and the 1st Tennessee finally secured trousers, shirts, blouses, underclothes, and shoes. Soldiers from the 1st Colorado and 7th California welcomed an issue of underwear.[222] The challenge for the quartermaster was to meet the troops' needs before shortages led to operational or welfare problems. Given the paucity of stocks combined with organizations arriving without equipment, Long and Pacific Department quartermaster officers did not always have the means to supply soldiers quickly.

The medical department confronted a situation similar to that of the quartermaster. Given limited military assets, it had to provide essential health care for troops. Organizations that converged on San Francisco brought their own medical support. Each Volunteer regiment was authorized one surgeon, two assistant surgeons, and three hospital stewards.[223] Such a small staff could be easily overwhelmed should virus or disease infect the 600 to 1,000 soldiers commonly manning these units.

Complicating the challenge facing regimental surgeons, higher headquarters possessed scant facilities to render medical assistance. The Department of California could access one military healthcare asset in the Bay Area: the Post Hospital, Presidio of San Francisco. The structure consisted of a small frame building large enough to accommodate "the ordinary number of sick of two companies."[224] Fortunately, the Presidio also served as home to a US Marine Hospital. Established on the reservation in 1875 "to combat cholera, yellow fever, and general unsanitary conditions existing among seamen," the Treasury Department operated the hospital. During the war, the Treasury Secretary allowed the Army Surgeon General to use vacant beds at this facility. Merritt's command tapped into the Marine Hospital shortly after camps were organized in the city.[225]

The Department of the Pacific did not establish a division hospital until 30 May. Composed of three large double hospital tents, the field facility was "capable of accommodating forty men."[226] Before that, military medical treatment came through meager unit resources or a brigade hospital formed from pooling regimental holdings.[227]

Unfortunately, sickness could not be postponed until Merritt's department prepared itself to meet medical emergencies. On 19 May, the *Call* reported a 2d Oregon Volunteer had been hospitalized with a case of measles.[228] By 21 May, several other cases developed within the regiment. A "rigid quarantine" helped to prevent the communicable disease from reaching epidemic proportions.[229] Nevertheless, measles infection spread to others. The 20th Kansas reported a case on 23 May.[230] Major W.O. Owen, chief surgeon in charge of the division hospital, noted that 50 patients were being treated for measles on 11 June.[231] Shortly thereafter, the disease threatened to infect much of the camp when the 1st Tennessee arrived at the Golden Gate with 18 cases already developed.[232] The field hospital, by that time in operation for nearly three weeks, took the lead to ensure the contagion stayed in check.

Over time, other maladies appeared among the troops. Unit surgeons reported treating nonlife-threatening "minor diseases usual in military camps" such as diarrhea, bronchitis, mumps, gonorrhea, and syphilis. Medical officials surmised that diarrhea could be traced to assorted causes: "exposure to cold and dampness" at campsites; poorly cooked food combined with an "irregularity of diet in the shape of overindulgence in pies, sweetmeats, fruits, etc., procured by the men or forced upon them by injudicious friends"; and "the excessive use of alcoholic stimulants in various forms indulged in by some of the men."[233] Surgeons believed that the health of the command would improve with an assault on wretched camp hygiene and poor personal habits. Until such corrections were made, however, medical officers feared that unchecked "minor disease," such as diarrhea, could exacerbate "epidemic diseases" like typhoid fever.[234] According to the Board of Medical Officers convened in September 1898 to investigate disease at Camps Merritt and Merriam (established on the Presidio as Camp Merritt closed), measles, pneumonia, cerebrospinal meningitis, and typhoid fever accounted for the most serious illnesses and deaths among the men.

This same board and several Army officers believed that Camp Merritt was a breeding ground for sickness in the expeditionary force. BG George M. Sternberg, US Army Surgeon General, described the location of Camp Merritt as "unsuitable. Its surface was a cold damp sand, continually exposed to chilly winds and heavy fogs, which saturated the tents, clothing, and bedding of the men with moisture."[235] LTC Henry Lippencott, chief surgeon, Department of the Pacific and VIII Corps, wrote how Camp Merritt was located on high ground that exposed it to winds and mists that perpetuated pneumonia.[236]

Some units' poor sanitary habits compounded the ills fostered by the camp's location. The Board of Medical Officers wrote, "It is known that great neglect existed among the men in this camp as regards the use of company sinks. It frequently occurred that men taken with diarrhea during the night would defecate in the company streets near and among the tents, covering up the deposit with a thin layer of sand." The board observed that "the longer this camp was maintained in one place the greater would be the amount of area of contaminated soil."[237] LTC Lippencott wrote that "vaults, covered with sheds, were dug for privies, but in many cases they had been put too near the kitchens and sleeping quarters of the men, no doubt due in many instances to the limited area of the camp. They were also not properly cared for." He would subsequently observe, "Another criticism in regard to the sinks is the closeness of most of them to the company kitchens, the distance between the two in many instances not exceeding 10 yards."[238] Strong breezes could blanket the campsite with sand, dried fecal matter, varied contaminants, and garbage that the men discarded.

Figure 65. Bird's-eye view of Camp Merritt, looking south.

MG Elwell S. Otis believed that one of the causes of sickness was the camp's location in "San Francisco, to which hucksters and immoral and depraved persons within the city had access. The camp should have been placed several miles from the city limits, where temptations for evil doing would have been farther removed."[239]

The Board of Medical Officers appeared to support Otis's views in part. Its report, dated 3 September 1898, found that "The general hygienic condition of Camp Merriam is much superior to that of Camp Merritt, owing to the fact that it being on a military reservation it is impossible to surround the men with and bring into their immediate view rum shops and other alluring means of debauchery, which circumstances it is known were important in lowering the general vitality of the command at Camp Merritt."[240]

Treatment for those sick within the encampments demanded medical aid that exceeded the military facilities' capabilities. To address this void, the Red Cross and several local civilian hospitals offered support. Their assistance proved an invaluable supplement to the Department of the Pacific's inadequate medical resources.

MG Merritt worked to secure the services of other general officers who could lead the department's brigade organizations in San Francisco and expeditions preparing to deploy overseas. MG Otis assumed command of Merritt's major subordinate unit, the Independent Division. Otis and his staff established procedures to organize, train, quarter, and equip the division's Regular and Volunteer forces assembling at the Golden Gate. In completing the latter tasks, the Department of the Pacific tapped into resources belonging to the Presidio and depot or arsenal assets that several staff departments—quartermaster, ordnance, subsistence, and medical—managed.

Merritt's command, however, did not depend exclusively upon military assistance in tending to expeditionary forces. Members of the San Francisco community donated land, facilities, goods, and services to support the many uniformed newcomers. In particular, several public and private organizations emerged to help clothe and care for troops when Army resources were lacking.

Notes

1. W. Merritt to the Adjutant-General, United States, 21 May 1898, in *Correspondence Relating to the War With Spain and Conditions Growing Out of the Same, Including the Insurrection in the Philippine Islands and the China Relief Expedition, Between the Adjutant-General of the Army and Military Commander in the United States, Cuba, Porto Rico, China, and the Philippine Islands, From April 15, 1898, to July 30, 1902*, volume II (Washington, DC: US Government Printing Office [GPO], 1902), hereafter cited as *Correspondence II*, 667; Francis B. Heitman, *Historical Register and Dictionary of the United States Army, From its Organization, September 29, 1789, to March 2, 1903*, volume 1 (Washington, DC: GPO, 1903), 292, 358, 448, 474-75, 936-37; Nelson A. Miles to the Honorable, the Secretary of War, 16 May 1898: "I have the honor to recommend the following assignments of general officers to commands" in Record Group 94, Office of the Adjutant General Document File, Document No. 81545, Box 604: 81394-81577 (Washington, DC: National Archives). Chaffee and Sumner were cavalrymen. Davis, an infantryman, had served as aide-de-camp to Lieutenant General Phillip Sheridan, a cavalryman.

2. R.A. Alger, 16 May 1898: "The following assignment of General Officers to command is hereby made by the President," in Record Group 94, Office of the Adjutant General Document File, Document No. 81545, Box 604: 81394-81577 (Washington, DC: National Archives).

3. General Orders, No. 50, Headquarters of the Army, Adjutant General's Office, 20 May 1898, in Record Group 94, Office of the Adjutant General Document File, filed with Document No. 81545, Box 604: 81394-81577 (Washington, DC: National Archives).

4. G.A. Garretson to Gen. H.C. Corbin, 28 May 1898 (Received 29 May 1898), in *Correspondence II*, 679-80.

5. F.V. Greene to Adjutant-General, 28 May 1898—4:36 p.m., in *Correspondence II*, 679.

6. Theo. F. Rodenbough, General Index, *Journal of the Military Service Institution of the United States*, volumes I-XXXIV, 29, 45.

7. "Generals King, Greene and H.G. Otis to go With Philippine Reenforcements," *San Francisco Chronicle*, 29 May 1898, 15.

8. Don E. Alberts, *Brandy Station to Manila Bay, A Biography of General Wesley Merritt* (Austin, TX: Presidial Press, 1980), 248.

9. Merritt to Brig. Gen. Charles King, 27 May 1898, *Army and Navy Journal*, 4 June 1898, 798.

10. W. Merritt, Major-General, Commanding, to Adjutant-General, 31 May 1898 (Received 4:20 p.m.), in *Correspondence II*, 683; Kenneth Ray Young, *The General's General: The Life and Times of Arthur MacArthur* (Boulder, CO: Westview Press, 1994) 152-57. MacArthur instructed in the Infantry and Cavalry Training School at Fort Leavenworth, Kansas, from September 1886 until July 1889; Alberts, 271-84. Merritt served at Fort Leavenworth between July 1887 and July 1890 as commander of the Department of the Missouri.

11. "General MacArthur is Here," *San Francisco Call*, 13 June 1898, 5; "General M'Arthur has Reached Here," *The Examiner*, 12 June 1989, 15.

12. H.C. Corbin to Major-General Merritt, 28 May 1898, in *Correspondence II*, 678; W. Merritt, Major-General, Commanding, to Adjutant-General, 31 May 1898 (Received 4:20 p.m.), in *Correspondence II*, 683.

13. Letter, Karl Kraemer, Co H, 51st Iowa Infantry, to "Dear Grand. Pa.", 9 July 1898 (Carlisle Barracks, PA: US Army Military History Institute).

14. Heitman, 673, 762.

15. H.C. Corbin, Adjutant-General, to Major-General Otis, 14 May 1898, in *Correspondence II*, 641.

16. "General Otis Arrives," *San Francisco Daily Report*, 18 May 1898, 3; "General Otis Arrives," *The Examiner*, 18 May 1898, 3.

17. General Orders, No. 2, Headquarters, U.S. Expeditionary Forces, San Francisco, Cal., 20 May 1898, in US Army, Department of the Pacific and Eighth Army Corps, Adjutant General's Office, *Index to General Orders and Circulars: Philippine Islands Expeditionary Forces, 1898*; General Orders, No. 1, Headquarters, Independent Division, Philippine Islands Expeditionary Forces, Camp Merritt, San Francisco, Cal., 1 June 1898 in US Army, Department of the Pacific and Eighth Army Corps, Adjutant General's Office, *Index to General Orders and Circulars: Philippine Islands Expeditionary Forces, 1898*; General Orders, No. 12, Headquarters, Independent Division, Eighth Army Corps, San Francisco, Cal., 29 June 1898 in US Army, Department of the Pacific and Eighth Army Corps, Adjutant General's Office, *Index to General Orders and Circulars: Philippine Islands Expeditionary Forces, 1898*.

18. General Orders, No. 1, Headquarters, U.S. Expeditionary Forces, San Francisco, Cal., 20 May 1898 in US Army, Department of the Pacific and Eighth Army Corps, Adjutant General's Office, *Index to General Orders and Circulars: Philippine Islands Expeditionary Forces, 1898*; "General Otis in Charge," *San Francisco Daily Report*, 18 May 1898, 3; "Transfer of the Troops," *San Francisco Call*, 24 May 1898, 12.

19. "Generals Consult," *San Francisco Call*, 29 May 1898, 7.

20. Apparently Merritt and his staff first occupied part of the Phelan Building's fourth floor. Later, they moved to offices on the second floor, which Otis took upon Merritt's departure for the Philippines. "Headquarters of General Wesley Merritt," *The Examiner*, 31 May 1898, 3; "Major-General Otis Changes His Headquarters," *The Examiner*, 30 June 1898, 2.

21. "Camp Merritt Inspected," *San Francisco Call*, 31 May 1898, 5; "Troops in Camp Merritt," *San Francisco Call*, 1 June 1898, 4.

22. "Wyoming Battery Joins the Troops," *San Francisco Chronicle*, 29 June 1898, 3; "Major-General Otis Changes His Quarters," *The Examiner*, 30 June 1898, 2; "Headquarters Changed," *San Francisco Call*, 29 June 1898, 5; "Army Headquarters," *San Francisco Call*, 30 June 1898, 5.

23. H.S. Crocker Company, *Crocker-Langley San Francisco Directory For Year Commencing April 1896* (San Francisco: H.S. Crocker Co., 1899), 1558.

24. "Major-General Otis Changes His Headquarters," *The Examiner*, 30

June 1898, 2; H.S. Crocker Company, 1558.

25. "The First California," *San Francisco Call*, 10 May 1898, 7; "Oregon's Volunteers Now in Camp," *San Francisco Call*, 14 May 1898, 7.

26. William Doxey, *Doxey's Guide to San Francisco and the Pleasure Resorts of California* (San Francisco: Doxey Press, 1897), 91; Crocker's Guide Map of the City of San Francisco, Compiled from the Official Surveys and for the Crocker-Langley San Francisco Directory, 1896.

27. H.S. Crocker Company, 1558; "Thousands Visit the Boys in Blue," *San Francisco Call*, 9 May 1898, 5; H.S. Crocker Company, *Crocker-Langley San Francisco Directory For Year Commencing April 1899* (Washington, DC: GPO, 1898), 68.

28. Report of Lieut. Col. Henry Lippincott, U.S.A., Chief Surgeon, Department of the Pacific and Eighth Army Corps, dated Manila, P.I., January 31, 1899, in US War Department, *Annual Reports of the War Department for the Fiscal Year Ended June 30, 1899. Reports of the Chiefs of Bureaus*. Report of the Surgeon-General (Washington, DC: GPO, 1898), 469.

29. "Headquarters of General Wesley Merritt," *The Examiner*, 31 May 1898, 3; "The Stars at Camp Merritt," *The Examiner*, 11 June 1898, 2.

30. "On His Way to Rule the Isles that Dewey Won," *San Francisco Chronicle*, 27 May 1898, 9.

31. "Fleet Not Likely to Move for a Week Yet," *San Francisco Chronicle*, 5 June 1898, 23.

32. Doxey, 82; "General Merritt Talks About the Volunteers to Alice Rix," *The Examiner*, 5 June 1898, 5.

33. "General Merritt's Words of Farewell to San Francisco," *The Examiner*, 30 June 1898, 1.

34. "Governor of the Philippines Departs To-Day," *San Francisco Chronicle*, 29 June 1898, 3.

35. Wesley Merritt to Hon. R.A. Alger, 17 May 1898, as published in *San Francisco Call*, 18 May 1898, 3.

36. W. Merritt to Secretary of War, 27 June 1898, in *Correspondence II*, p. 715.

37. "Monday in the Camp," *San Francisco Daily Report*, 6 June 1898, 3; "At Camp Merritt" and "At Headquarters," *San Francisco Daily Report*, 13 June 1898, 6; "Troops Inspected," *San Francisco Call*, 14 June 1898, 5; "Army Headquarters," *San Francisco Call*, 17 June 1898, 5; "King's Brigade for the Philippines," *San Francisco Call*, 18 June 1898, 7.

38. "Troops Inspected," *San Francisco Call*, 14 June 1898, 5.

39. Testimony of Maj.Gen. Wesley Merritt, 21 December 1898, in US Senate, *Report of the Commission Appointed by the President to Investigate the Conduct of the War Department in the War with Spain*, volume VII, *Testimony* (Washington, DC: GPO, 1900), hereafter cited as *Report VII*, 3272.

40. Doxey, 25; Michelin Travel Publications, *Michelin Green Guide to San Francisco*, 1st edition (Fort Worth, TX: Motheral Printing Co.), 51-52.

41. Alberts, 284.

42. "In Honor of Gen. Merritt," *San Francisco Call*, 9 June 1898, 7.

43. "Citizens Will Greet General Merritt," *The Examiner*, 2 June 1898, 4; "What is Won Must be Kept," *The Examiner*, 10 June 1898, 12; "General Merritt Wants No Big Public Banquet," *San Francisco Chronicle*, 4 June 1898, 9; "Banquet in Honor of General Merritt," *San Francisco Chronicle*, 10 June 1898, 7; "Troops at Richmond Will be Moved to the Reservation," *San Francisco Call*, 10 June 1898, 5.

44. "Minnesota Volunteers at Drill," *San Francisco Call*, 18 June 1898, 14.

45. "General Merritt at the Orpheum," *San Francisco Call*, 20 June 1898, 5.

46. "Ready for the Second Movement to Manila," *San Francisco Chronicle*, 13 June 1898, 5.

47. "Greene Ready for Manila," *The Examiner*, 12 June 1898, 15.

48. "Sudden Change of Plans for the Third Fleet," *San Francisco Chronicle*, 19 June 1898, 23; H.S. Crocker Company, *Crocker-Langley San Francisco Directory for Year Commencing May 1899*, 1550; *San Francisco: Its Builders Past and Present*, volume I, 99.

49. "Sudden Change of Plans for the Third Fleet," *San Francisco Chronicle*, 19 June 1898, 23.

50. "Rivalry Among the Regiments," *San Francisco Call*, 28 May 1898, 5; "Visitors Soon to be Barred," *The Examiner*, 31 May 1898, 3.

51. "Diagram of the Camp at the Bay District," *The Examiner*, 31 May 1898, 3.

52. Doxey, 99-106.

53. Ibid., 29-30.

54. "Major-General E.S. Otis in His Tent at the Camp Headquarters," *The Examiner*, 3 June 1898, 3.

55. "Diagram of the Camp at the Bay District," *The Examiner*, 31 May 1898, 3.

56. "Major-General E.S. Otis in His Tent at the Camp Headquarters," *The Examiner*, 3 June 1898, 3.

57. "Visitors Soon to be Barred," *The Examiner*, 31 May 1898, 3; "The Stars at Camp Merritt," *The Examiner*, 11 June 1898, 2.

58. "Army Headquarters," *San Francisco Call*, 21 May 1898, 5.

59. "The Stars at Camp Merritt," *The Examiner*, 11 June 1898, 2.

60. "Will Sail To-Morrow," *San Francisco Daily Report*, 24 May 1898, 1.

61. "The Day in Camp," *San Francisco Daily Report*, 31 May 1898, 3.

62. Ibid.; "In the Camp," *San Francisco Daily Report*, 3 June 1898, 2.

63. "Troops at Camp Merritt," *San Francisco Call*, 2 June 1898, 5.

64. Wesley Merritt to Hon. R.A. Alger, 17 May 1898 as published in *San Francisco Call*, 18 May 1898, 3.

65. "General Otis in Command," *San Francisco Call*, 18 May 1898, 5.

66. "The Day in Camp," *San Francisco Daily Report*, 31 May 1898, 3.

67. "Notes of the Camps," *San Francisco Chronicle*, 6 June 1898, 5.

68. "Has Asked for No Report on the Camp," *The Examiner*, 8 July 1898, 7; "Our Boys Are Favored by Gen. Otis," *The Examiner*, 10 July 1898, 16.

69. "When Will the Transports Sail?" *San Francisco Daily Report*, 16 May 1898, 2.

70. Ibid.; "The Charleston Has Sailed," *San Francisco Daily Report*, 18 May 1898, 3.

71. "Drilling at the Presidio," *The Examiner*, 11 May 1898, 3.

72. "One Army to Go and One to Wait Orders," *San Francisco Chronicle*, 13 May 1898, 4.

73. General Orders, No. 2, Headquarters, Independent Division, Philippine Islands Expeditionary Forces, Camp Merritt, San Francisco, Cal., 2 June 1898.

74. Letter, Charles F. Robe, Major, 14th Infantry, Commanding, to Adjutant General, First Brigade, 8 June 1898, in Record Group 395, Preliminary Inventory of the Records of U.S. Army Overseas Operations and Commands, 1898-1942, Entry 887: 8th Army Corps, Independent Division, July-December 1898, Letters Received June-September 1898, Box No. 1: General, Special Orders and Circulars, 1898 (Washington, DC: National Archives); Letter, D.D. Van Valzah to the Adjutant General, 1st. Brigade, Ind. Division, Camp Merritt, 8 June 1898, in Record Group 395, Preliminary Inventory of the Records of U.S. Army Overseas Operations and Commands, 1898-1942, Entry 887: 8th Army Corps, Independent Division, July-December 1898, Letters Received June-September 1898, Box No. 1: General, Special Orders and Circulars, 1898 (Washington, DC: National Archives).

75. Letter, Charles F. Robe to Adjutant General, First Brigade, 8 June 1898, in Record Group 395.

76. Letter, D.D. Van Valzah to the Adjutant General, 1st. Brigade, Ind. Division, Camp Merritt, 8 June 1898, in Record Group 395.

77. Letter, Samuel Ovenshine, Colonel 23d Infantry, Commanding, to Adjutant General, 1st Brigade, 8 June 1898, in Record Group 395, Preliminary Inventory of the Records of U.S. Army Overseas Operations and Commands, 1898-1942, Entry 887: 8th Army Corps, Independent Division, July-December 1898, Letters Received June-September 1898, Box No. 1: General, Special Orders and Circulars, 1898 (Washington, DC: National Archives).

78. Circular, Headquarters, 1st Brigade, Independent Division, Eighth Army Corps, Camp Merritt, 3 July 1898, in Record Group 395: Preliminary Inventory of the Records of U.S. Army Overseas Operations and Commands, 1898-1942, Entry 887: 8th Army Corps, Independent Division, July-December 1898, Letters Received: June-September 1898, Box No. 1: General, Special Orders and Circulars, 1898.

79. General Orders, No. 14., Headquarters Independent Division, Eighth Army Corps, San Francisco, Cal., 5 July 1898.

80. Ibid.

81. "The Army at the Old Track," *The Examiner*, 25 May 1898, p. 5.

82. Private James Camp, *Official History of the Operations of the First Idaho Infantry, U.S.V. in the Campaign in the Philippine Islands*, n.p., n.d., 3.

83. "No Place to Drill," *San Francisco Daily Report*, 28 May 1898, 4.

84. "Seventh California," *San Francisco Call*, 26 May 1898, 2.

85. Map, Presidio of San Francisco, California, 1897-1909, Post Engineer.

86. "Visitors Soon to be Barred," *The Examiner*, 31 May 1898, 3.

87. Edward S. Farrow, *A Dictionary of Military Terms* (New York: Thomas Y. Crowell Co., 1918) 550; "Vigorous Sham Battle," *San Francisco Call*, 16 June 1898, 8.

88. Lieutenant Alexander Laist, *Official History of the Operations of the First Montana Infantry, U.S.V. in the Campaign in the Philippine Islands*, n.p., n.d., 5-6.

89. Captain Frank W. Medbery, *Official History of the Operations of the First South Dakota Infantry, U.S.V. in the Campaign in the Philippine Islands*, n.p., n.d., 5.

90. "Drilling at the Presidio," *The Examiner*, 11 May 1898, 3; "One Army to Go and One to Wait Orders," *San Francisco Chronicle*, 13 May 1898, 4; "Presidio Camp Routine," *San Francisco Call*, 18 May 1898, 5; "Visitors Soon to be Barred," *The Examiner*, 31 May 1898, 3; "The Day in Camp," *San Francisco Daily Report*, 28 May 1898, 3.

91. Perry D. Jamieson, *Crossing the Deadly Ground: United States Army Tactics, 1865-1899* (Tuscaloosa, AL: University of Alabama Press, 1994), 112.

92. Ibid., 104.

93. US War Department, *Infantry Drill Regulations, United States Army* (New York: D. Appleton and Co., 1898), 14.

94. Medbery, 5.

95. Captain Jonathan M. House, *Toward Combined Arms Warfare: A Survey of 20th-Century Tactics, Doctrine, and Organization*, Research Survey No. 2 (Fort Leavenworth, KS: Combat Studies Institute, August 1984), 17-18.

96. Madison U. Stoneman, *Official History of the Operations of the First Battalion Wyoming Infantry, U.S.V. in the Campaign in the Philippine Islands*, n.p., n.d., 5.

97. Camp, 3.

98. Diary of Private William Henry Barrett, 2d Oregon Infantry, entry for 11 July 1898 (Carlisle Barracks, PA: US Army Military History Institute).

99. Letter, Karl Kraemer, Co H, 51st Iowa Infantry, to "Dear Sister," 7 July 1898 (Carlisle Barracks, PA: US Army Military History Institute).

100. Ibid.

101. "Doings in the Camp," *San Francisco Daily Report*, 27 May 1898, 3.

102. Special Orders, No. 6, Headquarters, Independent Division, Philippine Islands Expeditionary Forces, Camp Merritt, San Francisco, Cal., 6 June 1898, in Record Group 395, Preliminary Inventory of the Records of U.S. Army Overseas Operations and Commands, 1898-1942, Entry 887: 8th Army Corps, Independent Division, July-December 1898, Letters Received June-September 1898, General, Special Orders and Circulars, 1898 (in bound stack labeled "Independent Division 8th A.C. G.O., S.O., & Circulars 1898") (Washington, DC: National Archives); "The First Pay Day," *San Francisco Daily Report*, 7 June 1898, 3; "Seventh's Men Are Hopeful," *The Examiner*, 8 June 1898, 6.

103. "General Greene at Work," *San Francisco Call*, 9 June 1898, 5; "Rifle Practice for Keystone Regiment," *San Francisco Chronicle*, 9 June 1898, 3; "The First Pay Day," *San Francisco Daily Report*, 7 June 1898, 3;

"Seventh's Men Are Hopeful," *The Examiner*, 8 June 1898, 6.

104. "Camp Merritt Troops," *San Francisco Call*, 12 June 1898, 8; "Camp Merritt Notes," *San Francisco Call*, 20 June 1898, 5; "Division Headquarters," *San Francisco Call*, 22 June 1898, 5; "Tennesseans Hold a Levee," *San Francisco Chronicle*, 20 June 1898, 5; "At Camp Merritt," *San Francisco Daily Report*, 18 June 1898, 2.

105. "A Gap in the Camp," *San Francisco Call*, 27 June 1898, 10; "Camp Merritt," *San Francisco Call*, 25 July 1898, 5; "Wyoming Battery Joins the Troops," *San Francisco Chronicle*, 29 June 1898, 3; Letter, Kraemer to Grand. Pa., 9 July 1898.

106. "Echoes From the Camp," *San Francisco Chronicle*, 28 June 1898, 4.

107. Letter, Kraemer to Grand.Pa., 9 July 1898.

108. US War Department, *Infantry Drill Regulations, United States Army*, 14.

109. "At the Presidio," *San Francisco Daily Report*, 9 May 1898, 1.

110. "The First California," *San Francisco Call*, 10 May 1898, 7.

111. "Notes of the Camp," *San Francisco Call*, 16 June 1898, 8.

112. "Calisthenic Drill for the New Recruits at Camp Merritt," *San Francisco Chronicle*, 20 June 1898, 5.

113. "Wyoming Battery Joins the Troops," *San Francisco Chronicle*, 29 June 1898, 3.

114. Letter, Hugh E. Clapp, 1st Nebraska Infantry, to "Lieben Dad," 31 May 1898 (Carlisle Barracks, PA: US Army Military History Institute).

115. Letter, Louis W. Hubbard, 1st South Dakota, to "My Dearest Mother," 28 June 1898.

116. Letter, Kraemer to Sister, 11 August 1898.

117. "Camp Merritt Inspected," *San Francisco Call*, 31 May 1898, 5.

118. "Troops for the Parade," *San Francisco Daily Report*, 2 July 1898, 2; "The Parade by Divisions," *San Francisco Chronicle*, 5 July 1898, 9.

119. "Fine Parade on Oakland Streets," *The Examiner*, 5 July 1898, 10.

120. Laist, 6; "Oakland Celebrates the Glorious Fourth," *San Francisco Chronicle*, 5 July 1898, 10.

121. "Parade of Soldiers and Civilians," *The Examiner*, 5 July 1898, 10.

122. "Minnesota Men to Give an Exhibition," *The Examiner*, 12 June 1898, 21; "Iowa Boys Drill to Pleased Crowds," *The Examiner*, 29 June 1898, 3; "Native Daughters Arrange a Drill," *The Examiner*, 13 July 1898, 5; "Tennessee Regiment Drill in the Pavilion," *The Examiner*, 14 July 1898, 4; "Kansas Regiment in Fancy Drill," *The Examiner*, 27 July 1898, 9; "Drilled for Charity," *San Francisco Call*, 31 July 1898, 8.

123. Joseph I. Markey, *From Iowa to the Philippines: A History of Company M, Fifty-First Iowa Infantry Volunteers* (Red Oak, IA: Thos. D. Murphy Co., 1900), 62-63.

124. Lieutenant Martin E. Tew, *Official History of the Operations of the 13th Minnesota Infantry, U.S.V. in the Campaign in the Philippine Islands*, n.p., n.d., 3-4; "The Red Cross Benefit Draws Thousands to Mechanics' Pavilion,"

San Francisco Call, 18 June 1898, 14; "Were Praised By Merritt," *San Francisco Chronicle*, 18 June 1898, 14; "Drilled for the Red Cross," *The Examiner*, 18 June 1898, 18.

125. "A Crack Regiment Needed," *San Francisco Daily Report*, 18 June 1898, 4.

126. "Honors for Iowa's Sons," *San Francisco Call*, 29 June 1898, 7; "The Iowa Men Will Drill," *San Francisco Chronicle*, 28 June 1898, 7; "Drill and Review for the Red Cross Benefit," *San Francisco Chronicle*, 29 June 1898, 5.

127. Markey, 63; "Drill and Review for the Red Cross Benefit," *San Francisco Chronicle*, 29 June 1898, 5; "Iowa Boys Drill to Pleased Crowds," *The Examiner*, 29 June 1898, 3.

128. "Tennessee Boys Drill Before a Large Audience at the Pavilion," *San Francisco Call*, 15 July 1898, 9; "Tennessee Drill Tonight," *San Francisco Chronicle*, 14 July 1898, 5; "Madly Cheered for Dixie Land," *The Examiner*, 15 July 1898, 14; "Drill of Tennessee Troops," *San Francisco Daily Report*, 15 July 1898, 2.

129. "Seventh Regiment Drill," *San Francisco Call*, 21 July 1898, 5, 7; "Southern Californians in an Exhibition Drill," *San Francisco Chronicle*, 22 July 1898, 5; "The Seventh Drills for the First," *The Examiner*, 22 July 1898, 2; "Drill of the Kansans," *San Francisco Call*, 5 August 1898, 7; "Kansas Regiment to Drill," *San Francisco Chronicle*, 26 July 1898, 7; "Kansas Regiment Drill," *San Francisco Chronicle*, 27 July 1898, 8; "Kansas Boys Drill," *San Francisco Chronicle*, 5 August 1898, 7; "Exhibition Drill by the Kansas Men," *The Examiner*, 5 August 1898, 5.

130. "Orders From General Merriam," *San Francisco Call*, 7 May 1898, 8.

131. "The First is Under Orders," *San Francisco Call*, 7 May 1898, 8.

132. "The First California," *San Francisco Call*, 10 May 1898, p. 7; "Answer the Call to Arms," *The Examiner*, 9 May 1898, 3.

133. "The First California," *San Francisco Call*, 10 May 1898, 7.

134. "Discipline Now Strict," *San Francisco Chronicle*, 17 May 1898, 5.

135. "Doings in the Camp," *San Francisco Daily Report*, 27 May 1898, 3.

136. General Orders, No. 1, Headquarters, U.S. Expeditionary Forces, San Francisco, Cal., 20 May 1898.

137. General Orders, No. 1, Headquarters, Independent Division, Philippine Islands Expeditionary Forces, Camp Merritt, San Francisco, Cal., 1 June 1898.

138. General Orders, No. 2, Headquarters, Independent Division, Philippine Islands Expeditionary Forces, Camp Merritt, San Francisco, Cal., 2 June 1898.

139. General Orders, No. 1, Headquarters, Independent Division, Philippine Islands Expeditionary Forces, Camp Merritt, San Francisco, Cal., 1 June 1898.

140. "At Camp Merritt," *San Francisco Daily Report*, 23 June 1898, 1; "Immediate Example," *San Francisco Call*, 29 June 1898, 5; "Eighth Army Corps," *San Francisco Call*, 22 July 1898, 5.

141. "Immediate Example," *San Francisco Call*, 29 June 1898, 5.

142. "At Camp Merritt," *San Francisco Daily Report*, 9 June 1898, 3; "Local War Notes," *San Francisco Daily Report*, 21 June 1898, 2; "Will Sail on

Monday," *San Francisco Daily Report*, 22 June 1898, 2; "The Orders to Embark," *San Francisco Call*, 21 June 1898, 5.

143. "Health of Soldiers," *San Francisco Call*, 4 August 1898, 7.

144. "Local War Notes," *San Francisco Daily Report*, 30 June 1898, 2.

145. "Military Justice for Enlisted Men," *San Francisco Chronicle*, 6 July 1898, 3; "A Brigade Drill," *San Francisco Daily Report*, 11 July 1898, 3; "Soldiers Imprisoned," *San Francisco Daily Report*, 13 July 1898, 3; "Court-Martial Cases," *San Francisco Call*, 6 July 1898, 5; "Local War Notes," *San Francisco Daily Report*, 13 July 1898, 3.

146. "Tennessee Men," *San Francisco Daily Report*, 17 June 1898, 6.

147. Laist, 6.

148. "Holiday and No Holiday," *San Francisco Chronicle*, 31 May 1898, 3.

149. "The South Dakota Troops Arrive," *San Francisco Daily Report*, 2 June 1898, 3.

150. "Eighth Army Corps," *San Francisco Call*, 22 July 1898, 5.

151. Letter, Kraemer to Sister, 11 August 1898.

152. "The First California," *San Francisco Call*, 10 May 1898, 2.

153. "Drilling at the Presidio," *The Examiner*, 11 May 1898, 3.

154. General Orders, No. 2, Headquarters, Independent Division, Philippine Islands Expeditionary forces, Camp Merritt, San Francisco, Cal., 2 June 1898.

155. "Richmond's Tented Field," *San Francisco Call*, 3 June 1898, 7.

156. "The Band and the Guard Were Mounted," *San Francisco Call*, 19 June 1898, 7.

157. "Camp Merritt Notes," *San Francisco Call*, 20 June 1898, 5.

158. Letter, Kraemer to Sister, 7 July 1898.

159. "Eighth Army Corps," *San Francisco Call*, 14 July 1898, 8.

160. "The First Pay Day," *San Francisco Daily Report*, 7 June 1898, 3; "Seventh's Men are Hopeful," *The Examiner*, 8 June 1898, 6; "Troops at Camp Merritt," *San Francisco Call*, 3 July 1898, 7.

161. "City of the Soldiers Drenched and Soaked," *San Francisco Chronicle*, 15 May 1898, 23.

162. "The Second Expedition," *San Francisco Daily Report*, 15 June 1898, 2.

163. "Camp Streets to be Closed," *San Francisco Chronicle*, 24 June 1898, 5.

164. Stoneman, 5.

165. "The Day at the Camp," *San Francisco Daily Report*, 8 June 1898, 3.

166. "The Presidio Scandal," *San Francisco Daily Report*, 24 June 1898, 4; "Camp Streets to be Closed," *San Francisco Chronicle*, 24 June 1898, 5.

167. "More Rigid Rules for Camp Merritt," *San Francisco Chronicle*, 30 June 1898, 3; "Local War Notes," *San Francisco Daily Report*, 30 June 1898, 2; "Stringent Orders Issued," *San Francisco Call*, 30 June 1898, 5.

168. Stoneman, 5.

169. Letter, Clapp to Dad, 31 May 1898.

170. "Too Many Groggeries Around Camp Merritt," *San Francisco Chronicle*, 8 June 1898, 5; "Police Commissioners Call a Halt on Increase of Saloons at Camp Merritt," *San Francisco Chronicle*, 9 June 1898, 3.

171. "Richmond Asks Relief," *San Francisco Daily Report*, 8 June 1898, 3.

172. "Military Items Condensed," *San Francisco Chronicle*, 10 June 1898, 9.

173. "Local War Notes," *San Francisco Daily Report*, 27 June 1898, 2.

174. "The Provost Guard Waited," *San Francisco Chronicle*, 25 June 1898, 9.

175. Stoneman, 5.

176. "Four Thousand More Soldiers Now on Transports for Manila," *San Francisco Daily Report*, 14 June 1898, 1.

177. "Local War Notes," *San Francisco Daily Report*, 27 June 1898, 2.

178. "News of the Camps," *San Francisco Chronicle*, 29 May 1898, 23.

179. *History of the Operations of the First Nebraska Infantry, U.S.V. in the Campaign in the Philippine Islands*, n.p., n.d., 6.

180. Doxey, 99-106; "Soldiers' Sunday in Golden Gate Park," *San Francisco Chronicle*, 6 June 1898, 7.

181. "Soldiers at the Park," *San Francisco Chronicle*, 23 May 1898, 10.

182. Stoneman, 5; Markey, 63; *History of the Operations of the First Nebraska Infantry, U.S.V. in the Campaign in the Philippine Islands*, 5.

183. Crocker's Guide Map of the City of San Francisco, Compiled from the Official Surveys and for Crocker-Langley San Francisco Directory, 1896.

184. Doxey, 112-113.

185. "The Day in Camp," *San Francisco Chronicle*, 30 May 1898, 3; "Military News in Brief," *San Francisco Chronicle*, 7 June 1898, 4; "Welcome Paymaster," *San Francisco Call*, 7 June 1898, 7; "Shoddy Clothing," *San Francisco Call*, 14 June 1898, 5; "The Presidio Camp," *San Francisco Call*, 17 July 1898, 8; "Crowds at the Presidio," *San Francisco Call*, 18 July 1898, 5; "The Presidio Camp," *San Francisco Call*, 20 July 1898, 7; "Monday in the Camp," *San Francisco Daily Report*, 6 June 1898, 3; "The Second Expedition," *San Francisco Daily Report*, 15 June 1898, 2; "At Camp Merritt," *San Francisco Daily Report*, 16 June 1898, 1.

186. "Soldiers in the Swim," *San Francisco Chronicle*, 9 July 1898, 8.

187. "Military News in Brief," *San Francisco Chronicle*, 7 June 1898, 4; "Volunteers Race for Prizes in the Swim," *San Francisco Chronicle*, 20 June 1898, 5; "Shoddy Clothing," *San Francisco Call*, 14 June 1898, 5; "Soldiers at Sutro Baths," *San Francisco Call*, 27 June 1898, 10; "Tennessee Men," *San Francisco Daily Report*, 17 June 1898, 6; "Local War Notes," *San Francisco Daily Report*, 20 June 1898, 2.

188. "Local War Notes," *San Francisco Daily Report*, 30 June 1898, 2.

189. "Soldier Guests at the Lurline Baths," *San Francisco Call*, 22 May 1898, 7; "Soldiers in the Swim," *San Francisco Call*, 24 May 1898, 2.

190. "When Will the Transports Sail?" *San Francisco Daily Report*, 16 May 1898, 2.

191. "Camp at the Presidio," *San Francisco Call*, 9 August 1898, 12.

192. Letter, Eugene F. Bert to Major General Wesley Merritt, 28 May 1898, in Memorandum to the Commanding General, 1st Brigade, from Headquarters, Independent Division, 8 June 1898, in Record Group 395, Preliminary Inventory

of the Records of U.S. Army Overseas Operations and Commands, 1898-1942, Entry 887, No. 33: 8th Army Corps, Independent Division, July-December 1898, Letters Received June-September 1898, Box No. 1: General, Special Orders and Circulars, 1898 (Washington, DC: National Archives).

193. "Baseball for Red Cross," *The Examiner*, 8 June 1898, 5; "Soldiers to Play," *San Francisco Daily Report*, 3 June 1898, 6; "Military Baseball," *San Francisco Daily Report*, 7 June 1898, 3; "Minnesota Loses to San Francisco," *San Francisco Chronicle*, 10 June 1898, 9.

194. "California Bests Iowa," *San Francisco Chronicle*, 7 August 1898, 32.

195. "Volunteer Athletes Arranging Contests," *San Francisco Chronicle*, 12 June 1898, 23; "Minnesota Soldiers Against Montana Men," *San Francisco Chronicle*, 18 June 1898, 7; "Soldiers on the Gridiron," *San Francisco Chronicle*, 19 June 1898, 22; "The Soldiers Defeated," *San Francisco Call*, 22 June 1898, 5; "Will Sail on Monday," *San Francisco Daily Report*, 22 June 1898, 2; "Memorial Day in Camp," *San Francisco Daily Report*, 30 May 1898, 3; "Local War Notes," *San Francisco Daily Report*, 14 June 1898, 2; "Soldiers Play," *San Francisco Daily Report*, 18 June 1898, 3; "The Soldiers at Football," *San Francisco Daily Report*, 20 June 1898, 2.

196. Testimony of Maj.Gen. Wesley Merritt, 21 December 1898, in *Report VII*, 3265.

197. James J. Huston, *The Sinews of War: Army Logistics, 1775-1953* (Washington, DC: Office of the Chief of Military History, 1966) 280; Robert B. Roberts, *Encyclopedia of Historic Forts: The Military, Pioneer, and Trading Posts of the United States* (New York: Macmillan Publishing Co., 1988), 61-62; Workers of the Writers' Program of the Work Projects Administration in Northern California, *The Army at the Golden Gate: A Guide to Army Posts in the San Francisco Bay Area*, nd, np, 96-98.

198. Roberts, 62.

199. H.C. Corbin to Col. L.S. Babbitt, 14 May 1898, in *Correspondence II*, 641.

200. H.C. Corbin to Colonel Hawkins, 18 May 1898, in *Correspondence II*, 659; H.C. Corbin's Memorandum for the Chief of Ordnance, 18 May 1898, in *Correspondence II*, 659.

201. "Equipping the Regiments," *San Francisco Chronicle*, 28 May 1898, 9; "Memorial Day in Camp," *San Francisco Daily Report*, 30 May 1898, 3; "Troops at Camp Merritt," *San Francisco Call*, 1 July 1898, 7; "Eighth California," *San Francisco Call*, 23 July 1898, 5; "Camp Merritt," *San Francisco Call*, 25 July 1898, 5; Laist, 7.

202. General Orders, No. 6, Headquarters, Independent Division, Philippine Islands Expeditionary Forces, Camp Merritt, San Francisco, Cal., 13 June 1898.

203. Erna Risch, *Quartermaster Support of the Army: A History of the Corps, 1775-1939*, (Washington, DC: Office of the Quartermaster General, 1962), 492; US War Department, *Annual Reports of the War Department for the Fiscal Year Ended June 30, 1898. Report of the Secretary of War. Miscellaneous Reports.*

Report of the Commissary-General of Subsistence (Washington, DC: GPO, 1898), 582.

204. Risch, 492.

205. "To Increase the Army at Bay District," *San Francisco Call*, 1 June 1898, 5.

206. H.S. Crocker Company, 57; "A Timely Lesson," *San Francisco Call*, 11 June 1898, 5.

207. "Affairs at Camp Merritt," *San Francisco Chronicle*, 6 August 1898, 9.

208. "The Presidio Camp," *San Francisco Daily Report*, 20 May 1898, 3; "The Day in Camp," *San Francisco Daily Report*, 28 May 1898, 3; "Salmon for Soldiers," *San Francisco Daily Report*, 6 June 1898, 3; "Camp Merritt Will Not be Quite Deserted," *San Francisco Chronicle*, 14 June 1898, 14; "Affairs at Camp Merritt," *San Francisco Chronicle*, 6 August 1898, 9; "Division Headquarters," *San Francisco Call*, 23 June 1898, 5.

209. US War Department, *Annual Reports of the War Department for the Fiscal Year Ended June 30, 1898. Report of the Secretary of War. Miscellaneous Reports*. Report of the Quartermaster-General (Washington, DC: GPO, 1898), 380.

210. Letter, E.S. Otis to Col. Charles Denby, 19 November 1898, in US Senate, *Report of the Commission Appointed by the President to Investigate the Conduct of the War Department in the War With Spain*, volume VIII, *Correspondence* (Washington, DC: GPO, 1900), p 178, hereafter cited as *Report VIII*, 178.

211. Oscar F. Long to Quartermaster General, U.S. Army, 25 August 1898, in Record Group 92, Office of the Quartermaster General Document File, 1800-1914, Case 115533 (Washington, DC: National Archives).

212. "Preparing for an Early Movement," *San Francisco Chronicle*, 12 May 1898, 1.

213. Oscar F. Long to Quartermaster General, U.S. Army, 25 August 1898, in Record Group 92, Office of the Quartermaster General Document File, 1800-1914, Case 115533.

214. Oscar F. Long to Quartermaster General, U.S. Army, 1 October 1898, in Record Group 92, Office of the Quartermaster General. Document File, 1800-1914, Case 120579.

215. Ibid.

216. "Came in From Other States," *The Examiner*, 23 May 1898, 2.

217. "Outfitting the Soldiers," *San Francisco Chronicle*, 17 May 1898, 5.

218. "Shoes for the Soldiers," *San Francisco Call*, 10 July 1898, 8; US War Department, *Annual Reports of the War Department for the Fiscal Year Ended June 30, 1898. Report of the Secretary of War. Miscellaneous Reports*. Report of the Quartermaster-General (Washington, DC: GPO, 1898), 451.

219. Oscar F. Long to Quartermaster General, U.S. Army, 25 August 1898, in Record Group 92, Office of the Quartermaster General Document File, 1800-1914, Case 115533.

220. US War Department, *Annual Reports of the War Department for the Fiscal Year Ended June 30, 1898. Report of the Secretary of War. Miscellaneous*

Reports. Report of the Quartermaster-General (Washington, DC: GPO, 1898), 462.

221. Oscar F. Long to Quartermaster General, U.S. Army, 1 October 1898, in Record Group 92, Office of the Quartermaster General Document File, 1800-1914, Case 120579.

222. "The Presidio Camp Completed," *San Francisco Daily Report*, 18 May 1898, 3; "Doings in the Camp," *San Francisco Daily Report*, 27 May 1898, 3; "The Day in Camp," *San Francisco Daily Report*, 1 June 1898, 2; "Monday in the Camp," *San Francisco Daily Report*, 6 June 1898, 3; "Equipping the Expedition," *San Francisco Chronicle*, 28 May 1898, 9; "Hard Service at the Camp," *San Francisco Chronicle*, 8 July 1898, 7; "Division Headquarters," *San Francisco Call*, 23 June 1898, 5; "Eighth Army Corps," *San Francisco Call*, 23 July 1898, 5.

223. US War Department, *Annual Reports of the War Department for the Fiscal Year Ended June 30, 1898. Report of the Secretary of War. Miscellaneous Reports*. Report of the Surgeon-General (Washington, DC: GPO, 1898), 703.

224. John Phillip Langellier, "Bastion by the Bay: A History of the Presidio of San Francisco, 1776-1906," Unpublished Dissertation (Manhattan, KS: Kansas State University, 1982), 102-103; Workers of the Writers' Program, 71.

225. Workers of the Writers' Program, 76; US War Department, *Annual Reports of the War Department for the Fiscal Year Ended June 30, 1898. Report of the Secretary of War. Miscellaneous Reports*. Report of the Surgeon-General (Washington, DC: GPO, 1898), 716.

226. "The Field Hospital," *San Francisco Call*, 30 May 1898, 5.

227. "Camp of the Volunteers," *San Francisco Call*, 11 May 1898, 7; "Oregon's Volunteers Now in Camp," *San Francisco Call*, 14 May 1898, 7.

228. "Nurses to Go With the Soldiers," *San Francisco Call*, 19 May 1898, 8; Report of the Board of Medical Officers Convened at the Presidio, San Francisco, 3 September 1898, in *Report VIII*, 170.

229. "A Significant Detail," *San Francisco Call*, 21 May 1898, 5.

230. "The Richmond Camp," *San Francisco Call*, 24 May 1898, 2.

231. General Orders, No. 12, Headquarters, Independent Division, Eighth Army Corps, San Francisco, Cal., 29 June 1898; "Measles in Camp," *San Francisco Daily Report*, 13 June 1898, 6; "Fighting a Threatened Epidemic of Measles," *San Francisco Call*, 12 June 1898, 8.

232. Report of the Board of Medical Officers Convened at the Presidio, San Francisco, 3 September 1898, in *Report VIII*, 170; "War Incidents," *San Francisco Call*, 18 June 1898, 7.

233. Report of the Board of Medical Officers Convened at the Presidio, San Francisco, 3 September 1898, in *Report VIII*, 171-72.

234. Ibid.

235. Geo. M. Sternberg, Reply of Surgeon-General, in US Senate, *Report of the Commission Appointed by the President to Investigate the Conduct of the War Department in the War With Spain*, volume 1, 658.

236. US War Department, *Annual Reports of the War Department for the Fiscal Year Ended June 30, 1899. Reports of the Chiefs of Bureaus*. Report of the

Surgeon-General (Washington, DC: GPO, 1899), 472.

237. Report of the Board of Medical Officers Convened at the Presidio, San Francisco, 3 September 1898, in *Report VIII*, 171.

238. US War Department, *Annual Reports of the War Department for the Fiscal Year Ended June 30, 1899. Reports of the Chiefs of Bureaus*. Report of the Surgeon-General (Washington, DC: GPO, 1899), 472.

239. Letter, E.S. Otis to Col. Charles Denby, 19 November 1898, in *Report VIII*, 177-78.

240. Ibid., 172.

Chapter V
The Relief Societies

President William McKinley directed the Philippine expeditions to concentrate in San Francisco and prepare for overseas duty. McKinley chose the site because the Bay City featured excellent port facilities and an established military infrastructure. Unfortunately, the Army did not possess sufficient resources to accommodate the welfare needs of all soldiers assembled at the Golden Gate. San Franciscans rallied to offer assistance. One unforeseen and fortuitous dividend of the president's selection was the extent to which the civilian community embraced its uniformed visitors.

Specifically, citizens supported relief societies that emerged to care for soldiers in myriad ways. Politicians, businessmen, entrepreneurs, educators, and clergymen joined Bay Area residents to establish and sustain Red Cross organizations that were devoted to troop welfare. Working closely with the military, the state association and local society embarked on projects that augmented the medical care, equipment issue, and dietary offerings extended to thousands of soldiers encamped about San Francisco.

Some of these same civilian patrons supported another relief society that formed to look after Volunteers' family members. The Patriotic Home Helpers offered food and shelter to needy wives and children of community men who joined the military. San Francisco demonstrated a willingness to support others as well as its own during the war against Spain.

The Red Cross

Background

On 24 December 1897, Secretary of State John Sherman petitioned the general public on behalf of the President of the United States. In an open letter to the American citizenry, Sherman appealed for support in providing humanitarian assistance to the Cuban people. Many of the island's inhabitants suffered materially in the wake of their revolution against Spain begun in February 1895. Thousands of Cubans faced terrible sanitation conditions, inadequate food, and deadly disease in "reconcentration" camps that General Valeriano Weyler y Nicolau established.[1]

Clara Barton's American National Red Cross responded to Sherman's plea by committing to relief efforts on behalf "of the sufferers in Cuba."[2] Yet only four months after the secretary of state solicited help for Cubans, the United States' declaration of war substantially altered the scope of assistance needed from benevolent organizations. The president's call for thousands of military Volunteers expanded support requirements to include those Americans gathered to join the Army who were located in state and federal camps. By 1 May 1898, the geographic magnitude of the welfare task changed as well, embracing an island 90 miles off the Florida coast and a Pacific archipelago more than 7,000 miles west of San Francisco.

The National Red Cross responded to American servicemen's needs by pledging "to render auxiliary medical and hospital service during the war."[3] Representatives served "oral notice of the intention of the Red Cross to be ready to furnish any supplemental aid that might be required by the armies in the field."[4] On 9 June 1898, Secretary of War Russell A. Alger officially accepted the Red Cross's offer to assist in caring for troops. Through a letter issued by the Surgeon General, he alerted chief surgeons in the field that Barton's organization had "full authority to send agents and supplies to all our camps."[5]

Alger's official sanction merely confirmed what had already been practiced thousands of miles from Washington, DC for nearly a month. During May 1898, Red Cross societies in the trans-Mississippi west had begun their work in support of units mobilizing to serve in the war. Specifically, San Francisco Bay Area organizations evolved to assist the Regular and Volunteer units that concentrated about the Golden Gate.

Organization

California's Red Cross effort to support Volunteers appeared shortly after Congress declared war on Spain. Throughout the state, local societies took root. Most commonly, these organizations developed in communities preparing to send federalized National Guardsmen to war. The city of San Francisco had one complete infantry regiment intent upon gaining Volunteer Army status. Although this goal provided enough incentive to establish a Red Cross organization in the city, Alger offered an additional stimulus on 26 April 1898. In a letter to California governor James H. Budd, Secretary of War Alger announced that California National Guard units would rendezvous at San Francisco.[6]

In response to these developments, citizens were invited to attend the first meeting of the "Red Cross League and Sanitary Commission of California" on 2 May 1898. Members of the San Francisco community were encouraged to support a society dedicated to providing for state Volunteers. The invitation to constitute a Red Cross indicated that "This organization has been formed to provide California troops, called to defend their flag and country, with medical and other supplies, and to care for our soldier boys in camp and hospital."[7]

Figure 66.

The 2 May meeting at the California Hotel actually welcomed representatives from Bay Area Red Cross organizations. One woman who attended proclaimed, "We're fighting as surely for our country in this full membership of ours under the Red Cross as though we had shouldered muskets and marched away."[8] Other delegates who shared her sense of duty joined in chartering the California Red Cross Society. Representatives empowered the league to pursue local branch issues. An executive committee composed of key political figures and spiritual leaders, "the leading philanthropic women and foremost business men of the city," was named to supervise the organization's activities.[9]

Executive committee women, led by the society's president, Mrs. Willard B. Harrington, established numerous Red Cross subcommittees that defined the league's special areas of interest: constitution, finance, schools, subscription solicitations, nurses, entertainment, and clubs. These groups toiled to achieve the league's main objective to care for California men going to war. Pursuing this goal was no small task, given the military's questionable ability to clothe, equip, and care for thousands of new soldiers. Harrington observed that the federal government provided

141

Figure 67. Mrs. Willard B. Harrington.

the "barest of necessities" for its Volunteers. She added, "It is our duty . . . to see that the boys who go to fight for us, while we remain at home in comfort and safety, should be provided for to the best of our ability."[10] The society, therefore, intended to work closely with the military to identify and meet the needs of soldiers who marshaled in San Francisco.

Harnessing suitable resources to assist the military simply exceeded the capacity of only one Red Cross chapter. The San Francisco-based California Red Cross Society therefore set out to coordinate the work of branches across the state. Two developments assisted the society in realizing this goal: emerging Red Cross branches in Los Angeles, Visalia, Alameda, and Vallejo supported establishing a state-wide organization and the designation of San Francisco as the assembly point for Regular and Volunteer units bound for the Philippines.[11]

On 25 May 1898, the California Red Cross Society assisted in setting up a coordinating authority when it reorganized into two bodies.[12] The first organization, the San Francisco Red Cross Society, emerged to supervise activities that had a local focus. Mrs. John F. Merrill was elected president. The second organization, the California State Red Cross Association or Auxiliary, evolved to orchestrate the efforts of organizations across the state. Harrington as-

Figure 68. Mrs. John F. Merrill.

sumed the presidency of the new state body. In keeping with its broader charter, the state association announced that local Red Cross organizations should "equip their own troops. . . . In the field the general society would look after all the troops and thus there would be no conflict of the main and subordinate organizations."[13]

Red Cross personnel who formed the California state association chose to be administered by a board of managers. Composed of 15 members, the board represented the state's largest local organizations. Given their proximity to "the scene of embarkation," San Francisco and Alameda county achieved the greatest numeric advantage on the board. The association accorded San Francisco six members and Alameda county four representatives (Oakland, two; Alameda, one; Berkeley, one). The remaining five delegates hailed from Los Angeles, Sacramento, Marin, Santa Clara, and San Joaquin.[14]

Figure 69. Mrs. Phoebe Hearst.

The state association established a headquarters in two rooms on the second floor of *The Examiner*, or Hearst, Building.[15] Mrs. Phoebe A. Hearst, a noted philanthropist and William Randolph Hearst's mother, donated rooms rent-free to the Red Cross.[16] The state organization did not employ salaried officers. Volunteer workers attended the offices between 0900 and approximately 1800.[17] Operating out of rooms at this location gave Red Cross officials easy access to critical military agencies. The Hearst Building was positioned at the southeast corner of Market and Third Streets in downtown San Francisco. It stood less than a block from Phelan Building offices of the US Army's Pacific and California territorial departments and only several blocks from the depot quartermaster at 36 New Montgomery Street.[18]

The San Francisco Red Cross Society also enjoyed a favorable proximity to the same military facilities. The local society established its headquarters in the Claus Spreckels Building on Market and Third Streets, adjacent

143

to the Hearst Building and state association offices.[19] League volunteers operated from second-floor rooms provided by Spreckels, a wealthy entrepreneur who amassed a fortune through investing in the sugar industry.[20] Beginning 7 May, a local Red Cross representative moved about Rooms 204 to 207, tending to society business from 1000 to 1700.[21]

The state association and local society operated in tandem. Key members occasionally held positions in both organizations. Harrington, Merrill, and Mrs. L.L. Dunbar, secretary of the California State Red Cross Association, collaborated to orchestrate the subcommittees' efforts; they met daily with civilian volunteers.[22] Both the state and local Red Cross shared the use of a 16 Post Street warehouse loaned by the estate of "Bonanza King" James G. Fair. There, the organizations received donations and stored a "multiplicity of things received."[23]

Fundraising

Initially, the California Red Cross Society sought a type of donation that would have been better stored in a safe than a warehouse—money. Doctor William E. Hopkins, Surgeon General, California National Guard, estimated that "about $9000 would be required . . . to fit the medical corps for a campaign."[24] That figure pertained to requirements generated by California Volunteers only. As the War Department designated more units for service in Manila, the financial obligation to care for additional units increased. To generate monetary support intended to care for troops, the Governor of California, Mayor of San Francisco, and Red Cross officials issued a proclamation on 5 May 1898: "Let us rally to the aid of our country's defenders. We need money for necessities, not for luxuries. And as time is pressing, the money should be given at once."[25]

Mrs. F.G. Sanborn, chairman of the California Red Cross Society's subscription committee, circulated her own announcement. On 9 May, she and other Red Cross officials asked for assistance in raising a fund to provide "such articles for the care of the sick and wounded soldiers and sailors as are not provided for by the Government of the United States." Members of her committee thrust pledge books into the hands of eager volunteers prepared to solicit and record contributions. The organization also maintained subscription lists at several newspaper offices and placed donation boxes at various points in the city.[26]

Revenues "began to flow in slowly but surely" to Red Cross headquarters.[27] Starting in mid-May, the *San Francisco Call* and *San Francisco Daily Report* published information on Red Cross activities, solicitations, and funds several times a week. By 17 May, less than two weeks after announcing its initial appeal, the California Red Cross Society gathered subscriptions of $13,662.[28] On 27 June, Mrs. W.P. Morgan, the local organization's finance chairman, listed revenues at $47,277.[29] Just over two weeks later, the San Francisco Red Cross Society reported $51,866.[30] By the time of the peace protocol, the finance committee accounted for revenues that totaled $58,139.[31]

ENTHUSIASTIC COLLECTORS FOR THE RED CROSS

San Francisco Call, 25 May 1898

Figure 70.

The San Francisco society secured funds through a variety of sources. Morgan organized her 31 May statement of contributions in eight categories: general subscriptions; schools; clubs, churches, and associations; San Francisco Fire Department; San Francisco Produce Exchange; Stock and Bond Exchange; monthly subscriptions; entertainment; and benefits. Of the total receipts, "general subscriptions" accounted for slightly more than 66 percent.[32]

The dominance of "general subscriptions" could be traced to individual contributors' donations. Some were among the more noteworthy of the San Francisco region; others gave anonymously or subscribed from afar. Mayor James D. Phelan was among the first to respond to the early May solicitation when he wrote a check for $200.[33] Claus Spreckels contributed $1,000 toward the end of the month. Mrs. A.S. Townsend, a local philanthropist and one of the Red Cross's greatest supporters, gave $1,000 on 26 May.[34] Spreckels and Townsend accounted for the largest single donations given in spring and summer 1898. Many others gave smaller sums, including A.B. McCreery, $100; three little girls' fireworks money, $10; a "friend", $27; and a soldier, $1.[35]

Schools, too, routinely made contributions. At the organizational meeting on 2 May, discussion included how to include school children in the Red Cross effort. During May and June, the local society seldom released a report on its finances without noting money, no matter how seemingly insignificant, that the school children offered. For example, the Golden Gate Primary School gave 75 cents for its second subscription.[36] The Sutro Primary School delivered $10.[37] Others contributing included the school children of Mill Valley, $20; Monroe School, $10; Humbolt School, $1; and Girls Mission High School, $38.[38] Schools also participated in "entertainments and benefits," activities that generated revenue for the Red Cross. The Strawberry Festival at Clement Grammar School, for example, netted more than $112.[39]

Sports, cultural events, and military activities raised the most money in this category. "Red Cross Day" observed on Friday, 27 May, at the Oakland Race Track yielded $1514 from the California and Pacific Coast Jockey Clubs.[40] A 9 June baseball game at Recreation Park between the 13th Minnesota Volunteers and the San Francisco Baseball Club produced $77.[41] Mr. Fritz Scheel conducted the San Francisco symphony orchestra at a 2 June matinee performance in the Baldwin Theater. The concert before an audience described as "not over large" generated proceeds of $219.[42] The San Francisco Press Club hosted the sale of pictures by artists and art students in mid-June, raising $706.70 for the Red Cross.[43]

The San Francisco Red Cross Society also conceived of a benefit that tapped Volunteer regiments' services. On Friday evening, 17 June, the local organization sponsored a "reception" for 13th Minnesota Volunteers at the Mechanics' Pavilion. Society members invited the public to purchase admission tickets and watch the regiment perform various drills.

The program included physical exercise with arms, guard mount, bayonet exercise, company drill, and a review by MG Wesley Merritt.[44] The benefit raised nearly $700.[45] Eleven days later, troops from the 51st Iowa offered a similar fundraising program at the Mechanics' Pavilion. MG Elwell Otis served as reviewing officer. The Native Daughters of the Golden West, who sponsored the Red Cross benefit, charged patrons 25 cents for a seat in the gallery or 50 cents for one on the main floor. Proceeds netted more than $322.[46]

Figure 71.

A number of donations from various professional, business, and government organizations also added revenues to the local Red Cross. The Retail Liquor Dealers gave a whopping $1,132 in early July.[47] During June, the San Francisco Post Office Branch of the Red Cross Society pledged $100 per month.[48] Its August contribution reached $150.[49] Other notable donors were the Japanese Society, $160; the Japanese Bank, $25; the

Sam Yups of Chinatown, $112; Risdon Iron Works employees, $110; San Francisco Bar Association, $25; and not to be outdone, Merrill, Barker, and Hill's Guinea Pig Show, $50.[50]

Goods and Services

In addition to cash, the Red Cross encouraged gifts of goods and services. Early donations included essentials to get the Red Cross operational. Mrs. Phoebe Hearst and Claus Spreckels offered rent-free rooms in Market Street office buildings for use as Red Cross headquarters. To furnish state association offices, the Fuller Desk Company provided chairs and desks. Sloane and Company gave rugs.[51] A telephone company installed a phone "and allowed the use of it absolutely free for eight months."[52] The Hicks-Judd Company, a publishing enterprise that subsequently printed Volunteer unit histories as part of *Campaigning in the Philippines* by Karl Irving Faust, supplied the league with stationery and printing free of charge.[53] Western Union and Postal Telegraph Companies allowed the Red Cross to use their wires at no cost.[54] John Monahan and Company, commercial book and job printers, contributed 1,000 subscription blanks, enabling the Red Cross to collect pledges.[55]

Once organized, the society asked citizens for clothing and personal articles or the materials to make them. In some instances, civilian volunteers solicited specific items based on requests made by the military of the Red Cross. On 18 May, the *Daily Report* announced that "the society has issued a call for donations of muslin for pillow cases and sheeting. . . . A large supply of flannel is wanted for abdominal bandages. The Government has asked the society for 6000 of them."[56]

Organizations and individuals responded. The Needlework Guild donated 4,234 handkerchiefs and towels. Greenbaum, Weil, and Michels, importers and manufacturers of men's furnishing goods, offered the society one day's work on the factory's 200 sewing machines.[57] Mrs. A.S. Townsend sent 500 yards of muslin for bandages.[58] The Oregon Red Cross donated 600 caps and 1,000 bandages in early June.[59] Redington and Company, importers and jobbers, provided 500 fans.[60] The Native Daughters of the Red Cross furnished 300 caps and bandages.[61]

The Red Cross also regularly asked for "comfort bags." These personal items were made of denim and measured 7 inches long and 2 inches wide when opened. The bags contained buttons, thread, needles, pins, and safety pins. Society volunteers encouraged the public to include "coarse needles . . . as men at best are never good sewers, and it would be a difficult matter for the soldiers to thread a fine needle."[62]

San Francisco Call, 19 May 1898

A SOLDIER'S COMFORT-BAG

Figure 72.

The Red Cross also solicited and received assorted other goods and services from numerous donors. "All mothers of the soldiers are requested to go to the society's rooms, 16 Post Street, and assist in sewing."[63] The Red Cross also conceived of a role for children beyond their school relief projects: "Boys can do good service at 16 Post street, as messengers, on Saturday afternoons or after school hours."[64] Merchants, manufacturers, and producers were urged to contribute canned and preserved fruits, beef extracts, and other foods.

The public responded in much the same way as they had to requests for money. Townsend donated 5,000 pounds of dried fruit.[65] The State Board of Trade sent 225 boxes of fruit to the society's hospitality rooms at the Ferry Building by the bay. The Union Ice Company contributed all the ice needed in the hospital department.[66] Belmont School sent 12 gallons of milk daily to Camp Merritt to be apportioned among the regiments.[67] The American Union Fish Company dispatched 3,000 pounds of fish to the Colorado, Wyoming, Utah, and Montana Volunteers.[68] Fish and Game Warden Joseph A. Mogan conducted "another" raid on fishermen and sent 1,000 pounds of confiscated fish to the Red Cross.[69] The Trinity Church ladies prepared 565 lunches, and Grace Church sent 124 packages of food to the Ferry Building hospitality rooms.[70]

Others who offered donations included Messieurs Grey, Mitchell, and A.A. Hold who secured wood for hospital tent floors at Lime Point, Fort Baker, and other areas that accommodated troops. These men inspired six lumber companies to each donate 1,500 feet of lumber.[71] The Pacific Pine Lumber Company subsequently presented floor covering for five hospital tents.[72] Mrs. Alferitz and sons donated 1,700 postals, a popular item among the soldiers. The Red Cross noted toward the end of June that 10,316 postals had been distributed to the Volunteers.[73] G.M. Joselyn and Company of San Francisco, ship chandlers, donated a large quantity of bunting "for Red Cross flags to go to Manila."[74]

Arrivals

After the 2d Oregon's lead units slipped unnoticed into San Francisco on 13 May, California Red Cross Society volunteers resolved to establish

149

a welcome for troops. The organization learned at a meeting on 17 May that large numbers of soldiers were expected to arrive within 24 hours. Reverend Jacob Voorsanger, rabbi of the Temple Emmanu-El Synagogue and member of the Red Cross advisory board, "had already proposed that something be done in the way of cheer for the stranger at the ferry landing."[75] A Red Cross executive committee report recorded concern that men were likely to arrive "hungry and travel worn, with the prospect of a long march through a strange city, and the further probability of waiting for food for hours after arriving at their destination."[76] Spurred by offers of assistance from the Salvation Army and Mayor Phelan, the society elected to provide refreshments for newly arrived forces. Through this activity, the organization intended to offer uniformed newcomers "a practical California welcome" and "an introduction to the Red Cross Society."[77]

On 18 May, society volunteers implemented the program. Perhaps a little overzealous in their execution, Red Cross personnel crossed the bay and fed one of Oregon's battalions just after the troops reached Oakland. When other comrades arrived from the same state and boarded a bay ferry at Oakland, the Red Cross embarked and served refreshments during the short trip to San Francisco.[78]

That venture was the only instance in which members of the San Francisco society crossed the bay to greet troops. Thereafter, the local organization instituted welcoming festivities at San Francisco's Ferry Building. To prepare for inbound units, members of the Red Cross hospitality committee coordinated with Southern Pacific officials who operated both railroad and ferry services. Exact arrival times were often difficult to establish; therefore committee volunteers gathered at the depot around 0600 when the first ferries departed Oakland for San Francisco.[79]

The *Call* described a typical Red Cross wel-

Figure 73. Ready for work at the Ferry Building.

come. Normally troops offloaded ferries, then stacked their weapons and grounded other pieces of equipment. After forming into ranks, the men moved to the Ferry Building, marching to music the Merchants' Association band or a recently arrived regiment provided. Soldiers entered Red Cross hospitality rooms that had the "appearance of a flower show owing to the great quantity of exquisite blossoms hanging in garlands" and adorning tables.[80]

Once inside, men passed through lines of volunteer servers who offered hot coffee and an assortment of food: stew, hard-boiled eggs, pork and beans, hot bread and butter, sandwiches, cheeses, doughnuts, fruits, pies, and cakes.[81] Many troops devoured their first home-cooked food in weeks. Acting on requests from the Red Cross, local churches, synagogues and the general public provided much of the food.[82] On one occasion when the number of soldiers served virtually exhausted supplies, restaurants near the Ferry Building sent provisions.[83]

Figure 74. Dispensing hospitality at the Ferry Building.

The Red Cross welcome made an immediate, lasting impression on troops. Private William S. Christner, 10th Penn-sylvania, wrote his parents on 26 May 1898, "When we arrived at Frisco the ladies of the Red Cross society met us and such a breakfast the boys had not eaten for some time. Then they packed our haversacks with sandwiches, oranges, and bananas. Grapes and apricots were given us in plenty."[84]

Another Volunteer, Private A.G. Baker, 1st Colorado, recalled the experience in his personal narrative of the war. As he prepared to disembark near the ferry depot on 21 May, Baker and his fellow Coloradans believed they would not be fed until completing the 4-mile march to Camp Merritt. To their surprise, the ladies of the Red Cross awaited with food prepared. Members of the regiment were ushered into a large room "decorated with flags and patriotic colors. In the center of the room was an immense lunch counter laden with everything a hungry soldier could desire." Baker wrote that the ladies "served rich brown coffee, dainty sandwiches, cold meats of all kinds, cakes, cookies, pies and other deserts. Then apples, oranges, bananas, peaches and grapes, products of our modest sister state, were passed around."[85] Other Volunteer and Regular forces enjoyed a similar experience.

Figure 75. A cup of coffee at ferry Red Cross room.

As troops prepared to depart the Ferry Building for their camps in the city, the Red Cross and military units exchanged salutes. Mr. James B. Stetson, president of the California Street Cable Railroad and North Pacific Coast Railroad, usually served as toastmaster. Dubbed the "Ferry

Godfather" by fellow Red Cross volunteers, Stetson organized and led the festivities.⁸⁶ Each unit honored its hostesses with "three cheers and a tiger" for tendering such a splendid welcome. Other regiments offered more tangible expressions of thanks. For example, the 1st Montana presented "a beautiful gold mounted watch chain, made of sorrel horsehair, for the president of the Red Cross, Mrs. Merrill."⁸⁷ One soldier among recruits of the 18th and 23d Infantry Regiments left a dollar in appreciation for the society's reception.⁸⁸

Figure 76. Good cheer at the Ferry Building.

As troops moved out of the ferry depot, some with food stuffed in their pockets, the Red Cross offered blank postal cards to soldiers who could then write friends and relatives at home. The ladies also presented each soldier "with choice flowers with which to adorn themselves, giving them a picturesque appearance along the line of march."⁸⁹ The *Call* recorded that "the boys like to decorate and adorn their belts with roses, and embellish their gun barrels with calla lilies."⁹⁰ (See figure 77.)

Between 18 May and the battle for Manila on 13 August, Red Cross volunteers stood watch at San Francisco's Ferry Building, ready to greet every unit that entered the city. On at least one occasion, the society's workers offered more than the usual welcome of food and flowers. When 16 recruits from Texas arrived for duty with the Regular Army, they brought nothing but the clothes they wore. Red Cross members provided

Figure 77.

the men with food, clothing, and streetcar fare to the Presidio where they were assigned to their units.[91]

Departures

As expeditions prepared to leave San Francisco for the Philippines, Red Cross volunteers worked on several fronts to ready troops for their journey. The society gathered meals to give to soldiers who awaited dockside. The ladies also provided other services intended to comfort the troops as they braced for their long voyage overseas.

Units of the first expedition began to break camp and converge on three steamers during the fourth week of May. Near the ferry depot, Mrs. C.S. Wright managed the distribution of 11,000 lunches that were collected after the First Presbyterian Church issued a call for support.[92] Members of the 1st California Regiment boarded a troop transport, the *City of Peking*, to find chests and ammunition boxes "arranged on deck, in lieu of tables, and on these was spread the repast for officers and men."[93] When a baggage mix-up forced the 2d Oregon Regiment to remain dockside for hours before boarding the *Australia*, the Red Cross provided food.[94] After troops completed loading the *City of Sydney*, all three ships entered the stream and prepared to depart. While at anchor, each transport received a visit from Red Cross volunteers aboard the tugboats *Reliance* and *Monarch*. The organization's workers aboard these vessels transferred packages to troops on the steamers.[95]

The Red Cross offered additional aid to units that departed in June. Mrs. Merrill, president of the San Francisco society, appealed to the public for food donations as soldiers marshaled for the second expedition.[96] Response from the citizenry enabled a Red Cross delegation to provide the men with a lunch of coffee and sandwiches.[97] The Oakland and San Francisco societies distributed identification (ID) badges to Volunteers and Regulars who embarked the same month.[98]

The society renewed its call for public assistance as the third expedition prepared to sail. On 26 June, the *Call* published an announcement that solicited help: "As the soldiers will go aboard the transports to-day, it is asked that all lunches be sent to Mrs. Lowenberg, chairman of the hospitality committee."[99] Local community organizations and churches answered the appeal. Sherith Israel Congregation, St. Luke's Episcopal, First Presbyterian, and Temple Emanue-El collectively provided thousands of lunches.[100] Each soldier accepted homemade meals in individual packages "consisting of two meat sandwiches, a hard-boiled egg, cheese, cakes and doughnuts, and an orange or an apple." Troops also received pencils and postcards to write friends and loved ones farewell messages.[101]

Red Cross preparations for July's fourth expedition followed much the same course. The day before units boarded vessels, Trinity and Grace Churches prepared

Figure 78. Lunching before sailing from the transport dock.

lunches and delivered them to the Red Cross. Food donations poured into the organization's hospitality quarters at the Ferry Building.[102] On 15 July, the river steamer *Alvira*, with Red Cross representatives and friends of soldiers aboard, cruised the bay to visit departing transports.[103]

In Camp

The Red Cross was the most visible and active relief organization in the encampments. Troops saw the society's volunteers everywhere. The *Call* observed, "There is no day of rest for the ladies of the Red Cross. Visiting hospitals, comforting the sick and supplying the many wants of the boys in blue in these busy war times gives them very little time for recreation."[104]

Much of the Red Cross work in the various San Francisco camps focused on providing "necessaries for the care and comfort of the soldiers in cases where the Government does not supply such necessaries."[105] That broad mandate covered medical care, food and clothing, and in some cases, strong advice to the Army on how to improve troop welfare. The Red Cross exerted influence over the military unlike any other private organization of the era. While careful not to abuse its relationship with the Army, Red Cross officials nevertheless prodded the service to take action on issues related to the well-being of those in uniform.

Certainly, the Red Cross prioritized medical care. Work in this area constituted the organization's greatest contribution to soldiers who assembled in San Francisco. During May, in particular, when Merritt's command struggled to establish adequate medical facilities, the Red Cross moved to assist the military. On 13 May, members of the society's executive committee secured permission from the Presidio's chief surgeon to erect a large hospital tent on the military installation.[106] Through this activity, the organization offered to manage the "more serious cases" admitted to the installation's brigade hospital.[107] By 18 May, the Red Cross tent on the Presidio included 13 patients who variously suffered from a fractured ankle, measles, and tonsillitis. Three experienced male nurses volunteered their services to help oversee operations.[108]

As more troops poured into San Francisco and expanded the camps, demand for medical care became even more acute. Using vacant beds in the Treasury Department's Marine Hospital on the Presidio assisted military surgeons; it did not, however, alleviate the need for more facilities.[109] To cope with this predicament, both the military and the Red Cross welcomed assistance from local civilian hospitals. The hierarchy of the California Red Cross Society played a critical role in both encouraging and securing support from several of the city's care facilities. Mrs. Willard B. Harrington, Mrs. John F. Merrill, and Mrs. L.L. Dunbar, the leading officials and advocates of Red Cross work, served together on the Board of Directors, Hospital for Children and Training School for Nurses.[110] Their ties to other medical enterprises in the city reaped dividends for MG Merritt's beleaguered medical staff.

As early as 21 May, three days after troops poured into the Bay District Racetrack area, San Francisco's French Hospital offered to open a ward to military patients.[111] The proposal was attractive to Merritt's command for several reasons. First, the facility promised to relieve pressure on the Hospital Corps at a time when scant military dispensaries existed. Second, the French Hospital accorded medical care at no charge to the Army. Third, the facility, located at 5th and Point Lobos Avenues, was situated next to the new encampment selected by MG Merriam.[112] Patients could be evacuated expeditiously from the camp to the hospital.

Merritt's command consented, and the Red Cross assisted in moving soldiers who were afflicted with serious maladies to the French Hospital. Major Clayton H. Parkhill, brigade surgeon, referred four soldiers to the civilian facility for treatment on 25 May. Parkhill observed, "We were without proper means to care for the men at the time and we appreciated their generous offer very much."[113] Over the next 10 days, the hospital tended a total of 100 troops.[114] Major W.O. Owen, commander of the division hospital, would subsequently convey his appreciation to the superintendent of the French Hospital. Owen wrote of "the gratitude I entertain for you and the hospital under your direction for your benevolence in receiving our many sick when we were located at Camp Merritt." Owen referred to the serious cases taken "without charge and with that unfailing courtesy which I shall never cease to remember with the deepest gratification."[115]

On 13 June, the French Hospital reported

Figure 79.

that 40 soldiers occupied beds in its free ward.[116] Troops sent to the hospital often suffered from pneumonia, meningitis, typhoid fever, and bronchitis.[117] To alleviate some of the demand for care, the Red Cross opened another medical tent furnished with "iron bedsteads, bed clothing, wardrobes, and other necessary equipments" adjacent to the French Hospital.[118] By 20 July, the French Hospital patient count had dropped to 23 soldiers, in part because other civilian hospitals had volunteered to assist the military.[119]

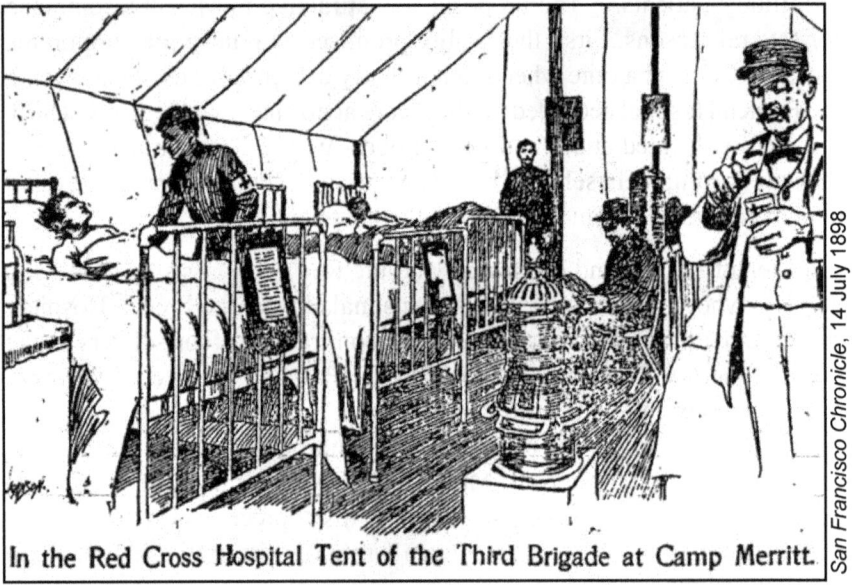

In the Red Cross Hospital Tent of the Third Brigade at Camp Merritt.

Figure 80.

One week after the French Hospital tendered its services, the German Hospital followed suit. The facility extended free care to troops who were too ill to be treated in the Red Cross tents.[120] Later, St. Luke's Hospital made a similar offer.[121] Essentially, the Red Cross and San Francisco area medical facilities joined in a patient evacuation process that dispatched soldiers through four progressive stages: regimental, brigade/division, Red Cross, and local civilian hospitals.

Sometimes hospital care could not prevent death. Even in those instances, the Red Cross extended comfort to the affected troops. On 30 May 1898, a Minnesota Volunteer who had battled typhoid pneumonia passed away at the French Hospital. The *Call* described the Red Cross assistance that was rendered: "The young man was without friends in this State.... The Red Cross Society provided delicacies and their representative, Miss

Frank, was at his bedside when the final moment came. The Red Cross will immediately write to the mother of the unfortunate boy, telling her of the care that was shown him and of the efforts to save his life."[122]

Red Cross volunteers worked to enhance medical care in other ways. The society erased medicine shortages that plagued the 1st Nebraska Infantry.[123] Surgeons of the 20th Kansas asked the organization to provide nourishment for hospitalized troops because the unit had no means to prepare sustenance for the sick.[124] The Oakland Red Cross also assisted military patients who were recovering from measles and pneumonia by securing appropriate food for them. The organization's hospital committee solicited the public for "clam juice, jelly, canned soup, fresh eggs, beef extract and malted milk."[125]

Another way the Red Cross looked after the welfare of Merritt's command was to provide each soldier with two bandages and the expertise on how to dress them. Volunteers from the Red Cross and Sanitary Corps conducted 30-minute drills in camp on how to use emergency bandages. Civilians conducting the class employed a chart to exhibit how to care for wounds. Soldiers used a "square of muslin cut diagonally" without stitching to practice their dressing.[126]

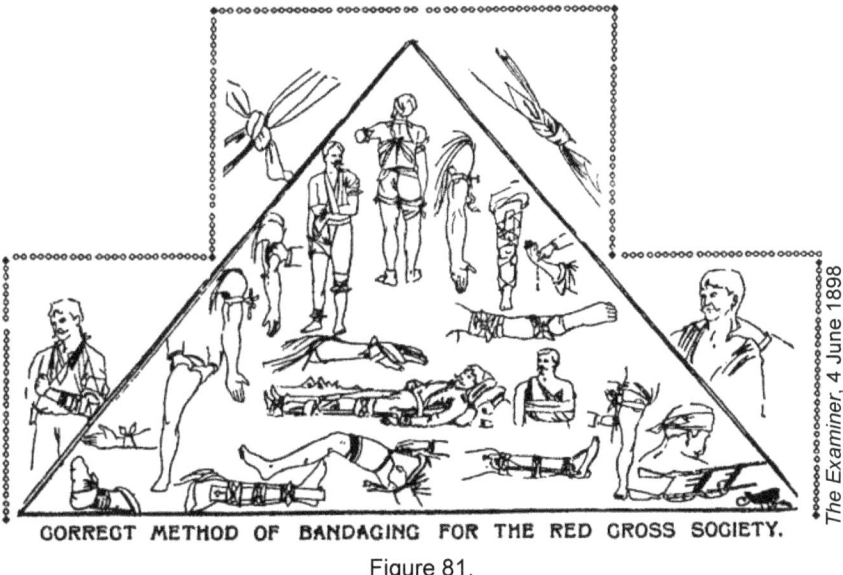

CORRECT METHOD OF BANDAGING FOR THE RED CROSS SOCIETY.
Figure 81.

Troops needed little instruction in finding more practical uses for bandages. When the Red Cross distributed two per man within the 1st South Dakota Infantry, the *Call* reported that Volunteers welcomed the dressings.

Wrappings proved "to be as great a preventive against cold in this climate as against more serious complaints in the tropics."[127]

In addition to medical care, the Red Cross also busied itself looking after the troops' quality of life. Units frequently arrived in camp with men who lacked essentials. Red Cross representatives furnished camp equipment, clothing, and financial assistance to many in need. The organization donated stoves to the California Heavy Artillery Batteries quartered in the Fontana warehouse.[128] The society also advanced artillerymen $500 to purchase basic supplies.[129] Some Volunteers from the 6th California Infantry lacked proper shoes; the Red Cross provided footwear.[130] In July, the society distributed "shoes and other necessities" to 1st Nebraska Infantry recruits who arrived at Camp Merritt partially equipped.[131] On 11 August, the Red Cross furnished meal money to several 1st Tennessee Infantry troops who were going home on sick leave.[132]

The organization also worked to provide all Volunteers and Regulars with an ID badge. Inspired by "the long list of unknown dead of the Civil War," the San Francisco Red Cross Society claimed the idea originated locally "and that no such means of identification were taken in the east." About the size of a "half dollar," the aluminum badge was "inscribed with the company, regiment, and number of each soldier."[133] Some badges displayed a cross on one side.[134] When several states failed to furnish aluminum medals for their Volunteers, the Red Cross pledged to supply them.[135] The society distributed badges before regiments embarked for the Philippines.[136] Nearly two decades later, the US Army would issue ID disks to all combat soldiers during World War I. Troops would subsequently refer to their ID disks as "dog tags."[137]

Volunteers and Regulars in the San Francisco camps benefited from Red Cross efforts in another quality-of-life area: sustenance. Aided by local restaurants and hostelries in early June, the society assisted South Dakotans who went into camp without food.[138] The same month, the Red Cross learned of 5,200 pounds of striped bass a local fish commissioner had confiscated. Shortly before the consignment was to be destroyed, the Red Cross purchased and dispatched the lot of 26 boxes to Camp Merritt. Captain W.B. Widner, 51st Iowa Infantry, wrote to the Red Cross Society, "I have the honor of acknowledging the receipt of a liberal supply of fish and four boxes of oranges, to be distributed among the Iowa Volunteers. Allow me to say that I consider both gifts very appropriate and assure you that it was delivered as per your request. I thank you for the entire regiment for this and many other favors received."[139] Later that month, the organization sent a wagonload of fresh vegetables to the North Dakota regiment, the first such addition to their diet since arriving in camp.[140]

The Red Cross also maintained hospitality rooms at the Ferry Building. Soldiers during their free time away from camp could visit and enjoy homemade foods that local citizens prepared. On 4 July, the San Francisco and Oakland societies joined forces to host soldiers at the depot during the holiday. The Red Cross "provided writing material and turned the entertainment into an 'at home.'"[141] The *Daily Report* quoted one Volunteer from Kansas describing the generous spreads in the hospitality rooms available to soldiers, "Just like a Baptist picnic at home . . . something good to eat and ladies to wait on you."[142] The harbor area remained a popular attraction for the troops who gathered in San Francisco and the Red Cross hospitality rooms a special place where all could relax away from the camps.

Finally, the Red Cross became involved in one other area of soldier welfare. The organization advised the military on quality-of-life issues. When camp sick lists grew during summer 1898, the society's hospital committee offered this perspective: "If more attention were given to the supplying of blankets and proper clothing to the incoming regiments and particularly to the unequipped recruits, we should have less pneumonia, sore throats and bowel troubles to chronicle and probably fewer deaths. . . . this neglect which may seem trifling now to those who are responsible for it, may assume alarming proportions when realized by the nation in the form of largely increased pension roll."[143] The organization also argued that soldiers needed an improved diet. The same committee report cited above maintained that "One of the greatest needs of all the men, whether sick or well, is an occasional supply of fresh vegetables."[144] The preceding month, a Red Cross ladies' visit to the military hospitals prompted an appeal for milk for the patients.[145]

An editorial in the *Daily Report* implicitly acknowledged the Red Cross Society's influence in this area. For weeks, the newspaper had advocated closing unsanitary Camp Merritt and displacing units to the Presidio. An editor wrote, "Meanwhile, we hope the Board of Health will exert itself to the utmost to abate the nuisance caused by the camp, and so avert the threatened epidemic. The Red Cross, Catholic Truth and other kindred societies could not do better service to the soldiers than by using their great influence along the same lines."[146]

Fitting Out for the Voyage

A unit's departure preparations did not mark the end of Red Cross assistance. The society worked to outfit expeditions with articles that would maintain troop comfort during their long voyage to the Philippine archipelago. In several instances, the organization worked through or at the behest of quartermasters to furnish specific items that the Army requested.

The first official business of the newly organized California State Red Cross Association addressed the initial expedition to Manila. Executive committee members decided to supply the troops with "onions as being a good article of diet." Accordingly, the president of the organization directed the purchasing committee "to buy a large quantity of them and have them immediately transferred in equal quantities" to each of the expedition's three transports.[147]

The Red Cross intended to care for members of the first expedition in other ways. Before soldiers boarded the transports, the society ensured that each soldier received a comfort bag, an abdominal belt, and a flannel cap.[148] The society also assisted the 2d Oregon, one of the Volunteer regiments deploying units with the first expedition. Having recently arrived in San Francisco without a regimental fund, the 2d Oregon petitioned the Red Cross for money to purchase supplies, mostly medicines, for use after departing San Francisco. The society decided to advance the regimental surgeon 25 cents per man, assuming that Oregon's Red Cross would later reimburse their brethren in California.[149]

Red Cross assistance grew considerably more sophisticated when the second expedition departed on 15 June. The society provided each of the transports with an extensive array of items to be used during the voyage. The items included:

2 cases Phillips' cocoa	4 dozen bottles lime juice
1 case condensed milk	6 large bottles of malted milk
1 case of alcohol	2 boxes unsweetened chocolate
20 pounds permanganate potash	500 pounds dried fruit
1 gallon Jamaica ginger	1 sack (501 pounds) farina
1 keg insect powder	2 cases whisky
1 case clam juice	3 bottles brandy
2 pails anchovies	1 case claret
10 pounds chipped beef	12 dozen towels
90 pounds steamed oatmeal	12 dozen handkerchiefs[150]

The link between the Army and Red Cross was illustrated in the issue over the quantity of dried fruit to be loaded aboard each ship. Specifically, the *Daily Report* revealed that the depot quartermaster, Major Oscar Long, informed the Red Cross that he wanted "1000 pounds of dried fruits for each of the five ships in the next fleet of transports."[151]

For the third and fourth expeditions, Red Cross volunteers intended to bolster troop welfare during the voyage by calling for additional items they had not solicited earlier. The society continued its practice of outfitting deploying troops with bandages and caps.[152] By late June, however, the organization's volunteers asked for games, cards, puzzles, and other items that soldiers could use to pass the time during a voyage that lasted nearly four weeks.[153]

Attention that Red Cross officials gave to this aspect of troop welfare did not go unrecognized. One 1st California officer wrote from Hawaii during a stop on his voyage to the Philippines, "The books, magazines and papers donated by the Red Cross Society have proved a great source of pleasure to all hands and have lessened the monotony of the run here to a great extent. The next expedition should be furnished with a good supply of salt water soap in order that the men may be able to use salt water to wash with, as it is not practicable to furnish enough fresh water for this purpose." Mrs. Harrington, president of the state Red Cross, responded to the letter by directing that the next expedition include those items the officer suggested.[154]

Soldiers were quite appreciative of the Red Cross's efforts to attend to troop welfare. Most regiments acknowledged the organization's work by writing letters of praise that were published in San Francisco newspapers. When the 13th Minnesota Infantry prepared for departure, the unit's commanding officer, COL McReeve, wrote to the president of the local society: "I beg leave to acknowledge receipt, through our quartermaster, on board the steamer City of Para, thirty-three boxes containing necessities and delicacies for the use of our enlisted men on the voyage to Manila. This very handsome donation, so entirely unexpected by us, adds but another to the many obligations under which we rest to your noble society for your intelligent and unremitting attentions to the wants and comforts of our regiment ever since we have been in your midst."[155]

Initiatives to Care for Troops Abroad

Even before the first expedition departed San Francisco, the Red Cross tackled the challenge of providing for the soldiers who would serve in the Philippines. An editor for the *Daily Report* who lauded the society's work in the city wrote, "The serious business of the Red Cross is to come. . . . The Philippine Islands are going to keep our Red Cross busy a long time, and the society is laying its plans for systematic and thorough work there and here."[156] The society still abided its mandate to dispense food and clothing to soldiers in need throughout the camps; however, providing medical care for those who would fight in the Philippines became one of the organization's foremost priorities.

The organization promoted Red Cross nurse care overseas for Regulars and Volunteers. Less than a week after Dewey's victory in Manila Bay, the California Red Cross Society made plans to dispatch nurses and medical supplies to the Philippines.[157] When men of the first expedition departed on 26 May 1898, they were joined by two Red Cross nurses who volunteered for service abroad. A. Parker Lewis and C.M. Waage, both males, secured permission to accompany the troops and established a Red Cross operation near Manila.[158]

While the organization pondered the need for additional nurses overseas, the Army called with a request. On 18 May, Major Robert H. White, Chief Surgeon, US Expeditionary Forces, asked the society to equip and provide 25 trained nurses for duty in the Philippines. "Only strong able-bodied men are wanted and they must be experienced in the care of the sick and wounded." Nurses, however, would be obligated to enlist in the Army for duty in hospitals. Essentially, these nurses would forfeit their Red Cross identity should they become affiliated with Merritt's command.[159]

The phrase "only strong able-bodied men are wanted" did not deter the Red Cross from championing an overseas role for female nurses. Mrs. Harrington, president of the California State Red Cross Association, was also president of the Hospital for Children and Training School for Nurses. The school was for women. Mrs. Wendell Easton, chairman of the society's Committee of Nurses and a member of the Board of Directors at Children's Hospital, observed, "Despite the fact that it has been publicly and semi-officially stated that women nurses will not be used at Manila, we have had constant and earnest appeals from women asking that their services in the camp and field be accepted. Considering that the decree has gone forth debarring women from this work, the number of women volunteers for this service is surprisingly large. The majority of them are trained graduate nurses and give the best of reference as to their ability and moral character."[160]

At mid-June, the organization issued a public proposal that challenged the male nurse policy. The society advocated the purchase of a hospital ship to be staffed by female nurses. Mrs. Easton offered the following outline: "This plan is to buy a ship with large decks suitable to that tropical climate, and to send a large body of nurses over on this vessel. At Manila, this vessel could be used as a hospital and the sick soldiers moved to it. The nurses could be divided into squads, each squad under an efficient head, and a general authority over all."[161]

Confronted by the need for medical care abroad and the welcomed offer of assistance from the Red Cross, MG Merritt, according to the *Call*, gave his permission for women to serve as nurses overseas.[162] Energized by this news, the Red Cross executive committee proposed to contact the Secretary of War to "ascertain under what conditions a hospital ship, paid for by the citizens of this city, would be received."[163] Noting that the "Atlantic coast cities have sent four hospital ships to Cuba," a *Daily Report* correspondent wrote that Mrs. Harrington "wants someone to suggest a plan of how to get one."[164]

Merritt advised that a Red Cross hospital ship could be forthcoming from a converted Spanish vessel Dewey captured at Manila Bay.[165] The society petitioned the government to furnish one of the prizes the Asiatic Squadron seized.[166] To outfit the ship, the organization's executive committee tentatively "decided to ask every bank and every newspaper west of the Rocky Mountains to receive subscriptions for the hospital ship enterprise." A subsequent meeting would "decide on a definite program."[167] The society intended to solicit donations from Western states.[168] By 9 July, the Red Cross received its first donations for a hospital ship. Two ladies, one from Ontario and the other from San Francisco, each contributed $1.[169]

The fund never had a chance to grow. Senator Stewart of Nevada notified the state Red Cross that the federal government committed to pay for the hospital ship project.[170] The *Scandia*, one of the first vessels purchased to form a permanent transport fleet for troops deploying to the Philippines, became America's floating hospital for service between San Francisco and the archipelago. The vessel, though it did not sail until after the peace protocol, transported male nurses only among its passengers.[171]

The Red Cross continued to place a priority on ensuring that Regulars and Volunteers deployed with bandages. Oakland's society sent 1700 bandages on the *City of Peking*.[172] The society worked through the depot quartermaster, Major Long, to issue two bandages to all who sailed. On 13 June, ladies of the Red Cross sent 4,800 bandages to Long for those assigned to the second expedition, and 4,294 bandages for soldiers due to sail with the third expedition.[173]

The Red Cross also prepared soldiers for duty in the Philippines by acquainting them with the environment they would encounter. Each soldier received a "useful little folder giving hints in the care of the health in the tropics."[174] Some troopers probably boarded their transports with at least a slight understanding of Spanish. The Red Cross had donated 100 Spanish primers that a citizen volunteer used to teach language fundamentals to soldiers encamped at San Francisco.[175]

Deployments of expeditions in June afforded the Red Cross an opportunity to dispatch funds to support those in the Philippines. The second expedition took $1,000 from the society to hire nurses in Manila for the troops stationed in the archipelago.[176] The third expedition carried $1,500 from the local society to spend on California units' welfare.[177]

Patriotic Home Helpers

Organization

One unique relief organization emerged in San Francisco that was unaffiliated with any international society, national association, or religious denomination. According to the *Daily Report*, the Patriotic Home Helpers formed to assist "the families of the soldiers and sailors who enlisted in the present war."[178] Like the Red Cross, however, women managed and energized the organization, giving it the ability to help those in need.

Just after the first expedition departed for the Philippines, the *Daily Report* and *San Francisco Chronicle* apprised the public of an intent to form a league for the benefit of "needy women, children or other dependents of volunteers." The *Chronicle* extended an invitation to "all patriotic people" to attend an organizational meeting at the Occidental Hotel on Friday, 27 May 1898.[179]

When finally formed on 3 June, the organization adopted the name Patriotic Home Helpers. A number of leading citizens took positions on the Helpers' various boards. Former Associate Justice of the Supreme Court Van R. Paterson presided over the meeting that produced the following appointments: US Circuit Judge W.W. Morrow, president; Mayor James D. Phelan, first vice president; and Major William B. Hooper, second vice president. Hooper had been one of the forces behind establishing the league. Mrs. Hester A. Harland accepted the Helpers' secretary position and subsequently emerged as the main volunteer responsible for routine organization business. She maintained office hours at Room 55 of the Occidental Hotel every morning from 1000 until noon.[180]

As early as 1 June, Hooper reported the receipt of numerous requests for assistance in meeting rent and food shortages. He anticipated petitions would continue until payday when some Volunteer dependents would likely be able to cover expenses. Hooper acknowledged others would not.[181] Paterson, noting that pay for the soldier amounted to only about $15 per month, cautioned that "it will be some time before he can remit this little sum and generally he will need it all for himself." Paterson also expressed concern over the potential magnitude of meeting the organization's goal, "We (California) have about 7000 men who have responded to the call for troops. Naturally there will be many dependents left in distress."[182]

Believing the cause essential but anticipating limited resources, the Patriotic Home Helpers turned early in June to the city's Associated Charities for an important function. The charities had a network of agents who could "investigate the cases of distressed families of soldiers, learn their needs and report to the Patriotic Home Helpers."[183] Essentially, the Helpers solicited assistance in determining the validity of requests for aid and identifying the most pressing claims.

The *Call* offered two examples of cases that warranted Helpers' aid. The first was a woman with six children. One son supported the family, and he enlisted, leaving his mother and siblings without any means of support. The second example featured a woman living in poverty and in need of medical assistance. Her husband had joined the Navy.[184]

With limited assistance available and the potential for charity cases to escalate, the Helpers had to establish a set of criteria for applicants to qualify for aid. A discriminator became the soldier or sailor's residence. The Patriotic Home Helpers was not a national organization and therefore focused on those with local roots. On 3 June, Hooper encouraged the Helpers to assist "dependent relatives of the California volunteers."[185] Apparently, members of the organization believed that condition was too broad. In less than two weeks, the organization further restricted eligibility. On 15 June, the *Chronicle* reported that the Helpers' object would be to aid dependents of soldiers and sailors "as were residents of this city at the time of their enlistment and who or may be engaged in the present war."[186]

Another rule the society adopted considered the number of dependent children in a family. If a mother cared for "from three to seven children in need of wearing apparel," the Helpers tried to assist. *The Examiner* reported on 1 July that "a worthy woman with six children" received clothing for her sons and daughters from a donation secured by the Helpers on the same day.[187]

The Helpers' relief committee ultimately had to make some difficult decisions based upon information the Associated Charities gathered. On 29 June, the *Chronicle* reported that Helpers rejected several cases "as undeserving of assistance."[188] This outcome may have been more a matter of available resources than one of residency. The *Daily Report* had observed earlier "that the demand is too great for the present resources of the society."[189]

Nevertheless, Helpers assisted dependents of several California

Volunteers. On 13 July, the organization found better shelter and paid a month's lodging for one soldier's family. Helpers assumed the rent for another family that would have lost its housing and dispatched groceries, coal, medicine, and clothing to others.[190] The organization was quite careful in the way it dispensed aid. Helpers did not give money directly to indigent families. Instead, a relief committee person compensated property owners for dependents' rent. League members provided groceries if the soldier's family needed food.[191]

Helpers also attempted to find jobs for the troops' needy family members, particularly wives and mothers. Local papers that published stories on league activities occasionally reported that applicants for aid were "more than anxious to get employment."[192] The organization took the somewhat extraordinary step of forming a committee to approach the depot quartermaster, Major Long, on behalf of "the widows, wives, mothers and daughters of soldiers." The committee was charged to seek for these women "a share in the work of making soldiers' uniforms, etc., contracts for which are being let every few days." *The Examiner* reported that Mrs. Oscar F. Long, an officer in the Red Cross and wife of the depot quartermaster, promised to intercede on behalf of "any applicant for Government work who should present a card from any member of the society."[193]

Fundraising and Material Donations

Not being associated with a larger regional, national, or international affiliate like the Red Cross, the Patriotic Home Helpers never had the ability to solicit financial support from a parent organization. Funding for assistance the Helpers

Figure 82. Mrs. Oscar Fitzallen Long.

rendered depended exclusively on local sources. Not unlike other organizations, however, individual contributions from Bay Area citizens constituted the mainstay of the group's revenues. The society urged "all patriotic persons" to become members by paying subscriptions of 50 cents a month. Those who were unable to give money were asked to donate clothing and provisions "or to assist in procuring employment for members of dependent families."[194]

Many of those willing to contribute financially gave more than the amount required to obtain membership. Major Hooper, one figure who was instrumental in establishing the society, presented "$25 and said he would contribute the same sum every month as long as the war continued." Several other committee members within the Helpers organization made similar pledges. Monthly donations frequently ranged from $1 to $25. Single contributions fell into a similar bracket with some notable exceptions. Claus Spreckels presented $1,000. M.J. Wall, Lewis Gerstie, and F.H. Woods each gave $100. Shreve and Company, cutlery importers, contributed $150. Crown Distilleries offered $50. Levi Strauss and Company gave $25.[195]

Other benefactors emerged to assist the Helpers. When transports from the second expedition departed for the Philippines, the San Francisco and North Pacific Railway Company sold tickets to citizens who wanted to bid farewell from the bay. The railway offered to take 1,000 passengers aboard the company's steamer *Ukiah* at 50 cents a person. Mr. Arthur W. Foster, president of the railway company, donated all excursion receipts to the Patriotic Home Helpers.[196]

One other group rendered assistance. Court Marin, Foresters of America No. 73, gave an entertainment and ball on Thursday, 30 June, for the benefit of the Home Helpers. Apparently, tickets for the event raised enough money to contribute $102.50 to the Helpers by 16 July.[197]

The San Francisco community assumed an invaluable role in caring for Army troops who gathered at the Golden Gate. Often acting through or supporting the Red Cross, numerous hospitals, church groups, school children, and business people collaborated with others in the community to produce medical assistance, personal items, welcoming festivities, and financial support for the military. Some area residents joined to create the Patriotic Home Helpers, an organization that tended to local Volunteers' needy families. As these societies worked to improve the health and care of their target recipients, other organizations emerged to look after the troops' moral welfare.

Notes

1. Thomas G. Paterson, J. Garry Clifford, and Kenneth J. Hagan, *American Foreign Relations: A History Since 1895*, 4th edition, volume II (Lexington, MA: D.C. Heath and Co., 1995) 11; Clara Barton, *The Red Cross in Peace and War* (Washington, DC: American Historical Press, 1899), 361-62.

2. Barton.

3. Ibid., 374.

4. Ibid., 375.

5. US War Department, *Annual Reports of the War Department for the Fiscal Year Ended June 30, 1898. Report of the Secretary of War. Miscellaneous Reports*. Report of the Surgeon-General (Washington, DC: US Government Printing Office [GPO], 1898), 724.

6. R.A. Alger to the Governor of California, 26 April 1898, in *San Francisco Call*, 3 May 1898, 7.

7. California State Red Cross, *A Record of the Red Cross Work on the Pacific Slope, Including California, Nevada, Oregon, Washington, and Idaho With Their Auxiliaries; also Reports From Nebraska, Tennessee, and Far-Away Japan* (Oakland, CA: Pacific Press Publishing Co., 1902), 73-76.

8. "California Ready to Aid the Sick and the Wounded," *San Francisco Call*, 3 May 1898, 14.

9. California State Red Cross, 79; "California Ready to Aid the Sick and the Wounded," *San Francisco Call*, 3 May 1898, 14.

10. "Hasten to Equip the Soldiers," *San Francisco Call*, 5 May 1898, 11.

11. W. McK. to the Secretary of War, 4 May 1898, in *Correspondence Relating to the War With Spain and Conditions Growing Out of the Same, Including the Insurrection in the Philippine Islands and the China Relief Expedition, Between the Adjutant-General of the Army and Military Commander in the United States, Cuba, Porto Rico, China, and the Philippine Islands, From April 15, 1898, to July 30, 1902*, volume II (Washington, DC: GPO, 1902), hereafter cited as *Correspondence II*, 635; "The Red Cross of California," *San Francisco Daily Report*, 24 May 1898, 3; "Merchants Prove Their Patriotism," *San Francisco Call*, 25 May 1898, 3.

12. California State Red Cross, 80.

13. Ibid., 11; "The Red Cross of California," *San Francisco Daily Report*, 24 May 1898, 3.

14. California State Red Cross, 11; "The Red Cross of California," *San Francisco Daily Report*, 24 May 1898, 3.

15. California State Red Cross, 13; Barton, 434; "The Red Cross," *San Francisco Daily Report*, 3 June 1898, 2.

16. *San Francisco: Its Builders Past and Present*, volume I, 31; California State Red Cross, 13.

17. California State Red Cross, 15.

18. William Doxey, *Doxey's Guide to San Francisco and the Pleasure Resorts of California*, (San Francisco: The Doxey Press, 1897), 83-84; H.S. Crocker

Company, *Crocker-Langley San Francisco Directory for Year Commencing May 1899* (San Francisco: H.S. Crocker Co., 1896), 57, 818.

19. H.S. Crocker Company, 1618; California State Red Cross, 81.

20. "The Red Cross," *San Francisco Daily Report*, 13 June 1898, 6; "Success for the Red Cross," *San Francisco Call*, 7 May 1898, 9; *San Francisco: Its Builders Past and Present*, 5-10.

21. "Success for the Red Cross," *San Francisco Call*, 7 May 1898, 9.

22. "Work of the Red Cross Society," *San Francisco Call*, 5 June 1898, 21.

23. California State Red Cross, 21-24; "The Red Cross," *San Francisco Daily Report*, 13 June 1898, 6; "The Red Cross," *San Francisco Daily Report*, 3 June 1898, 2; "Red Cross Badges are in Demand," *San Francisco Call*, 5 June 1898, 32.

24. "Ready Now for Work," *San Francisco Call*, 3 May 1898, 14; California State Red Cross, 78.

25. Letter to the people of California from James H. Budd, Governor; James D. Phelan, Mayor; Mrs. W.B. Harrington, President Red Cross Society; Mrs. John F. Merrill, Chairman Ladies' Executive Committee; "Success for the Red Cross," *San Francisco Call*, 7 May 1898, 9.

26. "Funds for Red Cross Needed," *San Francisco Call*, 9 May 1898, 7.

27. "Red Cross Badges are in Demand," *San Francisco Call*, 5 June 1898, 32.

28. "Red Cross Subscriptions," *San Francisco Daily Report*, 17 May 1898, 3.

29. Report of Executive Committee for Two Months Ending June 30, 1898, in *Overland Monthly*, September 1898, 191.

30. "Departing Soldiers to be Well Feasted," *San Francisco Call*, 13 July 1898, 14.

31. "Red Cross Notes," *San Francisco Call*, 13 August 1898, 12.

32. "The Red Cross," *San Francisco Daily Report*, 16 June 1898, 1.

33. "Success for the Red Cross," *San Francisco Call*, 7 May 1898, 9.

34. "Generous Checks to the Fund of the Red Cross," *San Francisco Call*, 27 May 1898, 7.

35. "Red Cross," *San Francisco Daily Report*, 2 July 1898, 2; "Red Cross," *San Francisco Daily Report*, 15 July 1898, 2.

36. "Red Cross Work," *San Francisco Daily Report*, 18 May 1898, 3.

37. "Red Cross Work," *San Francisco Daily Report*, 20 May 1898, 3.

38. "The Red Cross," *San Francisco Daily Report*, 3 June 1898, 2; "The Red Cross," *San Francisco Daily Report*, 11 June 1898, 6; "The Red Cross," *San Francisco Daily Report*, 16 June 1898, 1; "Red Cross," *San Francisco Daily Report*, 22 June 1898, 2.

39. "Thousands for the Red Cross," *San Francisco Call*, 3 June 1898, 14.

40. "Racing for Red Cross," *San Francisco Call*, 25 May 1898, 3; "Thousands for the Red Cross," *San Francisco Call*, 3 June 1898, 14.

41. "Baseball in Aid of the Red Cross," *San Francisco Call*, 9 June 1898, 4; "California Boys to be Cared For," *San Francisco Call*, 15 June 1898, 7.

42. "The Red Cross," *San Francisco Daily Report*, 28 May 1898, 3;

"Thousands for the Red Cross," *San Francisco Call*, 3 June 1898, 14.

43. "Baseball in Aid of the Red Cross," *San Francisco Call*, 9 June 1898, 4; "Red Cross," *San Francisco Daily Report*, 20 June 1898, 2.

44. "Minnesota Volunteers at Drill," *San Francisco Call*, 18 June 1898, 14.

45. "A Good Sum Realized," *San Francisco Daily Report*, 18 June 1898, 2.

46. "Reception to Iowa's Troops," *San Francisco Daily Report*, 29 June 1898, 3; "Red Cross," *San Francisco Daily Report*, 2 July 1898, 2; "Will Banquet Iowa's Troops," *San Francisco Call*, 26 June 1898, 8.

47. "The Red Cross," *San Francisco Daily Report*, 5 July 1898, 2.

48. "The Red Cross," *San Francisco Daily Report*, 10 June 1898, 3.

49. "Red Cross Notes," *San Francisco Call*, 13 August 1898, 12.

50. "Red Cross," *San Francisco Daily Report*, 12 July 1898, 3; "Chinatown Aids the Red Cross," *San Francisco Call*, 7 June 1898, 10; "Red Cross," *San Francisco Daily Report*, 17 June 1898, 6; "Red Cross Work," *San Francisco Daily Report*, 2 June 1898, 3.

51. "Success for the Red Cross," *San Francisco Call*, 7 May 1898, 9.

52. California State Red Cross, 13-15; "Success for the Red Cross," *San Francisco Call*, 7 May 1898, 9.

53. H.S. Crocker Company, 842; "Soldiers Greet the Red Cross," *San Francisco Call*, 14 May 1898, 5.

54. Barton, 439; "California Boys to be Cared For," *San Francisco Call*, 15 June 1898, 7.

55. H.S. Crocker Company, 1238; "The Red Cross," *San Francisco Daily Report*, 13 June 1898, 6.

56. "Red Cross Work," *San Francisco Daily Report*, 18 May 1898, 3.

57. "Merchants Prove Their Patriotism," *San Francisco Call*, 25 May 1898, 3; H.S. Crocker Company, 748.

58. "The Red Cross," *San Francisco Daily Report*, 3 June 1898, 2.

59. "The Red Cross," *San Francisco Daily Report*, 4 June 1898, 2.

60. H.S. Crocker Company, 1439; "The Red Cross," *San Francisco Daily Report*, 6 June 1898, 3.

61. "The Red Cross," *San Francisco Daily Report*, 6 June 1898, 3.

62. "Nurses to Go With the Soldiers," *San Francisco Call*, 19 May 1898, 8.

63. "Red Cross Work," *San Francisco Daily Report*, 20 May 1898, 3.

64. "Will Direct the Local Efforts of the Red Cross," *San Francisco Call*, 31 May 1898, 7.

65. "California Boys to be Cared For," *San Francisco Call*, 15 June 1898, 7.

66. "Toiling Under the Red Cross," *San Francisco Call*, 1 June 1898, 12.

67. "Red Cross Badges are in Demand," *San Francisco Call*, 5 June 1898, 32.

68. "Toiling Under the Red Cross," *San Francisco Call*, 1 June 1898, 12.

69. H.S. Crocker Company, 1235; "Adjoining States Help the Red Cross," *San Francisco Call*, 25 June 1898, 7.

70. "Departing Soldiers to be Well Feasted," *San Francisco Call*, 13 June 1898, 14.

71. "Red Cross," *San Francisco Daily Report*, 22 June 1898, 2; "Iowa's

Troops to be Their Guests," *San Francisco Call*, 23 June 1898, 9.

72. "The Red Cross," *San Francisco Daily Report*, 11 July 1898, 3.

73. "Will Banquet Iowa's Troops," *San Francisco Call*, 26 June 1898, 8.

74. "The Red Cross," *San Francisco Daily Report*, 11 July 1898, 3; H.S. Crocker Company, 939.

75. Report of Executive Committee for Two Months Ending June 30, 1898, in *Overland Monthly*, September 1898, 179; H.S. Crocker Company, 1740.

76. California State Red Cross, 80.

77. "Soldiers Will be Welcomed," *San Francisco Call*, 18 May 1898, 7; "Red Cross Work," *San Francisco Daily Report*, 18 May 1898, 3.

78. "Oregon Volunteers," *San Francisco Call*, 19 May 1898, 5.

79. *San Francisco Call*, 19, 22, 25, 27 May 1898 and 14, 17, 23 June 1898; *San Francisco Daily Report*, 2, 6, 10, 16 June 1898.

80. "Toiling Under the Red Cross," *San Francisco Call*, 1 June 1898, 12.

81. Ibid.

82. California State Red Cross, 97.

83. "Noble Men From the Middle West," *San Francisco Call*, 22 May 1898, 7.

84. Letter, William S. Christner, 10th Pennsylvania Infantry Regiment, to parents, 26 May 1898 (Carlisle Barracks, PA: US Army Military History Institute).

85. A.G. Baker, 1st Colorado Infantry, The Colorado Volunteers (Carlisle Barracks, PA: US Army Military History Institute).

86. "Marching on to Camp Richmond," *San Francisco Call*, 21 May 1898, 5; "Local Musicians Will Give a Grand Concert in Aid of the Red Cross," *San Francisco Call*, 29 May 1898, 9; California State Red Cross, 75; H.S. Crocker Company, 1636.

87. "Local Musicians Will Give a Grand Concert in Aid of the Red Cross," *San Francisco Call*, 29 May 1898, 9.

88. "The Red Cross," *San Francisco Daily Report*, 11 June 1898, 6.

89. "Toiling Under the Red Cross," *San Francisco Call*, 1 June 1898, 12.

90. "Local Musicians Will Give a Grand Concert in Aid of the Red Cross," *San Francisco Call*, 29 May 1898, 9.

91. "Generous Checks to the Fund of the Red Cross," *San Francisco Call*, 27 May 1898, 7.

92. "Red Cross Work," *San Francisco Daily Report*, 23 May 1898, 6.

93. "On the Transport Ready for Sea," *San Francisco Call*, 24 May 1898, 1-2.

94. "Around the Transports," *San Francisco Daily Report*, 25 May 1898, 3.

95. "The Others Are Ready," *San Francisco Daily Report*, 25 May 1898, 3.

96. "Red Cross Appeal," *San Francisco Call*, 14 June 1898, 5.

97. Alice Rix, "Ships in the Stream and Ready," *San Francisco Call*, 15 June 1898, 1.

98. "The Red Cross," *San Francisco Daily Report*, 15 June 1898, 2.

99. "Will Banquet Iowa's Troops," *San Francisco Call*, 26 June 1898, 8.

100. "On Board the Transports," *San Francisco Daily Report*, 27 June 1898, 2.

101. "Filed Quietly Aboard," *San Francisco Call*, 27 June 1898, 10.

102. "Red Cross," *San Francisco Daily Report*, 12 July 1898, 3; "Departing Soldiers to be Well Feasted," *San Francisco Call*, 13 July 1898, 14.

103. "Regulars Sail for the Orient," *San Francisco Call*, 16 July 1898, 5.

104. "Guests of the Red Cross," *San Francisco Call*, 25 July 1898, 5.

105. "No Pies Wanted," *San Francisco Call*, 29 May 1898, 8.

106. "Soldiers Greet the Red Cross," *San Francisco Call*, 14 May 1898, 5.

107. "Camping in the Rain," *San Francisco Call*, 15 May 1898, 7.

108. "Nurses to Go with the Soldiers," *San Francisco Call*, 19 May 1898, 8.

109. Workers of the Writers' Program of the Work Projects Administration in Northern California, *The Army at the Golden Gate: A Guide to Army Posts in the San Francisco Bay Area*, nd, np, 76; US War Department, *Annual Reports of the War Department for the Fiscal Year Ended June 30, 1898, Report of the Secretary of War, Miscellaneous Reports*, Report of the Surgeon-General (Washington, DC: GPO, 1900), 716.

110. H.S. Crocker Company, 61.

111. "The French Hospital Opens a Free Ward," *San Francisco Chronicle*, 22 May 1898, 4.

112. H.S. Crocker Company, 673.

113. "The Day in Camp," *San Francisco Daily Report*, 25 May 1898, 3.

114. "Items of Interest From the Camp of Instruction," *San Francisco Chronicle*, 4 June 1898, 9.

115. W.O. Owen, Major and Brigade Surgeon, to the Superintendent, French Hospital, 4 August 1898, in US Senate, *Report of the Commission Appointed by the President to Investigate the Conduct of the War Department in the War With Spain*, volume 8, *Correspondence* (Washington, DC: GPO, 1900), hereafter cited as *Report VIII*, 167.

116. "Local War Notes," *San Francisco Daily Report*, 13 June 1898, 6.

117. J.V.D. Middleton, Deputy Surgeon-General, to the Surgeon-General, U.S. Army, 30 July 1898, in *Report VIII*, 164; "Red Cross Work," *San Francisco Daily Report*, 21 May 1898, 2; "Soldiers in the Hospitals," *San Francisco Chronicle*, 21 June 1898, 5.

118. "The Red Cross," *San Francisco Call*, 13 June 1898, 5.

119. "That Awful Camp Merritt," *San Francisco Daily Report*, 21 July 1898, 3.

120. "The Red Cross," *San Francisco Daily Report*, 28 May 1898, 3.

121. "The Red Cross," *San Francisco Call*, 13 June 1898, 5.

122. "Will Direct the Local Efforts of the Red Cross," *San Francisco Call*, 31 May 1898, 7.

123. "Red Cross Work," *San Francisco Daily Report*, 23 May 1898, 6.

124. "Doings in the Camp," *San Francisco Daily Report*, 27 May 1898, 3.

125. "Oakland Red Cross," *San Francisco Daily Report*, 9 June 1898, 3.

126. "Red Cross Donations," *San Francisco Daily Report*, 31 May 1898, 3.

127. "Inspection of Troops," *San Francisco Call*, 10 June 1898, 5.

128. "The Fontana Building," *San Francisco Call*, 19 May 1898, 5.

129. "The Red Cross of California," *San Francisco Daily Report*, 24 May 1898, 3.

130. "Camp of Volunteers," *San Francisco Call*, 25 May 1898, 2.

131. "Departing Soldiers to be Well Feasted," *San Francisco Call*, 13 July 1898, 14.

132. "War Incidents," *San Francisco Call*, 12 August 1898, 10.

133. California State Red Cross, 81-82.

134. "At Camp Merritt," *San Francisco Daily Report*, 9 June 1898, 3.

135. "The Red Cross," *San Francisco Daily Report*, 7 June 1898, 7.

136. "At Camp Merritt," *San Francisco Daily Report*, 9 June 1898, 3; "Troops at the Presidio," *San Francisco Call*, 28 July 1898, 8.

137. Richard W. Wooley, "A Short History of Identification Badges," *Quartermaster Professional Bulletin*, December 1988, 16.

138. "Adding to the Army," *San Francisco Call*, 3 June 1898, 7; "Skirmished for Rations," *San Francisco Call*, 3 June 1898, 7.

139. Captain W.B. Widner to the Red Cross Society, 16 June 1898, *San Francisco Call*, 18 June 1898, 12.

140. "Adjoining States Help the Red Cross," *San Francisco Call*, 25 June 1898, 7.

141. "The Ladies' Holiday," *San Francisco Daily Report*, 5 July 1898, 2.

142. "Soldiers Coming," *San Francisco Daily Report*, 8 June 1898, 3.

143. "Some Sound Advice," *San Francisco Daily Report*, 1 July 1898, 2.

144. Ibid.

145. "Local War Notes," *San Francisco Daily Report*, 20 June 1898, 2.

146. "More Dangerous Every Day," editorial, *San Francisco Daily Report*, 21 June 1898, 4.

147. "Merchants Prove Their Patriotism," *San Francisco Call*, 25 May 1898, 3; "The Red Cross of California," *San Francisco Daily Report*, 24 May 1898, 3.

148. "Urgently Request Help," *San Francisco Call*, 23 May 1898, 5.

149. "Merchants Prove Their Patriotism," *San Francisco Call*, 25 May 1898, 3; "The Red Cross of California," *San Francisco Daily Report*, 24 May 1898, 3.

150. "California Boys to be Cared For," *San Francisco Call*, 15 June 1898, 7.

151. "Local War Notes," *San Francisco Daily Report*, 11 June 1898, 6.

152. "Preparing for the Next Expedition," *San Francisco Call*, 18 June 1898, 12.

153. "Red Cross," *San Francisco Daily Report*, 18 June 1898, 2.

154. "Will Furnish a Hospital Ship," *San Francisco Call*, 29 June 1898, 7.

155. Colonel C. McReeve, 13th Minnesota Regiment, to Mrs. John F. Merrill, President Red Cross Society, *San Francisco Call*, 26 June 1898, 8.

156. "Remember the Red Cross," editorial, *San Francisco Daily Report*, 6 July 1898, 14.

157. "Local War Notes," *San Francisco Daily Report*, 4 May 1898, 3.

158. "Local War Notes," *San Francisco Daily Report*, 16 June 1898, 2; Barton, 435.

159. "Nurses to Go With the Soldiers," *San Francisco Call*, 19 May 1898, 8.

160. "Plan of the Red Cross to Fit Out a Hospital Ship to Send to the Fleet at Manila," *San Francisco Call*, 12 June 1898, 21.

161. Ibid.
162. "Hospital at Manila," *San Francisco Call*, 26 June 1898, 7.
163. "Will Furnish a Hospital Ship," *San Francisco Call*, 29 June 1898, 7.
164. "The Red Cross," *San Francisco Daily Report*, 25 June 1898, 2.
165. "Merritt Wants a Hospital Ship," *San Francisco Call*, 1 July 1898, 10.
166. "The Hospital Ship," *San Francisco Daily Report*, 12 July 1898, 3.
167. Ibid.
168. "Hospital Ship," *San Francisco Call*, 19 July 1898, 5.
169. "The Red Cross," *San Francisco Daily Report*, 11 July 1898, 3.
170. "Hospital Ship," *San Francisco Call*, 19 July 1898, 5.
171. Karl Irving Faust, *Campaigning in the Philippines* (San Francisco: Hicks-Judd Co. Publishers, 1899), 66.
172. "Oakland Red Cross," *San Francisco Daily Report*, 9 June 1898, 3.
173. "Thousands More are Coming," *San Francisco Daily Report*, 8 June 1898, 3; "The Red Cross," *San Francisco Daily Report*, 13 June 1898, 6.
174. "Filed Quietly Aboard," *San Francisco Call*, 27 June 1898, 10; "On Board the Transports," *San Francisco Daily Report*, 27 June 1898, 2.
175. "Soldiers Who Conquer the Spanish Verb," *San Francisco Call*, 8 July 1898, 6.
176. "The Red Cross," *San Francisco Daily Report*, 15 June 1898, 2.
177. "Will Banquet Iowa's Troops," *San Francisco Call*, 26 June 1898, 8; "The Third Manila Expedition," *San Francisco Daily Report*, 27 June 1898, 2.
178. "Aiding Soldiers' Families," *San Francisco Daily Report*, 15 June 1898, 1.
179. "To Aid the Women," *San Francisco Daily Report*, 23 May 1898, 6; "Brief Military Items," *San Francisco Chronicle*, 26 May 1898, 2.
180. "Those Left Behind not Forgotten," *The Examiner*, 4 June 1898, 3; "Patriotic Home Helpers," *San Francisco Call*, 14 June 1898, 5; "Local War Notes," *San Francisco Daily Report*, 28 June 1898, 2.
181. "To Help Soldiers' Families," *San Francisco Chronicle*, 1 June 1898, 3.
182. "Patriotic Home Helpers," *San Francisco Call*, 14 June 1898, 5.
183. "Patriotic Home Helpers," *San Francisco Chronicle*, 11 June 1898, 11.
184. "Iowa's Troops to be Their Guests," *San Francisco Call*, 23 June 1898, 9; "Patriotic Home Helpers," *San Francisco Chronicle*, 23 June 1898, 7.
185. "Those Left Behind Not Forgotten," *The Examiner*, 4 June 1898, 3.
186. "Patriotic Home Helpers," *San Francisco Chronicle*, 15 June 1898, 7.
187. "Are Helping the Families," *The Examiner*, 2 July 1898, 5.
188. "Soldiers Families are Aided," *San Francisco Chronicle*, 29 June 1898, 5.
189. "Local War Notes," *San Francisco Daily Report*, 28 June 1898, 2.
190. "Patriotic Home Helpers," *San Francisco Chronicle*, 14 July 1898, 5; "War Incidents," *San Francisco Call*, 13 July 1898, 7.
191. "Patriotic Home Helpers," *San Francisco Chronicle*, 3 July 1898, 30.
192. "Are Helping the Families," *The Examiner*, 2 July 1898, 5; "Patriotic Home Helpers," *San Francisco Chronicle*, 3 July 1898, 30.
193. "A Woman to Help Women," *The Examiner*, 14 July 1898, 4; "Work of

the Home Helpers," *San Francisco Daily Report*, 14 July 1898, 3.

194. "Aiding Soldiers' Families," *San Francisco Daily Report*, 15 June 1898, 1.

195. *San Francisco Daily Report*, 18, 29 June 1898 and 2, 8, 9 July 1898; *San Francisco Call*, 18, 25 June 1898 and 2, 13 July 1898; *San Francisco Chronicle*, 9, 19, 24, 29 June 1898 and 3, 9 July 1898; *The Examiner*, 4, 18, 24 June 1898 and 2, 6, 14 July 1898; H.S. Crocker Company, 1940.

196. H.S. Crocker Company, 661; "To Accompany the Troops," *San Francisco Daily Report*, 14 June 1898, 2; "A Chance for Farewell, *San Francisco Call*, 15 June 1898, 5; "Keeping the Needy Families of Soldiers," *The Examiner*, 19 June 1898, 21.

197. "For the Helpers' Society," *The Examiner*, 6 June 1898, 5; "Aid for Patriotic Home Helpers," *The Examiner*, 16 July 1898, 5.

Chapter VI
The Religious Organizations

San Franciscans worked through relief societies to care for soldiers at the Golden Gate. Some supported the Patriotic Home Helpers in an effort to help California Volunteers' indigent family members. Far more citizens and local organizations assisted Red Cross workers who mobilized the aid of city hospitals and provided troops with desperately needed medical care.

While the Red Cross led Bay Area attempts to look after the troops' physical well-being, other community alliances initiated programs aimed at the spiritual welfare of Merritt's command. The San Francisco Young Men's Christian Association (YMCA) urged evangelical Protestant denominations to sponsor activities that fortified the soul in the face of numerous "temptations" that surrounded the encampments.

Two other major groups emerged to render spiritual aid to the military. After initiating their own ecclesiastical projects on behalf of those in uniform, members of the Young People's Society of Christian Endeavor joined forces with the YMCA to accomplish similar ends. The Catholic Truth Society volunteered its services as well. The society conducted mass for troops of the Roman Catholic faith and performed a variety of services for soldiers regardless of their denomination.

Young Men's Christian Association

Background

First conceived in England during the 1840s as a service organization, the YMCA offered ways for youthful tradesmen to cope with an immoral urban environment.[1] Looking to establish an alternative to "the saloon" or "an attractive rival of the 'social glass,'" the YMCA rented rooms in London for lectures, foreign language instruction, and religious meetings. The association stocked these accommodations with newspapers, books, and magazines, and all were available to associates during their leisure time. Affiliation with the London group turned on one's religious standing. To join, a young man had to be either "a member of a Christian church" or have given "evidence of his being a converted character."[2]

During the 1850s, the organization took root in the United States and embraced other vocations. The association looked "to seek men where they are in their ordinary contacts of life."[3] Associations evolved that attracted qualified young men among students, railroaders, and soldiers.

Youth who joined the Union cause during the American Civil War found spiritual and material support through the YMCA's Army and Navy Christian Commission. Originally established as an evangelistic initiative dedicated to the religious well-being of military personnel, the commission also worked to augment the troops' medical care and subsistence.[4] Although the organization detached from the Army after the war ended in 1865, the YMCA reestablished contact with the military in the late 1880s. State associations pursued "tent work" at militia campsites, maintaining club room equipment within canvas shelters the troops from the National Guard used.[5]

The affiliation with the military had been established. When the United States went to war with Spain in 1898, members of the YMCA offered their assistance to the McKinley administration. The organization wanted to assist in looking after the personal welfare of citizens who joined a military that paid "only secondary attention to the desires, which may be very real needs, of the men as individuals."[6]

Local Organization

On Thursday, 12 May 1898, Secretary Henry J. McCoy of the San Francisco YMCA visited the Presidio. He viewed firsthand the various campsites of the 1st and 7th California Volunteers and parts of the 14th US Infantry Regulars. The encampment already boasted 2,672 Volunteers and 220 Regulars with the prospect of adding troops from Oregon within a day. Alerted to association members in uniform among the regiments, McCoy decided to form an Army YMCA chapter "after getting the permission of the chaplains in charge."[7]

By 18 May, after more units had arrived or had received orders to converge at the Golden Gate, the commander of the Presidio, LTC Louis T. Morris, approved McCoy's initiative to establish a YMCA branch on the reservation. The local association acquired a 40-foot by 50-foot tent to accommodate religious exercises and placed it between the 1st and 7th California Volunteers.[8] Subsequent to this boost the local association gave, Chaplain Alfred S. Clark, 7th California, took charge of the camp's YMCA branch and oversaw chapter activities that members assigned to the various regiments performed.[9]

Although a Presidio branch took hold within the military, McCoy and his San Francisco YMCA were not about to sever their connection with Merritt's command. The secretary subsequently learned of "hundreds of young men belonging to the association from all parts of the country who are to be temporarily located at San Francisco."[10] The 1st New York, for

Lieutenant Colonel Louis T. Morris U. S. A.
Figure 83.

example, included about 300 Christian Association members in its ranks.[11] As these men arrived with their military organizations, the encampment spread beyond the Presidio into the Richmond District and other more isolated areas around the Bay Area. To meet uniformed YMCA members' spiritual needs and to promote young Volunteers' moral welfare in general, McCoy's association erected tents in additional locations. By 5 June, three new canvas shelters adorned the Richmond District's Camp Merritt.[12]

More significantly, the San Francisco association served as a conduit through which the YMCA, local churches, and Christian societies pooled their support efforts. In early June, San Francisco newspapers carried stories on the resurrection of the YMCA's Army and Navy Christian Commission from the Civil War era. The North American Association's International Committee in New York secured permission to establish a commission that could work with the military services at home and abroad.[13] Spurred by several local clergymen, the San Francisco association hosted meetings to establish an Army and Navy Christian Commission of California.

On 8 June 1898, several prominent members of the Bay Area's religious community, including San Francisco's YMCA Secretary McCoy and representatives of six evangelical churches, met to explore a collaborative effort to "supplement the work of the Army chaplains in camp and on the battlefield."[14] One pastor in the assembly, Freeman D. Bovard, First ME Church, said an organized commission would attempt "to unite all the denominations under one large tent or tabernacle" and include within its fold young people's church societies engaged in similar work.[15] The group appointed a committee to draft a provisional constitution and report its recommendations in a subsequent gathering.[16]

The 16 June meeting organized the US Army and Navy Christian Commission of California "to spread the gospel among the soldiers, sailors and marines either going or who have already gone to the Philippines." Representatives from Christian societies and the Christian, Congregational, Baptist, Methodist, and Presbyterian churches adopted a constitution and bylaws. They elected the following commission officers: president, Dr. H.C. Minton, Presbyterian Church; secretary, Reverend A.T. Needham, Oakland Methodist Church; and treasurer, Henry J. McCoy, Secretary, San Francisco YMCA, representing participating Christian societies.[17]

At the YMCA building on 20 June, the commission completed its organization by electing a vice president, modifying its constitution, and selecting an executive committee. Since the commission was scheduled to meet only monthly, the executive committee was empowered to handle the Commission's routine business.[18]

In the Camps

One goal of the YMCA, and later its Christian Commission, was to establish a presence within the various Golden Gate campsites. The *San Francisco Chronicle* reported in June that the Christian Commission intended to assign at least one representative to each regiment encamped in the Bay Area.[19] Providing every designee with a "canvas sanctuary" that could be erected in the campsites created a focal point about which troops could congregate and a shelter from which the association could pursue its objectives.

To the four tents already in place by 5 June the YMCA erected additional shelters at the following locations: at Camp Merritt with the 1st Montana, 1st New York Engineers, 1st Tennessee, and 20th Kansas; at Camp Barrett in Oakland with the 8th California; and at Fort Point with the artillery batteries. By 27 July, the association had pitched 17 tents.[20] The organization placed an office near Camp Merritt's southern boundary on Fifth Avenue near the French Hospital.[21] As Richmond campsites diminished in late summer, the YMCA relocated on the Presidio reservation to minister to units waiting to deploy abroad.[22]

After 12 July, the YMCA established an affiliated claim to several tents that other organizations had already constructed. One of the objectives in creating a Christian Commission was to unify the work of various Christian organizations and denominations. As early as 8 June the *San Francisco Daily Report* cited the need for a central organization that could coordinate the assistance that various evangelical societies and churches rendered.[23] At a meeting of the Christian Commission on 11 July, representatives of unnamed Christian societies agreed to fly the YMCA's banner over their tents.[24] Pastor Bovard, a commission member who had urged such a unification, assured these organizations that the commission would play a management role "but in such a manner as to leave them free to operate their own plans." Each Christian society that deferred to YMCA management could transfer its existing operating debts to the commission. The commission would also absorb future expenses.[25]

In addition to these incentives, groups embraced unification because evangelical Christian groups pursued similar ends, including temperance. At an 11 July Commission meeting, Reverend E.R. Dille of the Methodist Church reminded the audience of a growing evil reminiscent of the one that inspired the London association to action some 50 years earlier. Dille condemned "the saloons that 'form a fringe of hell around Camp Merritt' and of the efforts made . . . to counteract their pernicious influences."[26]

Dille and his associates sponsored commission tent activities as a wholesome alternative to saloons. Soldiers could write letters on free stationery bearing the imprints of the Christian Commission and American flag. Envelopes and stamps were provided at no cost to the young men. One report in early June estimated that soldiers wrote 1,500 letters each day from commission tents. By 18 July, a revised assessment doubled the figure to 3,000. Another report calculated that troops were writing from 10,000 to 20,000 letters per week in the commission's larger facilities.[27]

Commission tents hosted other diversions shaped by YMCA objectives. Open every day from 0800 to 2200, these shelters offered a place for social gatherings where men could meet fellow soldiers from other regiments. Troops could play sundry games under the canvas or outdoors. Reading areas contained small libraries with magazines, pictorials, and secular or religious newspapers from San Francisco and several Eastern cities.[28]

Away from camp the San Francisco YMCA sponsored activities at its permanent buildings for the Volunteers and Regulars assembled at the Golden Gate. Basketball teams from the encampments scrimmaged with association members. The 13th Minnesota and 1st New York played the YMCA "Rushers" of the San Francisco association. McCoy's association gymnasium at Mason and Ellis Streets hosted the events.[29] On 22 June, the San Francisco YMCA held an open house and reception at its main building for all soldiers in the city. The 7th California band played musical selections, and several local instrumentalists and singers performed, including Miss Cordie Wetjen who offered whistling solos.[30]

The YMCA also offered its facilities to other organizations that entertained troops or gave benefits for them. Secretary McCoy donated the association's downtown auditorium to the Red Cross for its benefit concert on 3 June. On 16 July, the Pacific Coast Women's Press Association entertained the 1st Montana at the Christian Commission's tent, erected in the regimental campsite. The program featured vocal solos and readings. The local Press Club also sponsored entertainment for the men at another "Y" location on 6 August.[31]

Other commission pursuits reflected a stronger, more obvious, correlation to young men's spiritual vitality. The organization believed in ministry through music. Each tent contained song books and an organ. According to Richard C. Morse, general secretary, YMCA International Committee, soldiers spent much of their leisure time at the tents singing favorite songs. "In the evenings," wrote Morse, "gospel hymns were preferred to all others. Generally the evening closed with an informal song service and prayer."[32] At one commission meeting, the executive council voted to purchase sacred music for the 8th California's regimental band at Camp Barrett.[33]

The commission distributed free religious literature, testaments, and Bibles to Volunteers and Regulars.[34] Dr. Minton, president, Christian Commission of California, established a commission goal "to place a copy of the Scriptures in the hand of every soldier."[35] The International Committee's Christian Commission tried to help Minton achieve his objective. On 2 August, the local commission received 5,000 Bibles and testaments for the troops from D.L. Moody, chairman, International Committee Evangelistic Department.[36]

The Christian Commission also sponsored worship services as another way to minister to soldiers' spiritual needs. The commission regularly scheduled religious assemblies at the several campsites and in the association building's auditorium. On Sundays, tents hosted gospel meetings and Bible classes.[37] Regimental chaplains used some of these facilities for Sunday services.[38] Shortly after the YMCA and Protestant churches formed the commission, Secretary McCoy invited Moody to visit the Golden Gate and conduct services. Although Moody never visited, evangelist M.P. Crittenden arrived to lead a series of tent meetings in July for the benefit of soldiers in both San Francisco and Oakland.[39]

Although its activities focused on the soldiers' spiritual well-being, the commission did not ignore the troops' routine, material needs. The commission provided stoves to the 1st Tennessee's hospital tents.[40] Association workers operating commission tents provided refreshments to soldiers who visited. Larger structures frequently contained small, ad hoc kitchens where civilian volunteers made soup for guests or "delicacies" for the convalescent. Troops could find an abundance of bread and an ever-present pitcher or tank of ice water to consume.[41]

Young ladies and women with a familial, or at least emotional, attachment to the association formed a Mothers' Christian Commission Club to assist in the ministry of work. The ladies sewed and mended clothing for the troops and in many instances served as ad hoc tailors. More than 50 ladies would meet on Tuesday and Thursday afternoons at Camp Merritt to tend to the troops' clothing.[42] They also did their best to visit other campsites in the Bay Area to help those outside of the Richmond District.[43]

Initiatives to Care for Troops Abroad

Concurrent with its spiritual calling in San Francisco, the association worked to establish a military ministry with troops deploying overseas. In June, Secretary McCoy argued that "most of the gunpowder that would be used in Manila had been fired." Suggesting that "there were more dangerous things there than Spanish bullets," the secretary stated, "it was to help the soldiers withstand temptation that the Young Men's Christian Association wanted to practically supplement the work of the chaplains of the Army."[44]

In May, the *Daily Report* speculated that "a whole outfit" representing the YMCA would go with an expedition to Manila.[45] On 1 June, speculation became reality with the War Department's permission. In a letter to Secretary McCoy, George de Rue Meiklejohn, Assistant Secretary of War, authorized the association to send two representatives with equipment on one of the expeditions. MG Miles endorsed the action as did the commander of the expeditionary force, MG Wesley Merritt, and the depot quartermaster, Major Long.[46]

On Saturday, 11 June, Secretary McCoy announced that Frank A. Jackson and Charles A. Glunz would represent the Christian Commission in the Philippines. The Christian Commission of California picked Jackson, an assistant secretary of the San Francisco YMCA. A representative of the International Committee chose Glunz, who served as the assistant secretary of the Oakland association. In discussing the reasons for their selection, McCoy emphasized that "both were a few years past their majority, unmarried, and had been about two years in the positions they were about to leave."[47]

Figure 84.

After being feted at a reception given in their honor at the local YMCA on 22 June, Jackson and Glunz sailed on the *City of Para* with the third expedition that departed on 27 June 1898. They wore a military-style uniform that bore the initials "C.C." and a triangular patch on the left sleeve. Their goal on behalf of the commission was to work with the chaplains and to continue much of the same kind of services the association performed in the Bay Area camps. Specifically, they were to "minister to the spiritual and physical needs of the men" in all ways possible. To achieve these ends, the two men brought with them a church organ, songbooks, a library, 100,000 sheets of paper with envelopes, and a large tent to erect with the Army wherever it was located.[48]

About the time Jackson and Glunz departed, the commission apparently considered expanding the goals of the two in the Philippines. *The Examiner* reported that the commission intended to send a large number of Bibles printed in Spanish with a subsequent expedition, noting that the two men represented the entire evangelical church body of California. Perhaps that representation obligated Jackson and Glunz to perform missionary work among the indigenous population in the environs of Manila.[49] Secretary McCoy later announced that they were expected to arrive at Manila the week of 17-23 July 1898 "where they would carry on the commission work."[50]

One other geographic area commanded the commission's attention: Hawaii. Selected for garrison duty in Honolulu, part of the 1st New York sailed for its new assignment in early August. The commission ensured that "a library of interesting books" was placed aboard the *Lakme* and *Nelson* and that other general reading material was spread among the men.[51]

Fundraising

The national Army and Navy Christian Commission expended a considerable sum of money pursuing its objectives. Morse estimated that by late 1898, the commission had spent $139,596 in support of the American military at home and abroad. Of that amount, state committees provided $58,650. The cumulative cost, however, could have been steeper except for the War Department's willingness to provide free transportation for men and equipment. In other words, Jackson and Glunz, along with their tent and Bibles, sailed at government expense. But the government did not pay the tab of $1,000 a week for stamps that soldiers used to mail the letters they wrote in the commission tents. Nor did the War Department back the commission's offer to absorb past debts and future expenses of those organizations joining the YMCA enterprise. The commission incurred these expenditures.[52]

Financial support for the national association's work at federal campsites or overseas came principally from private sources. Morse claimed that "the entire expense was met by the contributions of generous and patriotic friends of the soldier and sailor." Oliver O. Howard, a delegate of the national commission, also reported that money was raised through "voluntary contribution."[53] For the most part, these observations on fundraising for the national association were just as applicable to revenue gathering for the Christian Commission of California.

The California Commission solicited donations in ways similar to those of the Red Cross and Patriotic Home Helpers. Local newspapers periodically reported on the association's efforts to raise funds. In July, for example, the *Chronicle* published an association resolution that appealed "to the public and especially our churches to immediately co-operate in the work of the commission. This work, so urgent, is in progress and the results most encouraging and it requires funds for its conduct at once. We need gifts of money."[54]

Between early May and the August peace protocol, donations came from individual citizens located in various parts of California. Most were small sums. For example, Morris Wenck of Stockton gave $1. H. Sheldon of San Diego offered $5. A few notable exceptions to this norm included David Jacks of Monterey who advanced $100 to the cause. Mrs. Phoebe A. Hearst, so active in supporting the Red Cross with donations, bestowed $100 on the commission.[55] The most notable monetary gift came from an out-of-state source. Secretary McCoy revealed that "a gentleman in the East" gave $1,000 to send a commission representative to Manila.[56] Funds to send the other delegate came from local subscriptions.

Like the offerings of individual citizens, contributions flowed in from statewide evangelical churches and assorted organizations. Between 1 May and 12 August 1898, several local newspapers identified donations that came from 14 different cities in California, including those in the Bay Area, San Diego, and Los Angeles. Among these sites, church congregations in San Francisco and Oakland submitted the greatest contributions. Denominations represented across the state included Presbyterians, Methodist Episcopalians, Congregationalists, Baptists, and English Lutherans. Church donations frequently ranged from $10 to $30. The Presbyterian and Methodist Episcopalian congregations bestowed monetary gifts most frequently. Three societies offered one-time donations. The Chautauqua Assembly of Pacific Grove gave $10, the Presbyterian Christian Endeavor Society donated $4, and the Sacramento YMCA gave $6.[57]

Although Morse and Howard emphasized the importance of voluntary contributions in keeping the national Christian Commission solvent, the commission's California department found another lucrative fundraising activity. Like the Red Cross, the local commission hosted benefit drills. With the Army's collaboration, the Christian Commission sponsored two military performances at the Mechanics' Pavilion in San Francisco before the protocol.

The 1st Tennessee performed at the initial drill on 14 July. "Hundreds of ladies" prepared refreshments for the evening. A ticket committee offered "cards of admission" to the drill at 25 cents per adult and 10 cents for each child. An additional 25 cents secured a reserve seat. The performance featured a battalion drill guard mount; company drill, extended order; battalion parade; and regimental marching salute. A chorus directed by J.J. Morris sang patriotic songs. Featured soloists Charles H. Van Orden presented the "Battle Hymn of the Republic," and Miss Grace Davis sang "The Star-Spangled Banner." The Tennessee Regimental Band provided musical selections, including "Dixie Land," and the audience joined in singing several songs. The performance netted $992.50 with additional returns still being accounted for into early August.[58]

The second benefit drill for the Christian Commission of California featured the 20th Kansas commanded by COL Frederick Funston. Held on 4 August, the presentation shared several similarities with the 1st Tennessee benefit that was performed in July: music, song, and march dominated the program. The commission also offered tickets at the gate and reserve seats in advance for the same price that was charged at the previous drill.

The 20th Kansas drill nevertheless had its distinctions. One addition to the program featured a living pyramid of flags created by the YMCA's athletic class. The commission also hoped to reach a wider audience. To support the event, Southern Pacific Railroad officials ran special excursions from several California cities, including Sacramento, Stockton, and San Jose. An initial tally three days after the drill showed the performance collected more than $650. Newspapers reporting the event observed that proceeds from the benefit would be used for commission activities, including the Glunz and Jackson mission to the Philippines.[59]

The commission and the military continued their association beyond the peace protocol. YMCA volunteers continued to support troops stationed at the Presidio after other San Francisco encampments closed. On 1 October, Private Karl Kraemer, 51st Iowa, wrote his sister, "Today the Iowa, Kansas, and Tennessee regiments gave a drill in a ball park a couple of blocks outside of the camp." Kraemer acknowledged the event raised money "for the Manila work of the Army and Navy Christian Commission." The second battalion of each regiment performed, and the private revealed that "the Iowans had a sham battle. There was a very large crowd down there. All three of the Bands played together."[60]

Christian Endeavor Society

Background

Nearly three decades after the YMCA was introduced in the United States, Francis E. Clark established the Young People's Society of Christian Endeavor in Portland, Maine. Clark, a minister, started the organization as a means to give roles to youths in his Williston Congregational Church.

According to Clark, Endeavorers worked "to lead the young people to Christ and into His Church, to establish them firmly in the faith, and to set them at work in the Lord's vineyard." The Endeavor idea spread to other "evangelical denominations" that, in turn, sponsored their own societies. These local groups affiliated with Clark's parent organization, the United Christian Endeavor, which by 1885 had become an international Protestant youth society.[61]

One organizational characteristic distinguished the Christian Endeavors' activities from the YMCA before 1898. The Endeavorers did not have a historical connection to the military services as best embodied in the Army and Navy Christian Commission. When seeking sanction for its military ministry in 1898, the YMCA could remind the War Department of its commission work with Union armies during the Civil War and among state militia in the last quarter of the 19th century. The Endeavorers enjoyed no comparable connection.

Local Organization

Christian Endeavorers at the Golden Gate worked "to make the soldiers comfortable and happy and keep them from the temptations of the city."[62] The California State Christian Endeavor Union was the first Endeavorer organization to support military units around the bay in 1898. In particular, the union's missions office located at 760A Harrison Street in San Francisco coordinated much of the Endeavorers' activities.

Miss Mindora L. Berry, state superintendent of missions, energized the initiative to establish a Christian Endeavor presence among soldiers encamped at the Golden Gate. For assistance, she called on a number of the 700 Christian Endeavor societies in California. Her office orchestrated the efforts of local organizations, including the Golden Gate Union, composed of 50 societies, the Alameda county societies, and those of Oakland and San Rafael.[63]

Endeavorer assistance to the military became more pronounced after Berry assembled "women in sympathy with the Christian Endeavor work at Camp Merritt" and formed the Mothers' Christian Endeavor Club, or Mothers' Club, on 31 May. In early June, the club literally positioned itself to pursue the Endeavorers' goals by establishing a headquarters contiguous to the Richmond encampment. They and other Endeavorers settled in a vacant building variously described as a barn, or warehouse, at Fifth Avenue and D street.[64] That location may have been selected after market forces intruded on Endeavorer plans. The *Chronicle* reported, "An effort was made by the Christian Endeavorers to establish a free entertainment and lunch room on one of the vacant lots near the tents to counteract the influence of the great number of cheap groggeries that have sprung up, but a liquor dealer got a lease of the property which the Endeavorers wanted."[65]

Christian Endeavorers ministered to soldiers in ways that closely parallelled the YMCA's activities. YMCA officials, however, maintained that the association's commission was the one organization through which evangelical churches and young people's societies should coordinate their efforts. Berry unwittingly challenged YMCA supremacy when she urged the United Christian Endeavor to dispatch a representative to the Philippines. She made the request of her parent Endeavor organization after YMCA officials had secured the privilege of sending delegates overseas.

Berry's request found its way into the *San Francisco Call*, prompting the "Y" to pursue its coordinating authority more vigorously.[66] Less than two weeks after the Endeavorer initiative became public, YMCA supporters moved to gain hegemony over all Protestant young people's societies. At an assembly to establish the "Y's" Christian Commission of California, Reverend Dr. E.R. Dille and Rolla V. Watt declared that "Endeavorers would hereafter have to work through the Christian Commission and subject themselves to its authority."[67] H.J. McCoy, general secretary, San Francisco YMCA, and newly appointed treasurer, Army and Navy Christian Commission of California, adopted a similar yet more appeasing position. He outlined his views in a letter to the editor of *The Examiner*, "The idea is to unite all the forces of these churches, as in other States, in one union effort. . . . known as the Christian Commission. . . . There is no desire whatever to interfere with any line of work now being done; all will receive due credit, but will be under a national organization."[68]

The Endeavorers subsequently embraced McCoy's vision of a unified evangelical ministry coordinated by the Christian Commission. The *Call* published an article noting that the Christian Endeavorers' national officers had advised societies in the eastern states to work through the YMCA's Christian Commission "so that there may not be any misunderstanding or conflict of forces."[69] The *Chronicle* subsequently reported that the Christian Endeavorers and other young people's societies from Oakland and Alameda "unanimously decided to co-operate with the Christian commission."[70]

Other indicators reflected the Endeavorers' acquiescence to the Christian Commission. In late June, the Young People's Society of Christian Endeavor, Epworth League, and other societies of Fresno county joined in arranging a benefit for the commission.[71] On 7 July, the Christian Endeavorers' Golden Gate Union met at the San Francisco YMCA and "decided in the future to direct all their efforts in the Army work through the Christian Commission."[72] When the 1st New York began to arrive in the city, a number of the unit's Christian Endeavorers asked the Christian Commission to provide a tent for their use.[73] The commission, therefore, had established itself as the coordinating authority among evangelical Christian groups operating within the camps.

Although the Christian Endeavorers and Mothers' Club acquiesced to the YMCA, they did not disappear. To the contrary, Endeavorer ministries flourished throughout the Bay Area to support the military. The local newspapers continued to cite the organization's contributions. Public recognition of their work reflected a fulfillment of McCoy's pledge that "all will receive due credit, but will be under a national organization."[74]

In the Camps

Christian Endeavorers worked to offer troops a comfortable environment, one that presented an attractive alternative to San Francisco's "darker" leisure activities. The Mothers' Christian Endeavor Club that formed on 31 May pursued three specific objectives in the camps: to furnish free writing materials and writing and reading tents to each regiment, to provide refreshments and entertainment each night at the headquarters on 5th Avenue and B Street, and to receive and distribute comfort bags to the soldiers.[75]

Members of the Mothers' Club aggressively pursued these goals. The Endeavorer organization, like the YMCA, moved rapidly to establish structures where soldiers could spend some of their free time reading, writing, and socializing. The "Y" and Christian Endeavors jointly sponsored a reading and writing room on the second floor of the Fontana warehouse, home of several units from the 1st Washington.[76] The first tent the Endeavorers erected went into the 20th Kansas encampment by 27 May.[77] Soldiers of the regiment pitched in and surprised the Endeavorers by constructing wooden floors for the structure.[78] By 6 June, seven regimental campsites included tents that the society provided. Later in June, Endeavorers erected shelters among the North and South Dakota regiments as well as the 14th and 18th Regulars.[79] Women took charge of tent activities during the day. Men supervised the facilities at night until 2200.[80]

Just as the YMCA canvas shelters offered diversions from military life, Endeavorer tents hosted activities designed to look after the troops' welfare. The society typically stocked money orders "and many little things which the young people think are needful." Mothers' Club ladies would mend Regulars' and Volunteers' clothing.[81]

Members of Merritt's command often visited the tents to correspond with family and friends. Inside these shelters, troops could shield themselves from the elements and sit at tables to write their letters. Endeavorers furnished ink, pens, paper, and envelopes.[82] At one tent on 11 June, 25 soldiers sat and composed letters while several hundred men stood in line, waiting their turn for a seat.[83] Both the *Call* and *The Examiner* published articles estimating that an average of 200 letters a day were written in each of the Endeavorer tents.[84]

Although the society engaged in activities that fostered the soldiers' material welfare, Endeavorers routinely tended to the Regulars' and Volunteers' religious well-being. Every evening through the week, Endeavorers conducted 30-minute religious services in regimental tents.[85] A reporter for the *Chronicle* observed in late June that the Christian organization received letters from soldiers' families and friends all over the country, "thanking the Endeavorers for the manner in which they are attending, not only to the material wants of the soldiers, but also to their spiritual needs."[86]

The Mothers' Club launched an initiative to meet its second objective on 6 June. That night, the Congregational Church provided entertainment for approximately 200 soldiers at the Endeavorers' Camp Merritt headquarters on 5th Avenue and B Street. Troops listened to recitations, vocal and instrumental music, and an address by Reverend F.B. Cherington. At the end of the program, guests enjoyed hot coffee, sandwiches and cakes the hosts provided.[87]

Thereafter, Endeavorers scheduled entertainment Monday through Saturday at their headquarters. Open from 0900 until after taps at 2200, the "commodious barn" gave troops a chance to relax in an environment that offered periodicals, games, secular and religious books, stationery, tables, chairs, and a piano. Each evening, one of the Christian Endeavor unions or a church organization in the San Francisco-Oakland area sponsored a program of music and "recitations and speeches, all of a patriotic character." Toward evening's end, as many as 400 soldiers could be served refreshments consisting of "coffee, sandwiches, and other acceptable things."[88] By mid-June, these social events attracted so many troops that some soldiers were turned away.[89] The Endeavorers subsequently expanded their capability to entertain at headquarters, occasionally hosting 700 to 800 troops a night.[90]

Later in June, the Endeavorers revised their evening programs at camp headquarters. Hosts took time from "socials" to conduct short "praise" services. The *Call* reported that "at a service held the other evening about forty rose to confess Christ."[91] The First Baptist Church led the evening program for soldiers on 24 June. *The Examiner* reported that the church pastor, Dr. E.A. Woods, requested of "those desiring to become Christians to rise, and twenty responded—truly, a very successful meeting."[92]

Headquarters activities also catered to soldiers in additional ways. Troops with colds and other maladies visited for medicines that the Endeavorers' medical department stocked.[93] Miss D. Brooks oversaw hospital work. Her committee delivered milk, soups, and flowers to sick troops in the camps. Next to the assembly hall, civilian volunteers at the headquarters maintained a large room that catered to readers and letter-writers. As they did in their other camp facilities, Endeavorers maintained a supply of paper, envelopes, and stamps for the soldiers. A mail carrier dropped in to collect letters. Two newspapers, the *Call* and *The Examiner*, furnished dailies each morning. The San Francisco News Company donated periodicals. Troops also availed themselves of the sewing and mending services that "many earnest workers" offered.[94]

Fitting Out for the Voyage

Sewing related very closely to the third objective the Mothers' Club pursued. The women stitched and distributed comfort bags before the troops departed on expeditions to the Philippines. Precedent existed for this activity. Several years before the war, "floating committees" of the California State Christian Endeavor Union began to provide sailors with kits of personal items, sometimes called "ditty bags" or "housewives." At least two weeks before the Mothers' Club formed, Endeavorers committed their state organization to provide personal kits to troops encamped at the Golden Gate.[95]

The state organization prescribed the contents of kits in a circular dispatched to all of California's 700 societies. Each ditty bag was to contain a small New Testament, marked; paper, envelopes, and a pencil; needles and pins; coarse black and white thread; court plaster; a bandage; and Vaseline. Endeavorers of the California Union asked that "a personal letter of Christian cheer" accompany each kit. The circular directed that societies forward complete kits to Mindora Berry at the missionary extension headquarters in San Francisco. Acknowledging that smaller societies would probably not be able to furnish all articles, the state union assured all that "donations of articles or money for the purchase of the same will be thankfully received."[96]

By the end of May, the Mothers' Christian Endeavor Club, which Berry helped to organize, had identified comfort bags as a priority activity.[97] Mrs. C.S. Wright, chairman, Mothers' Club of California, and an active member of the Red Cross, scheduled a meeting with churchwomen of San Francisco to give them the pattern for "housewives" and enlisted their support in preparing the kits for soldiers and sailors.[98] Endeavorers also petitioned young people's societies throughout the state for their assistance in creating the kits.[99]

Solicitations paid dividends. By Sunday, 19 June, an average of 200 comfort bags arrived each day at Endeavorer headquarters in Camp Merritt. By that date, the organization had amassed nearly 3,300 bags for the troops. Men of the 1st Colorado Regiment received theirs on 11 June. Endeavorers supplied the second expedition's remaining forces before they sailed for Manila on 16 June. These units included the 1st Nebraska, 10th Pennsylvania, Utah batteries, and battalions from the 18th and 23d US Infantry Regiments. As the third expedition prepared to depart on 27 June, Endeavorers passed out more than 4,000 bags. Mrs. Emily Fowden, a Mothers' Club volunteer who supervised the "efficient corps of workers who sew, supply stamps and find out those who are in need of more clothing or who are sick," managed the distribution.[100] Members of the second expedition also benefited from one other Endeavorer project. The California Christian Endeavor Union supplied ships with games, writing material, and hymn books that troops would use during their long voyage to the Philippines.[101]

Initiatives to Care for Troops Abroad

The issue over which, if any, evangelical Christian organization would coordinate the ministry efforts of Protestants at home and abroad was settled in June. The matter reached resolution when Endeavorers moved to extend the overseas work they had begun in San Francisco camps. After the state union appointed a representative to the Philippines, the YMCA's Christian Commission asserted and established its primacy in coordinating Protestant work with the military.

Miss Berry, state superintendent of missions for the California Christian Endeavor Union, triggered the confrontation. She urged the national Endeavor organization to appoint and dispatch a society representative to supervise a ministry among soldiers and sailors around Manila. On 5 June, Berry sent the following telegram to John Willis Baer, general secretary, United Society of Christian Endeavor, Boston: "Urge McKinley endorse work and subsistence Endeavorer Philippines. Worker ready. California financially responsible. Answer."[102] The worker about whom she wrote was Arthur P. Alexander of Oakland.[103]

Berry also wrote a letter to MG Merritt seeking permission for Alexander to accompany the force deploying to the Philippines. On 7 June, Merritt endorsed Berry's request and directed that he be assigned "transportation to one of the ships now preparing."[104] The following day the Mothers' Christian Endeavor Club of California pledged $40 to outfit Alexander.[105] By the middle of the month, the Union had purchased a 20- by 40-foot tent for Endeavorer work in Manila.[106]

Alexander never sailed. Shortly after Merritt approved Berry's request, the Christian Endeavorers' national officers directed member societies to work through the YMCA's Christian Commission.[107] The California Christian Endeavor Union conformed with the directive and supported troops at home and abroad through the commission. When Charles Glunz and Frank Jackson of the YMCA's Christian Commission sailed for Manila with the third expedition, they took with them an American flag presented by the Young People's Society of Christian Endeavor, First Presbyterian Church, Oakland.[108]

Alexander did not disappear. In what must have been intended a sign of good faith offered to the Endeavorers, the commission found a role for Alexander in San Francisco. *The Examiner* reported on 1 July, "A.P. Alexander of the Christian Endeavor Society has been employed by the Commission (YMCA) to have general charge of the tents at Camp Merritt and will enter upon his duties to-day."[109]

Fundraising

Endeavorer solicitations produced only a few contributions. A group called the King's Daughters donated $32. The Wellesley Hill Christian Endeavor Society gave $10. Mrs. C.A. Heffner and George M. Sponsler offered $1 and 50 cents respectively.[110] The *Call* reported on contributions that 1st Nebraska Volunteers made during one payday, "Wherever the men's pay amounted to odd cents the difference in change was given by the soldiers to the Christian Endeavor Society."[111]

The Endeavorers asked for money, but they did not solicit donations as vigorously as the Red Cross. The California Christian Endeavor Union requested financial assistance not only from societies in the state but also from those in other states that dispatched troops to the Philippines via San Francisco.[112] Results of these calls for assistance were not as widely publicized as the Red Cross or YMCA's Christian Commission's comparable efforts.

Goods and Services

The Christian Endeavor Society supported troops in San Francisco with goods and services donated by its members and those mobilized on behalf of its cause. Individual citizens often rallied to calls for assistance. Scott and McCord, commission and dealers in hay and grain, donated letter paper, envelopes, seals, and most significantly, a large barn on 5th Avenue and B Street. The structure became the Mothers' Club headquarters facility where Endeavorers hosted numerous activities for soldiers at Camp Merritt.[113] To assist in transforming the barn into an activities facility, Mrs. A.W. Scott provided 53 chairs. Other citizens offered lamps, reading material, stationery, and flowers. William Patterson gave one writing desk, writing material, one ham, six cans of fruit, and five cakes of soap. Major Johnson furnished two tents.[114] G.H.T. Jackson assisted in stocking the Endeavorers' medical department when he donated three cases of Napa soda.[115]

Various church groups and Endeavorer societies assumed responsibility for the California Christian Endeavor Union's tent work. Christian Endeavor sections, including those from the Alameda County Union, First Presbyterian Church, Central Methodist Episcopal, and Cavalry Society, each took charge of an Endeavor tent within regimental campsites.[116] Either a San Francisco or an Oakland church often sponsored socials held nightly at the Endeavorers' Camp Merritt headquarters.[117]

Other enterprises and organizations rendered valuable assistance. The Mills' College Red Cross sent 32 comfort bags. Lowell High School donated 14 lamps. Denman School gave 12 bandanna nightcaps and 54 button bags. Union Lumber Company supplied one load of lumber. Renton-Holmes Lumber Company contributed one tent, scantlings, and boards.[118] J.R. Gates and Company, wholesale and retail druggists, furnished a large supply of medicine for the sick.[119]

The Catholic Truth Society

Background

Like the YMCA, Catholic Truth Societies (CTSs) traced their origins to England. First conceived in 1872 but formally established in 1884, the original society evolved under the direction of Bishop Herbert Vaughn and James Britten, a layman in the Catholic church. The organization held two principal aims: to distribute inexpensive devotional and educational works among Catholics and to spread information on Catholicism among Protestants. Membership subscriptions provided most of the financial support for the society's projects.

The society spawned other organizations that pursued its goals in hospitals, workhouses, and various guilds. In 1891, members formed a special committee to work for Catholic seamen's spiritual welfare. The CTS established clubs and homes for the benefit of these men. By the late 19th century, the organization had spread to other countries as well, including the United States.[120]

Local Organization

In San Francisco, two Catholic priests exercised leadership responsibilities within the local Truth Society. The first, Reverend Father Philip O'Ryan of St. Mary's Cathedral, served as the organization's president.[121] He also exercised responsibilities as director, League of the Cross.[122] The other, Reverend Father Peter C. Yorke, emerged as a leading figure within the society's Executive Council.[123]

On 1 June, Yorke addressed the CTS and emphasized several themes that defined the organization. First, in reflecting on the regiments arriving in San Francisco, the priest proclaimed that Catholics were doing their fair share of military duty. He asserted that the ratio of Catholics to non-Catholics in these units exceeded the results of a similar comparison among the general populace. He claimed that Catholic manpower constituted 75 to 100 percent of several military organizations reaching the Bay Area.

Second, Yorke cautioned that while the CTS should take pride in these statistics, members should be concerned by the lack of "spiritual attention" Catholics in uniform received. Non-Catholics dominated both the leadership positions and chaplains' billets within each regiment. Characterizing the Army's leaders as "too broad minded to tolerate religious injustice," Yorke urged members to create public opinion to get Catholic chaplains appointed.

Third, he decried an example of religious persecution. He recounted that during the last week of May, ladies of the society were discouraged from distributing sepulchers, medals, and other religious symbols among members of the 13th Minnesota Infantry. The chaplain of the regiment, a Methodist clergyman, allegedly declared that soldiers of the Minnesota regiment would attend his service or none at all. Yorke argued that soldiers should be permitted to attend services conducted by clergymen of their own faith. To those ends, the reverend father announced that within a week the CTS would constitute a physical presence in the encampments.[124]

The incident involving the Protestant chaplain from Minnesota and CTS members, as relayed to Father Yorke second-hand, appears to have been an isolated incident in the camps. Newspapers did not follow up on what Yorke labeled religious persecution, nor did they report similar infractions.[125]

In the Camps

By 4 June, the CTS established a headquarters at Camp Merritt in a huge tent east of the Idaho Regiment at Fulton Street and Second Avenue. The shelter, dubbed "Father Yorke's Church," seated about 2,000 people. First and foremost, Catholics established the structure to provide the "spiritual attention" to members of the faith, particularly in those terms envisioned by Yorke. City priests agreed to provide day and night coverage for confessions. Reverend fathers conducted masses on weekdays and Sunday.[126]

Figure 85.

In sermons to the troops, priests emphasized proper moral conduct. On 5 June, during the first Sunday service performed in the CTS tent, Father Yorke advised soldiers to be prepared both to go to war and to meet their God "not cursing and swearing and blaspheming."[127] A week later, Yorke declared in his message that "it is calumny on your arms, and scandalous that anyone should think you cannot be good soldiers, and at the same time decent men."[128] On 19 June, Father O'Ryan urged the troops to take the League of the Cross pledge to "abstain from liquor and the frequenting of saloons." He warned those in attendance that "men who go to Manila with systems weakened by alcohol will surely fall victims to the climate."[129] In early July, the *Chronicle* reported that more than 150 soldiers had taken the pledge. Much work, however, remained to be done to secure promises of abstinence from Bay Area troops. The population of Camp Merritt had reached 10,900 by 1 July.[130]

In addition to its headquarters facility, the CTS worked out of smaller tents located in several regimental areas: 20th Kansas, 1st Montana, 1st South Dakota, and 1st Idaho.[131] When Camp Miller was established at the Presidio in late July, the CTS opened an operation on the reservation.[132] It also erected a tent at the 8th California encampment in Oakland.[133] The Catholic Ladies' Aid Society, working in support of the CTS, sustained troops with the 1st North Dakota, South Dakota Battalion, 51st Iowa, and later the 7th California.[134] Although religious services targeted Catholics, the organization pursued general activities to support all soldiers in the encampments.

Figure 86.

Women affiliated with the CTS or Catholic Ladies' Aid Society led support efforts. These civilian volunteers formed committees that organized around major tasks. Troops in need of services the military did not provide could find some relief. Members of the hospital committee, for example, were among the busiest female volunteers. Regimental surgeons and hospital corpsmen lacked the resources to care and provide for all of those warranting medical attention. To assist, the ladies threw themselves into a host of projects designed to alleviate the troops' suffering.

Like some women affiliated with Red Cross organizations, Catholic ladies visited the sick and convalescent among the regiments. Members of the hospital committee tended to those with minor ailments who were according to the *Chronicle*, "compelled to lie in their hot tents through the day without the care of a doctor and deprived of food other than coarse Army fare."[135] They brought soldiers food baskets composed of appropriate "delicacies."[136] Baskets often contained calf's-foot jelly, wine jelly, beef tea, oranges, and fresh eggs.[137]

The troops certainly appreciated their work. In a letter to the Catholic Ladies' Aid Society on behalf of those ill in Company D, Private Nathan McCorkle, 51st Iowa Regiment, thanked the women for the assistance they rendered. McCorkle expressed appreciation for the milk and "delicacies" that the ladies delivered to his comrades.[138]

One state commander in chief also recognized the work the Catholic ladies performed. On 18 July, Montana Governor Robert R. Smith wrote the society, thanking members for "the kind and generous ministration of your society to our sick and needy soldiers." He closed his note with an expression of hope that their "good work will meet with deserved recognition both in this world and in the life to come."[139] Governor Smith justifiably acknowledged the society's efforts on behalf of his state's Volunteers. Each morning a CTS worker checked with company first sergeants of the Montana regiment to learn of the men reported as being sick. The ladies used company stoves to prepare foods for those who were too ill to leave their tents.[140]

The ladies also worked among other military organizations. On 8 June, local hospitals dismissed 25 men from the 1st Idaho Regiment to recuperate from a bout with the measles. The troops reached the Idaho encampment late in the afternoon. Knowing the men would have to sleep on the ground with only one blanket, the regimental surgeon requested that the society provide one additional blanket to each for their recovery. Representatives found one dry goods store still open for business. They paid $5 for each blanket and donated them to the men.[141]

In a noteworthy exception to the otherwise superb relations between the society and the military, the *Daily Report* revealed on 8 June that "ladies of the Catholic Truth Society have complained that the people in charge of the field hospital do not give proper care to the patients."[142]

Certainly there were grounds for criticism. Physicians at the Independent Division's hospital did not have the necessary supplies to care for their wards. On 15 June, doctors asked the society for "linseed and cottonseed oil and other drugs for the ninety-five patients under their charge." The ladies dispatched the necessary medications.[143]

When demand for medical care exceeded the capabilities of both military and society, the Catholic ladies took steps to secure assistance. Just like the Red Cross, the CTS referred seriously ill troops to local hospitals. Unlike the Red Cross, the CTS did not operate medical facilities. The ladies secured beds in the civilian hospitals for soldiers who needed more advanced medical care than regimental surgeons could provide. Some of the sick were sent to the French Hospital. When patients began to exceed the 35-bed capacity of the "free ward," the society spent the "nominal sum" of $10 a week for additional patient care. The ladies sent others, some of whom were afflicted with pneumonia and tonsillitis, to St. Mary's, which offered 12 beds, and the Waldeck Hospital that provided free space for four patients.[144]

Women of the mailing department comprised another busy group among the CTS volunteers. Volunteers and Regulars could go to the organization's "Big Tent" at Fulton Street and Second Avenue or many of the smaller regimental facilities and find an environment conducive to writing. The ladies set up tables and provided paper, envelopes, and stamps at no charge to the troops.[145] One Volunteer wrote in a letter, "These people of the Catholic Truth Society are nice and obliging. While I am writing this there are at least 300 other soldiers doing the same. The society furnishes everything free."[146]

Due to the quantity of letters written throughout the week at the society's headquarters on Camp Merritt, two ladies worked continuously to post the soldiers' mail.[147] The society provided postage for a daily average of 1,800 to 2,000 letters by late June. At 2 cents apiece, stamps cost the society $250 to $280 each week.[148] Sometimes the CTS simply ran out of stamps and called for donations. On 11 July, nearly 1,000 letters could not be mailed because the society lacked sufficient postage.[149]

One other committee, the sewing department, performed a service that soldiers sincerely appreciated. Sometimes the society engaged from 30 to 35 ladies and five sewing machines to help soldiers who dropped in at the Big Tent.[150] In general, the women stayed busy "making, mending, and fitting clothes and fastening on stripes and chevrons."[151] The *Call* observed that quartermasters issued clothes but did "not bother to change for a better fit." The ladies of the CTS emerged to provide a rudimentary tailoring service.[152] For many of the troops, the headquarters tent offered troops one-stop services of sorts where they could read, write, and have their clothes mended.[153]

The society also addressed other needs from their headquarters, which the *Chronicle* described as "such wants attended to as arise from the lack of woman's care in a military camp."[154] The commissary department operated out of a kitchen arranged in the headquarters. Members of this committee worked to have food prepared for soldiers who visited the Big Tent over the course of the day. The literary department provided reading material, such as copies of the *Soldier's Manual*, to uniformed visitors.[155] By early June, the CTS had conceived a plan to print pocket-sized prayer books for the troops.[156] On 20 June, the organization published 5,000 copies.[157] Distributing to the troops an assortment of religious publications, particularly references that related to Catholicism, was a fundamental CTS goal.

Fitting Out for the Voyage

The CTS offered assistance to the first three expeditions destined for the Philippines. When the first expedition prepared for departure in May, the CTS placed a "good library" aboard each transport. One of the local newspapers observed of the contribution: "Novels, histories, biographies and travels were among the books, and none of them were trashy."[158] The society accorded special services to the second expedition's men just before their transports sailed in mid-June. Ladies focused on some last-minute mending.[159] Father Yorke announced during mass at the Society's tent on Sunday, 12 June, that another mass would be celebrated the next morning at 0700 for those who were departing.[160] Members of the CTS provided numerous items for the troops who departed on the third expedition in late June. The organization dispensed 600 abdominal bandages, 800 comfort bags, 560 caps, 22 suits of underclothes, and three cots.[161]

Initiatives to Care for Troops Abroad

Beginning in July, the CTS sponsored an activity in camp designed to benefit the troops once they reached the Philippines. The CTS sponsored Spanish classes. Two women, Mrs. Howard and Miss Heney, offered free Spanish lessons every day at 1600. They presented their first instruction in July. Soldiers could get their lessons by visiting the society's Big Tent on Camp Merritt.[162] The *Chronicle* reported in late July that the classes were "very popular, and a large number of enlisted men attend them throughout the afternoons."[163] (See figure 87.)

"QUE ES ESTO?" MRS. HOWARD TEACHING SPANISH TO IOWA VOLUNTEERS.

Figure 87.

Fundraising, Goods, and Services

The CTS operated facilities at Camp Merritt and the Presidio that incurred numerous expenses. To meet obligations, the society depended on daily contributions from those who were willing to respond to the organization's solicitations. The organization had no general fund to finance its efforts.[164] The margin between solvency and debt was frequently narrow. As of 3 July, for example, total receipts were $647. Of that amount, $371 was used to pay for stamps and $115 covered incidentals. The CTS had a balance of $161 to undertake any remaining projects.[165]

During the first half of June, most contributions came from individuals. Monetary donations received at Room 37, Flood Building, ranged from a few cents to several dollars. Citizens offered bread, beef, ham, raw fresh eggs, hard-boiled eggs, and beef tea to feed the troops or tend to the sick. Others gave blankets, comfort bags, books, magazines, stamps, writing material, eiderdown caps, flannel, and muslin in response to the society's requests.[166]

In the latter part of June and through the rest of the summer, various communities, organizations, and individuals joined in substantially assisting the society. Citizens from Vallejo sent 90 dozen eggs.[167] Several people in Virginia City, Nevada, sent a total of $39.[168] Three lumber companies pooled their assets and furnished a stove, coal oil, and 800 feet of lumber.[169] An anonymous "friend" made three separate $100 contributions.[170] Various Catholic Ladies' Aid Societies responded with contributions.[171] The Consumers' Ice Company gave a daily donation of ice. Numerous drugstores offered various medications and drugs, including cough medicines.[172] The Del Monte Milling Company dispatched "a liberal donation" of flour and meal.[173] Mr. J.D. Spreckels, president of the Western Sugar Refining Company, sent a 100-pound bag of sugar.[174] Mayor Phelan gave $25, and nine city supervisors contributed sums from $5 to $25.[175] The San Francisco Post Office Branch of the Red Cross Society also gave $100.[176]

Like other welfare organizations that operated from generated revenues, the CTS sponsored benefits to increase its funds. The first fundraising event occurred on Tuesday, 12 July, at Mission Parlor Hall on 17th and Valencia Streets. Hosted by the Thomas Aquinas Reading Circle, the benefit performance included piano and vocal solos. Company G, League of the Cross Cadets, performed a drill. Volunteers also participated in the "Military Promenade." Members of the 51st Iowa Regiment Band and 1st Tennessee Regiment Vocal Quartet performed at the 12 July event.[177]

On Friday, 29 July, Miss Ella McClosky and Miss Eva McClosky hosted a "musicale and literary entertainment" and dance in Turn Verein Hall on 18th Street near Valencia. Performers included "many of the well-known celebrities of the amateur stage." Tickets cost 25 cents per person, 10 cents for children under age 12. The performance netted more than $27. The League of the Cross scheduled a third event for Friday, 5 August, at Metropolitan Hall.[178]

Citizens of the Golden Gate region actively supported Merritt's command in a host of ways. Many contributed goods, money, or time on behalf of soldiers who prepared for missions abroad. Others labored as members of major local organizations, some of which were supported by larger national associations, that looked after troops in a variety of ways.

The YMCA, Christian Endeavors, and CTS focused on the Regulars' and Volunteers' spiritual welfare. While each group followed agendas that perpetuated the evangelical Protestant or Catholic faiths, all fought for the souls of troops assembled in the region. The three organizations gave precedence to spiritual pursuits in the camps. They assisted military chaplains, hosted worship services, and provided religious literature. Additionally, all ensured that part of their ministry was devoted to the material and physical well-being of the men who used their services.

Long before Army troops could rely on the United Service Organizations (USO) for morale support, soldiers in late 19th-century San Francisco discovered the welfare projects that local religious groups hosted. Often working out of tents or shelters established in the midst of encampments, YMCA, Endeavorers, and CTS volunteer workers labored to provide assorted activities for troops in their leisure time.

Notes

1. Richard C. Morse, *History of the North American Young Men's Christian Associations* (New York: Association Press, 1913), 3-5.
2. Ibid., 7-10.
3. William Howard Taft, et al., eds. *Service With Fighting Men: An Account of the Work of the American Young Men's Christian Associations in the World War* (New York: Association Press, 1922), 187.
4. Richard C. Lancaster, *Serving the U.S. Armed Forces, 1861-1986: The Story of the YMCA's Ministry to Military Personnel for 125 Years* (Schaumburg, IL: Armed Services YMCA of the USA, 1987), 6-11.
5. Taft, 50-52; Morse, 219-20.
6. Taft, 26.
7. "Great Military Camp at the Presidio Grows With Every Day," *San Francisco Chronicle*, 13 May 1898, 4.
8. "The Presidio Camp Completed," *San Francisco Daily Report*, 18 May 1898, 3.
9. Ibid.; "War Incidents," *San Francisco Call*, 18 May 1898, 5; "Christian Soldiers," *The Examiner*, 18 May 1898, 2.
10. "War Incidents," *San Francisco Call*, 18 May 1898, 5.
11. "Christian Commission," *San Francisco Call*, 22 July 1898, 5.
12. "Appreciated by Soldiers," *The Examiner*, 5 June 1898, 15; "Military News in Brief," *San Francisco Chronicle*, 5 June 1898, 24.
13. "Appreciated by Soldiers," *The Examiner*, 5 June 1898, 15; "Christian Commission," *The Examiner*, 12 June 1898, 15; "Christian Commission," *San Francisco Call*, 12 June 1898, 8; "Work Among the Soldiers," *San Francisco Daily Report*, 8 June 1898, 3.
14. "The Christian Commission," *San Francisco Chronicle*, 9 June 1898, 3.
15. "Religious Welfare of the Soldiers," *The Examiner*, 9 June 1898, 3.
16. "The Christian Commission," *San Francisco Chronicle*, 9 June 1898, 3.
17. "For Christian Work Among the Soldiers," *The Examiner*, 17 June 1898, 12.
18. "Christian Commission," *San Francisco Chronicle*, 21 June 1898, 12.
19. "The Christian Commission," *San Francisco Chronicle*, 9 June 1898, 3.
20. "Kansas Regiment to Drill," *San Francisco Chronicle*, 21 July 1898, 7.
21. "Laboring for Army and Navy," *The Examiner*, 17 June 1898, 7.
22. "Christian Commission Work Extending," *The Examiner*, 1 July 1898, 5; "Laboring for Army and Navy," *The Examiner*, 12 July 1898, 7; "Christian Commission," *San Francisco Chronicle*, 3 July 1898, 30; "Christian Commission," *San Francisco Chronicle*, 21 July 1898, 7; "Christian Commission," *San Francisco Call*, 22 July 1898, 5; "Christian Commission," *San Francisco Call*, 23 July 1898, 5.
23. "Work Among the Soldiers," *San Francisco Daily Report*, 8 June 1898, 3.
24. "All Are Now Under One Flag," *San Francisco Chronicle*, 12 July 1898, 7.
25. "Religious Welfare of the Soldiers," *The Examiner*, 9 June 1898, 3; "The Christian Commission," *San Francisco Daily Report*, 12 July 1898, 2.

26. "Laboring for Army and Navy," *The Examiner*, 12 July 1898, 7.

27. "Appreciated by Soldiers," *The Examiner*, 5 June 1898, 15; "Busy Workers of the Christian Commission," *The Examiner*, 18 July 1898, 5; Richard C. Morse, "The International Committee of Young Men's Christian Associations," in US Senate, *Report of the Commission Appointed by the President to Investigate the Conduct of the War Department in the War With Spain*, volume VIII, *Correspondence* (Washington, DC: US Government Printing Office [GPO], 1900), hereafter cited as *Report VIII*, 467.

28. Morse, *Report VIII*, 467; "Appreciated by Soldiers," *The Examiner*, 5 June 1898, 15; "Military News in Brief," *San Francisco Chronicle*, 5 June 1898, 24.

29. "Christian Workers at Camp Merritt," *The Examiner*, 19 June 1898, 21; "The Soldiers Defeated," *San Francisco Call*, 22 June 1898, 5; "Volunteers vs. Y.M.C.A.," *San Francisco Call*, 18 July 1898, 5; "Will Sail on Monday," *San Francisco Daily Report*, 22 June 1898, 2.

30. "A Reception to the Soldiers," *San Francisco Call*, 21 June 1898, 5; "Local War Notes," *San Francisco Daily Report*, 21 June 1898, 2.

31. "No Rest Under the Red Cross," *San Francisco Chronicle*, 31 May 1898, 3;"Christian Commission," *San Francisco Chronicle*, 18 July 1898, 5; "Busy Workers of the Christian Commission," *The Examiner*, 11 July 1898, 5; "Army Christian Commission," *San Francisco Call*, 6 August 1898, 7.

32. Morse, *Report VIII*, 467.

33. "Kansas Regiment to Drill," *San Francisco Chronicle*, 26 July 1898, 7.

34. "Appreciated by Soldiers," *The Examiner*, 5 June 1898, 15; "Laboring for Army and Navy," *The Examiner*, 12 July 1898, 7; Morse, *Report VIII*, 467.

35. "Will Present Bibles to the Soldiers," *The Examiner*, 28 June 1898, 5.

36. "Army Christian Commission," *San Francisco Chronicle*, 3 August 1898, 9.

37. Morse, *Report VIII*, 467.

38. "Christian Commission Work," *San Francisco Call*, 25 July 1898, 5.

39. Morse, *Report VIII*, 467; "Laboring for Army and Navy," *The Examiner*, 12 July 1898, 7; "The Christian Commission," *The Examiner*, 23 July 1898, 5; "Christian Commission," *San Francisco Chronicle*, 3 July 1898, 30; "The Christian Commission," *San Francisco Chronicle*, 13 July 1898, 12; "The Christian Commission," *San Francisco Chronicle*, 20 July 1898, 7; "Christian Commission," *San Francisco Chronicle*, 25 July 1898, 10; "Christian Commission Work," *San Francisco Call*, 23 July 1898, 5; "Army Christian Commission," *San Francisco Call*, 24 July 1898, 9; "Christian Commission Work," *San Francisco Call*, 25 July 1898, 5.

40. "Christian Commission," *San Francisco Chronicle*, 2 August 1898, 7.

41. Morse, *Report VIII*, 467; Testimony of Maj. Gen. Oliver Otis Howard, 23 December 1898, in US Senate, *Report of the Commission Appointed by the President to Investigate the Conduct of the War Department in the War With Spain*, volume VII, *Testimony* (Washington, DC: GPO, 1900) hereafter cited as *Report VII*, 3305; "Army Christian Commission," *San Francisco Call*, 6 August 1898, 7.

42. "Laboring for Army and Navy," *The Examiner*, 12 July 1898, 7;"Busy Workers of the Christian Commission," *The Examiner*, 18 July 1898, 5; "Christian Commission," *San Francisco Chronicle*, 18 July 1898, 5; "The Christian Commission," *San Francisco Chronicle*, 28 July 1898, 8.

43. "Christian Commission Work," *San Francisco Call*, 25 July 1898, 5.

44. "Will Go to Manila for the Christian Commission," *San Francisco Chronicle*, 13 June 1898, 3.

45. "The Presidio Camp Completed," *San Francisco Daily Report*, 18 May 1898, 3.

46. "Y.M.C.A. Army Work," *San Francisco Call*, 6 June 1898, 10; "Appreciated by Soldiers," *The Examiner*, 5 June 1898, 15; "Military Briefs," *San Francisco Chronicle*, 2 June 1898, 3; "Military News in Brief," *San Francisco Chronicle*, 5 June 1898, 24.

47. "Will Go to Manila for the Christian Commission," *San Francisco Chronicle*, 13 June 1898, 3.

48. "Christian Workers for Manila," *San Francisco Call*, 21 June 1898, 5; "Christian Workers at Camp Merritt," *The Examiner*, 19 June 1898, 21; "The Christian Commission," *San Francisco Daily Report*, 21 June 1898, 2; "Will Work for Christ in Manila," *The Examiner*, 28 June 1898, 14; "Christian Commission Going to the Front," *The Examiner*, 5 June 1898, 36.

49. "Will Work for Christ in Manila," *The Examiner*, 28 June 1898, 14.

50. "The Christian Commission," *San Francisco Call*, 18 July 1898, 5.

51. "Army Christian Commission," *San Francisco Call*, 6 August 1898, 7.

52. "The Christian Commission," *San Francisco Daily Report*, 12 July 1898, 2; Morse, *Report VIII*, 468.

53. Morse, *Report VIII*, 468; Testimony of Maj. Gen. Oliver Otis Howard, 23 December 1898, in *Report VII*, 3305.

54. "All are Now Under One Flag," *San Francisco Chronicle*, 12 July 1898, 7.

55. "The Christian Commission," *The Examiner*, 23 July 1898, 5; "Christian Commission," *San Francisco Call*, 23 July 1898, 5; "Kansas Regiment to Drill," *San Francisco Chronicle*, 26 July 1898, 7; "Army Christian Commission," *San Francisco Call*, 24 July 1898, 9; "Christian Commission," *San Francisco Chronicle*, 18 July 1898, 5.

56. "Will Go to Manila for the Christian Commission," *San Francisco Chronicle*, 13 June 1898, 3; "Y.M.C.A. Army Work," *San Francisco Call*, 6 June 1898, 10; "Appreciated by Soldiers," *The Examiner*, 5 June 1898, 15.

57. *San Francisco Chronicle*, 18 July 1898, 5; 21 July 1898, 7; 26 July 1898, 7; 28 July 1898, 8; 2 August 1898, ; *San Francisco Call*, 12 July 1898, 5; 22 July 1898, 5; 23 July 1898, 5; 24 July 1898, 9; 27 July 1898, 8; 29 July 1898, 5; 7 August 1898, 7; *The Examiner*, 18 July 1898, 5; 23 July 1898, 5.

58. "Tennessee Boys at the Pavilion," *The Examiner*, 7 July 1898, 7; "Tennessee Regiment Drill in the Pavilion," *The Examiner*, 14 July 1898, 4; "All Are Now Under One Flag," *San Francisco Chronicle*, 12 July 1898, 7; "Tennessee Drill To-night," *San Francisco Chronicle*, 14 July 1898, 5; "The Tennessee Regiment," *San Francisco Call*, 12 July 1898, 5; "The Christian

Commission," *San Francisco Daily Report*, 12 July 1898, 2.

59. "The Kansas Boys to Drill," *San Francisco Call*, 27 July 1898, 8; "The Kansas Boys to Entertain," *San Francisco Call*, 29 July 1898, 5; "Military Entertainment," *San Francisco Call*, 30 July 1898, 5; "Moving Their Tents," *San Francisco Call*, 12 July 1898, 5; "Kansas Regiment to Drill," *San Francisco Chronicle*, 26 July 1898, 7; "Kansas Regiment Drill," *San Francisco Chronicle*, 27 July 1898, 8; "The Christian Commission," *San Francisco Chronicle*, 28 July 1898, 8; "The Kansas Drill Next Week," *San Francisco Chronicle*, 30 July 1898, 5; "Christian Commission," *San Francisco Chronicle*, 2 August 1898, 7; "Army Christian Commission," *San Francisco Chronicle*, 3 August 1898, 9.

60. Letter from Karl Kraemer, Co H, 51st Iowa Infantry, Presidio, San Francisco, to "Sister and all," 1 October 1898 (Carlisle Barracks, PA: US Army Military History Institute).

61. F.E. Clark, *Young People's Society of Christian Endeavor . . . What It is and How It Works* (Boston: United Society of Christian Endeavor, 1894), 5, 8.

62. "Good Work of the Endeavorers," *The Examiner*, 11 June 1898, 2.

63. "Christian Endeavorers Lend Their Aid," *San Francisco Chronicle*, 16 May 1898, 5; "Notes of the Camps," *San Francisco Chronicle*, 30 May 1898, 3.

64. "Military News in Brief," *San Francisco Chronicle*, 1 June 1898, 3; "Work of the Mother's Club," *The Examiner*, 8 June 1898, 6.

65. "Items of Interest From the Camp of Instruction," *San Francisco Chronicle*, 4 June 1898, 9.

66. "Soldier Endeavorers," *San Francisco Call*, 6 June 1898, 10.

67. "For Christian Work Among the Soldiers," *The Examiner*, 17 June 1898, 12.

68. H.J. McCoy, Letter to the Editor, *The Examiner*, 20 June 1898, 3.

69. "Christian Commission," *San Francisco Call*, 12 June 1898, 8.

70. "Christian Commission," *San Francisco Chronicle*, 3 July 1898, 30.

71. "Christian Commission Going to the Front," *The Examiner*, 26 June 1898, 36.

72. "Under Christian Commission Flag," *San Francisco Chronicle*, 9 July 1898, 9.

73. "Christian Commission," *San Francisco Call*, 22 July 1898, 5.

74. McCoy, *The Examiner*, 20 June 1898, 3.

75. "Work of the Mother's Club," *The Examiner*, 8 June 1898, 6.

76. "Washington Soldiers," *San Francisco Call*, 1 June 1898, 4.

77. "At Bay District Camp," *San Francisco Chronicle*, 27 May 1898, 9.

78. "In the Christian Endeavorers' Hive," *The Examiner*, 26 June 1898, 36.

79. "Soldier Endeavorers," *San Francisco Call*, 6 June 1898, 10; "Christian Workers at Camp Merritt," *The Examiner*, 19 June 1898, 21.

80. "Good Work of the Endeavorers," *The Examiner*, 11 June 1898, 2; "Endeavorers are Accomplishing Much," *The Examiner*, 11 July 1898, 5.

81. "In the Christian Endeavorers' Hive," *The Examiner*, 26 June 1898, 36.

82. "At Bay District Camp," *San Francisco Chronicle*, 27 May 1898, 9.

83. "The Endeavorers Doing Good Work, *The Examiner*, 12 June 1898, 15.

84. "Christian Endeavor," *San Francisco Call*, 19 June 1898, 7; "Christian Workers at Camp Merritt," *The Examiner*, 19 June 1898, 21.

85. "Soldier Endeavorers," *San Francisco Call*, 6 June 1898, 10.

86. "Churches Aid the Soldiers," *San Francisco Chronicle*, 29 June 1898, 5.

87. "To Amuse the Boys," *San Francisco Call*, 7 June 1898, 7.

88. "Christian Endeavor Work," *San Francisco Chronicle*, 11 June 1898, 11; "To Amuse the Boys," *San Francisco Call*, 7 June 1898, 7; "Good Work of the Endeavorers," *The Examiner*, 11 June 1898, 2.

89. "War Incidents," *San Francisco Call*, 17 June 1898, 5.

90. "Endeavor Socials for the Soldiers," *The Examiner*, 5 July 1898, 9; "A Tennessee Night," *San Francisco Call*, 2 July 1898, 7.

91. "Christian Endeavorers in Camp," *San Francisco Call*, 23 June 1898, 5.

92. H.S. Crocker Company, *Crocker-Langley San Francisco Directory For Year Commencing May 1899* (Washington, DC: GPO, 1898), 1925; "In the Christian Endeavorers' Hive," *The Examiner*, 26 June 1898, 36.

93. "Women's Work in Camp," *San Francisco Daily Report*, 11 July 1898, 3; "In the Christian Endeavorers' Hive," *The Examiner*, 26 June 1898, 36; "Endeavorers' Aid for the Soldiers," *The Examiner*, 10 July 1898, 23.

94. "In the Christian Endeavorers' Hive," *The Examiner*, 26 June 1898, 36; "Endeavorers' Aid for the Soldiers," *The Examiner*, 10 July 1898, 23; "Christian Endeavor," *San Francisco Call*, 16 June 1898, 8; "Christian Endeavorers," *San Francisco Call*, 26 June 1898, 7; "Endeavorers are Accomplishing Much," *The Examiner*, 11 July 1898, 5; "Women's Work in Camp," *San Francisco Daily Report*, 11 July 1898, 3.

95. "Christian Endeavors Lend Their Aid," *San Francisco Chronicle*, 16 May 1898, 5; "Christian 'Housewives,'" *San Francisco Daily Report*, 16 May 1898, 2.

96. "Christian Endeavors Lend Their Aid," *San Francisco Chronicle*, 16 May 1898, 5; "Christian 'Housewives,'" *San Francisco Daily Report*, 16 May 1898, 2.

97. "Work of the Mother's Club," *The Examiner*, 8 June 1898, 6; "To Amuse the Boys," *San Francisco Call*, 7 June 1898, 7.

98. "Christian Endeavor Work," *San Francisco Chronicle*, 31 May 1898, 3.

99. "The Endeavorers Doing Good Work," *The Examiner*, 12 June 1898, 15.

100. Ibid.; "Christian Workers at Camp Merritt," *The Examiner*, 19 June 1898, 21; "In the Christian Endeavorers' Hive," *The Examiner*, 26 June 1898, 36; "Endeavorers are Accomplishing Much," *The Examiner*, 11 July 1898, 5; "Christian Endeavorers in Camp," *San Francisco Call*, 23 June 1898, 5; "Christian Endeavorers," *San Francisco Call*, 26 June 1898, 7; "Local War Notes," *San Francisco Daily Report*, 27 June 1898, 2.

101. "Christian Endeavorers are Kept Busy," *The Examiner*, 23 June 1898, 4; "Aiding the Volunteers," *San Francisco Call*, 23 June 1898, 5; "At Camp Merritt," *San Francisco Daily Report*, 23 June 1898, 1.

102. "Soldier Endeavorers," *San Francisco Call*, 6 June 1898, 10.

103. "Military News in Brief," *San Francisco Chronicle*, 9 June 1898, 3.

104. "Going to the Front," *San Francisco Call*, 8 June 1898, 8.

105. "Military News in Brief," *San Francisco Chronicle*, 9 June 1898, 3.

106. "Christian Endeavor Work," *San Francisco Chronicle*, 15 June 1898, 7; "Christian Endeavor," *San Francisco Call*, 16 June 1898, 8; "Local War Notes," *San Francisco Daily Report*, 15 June 1898, 2.

107. "Christian Commission," *San Francisco Call*, 12 June 1898, 8.

108. "Christian Commission Going to the Front," *The Examiner*, 26 June 1898, 36.

109. "Christian Commission Work Extending," *The Examiner*, 1 July 1898, 8.

110. "Christian Endeavorers," *San Francisco Call*, 26 June 1898, 7; "Good Work of the Endeavorers," *The Examiner*, 11 June 1898, 2; "Christian Workers to Camp Merritt," *The Examiner*, 19 June 1898, 21.

111. "Camp Merritt Troops," *San Francisco Call*, 12 June 1898, 8.

112. "News of Camp and Army," *San Francisco Chronicle*, 13 June 1898, 3.

113. H.S. Crocker Company, 1552; "Work of the Mother's Club," *The Examiner*, 8 June 1898, 6.

114. "Good Work of the Endeavorers," *The Examiner*, 11 June 1898, 2.

115. "Endeavor Socials for the Soldiers," *The Examiner*, 5 July 1898, 9.

116. "News of the Camps," *San Francisco Chronicle*, 28 May 1898, 11; "Christian Endeavor Work," *San Francisco Chronicle*, 3 July 1898, 30.

117. "Notes of the Camps," *San Francisco Chronicle*, 6 June 1898, 5.

118. "Good Work of the Endeavorers," *The Examiner*, 11 June 1898, 2.

119. H.S. Crocker Company, 696; "Women's Work in Camp," *San Francisco Daily Report*, 11 July 1898, 3.

120. *Encyclopedia of Catholicism* (San Francisco: Harper Collins, 1995) 287; Robert C. Broderick, *The Catholic Concise Encyclopedia* (St. Paul, MN: Catechetical Guild Educational Society, 1957) 80; *The Catholic Encyclopedia*, volume XV (New York: Robert Appleton Co., 1912), 77; *New Catholic Encyclopedia*, volume III (Washington, DC: Catholic University of America, 1967), 331.

121. H.S. Crocker Company, 53; "Soldiers Grateful for Deeds of Mercy," *The Examiner*, 12 September 1898, 4.

122. "A Society's Good Work," *San Francisco Daily Report*, 17 June 1898, 1.

123. "Catholic Truth Society," *San Francisco Call*, 17 July 1898, 8; "Catholic Truth Society," *San Francisco Chronicle*, 19 July 1898, 4.

124. "Father Yorke Protests," *San Francisco Daily Report*, 2 June 1898, 3; "Religion in the Regiments," *San Francisco Chronicle*, 2 June 1898, 9.

125. "Religion in the Regiments," *San Francisco Chronicle*, 2 June 1898, 9.

126. "Items of Interest From the Camp of Instruction," *San Francisco Chronicle*, 4 June 1898, 9; "Religion in the Regiments," *San Francisco Chronicle*, 2 June 1898, 9; "War Incidents," *San Francisco Call*, 3 June 1898, 7. "The Sunday Round at Camp Merritt," *San Francisco Chronicle*, 13 June 1898, 5.

127. "Notes of the Camps," *San Francisco Chronicle*, 6 June 1898, 5.

128. "Father Yorke to Soldiers," *The Examiner*, 13 June 1898, 3.

129. "Tennesseans Hold a Levee," *San Francisco Chronicle*, 20 June 1898, 5.

130. "Catholic Truth Society," *San Francisco Chronicle*, 1 July 1898, 12.

131. "For the Good They Can Do," *The Examiner*, 8 July 1898, 7.

132. "Truth Society at the Presidio," *The Examiner*, 20 July 1898, 5.

133. "Truth Society's Willing Workers," *The Examiner*, 16 July 1898, 5.

134. "Friends of the Soldiers," *San Francisco Chronicle*, 19 June 1898, 19; "Catholic Ladies' Aid," *San Francisco Chronicle*, 14 July 1898, 5.

135. "Thanks From Volunteers," *San Francisco Chronicle*, 3 July 1898, 30.

136. "Provisions Wanted," *San Francisco Daily Report*, 8 June 1898, 3; "Women's Work in Camps," *San Francisco Daily Report*, 6 July 1898, 3; "Catholic Aid for Soldiers in the Field," *The Examiner*, 11 June 1898, 3; "Christian Work for Volunteer Army," *San Francisco Chronicle*, 8 June 1898, 5; "Truth Society's Work," *San Francisco Chronicle*, 15 June 1898, 7; "Friends of the Soldiers," *San Francisco Chronicle*, 19 June 1898, 19; "Helping the Soldiers," *San Francisco Chronicle*, 23 June 1898, 7; "Catholic Truth Workers," *San Francisco Chronicle*, 27 June 1898, 7.

137. "Minister to the Soldiers," *The Examiner*, 12 June 1898, 25.

138. "Thanks From Volunteers," *San Francisco Chronicle*, 3 July 1898, 30.

139. Letter From the Governor of Montana to the Catholic Truth Society, San Francisco, *The Examiner*, 24 July 1898, 23.

140. "Catholic Truth Society," *San Francisco Chronicle*, 3 July 1898, 30.

141. "Truth Society's Work," *San Francisco Chronicle*, 15 June 1898, 7; "Catholic Ladies' Work," *San Francisco Chronicle*, 17 June 1898, 9; "Were Helped by the Truth Society," *The Examiner*, 27 June 1898, 3; "Helping the Troops," *San Francisco Daily Report*, 15 June 1898, 1.

142. "Local War Notes," *San Francisco Daily Report*, 27 June 1898, 2.

143. "Aid for Sick Soldiers," *The Examiner*, 16 June 1898, 4.

144. "Local War Notes," *San Francisco Daily Report*, 21 June 1898, 2; "For the Sick Soldiers," *San Francisco Daily Report*, 24 June 1898, 1, 6; "Local War Notes," *San Francisco Daily Report*, 27 June 1898, 2; "Catholic Truth Work," *San Francisco Chronicle*, 21 June 1898, 12; "Catholic Truth Workers," *San Francisco Chronicle*, 27 June 1898, 7; "Caring for the Sick," *San Francisco Chronicle*, 29 June 1898, 5; "Catholic Ladies' Aid," *San Francisco Chronicle*, 31 July 1898, 24; "Work of the Catholic Truth Society," *The Examiner*, 15 June 1898, 12; "Aid for the Sick Soldiers," *The Examiner*, 16 June 1898, 4; "Helping the Soldier Boys," *The Examiner*, 17 June 1898, 5; "They Labor in the Cause of Soldiers," *The Examiner*, 18 June 1898, 14; "Catholic Truth Society's Needs," *The Examiner*, 3 July 1898, 22.

145. "Christian Work for the Volunteer Army," *San Francisco Chronicle*, 8 June 1898, 5.

146. "Appreciate Truth Society Labors," *The Examiner*, 12 July 1898, 7.

147. "Aid for the Sick Soldiers," *The Examiner*, 16 June 1898, 4.

148. "Two Thousand Letters Daily," *The Examiner*, 28 June 1898, 5.

149. "Appreciate Truth Society Labors," *The Examiner*, 12 July 1898, 7.

150. "Generous Aid for the Volunteers," *The Examiner*, 14 July 1898,

4; "Generous Catholic Ladies," *San Francisco Daily Report*, 14 July 1898, 3; "Catholic Truth Work," *San Francisco Chronicle*, 21 June 1898, 12.

151. "Catholic Truth Work," *San Francisco Chronicle*, 21 June 1898, 12.

152. "Among the Volunteers," *San Francisco Call*, 26 June 1898, 7.

153. "Many Help the Truth Society," *San Francisco Chronicle*, 24 June 1898, 3; "A Daily Scene at Camp," *San Francisco Chronicle*, 29 June 1898, 5.

154. "Catholic Ladies' Work," *San Francisco Chronicle*, 17 June 1898, 9.

155. "For the Good They Can Do," *The Examiner*, 8 July 1898, 7.

156. "Religion in the Regiments," *San Francisco Chronicle*, 2 June 1898, 9.

157. "Tennesseans Hold a Levee," *San Francisco Chronicle*, 20 June 1898, 5.

158. "Religion in the Regiments," *San Francisco Chronicle*, 2 June 1898, 9.

159. "Helping the Troops," *San Francisco Daily Report*, 15 July 1898, 1.

160. "Father Yorke to Soldiers," *The Examiner*, 13 June 1898, 3.

161. "Were Helped by the Truth Society," *The Examiner*, 27 June 1898, 3.

162. "Good Work of the Truth Society," *The Examiner*, 11 July 1898, 5; "Truth Society's Willing Workers," *The Examiner*, 16 July 1898, 5; "Catholic Truth Society," *San Francisco Chronicle*, 14 July 1898, 5.

163. "Catholic Truth Society," *San Francisco Chronicle*, 27 July 1898, 8.

164. "Catholic Truth Society," *San Francisco Chronicle*, 9 July 1898, 9.

165. "Catholic Truth Society," *San Francisco Call*, 17 July 1898, 8.

166. *San Francisco Daily Report*, June 1898, 9, 10, 13, 15, 17-18, 20; July 1898, 6, 11, 14; *San Francisco Call*, 19 June 1898; *San Francisco Chronicle*, June 1898, 8, 15, 17, 19, 21, 23, 29; July 1898, 4, 14, 17, 21, 25, 28, 30-31; August 1898, 1, 2, 8, 12; *The Examiner*, June 1898, 10-11, 13, 15-20, 24, 27; July 1898: 2, 3, 8, 12, 17, 25, 30.

167. "Generous Vallejoites," *San Francisco Daily Report*, 21 June 1898, 2.

168. "Aiding the Good Work at the Camp," *The Examiner*, 7 July 1898, 7.

169. "Camp Merritt," *San Francisco Daily Report*, 22 June 1898, 1.

170. "Steamer Peru Saw the Transports," *San Francisco Daily Report*, 24 June 1898, 6; "Help for the Sick," *San Francisco Chronicle*, 24 June 1898, 9; "Truth Society at the Presidio," *The Examiner*, 20 July 1898, 5; "Catholic Truth Society," *San Francisco Chronicle*, 20 July 1898, 7.

171. "Delicacies for Soldiers," *San Francisco Chronicle*, 18 July 1898, 5.

172. "Catholic Truth Society Donations," *The Examiner*, 4 July 1898, 12; "Catholic Truth Society Donations," *The Examiner*, 6 July 1898, 4; "Generous Aid for the Volunteers," *The Examiner*, 14 July 1898, 4.

173. "Catholic Truth Society," *San Francisco Chronicle*, 9 July 1898, 9.

174. H.S. Crocker Company, 1618; "Masses in the Tent of the Truth Society," *The Examiner*, 18 July 1898, 5.

175. "Stamps are Needed for Soldiers' Letters," *The Examiner*, 3 August 1898, 9.

176. "Catholic Truth Society's Work," *The Examiner*, 23 August 1898, 10.

177. "Catholic Truth Society," *San Francisco Chronicle*, 9 July 1898, 9; "Flag Given the Truth Society," *San Francisco Chronicle*, 10 July 1898, 22; "For the Benefit of Sick Soldiers," *San Francisco Chronicle*, 13 July 1898, 12.

178. "Will Help the Truth Society," *The Examiner*, 23 July 1898, 5; "Catholic Truth Society," *San Francisco Call*, 23 July 1898, 5; "Will Aid the Soldiers' Hospital," *San Francisco Call*, 27 July 1898, 8; "Catholic Truth Society," *San Francisco Chronicle*, 3 August 1898, 9.

Chapter VII
Deployment Considerations

After his stunning victory at Manila Bay on 1 May 1898, Commodore George Dewey cabled Washington and requested a "fast steamer with ammunition."[1] From Cavite three days later, Dewey sent Navy Secretary John Long an intriguing assessment, "I control bay completely and can take city at any time, but I have not sufficient men to hold."[2] Dewey's announcement reinforced the McKinley administration's inclination to follow up the naval victory with a US Army occupation force, the size of which would have to be determined.

Even as Regulars and Volunteers assembled in San Francisco preparatory to duty in the Philippines, the military did not have the means to deploy sizable Army units across the Pacific. One officer observed at the time that "the Army had never done anything of this kind; we had never transported troops by sea; it was something new to the Army of the United States."[3] Securing the requisite steamers became one of the war's major undertakings. Outfitting each transport to accommodate troops and equipment overseas was a closely associated task.

The transportation challenge brought with it another vexing problem: Which units would deploy and when? Sufficient vessels could not be contracted or purchased to dispatch MG Merritt's command in one movement. What criteria would be used to designate regiments a part of a specific expedition? Merritt and MG Otis faced these questions and the often unsolicited advice of other military and political authorities as to which organizations to move abroad and in what order.

Departing expeditions impacted the campsites around San Francisco. Originally established in four locations, bivouac areas increasingly faced the scrutiny of newspaper reporters, medical officers, businessmen, and local citizens. These groups exerted pressure to reposition troops onto the Presidio. As units deployed and reduced the number of troops remaining near the Golden Gate, senior officers began moving units to the military reservation. All of the troops would eventually relocate but not before a peace protocol ended hostilities between the United States and Spain.

Securing the Transports

By the time McKinley announced the 12 August protocol, 19 chartered vessels had transported 15,719 officers and men to Manila.[4] Additionally, three coast steamers dispatched 982 troops (charging the Army a per capita rate) to Honolulu for garrison duty.[5] Transactions often involved the

Assistant Secretary of War, quartermaster officers, and senior leaders in the Department of the Pacific.

The first vessel secured for Pacific troop duty actually came into federal service without input from Army personnel. On 7 May 1898, Secretary Long informed Dewey that the *City of Peking* would sail with ammunition and stores to replenish the Asiatic station's naval force.[6] Responding to Dewey's request to resupply his squadron after the battle of Manila Bay, the Department of the Navy had chartered the *Peking* from the Pacific Mail Steamship Company for $1,000 a day. The 24-year-old ship measured 435 feet long and 48 feet wide. Engaged in Pacific trade since 1875, the vessel had completed 100 round trips between the United States and China by February 1898. Although signed in early May, the contract became effective at midmonth because the *Peking* was still at sea on a return voyage from Hong Kong.[7]

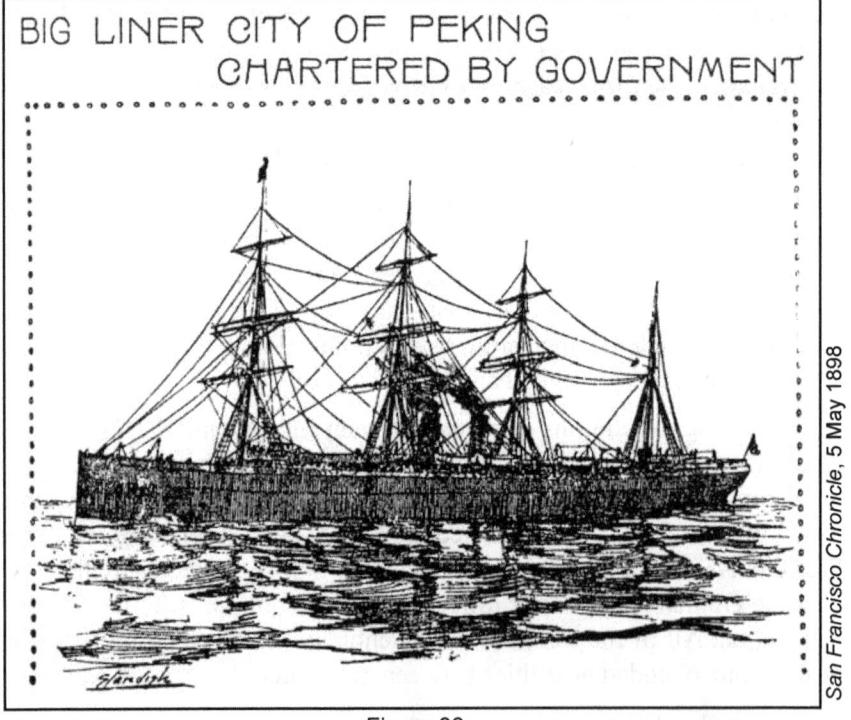

Figure 88.

Just after the ship docked at a San Francisco wharf on 9 May, Secretary Long offered the War Department space aboard the *Peking* to transport troops. In addition to supplies for Dewey, the ship could accommodate "1,200 men and 75 officers, including naval contingent."[8] While that number was impressive, it was well short of the 5,000 men the commodore desired and a fraction of the "12,000 men, or one army corps" figure the Adjutant General was considering for Philippine service on 13 May.[9]

The *Peking* would be the first and only vessel the Navy would charter that conveyed Army troops to the Philippines. On 10 May, War Department personnel began to procure oceanic transports for the thousands of men selected for duty in the Philippines.[10] From Washington, Assistant Secretary of War George de Rue Meiklejohn routinely worked charter issues.[11] William McKinley had appointed Meiklejohn, a Republican from Nebraska who had served two terms in the US House of Representatives, to the position on 14 April 1897.[12]

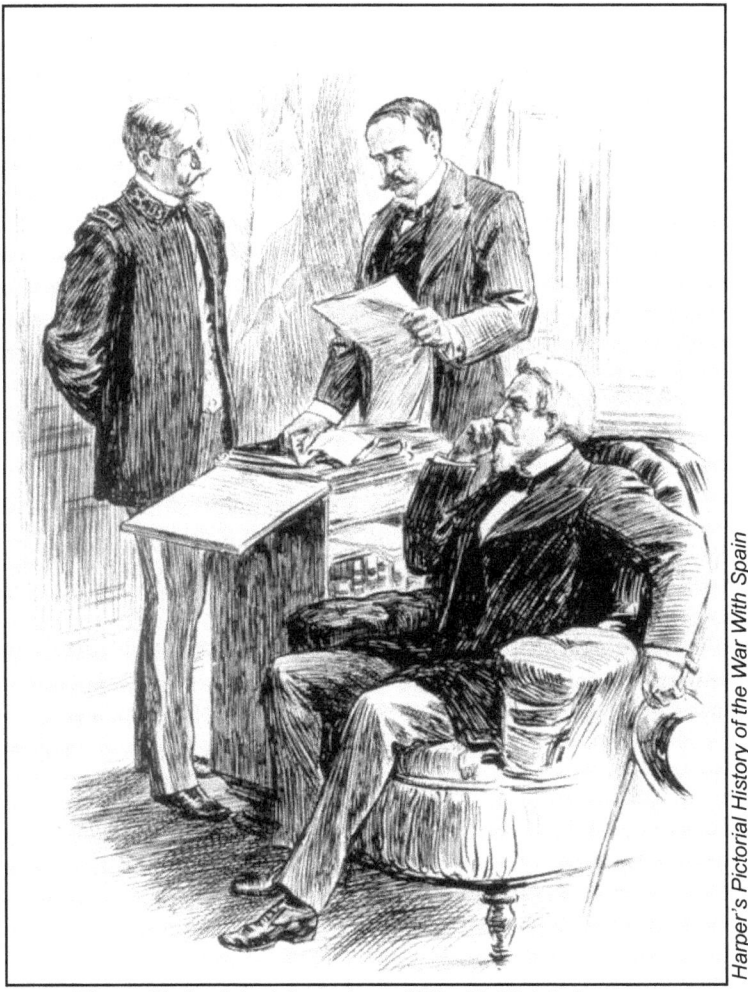

Figure 89. Assistant Secretary of War Meiklejohn's room.

Meiklejohn worked closely with officers from the Quartermaster Department who handled a myriad of details associated with securing vessels. At first, BG Marshall I. Ludington, Quartermaster General, designated COL Charles Bird to arrange for all water transportation.[13] Bird and Meiklejohn collaborated to establish bids for vessels, to negotiate with steamship companies, and to execute charters.[14] By 30 June, this team contracted through six companies to use 14 steamers that could transport 13,688 men and their equipment to destinations in the Pacific.[15]

From the vantage of commanders in San Francisco, War Department efforts that Meiklejohn and Bird led were not producing sufficient transports when needed. A day before the first expedition sailed, MG Otis wrote that other units were fit enough to deploy, but "the great obstacle to moving is vessel transportation."[16] On 2 June, Merritt cabled the AG, BG Corbin, that he had "more men ready to embark" than the then-contracted vessels could accommodate. The general ended his message, "It is important of course that additional transports be chartered at once."[17] Four days later in another dispatch to Corbin, Merritt reiterated how vessel shortages prevented more forces from deploying. "I consider it important that the authorities in Washington should know how matters are dragging with the Philippine expedition," began Merritt. First, the next deployment would be delayed "owing to changes necessary to be made in the chartered transports." Second, pronouncing "plenty of men as fit to go," the general highlighted the need to acquire more transports, asking "can they not be hurried? I am not complaining, but report the facts, as they do not seem to be understood in Washington."[18]

A day later, Merritt's frustration with available shipping spilled over into newspapers. On 7 June, the *Call* published an article giving the general's personal assessment of his command, including training, equipment, and deployments. Merritt observed, "The only complaint now is the delay in the furnishing of transports. I have represented to the War Department that the transports are coming in very slowly." Then, perhaps recalling an earlier need to offer "semi-retraction" statements when his alleged remarks about poorly disciplined Volunteers appeared in May's New York newspapers, Merritt added, "I do not wish to be understood as making any complaint or any criticism of the War Department. I am merely making a statement of facts in reply to your inquiries. I think the War Department is doing everything in its power to facilitate the rapid movement of troops to the Philippines. The shortage of transports is no fault of the War Department."[19]

Of course, that statement was more for public consumption, given the tone of his personal communiqués to Corbin. In actuality, Washington officials had been working diligently to meet the Department of the Pacific's needs. Between May and June, the Quartermaster Department engaged nearly all suitable vessels on the West Coast.[20] Nevertheless, shipping contracted over those two months could accommodate only about 70 percent of the troops allocated for duty in the Pacific.[21]

Responding to Merritt's appeals and the need for more shipping on the Atlantic Coast as well, the War Department changed tactics. Although three more Manila-bound vessels would be chartered before the 12 August peace protocol, the War Department in late June began to procure transport ships through outright purchase. The Secretary of War subsequently established a "division of transportation" in the Quartermaster Department to spearhead the effort.[22] Under the direction of COL Frank Hecker, a Detroit manufacturer commissioned in the Volunteers, the division used federal funds to buy 17 vessels, two of which were assigned to steam the Pacific.[23]

As much as the military needed ships to deploy forces, the Army refused to take all vessels offered. In recounting his experience working the purchase of ships, Hecker observed, "Ninety per cent of the ships tendered the Government were found wholly unsuited because of their age and unseaworthiness, because they would require immediate and extensive repairs to machinery, or because it was not practicable, in the short time at the disposal of the Department, to ventilate them, even partially." To this list of shortcomings he also could have included exorbitant costs. For example, Hecker recalled how the Canadian Pacific Railway Company offered two steamers at a price he considered too inflated, given their "history." Negotiations for both ships continued throughout the war but were never completed.[24]

Although War Department officials played a key role in acquiring or rejecting ships offered for Pacific service, their decisions were often shaped by information they received from military authorities on the West Coast. Merritt, for example, seemingly acquired considerable authority to secure steamers after he complained that a lack of shipping hindered timely deployments. Corbin informed Merritt that "any action on your part looking to speedy supply of transportation will be approved." After apprising Merritt of the need to keep his office informed of efforts made, Corbin assured him that "the President as well as the Secretary of War give you the widest latitude in this matter."[25]

About a month after receiving this cable, Merritt requested that the government purchase the *Newport*, a chartered steamer on which he was taking passage to the Philippines. He recounted the ship's attractive features, calling the "vessel admirably adapted in every way for one of the permanent fleet of transports."[26] COL Hecker, who ultimately considered Merritt's request, found the asking price "so much in excess of her intrinsic value that it would not be advantageous for the Government to purchase her."[27] The Secretary of War concurred with Hecker's assessment, leaving Corbin with the task of informing Merritt that the ship would retain its charter status only.[28]

Others in San Francisco exerted a decidedly greater influence in the transport appropriation process. Before Merritt's late May arrival in the city, MG Otis offered the War Department extensive observations on ships considered for charter. On 18 May, a day after reaching San Francisco, Otis submitted a report to BG Corbin assessing the readiness of ships already contracted. He also named several vessels suitable for troops that could be available in the future and identified a few ships that possibly would be "available only by seizure." He deemed one particular vessel, the *Conemaugh*, "not suited for troops but adapted for animals and freight."[29] That ship was never chartered for any units of the Philippine expeditionary force.

On 19 May, Otis received instructions from Secretary Alger to assume command of expeditionary troops and directions to confer with the president of Pacific Mail Steamship Company "to ascertain from him whether it is not possible to get charter of other ships." In the meantime, Otis was to report the largest number of soldiers who could be accommodated by ships that already were chartered. If contracted vessels could not give passage to all troops, then Alger believed that other ships might have to be pressed into service.[30]

MG Otis met with representatives of Pacific Mail and discussed chartering two vessels. The War Department subsequently contracted both ships.[31] After Merritt departed at the end of June, Otis personally directed the charter of two additional watercraft: the *St. Paul*, another troopship, and the *Tacoma*, a vessel used to move stock and forage to the archipelago.[32] The War Department supported his initiative and executed contracts for both vessels. At the same time, the department opted not to complete a contract for the *Titania* after Otis communicated his reservations about the vessel to the Assistant Secretary of War.[33] The *Chronicle* reported that the vessel was "unsuited for troops, and would have to undergo many repairs and changes before she could be made habitable."[34] Meiklejohn trusted Otis's judgment, so much so that on 10 July he gave

The Examiner, 4 August 1898

Figure 90.

Otis the authority to "make all arrangements necessary for the charter of steamers for transportation of troops to Hawaii."[35]

A major reason for Otis's ability to render such an informed judgment on acquiring or rejecting ships rested with his willingness to conduct personal inspections of vessels or to accept reports from others on the conditions of potential transports. The general "inspected nearly all of the vessels used" to dispatch troops abroad.[36] Those not contracted may well have been eliminated because of observed shortcomings noted through personal assessments.

The *Centennial*, for example, failed to pass inspections in San Francisco and never joined the chartered transport fleet to the Philippines. The War Department looked to contract the ship from Peter Larsen of Seattle a little more than a month into the war. When the vessel docked at San Francisco's Folsom Street wharf on 4 June, the depot quartermaster and a medical board of survey conducted an examination for its fitness to carry troops. They reported considerable concern over the space allocated for soldiers, suggesting the ship needed "to be overhauled and entirely renovated before she will be ready for sea."[37]

Alerted to potential problems with the *Centennial*, Secretary Meiklejohn ordered an extensive inspection. MG Merritt reported that Lieutenant Lopez and Naval Constructor Snow found the ship unseaworthy.[38] In addition to limited troop space, the boilers' poor condition precluded the ship from joining the transport fleet.[39] Although the owners threatened to sue and the US Senate heard arguments as to possible collusion among shipowners in San Francisco, the *Centennial's* charter was not executed.[40]

Had legal action been taken, those representing the *Centennial* could not have based their argument on the premise that it was the only ship not taken after an inspection. Military authorities examined numerous vessels that never received a contract. Local newspapers reported that the *Belgic*, *Cleveland*, *Whitgift*, *Titania*, *Conemaugh*, and *Roanoke* underwent formal scrutiny, but the War Department declined to charter them.[41]

Major Oscar Long, the depot quartermaster, was another military officer in San Francisco who exerted considerable influence over the transport appropriation process. With the War Department having assigned the Quartermaster General responsibility for securing steamers, Long served a critical role at the expeditionary force's port of embarkation. Although ships were chartered in Washington, Long led the effort "to inspect them and to certify to their fitness."[42]

Through May into early June, Long and other inspectors often boarded vessels to evaluate specific areas related to transporting troops. The US Inspectors of Steam Vessels toured the first expedition's *City of Peking*, *City of Sydney*, and *Australia* "and found that the extra berths were properly made and that there were enough life-preservers on board."[43] A Sanitary Commission examination of the *Peking* contributed to MG Otis's decision to decrease the number of troops aboard given space restrictions.[44] A medical examining board that consisted of Army surgeons scrutinized the second expedition's *China*, *Colon*, and *Zealandia* before receiving orders to check the *Morgan City* and *Senator* "as to their capacity, sanitary condition and needed changes."[45]

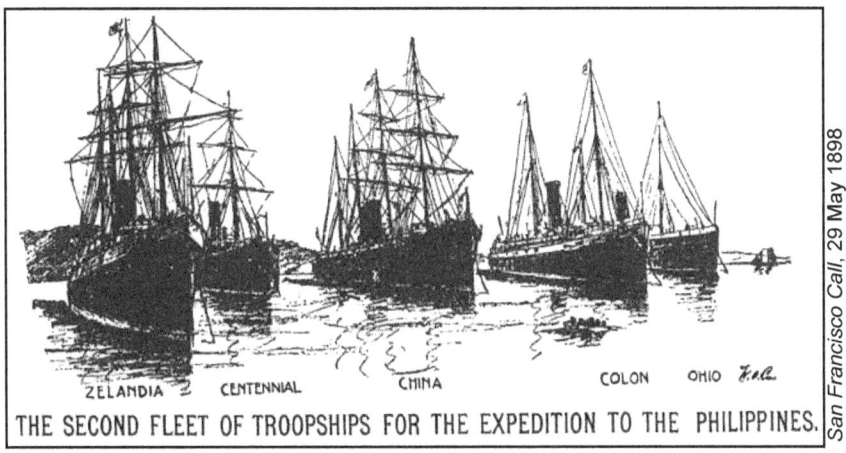

THE SECOND FLEET OF TROOPSHIPS FOR THE EXPEDITION TO THE PHILIPPINES.

Figure 91.

A day after Long and his medical survey team assessed the *Centennial*, two additional examinations were scheduled. Captain John H. Bermingham, supervising inspector of hulls and boilers, was scheduled to "go over the steamer and see that she conforms to all the requirements of law and a board of naval officers will see to it that she is fit to act as a United States troopship."[46]

Shortly after reporting the *Centennial's* shortcomings to Washington, MG Merritt reassessed the inspection process and appointed his own board "for the purpose of hastening the preparations" of the Philippine expeditions. Knowing Major Long, who never belonged to his command, to be overwhelmed "with the depot quartermaster's affairs," Merritt named two Army quartermasters and a Navy lieutenant to check vessels for transport suitability. The general, however, instructed his board to work closely with Long in their endeavor.[47] This board became a part of an inspection process that, by 19 June, the *Call* reported as constituted by "four examinations in all, and every one of the strictest character." Those included assessments that "officials of the Treasury Department, Navy Department, Medical Board and Quartermaster's Department" rendered.[48]

Merritt also instructed the quartermaster officers of his inspection team to perform one other Herculean task associated with deployment. The general ordered them "personally [to] superintend the fitting and preparation of the ships for the reception of troops." Merritt asserted that Major Long, as the depot quartermaster, would "provide the material and labor necessary for the outfitting of the ships" in addition to other required assistance.[49]

Transforming vessels into troop transports often required the performance of numerous tasks, depending on the findings of the several inspection teams. COL Charles Bird estimated that 10 days were required in San Francisco to prepare the steamers as oceanic troop carriers.[50] That figure likely did not include the amount of time taken to offload cargo on many vessels that docked in the city about the time their charters would take effect.

On 1 October 1898, Long wrote the Quartermaster General, "Our transports were provided with every modern convenience which intelligent foresight or thought could secure for the welfare and comfort of the troops."[51] Recalling the work done to chartered vessels during his duty tour in San Francisco, MG Otis wrote, "Cooking and cold-storage facilities were improved and enlarged; comfortable bunks and means of ventilation were provided; the vessels were thoroughly policed."[52]

While both officers' observations give a sense of what was generally accomplished to prepare transports, Major Long and his quartermaster peers supervised or observed considerably more work to prepare vessels for departure. First, ships were "thoroughly cleaned from stem to stern . . . then fumigated and otherwise disinfected."[53] Ships had to be coaled for the approximately 7,000-mile journey lasting 25 days.[54] Carpenters, joiners, and mechanics worked to paint; put up bunks; and build extra galleys, lavatories, and closets where needed.[55] Several ships stocked additional life preservers after the inspectors of steam vessels called for them.[56]

Stevedores and troops hauled aboard stores and unit equipment.[57] Supplies loaded on the four vessels of the second expedition included "boxes of roast beef, barrels of sugar, bags of salt and other provisions."[58] The *Daily Report* observed vessels in the third expedition taking on "canned goods of every kind, lumber, telegraph wire, barbed wire, lumberor houses, probably officer's quarters; cement, picks, shovels and wheelbarrows."[59]

Figure 92.

Sometimes the loading process did not go smoothly or was not thought through carefully. The *Daily Report* complained that for the first expedition's *City of Peking*, "the loading has proceeded very, very slowly, being done and undone, and done over again."[60] CPT W.E. Birkhimer, 3d US Infantry, who sailed on the third expedition's *Ohio*, wrote, "Nothing is plainer than this fact: in loading a vessel it is important to have everything conducted in a systematic, pre-arranged, and orderly manner, so that everything will have an ascertained place and be placed just there." Apparently, that advice had not been heeded when the *Ohio* was loaded. Birkhimer lamented, "There was not, perhaps, in the military community on board the ship, one person who did not, at various times during the voyage, have reason to regret the want of well established order in loading the supplies intended for this convenience or necessities."[61]

Some ships received special attention. For example, laborers lashed four 4-pound Hotchkiss guns to the deck of the *Peking* should some protection be needed against armed Spanish ships.[62] When the Utah Battery deployed with the second expedition, three of its guns remained intact, one each mounted aboard the *Colon, Zealandia,* and *China*.[63]

LOADING UTAH'S LIGHT ARTILLERY ON BOARD THE STEAMER CHINA.
Figure 93.

Selecting the Units

The US Army dispatched seven expeditions to the Philippines before 12 August. These deployments occurred as steamers became available. The first three expeditions, the only ones to participate in combat operations against the Spanish at Manila, traveled in clusters of three to five ships. Recognizing that the need for haste coupled with limited troopship availability precluded dispatching the entire command in one deployment, department officers had to make decisions on the organization of each force that sailed from San Francisco.

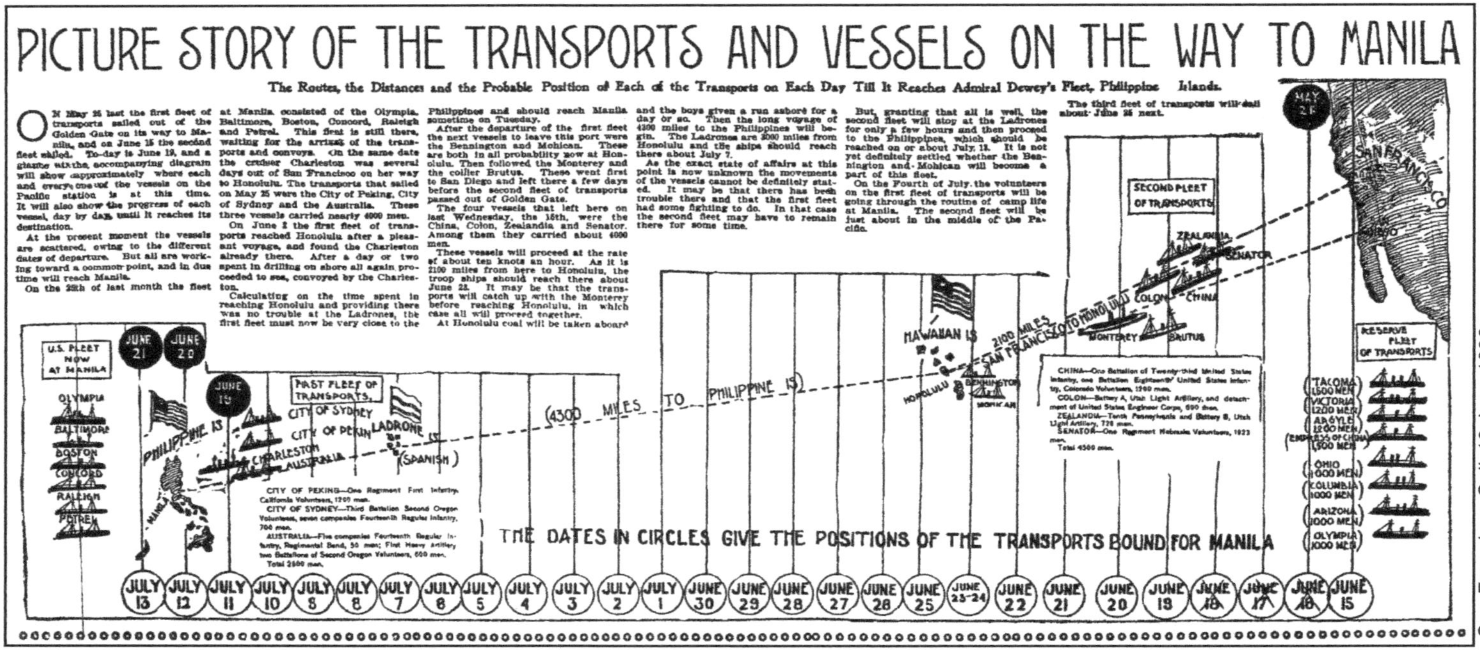

PICTURE STORY OF THE TRANSPORTS AND VESSELS ON THE WAY TO MANILA

The Routes, the Distances and the Probable Position of Each of the Transports on Each Day Till It Reaches Admiral Dewey's Fleet, Philippine Islands.

On May 25 last the first fleet of transports sailed out of the Golden Gate on its way to Manila, and on June 15 the second fleet sailed. To-day is June 19, and a glance at the accompanying diagram will show approximately where each and every one of the vessels on the Pacific station is at this time. It will also show the progress of each vessel, day by day, until it reaches its destination.

At the present moment the vessels are scattered, owing to the different dates of departure. But all are working toward a common point, and in due time will reach Manila.

On the 25th of last month the fleet at Manila consisted of the Olympia, Baltimore, Boston, Concord, Raleigh and Petrel. This fleet is still there, waiting for the arrival of the transports and convoys. On the same date the cruiser Charleston was several days out of San Francisco on her way to Honolulu. The transports that sailed on May 25 were the City of Peking, City of Sydney and the Australia. These three vessels carried nearly 4000 men.

On June 2 the first fleet of transports reached Honolulu after a pleasant voyage, and found the Charleston already there. After a day or two spent in drilling on shore all again proceeded to sea, convoyed by the Charleston.

Calculating on the time spent in reaching Honolulu and providing there was no trouble at the Ladrones, the first fleet must now be very close to the Philippines and should reach Manila sometime on Tuesday.

After the departure of the first fleet the next vessels to leave this port were the Bennington and Mohican. These are both in all probability now at Honolulu. Then followed the Monterey and the collier Brutus. These went first to San Diego and left there a few days before the second fleet of transports passed out of Golden Gate.

The four vessels that left here on last Wednesday, the 15th, were the China, Colon, Zealandia and Senator. Among them they carried about 4000 men.

These vessels will proceed at the rate of about ten knots an hour. As it is 2100 miles from here to Honolulu, the troop ships should reach there about June 23. It may be that the transports will catch up with the Monterey before reaching Honolulu, in which case all will proceed together.

At Honolulu coal will be taken aboard and the boys given a run ashore for a day or so. Then the long voyage of 4300 miles to the Philippines will begin. The Ladrones are 3000 miles from Honolulu and the ships should reach there about July 7.

As the exact state of affairs at this point is now unknown the movements of the vessels cannot be definitely stated. It may be that there has been trouble there and that the first fleet had some fighting to do. In that case the second fleet may have to remain there for some time.

But, granting that all is well, the second fleet will stop at the Ladrones for only a few hours and then proceed to the Philippines, which should be reached on or about July 13. It is not yet definitely settled whether the Bennington and Mohican will become a part of this fleet.

On the Fourth of July the volunteers on the first fleet of transports will be going through the routine of camp life at Manila. The second fleet will be just about in the middle of the Pacific.

The third fleet of transports will sail about June 25 next.

CITY OF PEKING—One Regiment First Infantry, California Volunteers, 1200 men.

CITY OF SYDNEY—Third Battalion Second Oregon Volunteers, seven companies Fourteenth Regular Infantry, 700 men.

AUSTRALIA—Five companies Fourteenth Regular Infantry, Regimental Band, 50 men; First Heavy Artillery two Battalions of Second Oregon Volunteers, 600 men.

Total 2500 men.

CHINA—One Battalion of Twenty-third United States Infantry, one Battalion Eighteenth United States Infantry, Colorado Volunteers, 1200 men.

COLON—Battery A, Utah Light Artillery, and detachment of United States Engineer Corps, 690 men.

ZEALANDIA—Tenth Pennsylvania and Battery B, Utah Light Artillery, 728 men.

SENATOR—One Regiment Nebraska Volunteers, 1923 men.

Total 4500 men.

San Francisco Call, 19 June 1898

Figure 94.

Some department leaders' decisions produced common features among numerous expeditions. General officers commanded the first four deployments and five of seven overall. Infantrymen sailed in numbers much greater than those of other service branches. State Volunteer organizations dominated the units composing each force, although Regulars formed the core.

REGULARS AND VOLUNTEERS MARCHING DOWN POST STREET. *The Examiner*, 15 June 1898

Figure 95.

Just as proximity to San Francisco became a key consideration for assigning a unit to MG Merritt's command, so, too, did this factor influence the makeup of the first expedition. On 14 May, in the absence of general officers at the Golden Gate, the War Department issued deployment orders to the 1st California and four companies of the 14th Infantry.[64] Although other California infantry and artillery Volunteers had reached San Francisco, only one steamer, the *City of Peking*, was available to carry abroad these troops and a small naval contingent. When military authorities on the West Coast reported that the *Australia* and *City of Sydney*, both chartered on 10 May, could be ready to sail with the *Peking* after 20 May, this development called for more troops to join the first expedition.[65]

MG Otis, who arrived in the city on 17 May, designated those troops. Two days later, after having "inspected the three vessels already chartered and casually the troops which have arrived," Otis designated "the regiment of Oregon volunteers now here and in fair shape" to sail with the 1st California and five companies of the 14th Regulars.[66] This decision would be the first of many that would leave troops bitter in the 7th California. From their perspective, the regiment would always be overlooked or ignored in favor of other state organizations that had more influence with military or political authorities.

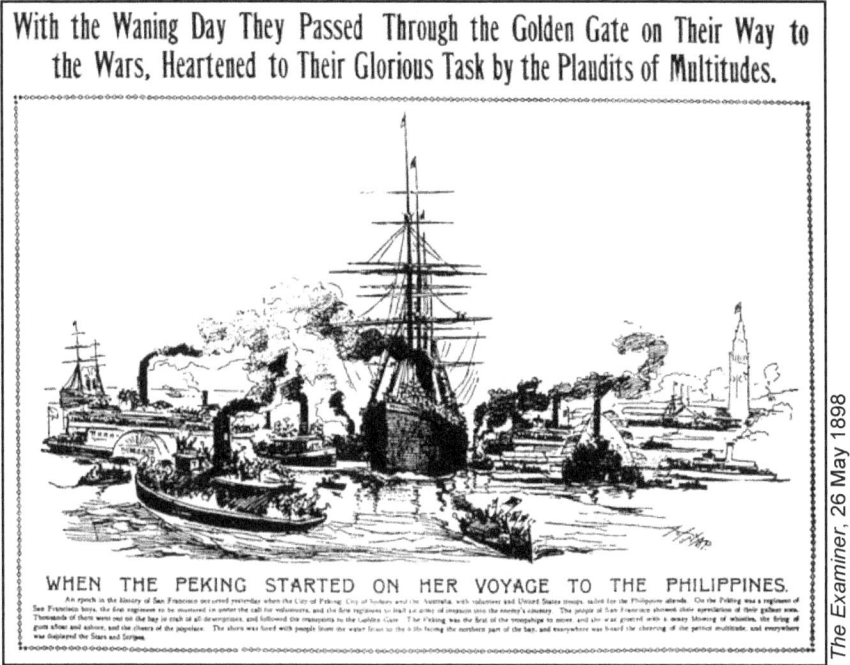

Figure 96.

In addition to these infantry units, Otis ordered deployed personnel representing two other service functions, the medical and artillery. He found sufficient space aboard the *Sydney* to billet hospital corpsmen. The general also manifested "an officer and 50 men detached from the battalion of heavy artillery California Volunteers, which includes all members who have any knowledge of the service of artillery."[67] Apparently Otis was not inspired by the "combined arms" concept that wedded two service functions on the battlefield. More appropriately, Private Charles R. Detrick, 1st California Infantry, suggested, "It was thought that with the taking of various strongholds of the Spaniards in the islands, the American forces would come into possession of much valuable ordnance, and the artillerymen would be needed to care for it, and even to man the captured cannon for use against the enemy."[68]

Regular infantry continued to form the core of the expeditionary forces in all subsequent deployments. Arriving in San Francisco on 29 May, the undermanned 18th and 23d Infantry Regiments each trained and prepared four companies for the second expedition that sailed on 15 June. Units from these two regiments that did not deploy remained in the city. They awaited recruits, some of whom were attached to four more companies from each

231

regiment that departed with the third expedition at the end of June. As the 18th and 23d Infantry continued to recruit and train new members of the regiment, five companies of the 14th Infantry either organized or arrived in the city to join the fourth expedition.[69]

When units from specific noninfantry service branches, whether Volunteer or Regular, arrived at the Golden Gate, Merritt and Otis frequently manifested them with the next force to leave San Francisco. This practice held true especially for artillerymen and engineers. Merritt had either requested or welcomed both kinds of troops in additional numbers.[70] The Astor Battery reached the city on 20 June and sailed with the third expedition on 27 June. An engineer company moved into camp on 29 May, then deployed in increments with the next two expeditions. Cavalrymen did not sail until the fourth expedition and failed to reach the archipelago before the peace protocol.[71]

With these priorities established, Merritt, Otis, and subsequently Merriam had to determine the deployment sequence of the state Volunteer infantry. After the first expedition, geography stopped favoring the selection of West Coast units to ship overseas. Volunteer organizations from Nebraska, Kansas, Wyoming, Colorado, Minnesota, Idaho, Utah, Pennsylvania, Montana, North Dakota, South Dakota, and Iowa reached San Francisco before 15 June and were available to be assigned to the second expedition. Given the paucity of transports to move troops, however, not all could go at once. Essentially, these organizations started on an equal footing in terms of being close to the port of embarkation. Other considerations, therefore, weighed more heavily in determining the composition of expeditions that deployed in June and July.

Militarily, the major discriminator dealt with unit readiness to deploy. From Merritt and Otis's viewpoint, the key component of readiness centered around state troops having the requisite individual and organizational equipment, including weapons and ammunition, to make the trip and stand garrison duty abroad. Neither of the expedition's most senior commanders conducted thorough troop inspections to determine readiness. Instead they depended on their inspectors general (IGs), COL Robert P. Hughes and CPT John S. Mallory, to assess the units encamped at San Francisco.

Mallory served on Otis's staff.[72] Shortly after reaching the city on 17 May, he began to examine the equipment at Camp Merritt and the Presidio. As the IG, Mallory scrutinized the 2d Oregon's haversacks and rifles and the 20th Kansas's tents and ovens.[73] Other commands stood ordnance inspection to determine their weapons' serviceability and whether state property could be federalized.[74] On 29 June, the *Call* reported that Mallory's inspection of National Guard weapons the 1st Tennessee brought revealed that most were "in a bad condition, and very few of them were accepted by him."[75]

After Hughes arrived in San Francisco to become Merritt's IG, the Department of the Pacific initiated a systematic inspection of all Volunteer infantry. These checks required organizations to move to the Presidio where they would be inspected in "heavy marching order" by both Hughes and Mallory. Private Karl Kraemer wrote that this formation called for troops to shoulder "blankets, haversacks, canteens and guns."[76] The *Chronicle* reported that the haversack was "a fifty-pound pack with everything needed for a campaign in the field."[77] For several weeks beginning 3 June, the team checked all Volunteer infantry in camp.[78] Their work provided an instant source of information for Merritt and Otis on the state of command readiness.

Newly Uniformed Infantry in Heavy Marching Order.

San Francisco Chronicle, 13 June 1898

Figure 97.

The two generals desperately needed this sort of unvarnished assessment of state Volunteer units. Several organizations presented incredibly positive, sometimes misleading, images of their logistics status to attain an overseas assignment. Writing after the 12 August protocol, Major Long observed that "in several instances those from States whose quotas were presumably perfectly equipped, and which had heralded their arrival by telegraphing in advance that they required nothing in this regard, were found, when their requisitions were filled, to be deficient in the most essential requirements of equipment. (This was the case with the Colorado, Iowa and Pennsylvania troops)."[79]

233

Dominated at first by logistics considerations, "readiness" evaluations did not initially include an assessment of a unit's drill proficiency. Three expeditions departed before the command established a procedure to appraise organizational training. On 27 June, two days before Merritt sailed for the Philippines, COL Hughes inspected and drilled the 7th California at the Presidio. The *Daily Report* noted that "each command has been assigned a day this week upon which it will have to go through the same maneuvers."[80] Hughes evaluated the 20th Kansas on 29 June and the 1st South Dakota on 30 June.[81] Drill proficiency then became a factor that could have influenced the selection of the 1st Montana and 1st South Dakota, the last two Volunteer regiments to sail for Manila before the United States and Spain signed the peace protocol.

While readiness to deploy may not have exclusively determined the precise order in which units sailed from San Francisco, this criterion was sufficient to award the lowest deployment priority to the 1st Tennessee. On 20 June, Merritt observed, "The Tennessee regiment, which just arrived, is completely destitute of equipment in any direction, and of instruction and drill to a great extent." He judged those Volunteers as "unlikely to be fit for some time to become a part in this expedition."[82]

Long wrote that along with the 1st Tennessee, the 20th Kansas and 1st Montana had arrived in San Francisco "almost entirely unequipped."[83] Merritt, too, found the 20th Kansas lacking, but for a different reason—regimental leadership. "The Kansas regiment has been here some time," Merritt noted, "and has made itself prominent by its want of capacity, so far as officers are concerned." He did, however, welcome the recent arrival of the regiment's commander, COL Frederick Funston, suggesting "the colonel may improve these conditions, but as it now stands the regiment is unfit to embark."[84] Funston worked to train and discipline his unit, but the effort did not expedite the Kansas Volunteers' deployment. Both the 20th Kansas and the 1st Tennessee were among the last units to sail for the Philippines in October and November 1898.[85]

Leadership, or more accurately leader preferences, may have accounted for the reason why specific units with readiness shortcomings deployed before others. Beginning with the second expedition, Merritt and Otis collaborated to choose the order in which Volunteer infantry would sail for Manila. They selected the 1st Colorado and 10th Pennsylvania, two regiments that Long judged "deficient in the most essential requirements of equipment" when they arrived in San Francisco on 21 and 25 May, respectively.[86] Quartermasters worked to erase these deficits, given the sailing priorities both general officers fixed.

Otis, who had most recently commanded the Department of the Colorado before his assignment to the Philippine expedition, showed a preference for Volunteers from the Rocky Mountain state shortly after his arrival. The *Daily Report* offered as an explanation for this policy, "General Otis was a resident of Denver for a long time, and is personally acquainted with a number of the officers of the Colorado regiment. He has seen the regiment at work and knows what he may expect of it." The newspaper suggested that the Coloradans would likely leave on the first available expedition.[87]

The newspaper surmised correctly. When an outbreak of measles threatened to eliminate the 2d Oregon from the first expedition, Otis recommended that the 1st Colorado take its place. In a telegraph to Corbin, Otis stated, "First Colorado, of full regimental strength, well equipped, well officered, and having superior medical officers, will arrive in morning, and I suggest that it be placed on vessel as soon as practicable."[88] Apparently, the measles did not spread within the Oregon regiment, and Otis discovered equipment shortfalls in the 1st Colorado. The 2d Oregon retained its position with the first expedition.

This outcome nevertheless failed to diminish Otis's advocacy of the Colorado Volunteers. On 24 May, he informed Corbin that "the Colorado, Minnesota, and Nebraska regiments are in fair condition; need to be outfitted with certain necessary stores not yet received, but arrive in two or three days. These regiments are being inspected to ascertain what ordnance is necessary. They can be placed in condition to sail early next week."[89]

The second expedition subsequently departed with the 1st Colorado and 1st Nebraska, but the 13th Minnesota gave way to the 10th Pennsylvania. One reason for the change may have been that limited space was available on the outgoing transports. If that were so, the smaller Pennsylvania regiment with 640 Volunteers may have been more feasibly manifested than the 13th Minnesota with 1,030 men.[90]

Yet another explanation acknowledges Merritt's preference for state troops from the East Coast. The 10th Pennsylvania came from one of the two largest National Guard programs in the country. The other belonged to New York, a state that subsequently provided a Volunteer regiment to garrison Hawaii. As commander, Department of the East, Merritt was familiar with both programs and had confidence in the abilities of units drawn from either state. The *Daily Report* claimed that "General Merritt has always been known to lean toward the Pennsylvania regiment, and was instrumental in having it brought hither."[91]

Aside from Merritt's preferences, the presence of the 10th Pennsylvania in San Francisco reflected the existence of political pressure in forming expeditions. Just as Congressman J.B. Showalter influenced the assignment of his state's regiment to Merritt's command, so, too, did other politicians urge specific units' inclusion in expeditions to the Philippines.[92] The *Chronicle* charged that officers from the 1st Nebraska solicited the aid of a senator and Assistant Secretary of War Meiklejohn, a former lieutenant governor and congressman from the state, to ensure that the organization sailed with the second expedition.[93]

This particular case was likely nothing more than allegation and coincidence, but plenty of evidence exists to indicate that prominent citizens and noted politicians sponsored organizations for subsequent expeditions. This pressure became quite overt in July, about the time Otis decided to man the fourth expedition with recruits that belonged to organizations that had already sailed. The fear was that the war would end before state Volunteers assembled in San Francisco could get overseas.

On 8 July, MG Otis urged that a California unit be sent into the Pacific to take station in Hawaii.[94] BG Corbin responded, "There is no objection to the Eighth California other than it is thought that as California has one regiment on the way to the Philippines the other States feel that details for service should be given to all the States alike. Two regiments from any one State are for these reasons objectionable. You have no idea the anxiety for service, and how any sign of favoritism is resented."[95] Decisions on assignments to locations in the Pacific were treated as discreetly as possible.

Essentially, the authorities in San Francisco began to receive strong suggestions from sources outside the Golden Gate on what units should go abroad. On 9 July, Secretary of War Alger advocated that the 1st South Dakota deploy.[96] Otis responded in the affirmative and the 1st South Dakota sailed with the sixth and seventh expeditions at the end of July.[97] From 10 July through 12 August, Merritt's command and the War Department entertained unsolicited requests on behalf of the 7th California, 8th California, 1st New York, 1st Montana, 51st Iowa, 20th Kansas, 1st Washington, and 1st Nevada.[98] By the end of November, all sailed for destinations in the Pacific except the two regiments from California. Neither organization deployed. As Corbin had reminded Otis, the 1st California had already sailed and represented the state overseas. (See appendix A.)

Restructuring the Camps and Commands

Troop organizations selected for expeditions often marched to the docks amidst the same pomp and ceremony that had characterized their arrival at the Golden Gate. The earliest departures were particularly noteworthy for the attention the San Francisco community gave them. Ordered on the first expedition, Private Charles Detrick, 1st California, wrote of his unit's march from the Presidio to the Pacific mail dock, "every foot of the way was crowded with the families, friends, and well-wishers of the boys."[99]

Figure 98.

June send-offs were comparably enthusiastic. The 1st Nebraska experienced a similar farewell according to its regimental scribe. Assigned to the *Senator* of the second expedition, the regiment marched from Camp Merritt on 14 June. The 1st Nebraska chronicler wrote, "In the settled portion of the city, and all the way down to the dock, the streets were literally packed with patriotic crowds; bands played inspiring music, steam whistles and calliopes were blown, and guns were fired, in honor of the passing troops." He added that near the ship "the Red Cross Society served an excellent supper, for which the men were highly grateful."[100]

A North Dakotan, First Sergeant Phil H. Shortt, described his organization's movement to the docks on 27 June. Shortt wrote of "the streets on the way to the steamer being filled with people who bade the regiment hearty farewells and wished it success and good luck. The scene at the wharf was beyond description. The docks were crowded with soldiers, and the ladies of the Red Cross were everywhere conspicuous."[101]

Figure 99. Volunteers on transport *Rio de Janeiro* leaving San Francisco for Manila.

Departures frequently necessitated restructuring campsites and reorganizing commands. After forces from the first expedition vacated their bivouac sites, Otis began to separate his Independent Division organizations from those belonging to Merriam's Department of California. At Camp Merritt, Otis maintained regiments, battalions, or detachments that were tentatively tagged for duty overseas. On the Presidio and at Fontana warehouse, Merriam retained the troops most likely to garrison Golden Gate posts or West Coast fortifications. In keeping with this concept, 7th California and 14th Infantry troops relocated to Richmond's Bay District Racetrack area in late May.[102] The 6th California and 1st Washington remained at the Presidio and Fontana sites, respectively, since both organizations would see garrison duty in the Golden Gate region through the end of hostilities with Spain.

Upon reaching San Francisco after the first expedition sailed, Merritt ordered the Independent Division organized into major subordinate commands. Led by MG Otis, the division separated into four brigades composed of all organizations identified for service in the Pacific. Senior regimental commanders who had reached the city by 30 May took charge of each brigade.[103]

In the days surrounding the departure of two expeditions in June, the division reorganized to accommodate changes in brigade leadership and composition. Three days before the second expedition sailed on 15 June, Otis revamped his division's structure. He named newly appointed brigadier generals to command each of his four brigades. He dropped units that sailed from the existing organization, retained all Regulars in the 1st Brigade, and placed the two least ready regiments, the 20th Kansas and 1st Tennessee, into the 2d Brigade.[104] About the time the third expedition and MG Merritt sailed in late June, Otis reorganized again. With the departures of one of his brigade commanders, BG Arthur MacArthur, and additional Volunteer and Regular forces, Otis consolidated the division into three brigades.[105]

Figure 100.

The most dramatic reorganizations within commands at the Golden Gate occurred when flotillas left the bay in July. As Otis prepared to leave with the fourth expedition on the 15th, he relinquished "command of all troops in this vicinity known as the 'Expeditionary Forces'" to the current 1st Brigade commander, BG Marcus P. Miller.[106] In a separate order, Otis directed that for the near term, units still in the city were to "be re-brigaded and constitute at least two brigades under division formation."[107] Miller saw to those details when, on 20 July, he closed out the 3rd Brigade and assigned Volunteer regiments to the remaining two.[108]

Major-General Otis Issues His Last Order at Headquarters

Figure 101.

San Francisco Chronicle, 16 July 1898

Otis's departure signaled one other major change in the command structure. After 15 July, the Department of the Pacific stopped exercising direct control over the Independent Division in San Francisco. In the absence of both Merritt and Otis, the department's highest-ranking officers, the War Department transferred authority over the division to MG Henry C. Merriam. On 10 July, Secretary of War Alger ordered that the "remaining troops heretofore destined for the Philippines will, until return transportation or other orders issued, report to the commanding general Department of California for his orders."[109] Merriam therefore resumed control over the command he had originally influenced for only a few days in May.

Merriam assumed his additional responsibilities as departures for the Philippines and the occupation of Bay Area defenses invited the restructuring of existing encampments. Nearly two weeks before Merriam took control of the Independent Division, four major campsites in the city had been reduced to three. The last troops to occupy Fontana's warehouse departed on 2 July when the 1st Battalion, 1st Washington, ferried to Angel Island to man defense works.¹¹⁰ Actually, the troop exodus from Fontana had begun only days after the California Heavy Artillery and 1st Washington occupied the structure during the second week of May. On 16 May, "a sharp report like that of a rifle shot" stirred troops trying to sleep on the second story's hardwood floor. Believing the structure about to collapse, all 600 artillerymen emptied Fontana and anxiously spent a night under the stars.¹¹¹

Figure 102.

Private Charles R. Detrick, 1st California, described the building as "a ramshackle affair" where the wind and fog rushed through its broken windows. Detrick hypothesized that troops who had trained inside the warehouse had loosened joints holding the second story's hardwood floor together.¹¹² The *Examiner* rendered similar observations, but also suggested that boisterous play may have taken its toll. The newspaper reported, "The march step of hundreds of men has had a tendency to shake the floors pretty lively. A few days ago 300 men indulged in a tug of war contest on the second floor. They shook things up so lively that the officers compelled them to cease the sport."[113] A civil engineer with the Department of California investigated and deemed the structure safe. He surmised that the cracking noises were caused by wood "'checking' from the heat engendered by a number of stoves" the Red Cross provided to keep the troops warm.[114]

The engineer's report failed to mollify artillerymen who were only too ready to bid farewell to Fontana. They relocated into permanent barracks at the Presidio on 18 May.[115] Unlike their California comrades, Volunteers from the 1st Washington never found the warehouse disagreeable. They remained billeted in the structure with Merriam's blessing until ordered out in early July. Adjutant William L. Luhn, 1st Washington, wrote, "The 1st and 2d Battalions in Fontana Barracks were very comfortably quartered compared to the many troops who were put in camp on the sand hills of San Francisco, known as Camp Merritt."[116]

That particular encampment, which included two sites in the Richmond District, referred to as the Bay District Racetrack and Jordan Tract, had become a target for criticism from several sources in the San Francisco area. Coincidentally, this scrutiny intensified as expeditions departed, reducing the number of troops bivouacked in the area. Ironically, the officer most active in establishing the Richmond encampment, MG Merriam, regained control over Camp Merritt and its troops in mid-July when objections to the area reached their zenith.

For more than a month leading up to that point, local newspapers ran articles and editorials that faulted Richmond sites and urged improvements to the Presidio. On 8 June, the *Daily Report* announced that Richmond citizens were about to petition MG Otis for help. The article observed that "the presence of 14,000 soldiers in Richmond has given local business a boom and in various ways benefited the region." The reporter nevertheless proclaimed that "some of the soldiers who patronize the saloons are getting a little too lively for the peace and comfort of quiet and orderly citizens. . . . There is another nuisance in the camp—the cesspool nuisance—which the people of Richmond are anxious to see abated."[117]

On 9 June, the *Chronicle* ran an editorial exposing the "sanitary, moral and military" shortcomings of Camp Merritt. First, filthy sinks dug in lieu of sewers posed a sanitation hazard by threatening the troops' "health and that of the city." Second, unlike the Presidio, this encampment stood on private property divided by city streets. Sentinels had no power to close thoroughfares into the camp. The inability to close streets poisoned the camps' moral environment by giving access to those the newspaper described as "disreputable people of both sexes." Just across the same streets, soldiers could find ample intoxicants available in numerous saloons or groggeries. Third, the camps were not conducive to military training. With 11,159 Volunteers and Regulars spread out over both Richmond sites, units had no place to drill unless they marched to Golden Gate Park or the Presidio.[118]

That same theme ran through editorials and articles of other newspapers. The *Call* questioned why the Army continued to maintain Camp Merritt and not work to accommodate more troops on the large military reservation by the bay.[119] A *Daily Report* editorialist urged the military to develop the Presidio for use as a campsite and warned that Camp Merritt invited "trouble" between soldiers and civilians.[120]

The newspapers found allies among others in San Francisco who joined in questioning the military's encampment decisions. On 20 June, a *Daily Report* editorial revealed that the city's Board of Health had warned that Camp Merritt, "owing to its lack of sewerage, threatened to cause an epidemic."[121] Acting on this report, the San Francisco Board of Supervisors, led by Mayor James Phelan, prepared a resolution for Secretary of War Alger. Reprinted in the *Chronicle*, the resolution stated that military authorities had established a camp "on private and unsewered blocks directly to the windward of the most populous portion of the city." Through their resolution, the board argued that "the placing of from 10,000 to 12,000 soldiers on these city blocks unnecessarily exposes the soldiers to demoralizing influences and also menaces their sanitary welfare and that of the city." City supervisors maintained that the military had actually few options other than to establish sites in the Richmond District because of the Presidio's inability to host a large body of troops. The supervisors urged Secretary Alger to support the kind of improvements to the Presidio that would lead to a greater accommodation of forces on the military reservation.[122]

Another development likely inspired the Board of Supervisors to act. After President McKinley issued a second call for Volunteers, California brought another regiment into federal service. Instead of joining their comrades at San Francisco encampments, members of the 8th California established their bivouac site in Oakland. In an article published on 22 June, the *Chronicle* quoted regimental commander COL Park Henshaw for an explanation of the site selection. Henshaw stated, "The reason for selecting some place other than San Francisco for the rendezvous is the desire to have a quiet and comparatively isolated spot where the men will be free from outside influence. They will be given all that is necessary for their welfare, and, being removed from temptations, will be better able to devote their time and attention to drills and military discipline."[123] Then, after the third expedition departed, the *Call* reported on 3 July that "Oakland residents are making a strong effort to have the First New York located here."[124] This particular regiment had recently been added to Merritt's command and was making its way west.

Still in command of the force at Camp Merritt, MG Otis took steps to address several of the problems that San Francisco papers and political authorities identified. On 23 June, he ordered all sinks in the Richmond encampment disinfected and that "Brigade Commanders will see to it that the sinks of each organization of their respective brigades are inspected daily by the regimental surgeon or medical officer attached."[125] By 1 July, he accepted the appointment of Major W.S.H. Matthews, 51st Iowa, as inspecting surgeon of Camp Merritt.[126] Soon after, Matthews' observations on the sanitary conditions of the camp found their way into the *Daily Report*. A new voice could be added to those heretofore nonmilitary sources arguing for changes at the camps.

On 5 July, the *Daily Report* commented on Matthews' efforts to assist the 1st Tennessee with its sinks. The paper's correspondent summarized, "No notice has been taken of this by the officers, and nothing toward remedying this evil undertaken. The odor from the sinks is bad enough when they are covered, and as they are at present it is intolerable."[127] A day later, the same newspaper revealed that Matthews ordered more sinks prepared, and then quoted him, "If we were to stay here for only a week or ten days more that might be good enough, but when we shall have to stay here or somewhere in this neighborhood for a month at least, as the prospects at present are, the only safe thing to do is to remove the camp."[128]

On 7 July, four days after Oakland announced its effort to acquire the 1st New York, Matthews rendered an official report to the division's chief surgeon, stating, "I have made an inspection of Camp Merritt and find that the sanitary conditions and the health of the men in this camp is not what it should be."[129] Still the camp did not move, nor were preparations made to improve the Presidio as a bivouac site.

The 1st New York's arrival on 13 and 14 July changed the situation. COL Thomas Barber, the regiment's commanding officer, objected to the Camp Merritt grounds where the 1st New York was assigned. Formerly occupied by the 23d Infantry since 29 May and only recently vacated, the block area was "one stretch of dry sand, mixed with debris and decayed matter." Barber ordered a sanitary inspection by his regimental surgeon who subsequently reported "that a permanent encampment at the place allotted to the First New York would be a menace to the health of the men."[130]

Barber took his concerns directly to MG Otis in the Phelan Building. He requested that the 1st New York relocate onto the Presidio reservation. In one of his final decisions as commander of the expeditionary forces assembled in San Francisco, Otis concurred. His decision was made easier in part because of the New York regiment's official status. Barber's infantry was bound for Honolulu. Hawaii fell within the Department of California's jurisdiction; any unit assigned duties there belonged to MG Merriam. Units assigned to the Department of California were quartered on the Presidio or at coast defense sites. Moving the 1st New York onto the Presidio could therefore be justified as assigning the organization to its parent headquarters.[131] Merriam approved Barber's appeal as well, and the New Yorkers established their bivouac at the Presidio on 15 July, the same day Otis sailed for the Philippines.[132]

Relocation fueled more protests over the Richmond camps' continued existence. On 16 July, Hugh Craig, president, San Francisco Chamber of Commerce, renewed his crusade to condemn Camp Merritt. He and other San Francisco businessmen had to be concerned about Oakland's challenge to secure military camps. The longer Richmond encampments existed, the greater the chance that military or political authorities could decide to relocate across the bay. This action would be a blow to San Francisco's commerce.

In early June, Craig had asked Secretary of War Alger for assistance in this endeavor, only to be referred to the local commander. This time he wired President McKinley. His message dated 16 July read: "Camp Merritt, in San Francisco, has been condemned by our Board of Supervisors because of its unsanitary condition, protested against by the neighbors, and is a blot upon the Administration. The ladies of the Red Cross are heartbroken at the increasing mortality, entirely unnecessary. The New York regiment, just arrived, would not accept quarters there and is now camped at the Presidio." He asked the president "to compel the removal of this disgraceful condition of affairs," while promising that the chamber would "sewer and supply with fresh water the Presidio grounds."[133]

Craig realized at least part of the solution that he desired. On 18 July, the AG, BG Corbin telegraphed MG Merriam: "Secretary War further directs that Camp Merritt be abandoned and these troops be placed in camp on the Presidio Reservation."[134] Alger's directive, however, did not mark the end but rather "the beginning of the end" for Camp Merritt. Merriam received no timetable for closing the Richmond sites. The Presidio could not be transformed hastily to accommodate all the troops in San Francisco awaiting deployment. Repositioning the forces too quickly would overburden the military installation's services. Merriam decided to gradually withdraw from the city, starting with displacing the division hospital to a barracks at the Presidio on 21 July. After three more expeditions departed with troops by 29 July, Merriam began to transfer regiments out of Richmond. Camp Merritt ceased to exist on 26 August when the last troops marched onto the Presidio.[135]

One of the military's remarkable accomplishments was acquiring ocean transports for Merritt's command. Quartermasters on both coasts and generals at the Golden Gate secured suitable vessels for Regulars and Volunteers. Each vessel was inspected for safety threats and health risks. Not all available ships were chartered or purchased. Some accepted into service had to be refurbished before admitting passengers and commencing the voyage.

The transportation challenge created an associated problem. The Department of the Pacific had to determine the order in which units deployed overseas. Merritt and Otis ultimately designated Regular infantry companies as the core of each expedition. Around this nucleus the generals added sections of Army medical personnel, artillerymen, and engineers as they became available. State Volunteer infantry constituted most of each deploying force. The order in which Volunteer units sailed depended on diverse criteria—proximity to the coast, logistics preparedness, drill proficiency, political influence, and general officers' preferences.

As the Department of the Pacific's strength dwindled about the Golden Gate, commanders reassessed the need for campsites. Originally established in four locations, bivouac areas increasingly became the subject of criticism levied by businessmen, newspaper reporters, local citizens, and some military officials. These groups advocated consolidating the troops on the Presidio reservation. Successive deployments reduced the number of military organizations remaining in the San Francisco area, which created the opportunity to close encampments. Toward the end of July, commanders began to move troops to the Presidio. All of the troops would eventually move out of city camps and relocate, either overseas or on the Presidio, but not before a peace protocol ended hostilities between the United States and Spain.

Notes

1. US Navy Department, Dewey to Secretary of the Navy, Hongkong, 7 May 1898, (Manila, 1 May), *Annual Reports of the Navy Department for the Year 1898, Appendix to the Report of the Chief of the Bureau of Navigation* (Washington, DC: US Government Printing Office [GPO], 1898), 68.

2. US Navy Department, Dewey to Secretary of the Navy, Hongkong, 7 May 1898, (Cavite 4 May), *Annual Reports of the Navy Department for the Year 1898*, 68.

3. Testimony of Colonel Charles Bird, Quartermaster, U.S. Volunteers, 2 December 1898, in US Senate, *Report of the Commission Appointed by the President to Investigate the Conduct of the War Department in the War With Spain*, volume VI, *Testimony* (Washington, DC: GPO, 1900), hereafter cited as *Report VI*, 2612.

4. US War Department, *Annual Reports of the War Department for the Fiscal Year Ended June 30, 1898, Report of the Secretary of War, Miscellaneous Reports*, Report of the Quartermaster-General of the Army (Washington, DC: GPO, 1898), 442-43.

5. Letter, Major Oscar Long to Quartermaster General, 25 August 1898, in Record Group 92, Office of the Quartermaster General, Document File 1800-1914, Document No. 115533 (Washington, DC: National Archives), 4; Telegram, Merriam, Major-General, to Adjutant-General, Washington, D.C., 9 August 1898 (Received 8:31 p.m.) in *Correspondence Relating to the War With Spain and Conditions Growing Out of the Same, Including the Insurrection in the Philippine Islands and the China Relief Expedition, Between the Adjutant-General of the Army and Military Commander in the United States, Cuba, Porto Rico, China, and the Philippine Islands, From April 15, 1898, to July 30, 1902*, volume II (Washington, DC: GPO, 1902), hereafter cited as *Correspondence II*, 748; Telegram, Merriam, Major-General, to Adjutant-General, Washington, D.C., 9 August 1898 (Received 9:28 p.m.) in *Correspondence II*, 748.

6. US Navy Department, Long to Dewey, Washington, 7 May 1898, in *Annual Reports of the Navy Department for the Year 1898*, 69.

7. US Navy Department, Report of the Secretary of the Navy in *Annual Reports of the Navy Department for the Year 1898, Report of the Secretary of the Navy, Miscellaneous Reports*, 21. "The City of Peking," *San Francisco Daily Report*, 5 May 1898, 1; "Why These Long Delays," *San Francisco Daily Report*, 21 May 1898, 7; "The Peking Arrives," *The Examiner*, 10 May 1898, 3.

8. John D. Long, Secretary, to the Honorable, the Secretary of War, Washington, 12 May 1898, in *Correspondence II*, 637.

9. US Navy Department, Dewey to Secretary of the Navy, Hongkong, 15 May 1898 (Cavite, 13 May), in *Annual Reports of the Navy Department for the Year 1898*, 97-98; H.C. Corbin, Adjutant-General, to General Merriam, Washington, 13 May 1898, in *Correspondence II*, 639.

10. US War Department, *Annual Reports of the War Department for the Fiscal Year Ended June 30, 1898, Report of the Secretary of War, Miscellaneous*

Reports, Quartermaster Department's Synopsis (Washington, DC: GPO, 1898), 172.

11. Testimony of Colonel Charles Bird, in *Report VI*, 2612-13; Testimony of Brigadier-General Marshall I. Ludington, Quartermaster-General, 16 December 1898, in US Senate, *Report of the Commission Appointed by the President to Investigate the Conduct of the War Department in the War With Spain*, volume VII, *Testimony* (Washington, DC: GPO, 1900), hereafter cited as *Report VII*, 3155; Telegram, Otis to Adjutant-General, U.S. Army, 21 May 1898, 11:20 p.m., in *Correspondence II*, 667-68; Telegram, Hugh C. Wallace to G.D. Meiklejohn, 25 May 1898 (Received 4:26 p.m.), in *Correspondence II*, 672; Telegram, Otis to Adjutant-General, U.S. Army, 8 July 1898 (Received 7:10 p.m.), in *Correspondence II*, 721-22; Telegram, H.C. Corbin to Major-General Otis, 10 July 1898, in *Correspondence II*, 725; "To Increase the Army at Bay District," *San Francisco Call*, 1 June 1898, 5; "Transports Hard to Find on the Coast," *San Francisco Chronicle*, 24 May 1898, 4; "More Ships Are Secured," *San Francisco Chronicle*, 8 June 1898, 5; "Major Long May Take any Pacific Vessel," *San Francisco Chronicle*, 22 June 1898, 3; "Centennial Rejected," *San Francisco Daily Report*, 8 June 1898, 3; "Chartering Transports," *San Francisco Daily Report*, 9 June 1898, 3.

12. *Biographical Directory of the American Congress, 1774-1996* (Alexandria, VA: CQ Staff Directories, 1997), 1509; *Who Was Who in America*, volume 1, 1897-1942 (Chicago: Marquis Who's Who, 1943), 828.

13. Testimony of Colonel Charles Bird, Quartermaster, U.S. Volunteers, 2 December 1898, in *Report VI*, 2607.

14. Ibid., 2613.

15. US War Department, *Annual Reports of the War Department for the Fiscal Year Ended June 30, 1898*, Report of the Secretary of War, Miscellaneous Reports, Quartermaster Department's Synopsis, 172; Ibid., Report of the Quartermaster-General of the Army, 388.

16. Otis to Adjutant-General, U.S. Army, 24 May 1898 (Received 5:24 p.m.), in *Correspondence II*, 671.

17. W. Merritt to Adjutant-General, 2 June 1898 (Received 4:56 p.m.), in *Correspondence II*, 685-86.

18. Merritt to Adjutant-General, 6 June 1898 (Received 6:30 p.m.), in *Correspondence II*, 691-92.

19. "General Merritt on the Shortage of Transports," *San Francisco Call*, 7 June 1898, 7.

20. Erna Risch, *Quartermaster Support of the Army: A History of the Corps, 1775-1939* (Washington, DC: Office of the Quartermaster General, 1962), 546; Testimony of Colonel Frank Hecker, Quartermaster, U.S. Volunteers, 7 December 1898, in *Report VI*, 2786.

21. By 29 May, the McKinley administration determined that 20,000 troops would comprise the Philippine expeditionary force. See H.C. Corbin to Major-General Merritt, 29 May 1898, in *Correspondence II*, 680.

22. US War Department, *Annual Reports of the War Department for the*

Fiscal Year Ended June 30, 1898, *Report of the Secretary of War*, *Miscellaneous Reports*, Report of the Quartermaster-General of the Army, 437.

23. Testimony of Colonel Frank Hecker, Quartermaster, U.S. Volunteers, 7 December 1898, in *Report VI*, 2767-68; US War Department, *Annual Reports of the War Department for the Fiscal Year Ended June 30, 1898*, *Report of the Secretary of War*, *Miscellaneous Reports*, Quartermaster Department's Synopsis, 173.

24. Testimony of Colonel Frank Hecker, Quartermaster, U.S. Volunteers, 7 December 1898, in *Report VI*, 2786-88.

25. H.C. Corbin to Major-General Merritt, 7 June 1898, in *Correspondence II*, 692.

26. W. Merritt to The Adjutant-General, U.S. Army, 6 July 1898 (Received 21 July 1898), in *Correspondence II*, 737.

27. Frank J. Hecker to Brig. Gen. H.C. Corbin, 27 July 1898, in *Correspondence II*, 741.

28. H.C. Corbin to the Commanding General, Eighth Army Corps and Department of the Pacific, 29 July 1898, in *Correspondence II*, 742.

29. Otis to Adjutant-General, U.S. Army, 18 May 1898 (Received 19 May 1898, 6:45 a.m.), in *Correspondence II*, 659-60.

30. H.C. Corbin to Gen. E.S. Otis, U.S. Army, 19 May 1898, in *Correspondence II*, 661.

31. Otis to Adjutant-General, U.S. Army, 21 May 1898, 11:20 p.m., in *Correspondence II*, 667-68; H.C. Corbin to Major-General Merritt, 31 May 1898, in *Correspondence II*, 683.

32. Otis to Adjutant-General, U.S. Army, 8 July 1898 (Received 7:10 p.m.), in *Correspondence II*, 721-22; Otis to Adjutant-General, U.S. Army, 8 July 1898 (Received 10:41 p.m.), in *Correspondence II*, 722.

33. H.C. Corbin to Gen E.S. Otis, 7 July 1898, in *Correspondence II*, 720; Otis to Adjutant-General, U.S. Army, 8 July 1898 (Received 7:10 p.m.), in *Correspondence II*, 721-22; Long to Quartermaster-General, 9 July 1898, in *Correspondence II*, 722.

34. "Hawaiian Annexation Changes All Plans," *San Francisco Chronicle*, 10 July 1898, 23.

35. H.C. Corbin to Major-General Otis, 10 July 1898, in *Correspondence II*, 725.

36. Letter, E.S. Otis to Col. Charles Denby, 19 November 1898, in US Senate, *Report of the Commission Appointed by the President to Investigate the Conduct of the War Department in the War with Spain*, volume VIII, *Correspondence* (Washington, DC: GPO, 1900), hereafter cited as *Report VIII*, 179.

37. "Held Back by Slight Repairs," *The Examiner*, 5 June 1898, 15; "Something About the Transport Centennial," *San Francisco Chronicle*, 5 June 1898, 23.

38. "Centennial's Charter Promptly Canceled," *San Francisco Chronicle*, 8 June 1898, 5; "Centennial Rejected," *San Francisco Daily Report*, 8 June 1898, 3.

39. "Transports are Waiting," *San Francisco Daily Report*, 7 June 1898, 3.

40. "Coast Ship-Owners Sharply Criticised," *San Francisco Chronicle*, 10 June 1898, 7; "Centennial's Owners May Sue Uncle Sam," *San Francisco Chronicle*, 11 June 1898, 11.

41. "The Transport Fleet," *The Examiner*, 11 May 1898, 3; "More Steamers to be Seized," *The Examiner*, 3 July 1898, 22; "More Ships for Manila," *San Francisco Daily Report*, 11 May 1898, 3; "Looking for Ships," *San Francisco Daily Report*, 1 June 1898, 2; "Chartering Transports," *San Francisco Daily Report*, 9 June 1898, 3; "Ships to be Seized," *San Francisco Chronicle*, 3 July 1898, 24.

42. "Cause of Delay," *San Francisco Daily Report*, 4 June 1898, 2.

43. "Brief Military Items," *San Francisco Chronicle*, 26 May 1898, 2.

44. Otis to Adjutant-General, U.S. Army, 19 May 1898 (Received 20 May 1898, 2:05 a.m.), in *Correspondence II*, 663; "Zealandia Chartered for Manila—Duty for Naval Reserves," *San Francisco Call*, 21 May 1898, 5.

45. "Transports for Manila," *San Francisco Call*, 9 June 1898, 5.

46. "Overhauling Troopships Improperly Fitted Up for Service," *San Francisco Call*, 4 June 1898, 7; "The Transports," *San Francisco Daily Report*, 17 June 1898, 1.

47. "Five Transports Will Soon be Ready," *San Francisco Chronicle*, 10 June 1898, 9; "Merritt Has Orders to Hurry to Dewey's Aid," *San Francisco Chronicle*, 11 June 1898, 9; "Inspection of Transports," *San Francisco Daily Report*, 10 June 1898, 3.

48. "Why the Brigade was Reorganized," *San Francisco Call*, 19 June 1898, 7.

49. "Inspection of Transports," *San Francisco Daily Report*, 10 June 1898, 3; "Five Transports Will Soon be Ready," *San Francisco Chronicle*, 10 June 1898, 9; "Merritt Has Orders to Hurry to Dewey's Aid," *San Francisco Chronicle*, 11 June 1898, 9.

50. Testimony of Colonel Charles Bird, Quartermaster, U.S. Volunteers, 2 December 1898, in *Report VI*, 2622-23.

51. Letter, Oscar F. Long to Quartermaster General, 1 October 1898, in Record Group 92, Office of the Quartermaster General, Document File 1800-1914, Document No. 120579, 3.

52. Letter, E.S. Otis to Col. Charles Denby, 19 November 1898, in *Report VIII*, 179.

53. "Why the Brigade Was Reorganized," *San Francisco Call*, 19 June 1898, 7.

54. "The Delayed Transports," *San Francisco Daily Report*, 13 May 1898, 2; "Transports Not Ready," *San Francisco Daily Report*, 16 May 1898, 2; "No Hurry Anywhere," *San Francisco Daily Report*, 17 May 1898, 3; "Dawdling at the Docks," *San Francisco Daily Report*, 18 May 1898, 3; "The Transports," *San Francisco Daily Report*, 3 June 1898, 2; "Slow Work on Transports," *San Francisco Daily Report*, 20 June 1898, 2; "The Transports," *San Francisco Daily Report*, 22 June 1898, 1; "Putting Stores on the Transports," *San Francisco Daily Report*, 9 July 1898, 2; "Fitting-Up the City of Peking for Duty with the Manila Expedition," *San Francisco Chronicle*, 18 May 1898, 3; "More Ships to Carry

Men," *San Francisco Call*, 9 June 1898, 5; "Going With a Rush," *San Francisco Call*, 21 June 1898, 5.

55. "Getting Ready for Manila," *San Francisco Call*, 12 May 1898, 5; "The Manila Expedition," *San Francisco Call*, 17 May 1898, 7; "More Ships to Carry Men," *San Francisco Call*, 9 June 1898, 5; "Ships in the Stream and Ready," *San Francisco Call*, 15 June 1898, 1; "Going With a Rush," *San Francisco Call*, 21 June 1898, 5; "Fitting-Up the City of Peking for Duty With the Manila Expedition," *San Francisco Chronicle*, 18 May 1898, 3; "Ocean Greyhound City of Peking, Now Fitting as a Troopship," *The Examiner*, 18 May 1898, 2; "The Delayed Transports," *San Francisco Daily Report*, 13 May 1898, 2; "Transports Not Ready," *San Francisco Daily Report*, 16 May 1898, 2; "No Hurry Anywhere," *San Francisco Daily Report*, 17 May 1898, 3; "Dawdling at the Docks," *San Francisco Daily Report*, 18 May 1898, 3; "The Transports," *San Francisco Daily Report*, 3 June 1898, 2; "The Delayed Transports," *San Francisco Daily Report*, 6 June 1898, 3; "The Four Transports Nearly Ready," *San Francisco Daily Report*, 16 June 1898, 1; "Slow Work on Transports," *San Francisco Daily Report*, 20 June 1898, 2; "Putting Stores on the Transports," *San Francisco Daily Report*, 9 July 1898, 2.

56. "Brief Military Items," *San Francisco Chronicle*, 26 May 1898, 2.

57. "Making Ready Ships for the Troops," *San Francisco Chronicle*, 16 May 1898, 5; "Fitting-Up the City of Peking for Duty With the Manila Expedition," *San Francisco Chronicle*, 18 May 1898, 3; "Hope to Sail by Tomorrow," *San Francisco Chronicle*, 21 May 1898, 9; "No Hurry Anywhere," *San Francisco Daily Report*, 17 May 1898, 3; "More Ships to Carry Men," *San Francisco Call*, 9 June 1898, 5; "At Camp Merritt," *San Francisco Daily Report*, 18 June 1898, 2; "Slow Work on Transports," *San Francisco Daily Report*, 20 June 1898, 2; "More Transports for Manila," *San Francisco Daily Report*, 8 July 1898, 3; "Putting Stores on the Transports," *San Francisco Daily Report*, 9 July 1898, 2.

58. "Four Transports Loaded and Waiting for the Regiments Bound to Manila," *San Francisco Chronicle*, 14 June 1898, 12.

59. "The Transports," *San Francisco Daily Report*, 22 June 1898, 1.

60. "Why These Long Delays," *San Francisco Daily Report*, 21 May 1898, 7.

61. Captain W.E. Birkhimer, "Transportation of Troops by Sea," *Journal of the Military Service Institution of the United States*, volume XXIII, 1898, 439-40.

62. "Arming of the City of Peking," *San Francisco Call*, 16 May 1898, 8; "Ocean Greyhound City of Peking, Now Fitting as a Troopship," *The Examiner*, 18 May 1898, 2; "Dawdling at the Docks," *San Francisco Daily Report*, 18 May 1898, 3.

63. "Preparing to Sail," *San Francisco Call*, 13 June 1898, 5.

64. Corbin to Col. James A. Smith, 14 May 1898, in *Correspondence II*, 640; Corbin to Commanding Officer, Battalion Fourteenth U.S. Infantry, 14 May 1898, in *Correspondence II*, 640.

65. Field to Adjutant-General, U.S. Army, 14 May 1898 (Received 11:48 p.m.), in *Correspondence II*, 643; Long to Quartermaster-General, 17 May 1898

(Received 8:23 p.m.), in *Correspondence II*, 653-54; Long to Quartermaster-General, 17 May 1898 (Received 8:50 p.m.), in *Correspondence II*, 654; Otis to Adjutant-General, U.S. Army, 18 May 1898 (Received 19 May 1898, 6:45 a.m.), 659-60.

66. Otis to Adjutant-General, U.S. Army, 18 May 1898 (Received 19 May 1898, 6:45 a.m.), in *Correspondence II*, 659-60; Otis to Adjutant-General, U.S. Army, 19 May 1898 (Received 20 May 1898, 2:05 a.m.), in *Correspondence II*, 663.

67. Otis to Adjutant-General, U.S. Army, 21 May 1898, 11:20 p.m., in *Correspondence II*, 667-68.

68. Private Charles R. Detrick, *History of the Operations of the First Regiment California U.S. Volunteer Infantry in the Campaign in the Philippine Islands*, n.p., n.d., 96-97.

69. Letter, D.D. Van Valzah to the Adjutant General, 1st. Brigade, Ind. Division, Camp Merritt, 8 June 1898, in Record Group 395, Preliminary Inventory of the Records of U.S. Army Overseas Operations and Commands, 1898-1942, Entry 887: 8th Army Corps, Independent Division, July-December 1898, Letters Received June-September 1898, Box No. 1, General, Special Orders and Circulars, 1898 (Washington, DC: National Archives); Letter, Samuel Ovenshine, Colonel, 23d Infantry, Commanding, to Adjutant General 1st Brigade, 8 June 1898, in Record Group 395; "Summary of the Principal Events Connected With Military Operations in the Philippine Islands," in US War Department, *Annual Reports of the War Department for the Fiscal Year Ended June 30, 1899, Report of the Major General Commanding the Army*, v-vi.

70. Merritt, Major-General, to His Excellency William McKinley, 13 May 1898, in *Correspondence II*, 643; W. Merritt to His Excellency William McKinley, 15 May 1898 (Received 16 May 1898), in *Correspondence II*, 645; W. Merritt to Adjutant-General, 21 May 1898, in *Correspondence II*, 666; W. Merritt to Adjutant-General, 21 May 1898, in *Correspondence II*, 666-67; Merritt to Adjutant-General, 30 May 1898, in *Correspondence II*, 681; H.C. Corbin to Major-General Merritt, 31 May 1898—12 midnight, in *Correspondence II*, 683; H.C. Corbin to Major General Merritt, 4 June 1898, in Record Group 94, filed with Document Number 82934, Box 612, 82867 to 83122.

71. "Summary of the Principal Events Connected With Military Operations in the Philippine Islands," in US War Department, *Annual Reports of the War Department for the Fiscal Year Ended June 30, 1899, Report of the Major General Commanding the Army*, v-vi.

72. General Orders No. 2, Headquarters, U.S. Expeditionary Forces, San Francisco, Cal., 20 May 1898; General Orders No. 1, Headquarters, Independent Division Philippine Islands Expeditionary Forces, Camp Merritt. San Francisco, Cal., 1 June 1898; General Orders No. 12, Headquarters, Independent Division, Eighth Army Corps, San Francisco, Cal., 29 June 1898.

73. "More Troops Embark To-Day," *The Examiner*, 24 May 1898, 2; "Nebraska Troops Mysteriously Ill, *The Examiner*, 28 May 1898, 3.

74. Otis to Adjutant-General, U.S. Army, 24 May 1898 (Received 5:24 p.m.),

in *Correspondence II*, 671; "The Day in Camp," *San Francisco Daily Report*, 25 May 1898, 3; "Camp Richmond," *San Francisco Call*, 29 May 1898, 7.

75. "Camp Merritt Troops," *San Francisco Call*, 29 June 1898, 5.

76. Letter, Karl Kraemer, Co H, 51st Iowa Infantry, to Dear Sister, 11 August 1898 (Carlisle Barracks, PA: US Army Military History Institute).

77. "Warm Weather Events Out at Camp Merritt," *San Francisco Chronicle*, 5 June 1898, 23.

78. "The Day in Camp," *San Francisco Daily Report*, 2 June 1898, 3; "In the Camp," *San Francisco Daily Report*, 3 June 1898, 2; "The Day at the Camp," *San Francisco Daily Report*, 8 June 1898, 3; "At Camp Merritt," *San Francisco Daily Report*, 18 June 1898, 2; "Richmond's Tented Field," *San Francisco Call*, 3 June 1898, 7; "Next Tuesday or Later," *San Francisco Call*, 4 June 1898, 7.

79. Letter, Oscar F. Long to Quartermaster General, 1 October 1898, in Record Group 92, Office of the Quartermaster General, Document File 1800-1914, Document No. 120579, 2.

80. "At Camp Merritt," *San Francisco Daily Report*, 27 June 1898, 1.

81. "Wyoming Battery Joins the Troops," *San Francisco Chronicle*, 29 June 1898, 3; "More Rigid Rules for Camp Merritt," *San Francisco Chronicle*, 30 June 1898, 3.

82. Merritt to The Adjutant-General, 20 June 1898, in *Correspondence II*, 707.

83. Letter, Oscar F. Long to Quartermaster General, 1 October 1898, in Record Group 92, Office of the Quartermaster General, Document File 1800-1914, Document No. 120579, 2.

84. Merritt to The Adjutant-General, 20 June 1898, in *Correspondence II*, 707.

85. "Summary of the Principal Events Connected With Military Operations in the Philippine Islands," in US War Department, *Annual Reports of the War Department for the Fiscal Year Ended June 30, 1899, Report of the Major General Commanding the Army*, viii.

86. Letter, Oscar F. Long to Quartermaster General, 1 October 1898, in Record Group 92, Office of the Quartermaster General, Document File 1800-1914, Document No. 120579, 2.

87. "The Day in Camp," *San Francisco Daily Report*, 2 June 1898, 3.

88. Otis to Adjutant-General, U.S. Army, 20 May 1898 (Received 4:40 p.m.), in *Correspondence II*, 663-64.

89. Otis to Adjutant-General, U.S. Army, 24 May 1898 (Received 5:24 p.m.), in *Correspondence II*, 671.

90. "Seven Thousand Men," *San Francisco Call*, 26 May 1898, 2.

91. "The Day in Camp," *San Francisco Daily Report*, 2 June 1898, 3.

92. J.B. Showalter to General Alger, 17 May 1898 (Received 18 May 1898), in *Correspondence II*, 658.

93. "Ships and Men for the Second Manila Expedition," *San Francisco Chronicle*, 4 June 1898, 9; *Who Was Who in America*, volume 1, 1897-1942, 828; "Nebraska Must Wait for Third Fleet," *San Francisco Chronicle*, 5 June 1898, 23.

94. Otis to Adjutant-General, U.S. Army, 8 July 1898 (Received 7:10 p.m.), in *Correspondence II*, 722.

95. H.C. Corbin to Major-General Otis, 10 July 1898, in *Correspondence II*, 724-25.

96. H.C. Corbin to Major-General Otis, 9 July 1898, in *Correspondence II*, 723.

97. Otis to Adjutant-General, U.S. Army, 9 July 1898 (Received 7:56 p.m.), in *Correspondence II*, 724; "Summary of the Principal Events Connected With Military Operations in the Philippine Islands," in US War Department, *Annual Reports of the War Department for the Fiscal Year Ended June 30, 1899, Report of the Major General Commanding the Army*, vi.

98. H.C. Corbin to Major-General Otis, 10 July 1898, in *Correspondence II*, 725; H.C. Corbin to Major-General Otis, 10 July 1898—midnight, in *Correspondence II*, 726; Otis to Adjutant-General, U.S. Army, 10 July 1898 (Received 11 July 1898, 3 a.m.), in *Correspondence II*, 726; H.C. Corbin to Major-General Otis, 11 July 1898, 4:35 p.m., in *Correspondence II*, 727; Lee Mantle to Hon. R.A. Alger, 16 July 1898 (Received 4:30 p.m.), in *Correspondence II*, 734; Harrison Gray Otis to Adjutant-General of the Army, 17 July 1898 (Received 18 July 1898, 1:50 a.m.), in *Correspondence II*, 734; Boies Penrose to Hon. George D. Meiklejohn, 18 July 1898 (Received 1:35 p.m.), in *Correspondence II*, 735; George C. Perkins to R.A. Alger, 18 July 1898 (Received 9:27 p.m.), in *Correspondence II*, 735; George C. Perkins to Adjutant-General Corbin, 18 July 1898 (Received 9:30 p.m.), in *Correspondence II*, 735; U.S. Grant, Jr., to Hon. R.A. Alger, 18 July 1898 (Received 11:28 p.m.), in *Correspondence II*, 736; John Gear to Honorable Secretary of War, 21 July 1898 (Received 8:47 p.m.), in *Correspondence II*, 739; Charles Curtis to Honorable Secretary of War, 22 July 1898 (Received 12:16 p.m.), in *Correspondence II*, 739; H.C. Corbin to General Merriam, 26 July 1898, 11:15 p.m., in *Correspondence II*, 741; H.C. Corbin to General Merriam, 27 July 1898, 3:30 p.m., in *Correspondence II*, 741; W.S. Leake to Hon. R.A. Alger, 1 August 1898 (Received 5:56 p.m.), in *Correspondence II*, 743; R.A. Alger to Hon. J.R. Rogers, Governor of Washington, 16 August 1898, in *Correspondence II*, 753.

99. Detrick, 2.

100. *History of the Operations of the First Nebraska Infantry, U.S.V. in the Campaign in the Philippine Islands*, n.p., n.d., 6-7.

101. First Sergeant Phil H. Shortt, *Official History of the Operations of the First North Dakota Infantry, U.S.V. of the Campaign in the Philippine Islands*, n.p., n.d., 1-2.

102. "Seventh California," *San Francisco Call*, 26 May 1898, 2; "Regulars Wanted," *San Francisco Call*, 26 May 1898, 2.

103. General Orders No. 2, Headquarters, U.S. Expeditionary Forces, and Department of Pacific, San Francisco, Cal., 30 May 1898.

104. General Orders No. 5, Headquarters, Independent Division, Philippine Islands Expeditionary Forces, Camp Merritt, San Francisco, Cal., 12 June 1898.

105. General Orders No. 11, Headquarters, Independent Division, Philippine

Islands Expeditionary Forces, Camp Merritt, San Francisco, Cal., 27 June 1898.

106. General Orders No. 17, Headquarters, Independent Division, Eighth Army Corps, San Francisco, Cal., 15 July 1898.

107. General Orders No. 16, Headquarters, Independent Division, Eighth Army Corps, San Francisco, Cal., 11 July 1898.

108. Special Orders No. 10, Headquarters, Independent Division, Eighth Army Corps, Camp Merritt, San Francisco, Cal., 20 July 1898, in *San Francisco Call*, 21 July 1898, 5.

109. H.C. Corbin to Major-General Otis, 10 July 1898, 9:10 p.m., in *Correspondence II*, 725; H.C. Corbin to Commanding General, Department of California, 10 July 1898, 9:15 p.m., in *Correspondence II*, 725-26.

110. "Washington Infantry," *San Francisco Call*, 17 June 1898, 5; Adjutant William L. Luhn, *Official History of the Operations of the First Washington Infantry, U.S.V. in the Campaign in the Philippine Islands*, n.p., n.d., 4; "Local War Notes," *San Francisco Daily Report*, 2 July 1898, 2.

111. "Slept on the Sand," *San Francisco Chronicle*, 18 May 1898, 3.

112. Detrick, 96.

113. "Fontana Barracks Deserted by Artillerymen," *The Examiner*, 19 May 1898, 2.

114. "The Fontana Building," *San Francisco Call*, 19 May 1898, 5; "Artillerymen Quit the Big Warehouse," *San Francisco Chronicle*, 19 May 1898, 4.

115. Detrick, 96; "The Fontana Building," *San Francisco Call*, 19 May 1898, 5; "Artillerymen Quit the Big Warehouse," *San Francisco Chronicle*, 19 May 1898, 4.

116. Luhn, 4.

117. "Richmond Asks Relief," *San Francisco Daily Report*, 8 June 1898, 3.

118. "A Misplaced Camp," *San Francisco Chronicle*, 9 June 1898, 6; "Fourteen Thousand," *San Francisco Call*, 3 June 1898, 7.

119. "An Army Mystery," *San Francisco Call*, 12 June 1898, 8.

120. "A Distinct Question," *San Francisco Daily Report*, 11 June 1898, 4; Editorial," *San Francisco Daily Report*, 14 June 1898, 4.

121. "A Plague Spot," *San Francisco Daily Report*, 20 June 1898, 4.

122. "Alger's Aid is Requested," *San Francisco Chronicle*, 21 June 1898, 9.

123. "New Regiment to Camp at Oakland," *San Francisco Chronicle*, 22 June 1898, 12.

124. "Camp Barrett Might Increase," *San Francisco Call*, 3 July 1898, 7.

125. Circular, Headquarters, Independent Division, Philippine Islands Expeditionary Forces, Camp Merritt, San Francisco, Cal., 23 June 1898, in Record Group 395, Preliminary Inventory of the Records of U.S. Army Overseas Operations and Commands, 1898-1942, Entry 887: 8th Army Corps, Independent Division, July-December 1898, Letters Received June-September 1898, Box No. 1, General, Special Orders and Circulars, 1898 (Washington, DC: National Archives).

126. "At Camp Merritt," *San Francisco Daily Report*, 1 July 1898, 2.

127. "At Camp Merritt," *San Francisco Daily Report*, 5 July 1898, 2.

128. "The Camp Must Move," *San Francisco Daily Report*, 6 July 1898, 3.

129. W.S.H. Matthews to the Chief Surgeon, Independent Division, Eighth Army Corps, 7 July 1898, in *Report VIII*, 164.

130. "Barber for Governor-General of Hawaii," *San Francisco Call*, 15 July 1898, 8.

131. H.C. Corbin to Major-General Otis, 10 July 1898, midnight, in *Correspondence II*, 726; Otis to Adjutant-General, 13 July 1898 (Received 9:49 p.m.), in *Correspondence II*, 729; H.C. Corbin to Major-General Otis, 14 July 1898, 12:45 a.m., in *Correspondence II*, 729; H.C. Corbin to Major-General Merriam, 14 July 1898, 3:45 p.m., in *Correspondence II*, 733; "Barber for Governor-General of Hawaii," *San Francisco Call*, 15 July 1898, 8.

132. *Annual Report of the Adjutant-General of the State of New York for the Year 1898* (New York: Wynkoop Hallenbeck Crawford Co., State Printers, 1899), 131; "Moved to the Presidio," *San Francisco Call*, 16 July 1898, 5; "At Camp Merritt," *San Francisco Daily Report*, 15 July 1898, 2; "New York Regiment to Leave Unhealthful Camp Merritt," *San Francisco Chronicle*, 15 July 1898, 5.

133. Hugh Craig to the President, Washington, 16 July 1898, in *San Francisco Daily Report*, 16 July 1898, 21; *San Francisco Chronicle*, 17 July 1898, 23; *San Francisco Call*, 17 July 1898, 8.

134. H.C. Corbin to Major-General Merriam, 18 July 1898, in *Correspondence II*, 734-35.

135. A special report on the subject of military camps in and about San Francisco from 6 May to 1 September 1898 by Lieut. Col. J.V.D. Middleton, deputy surgeon-general, US Army, 10 September 1898, in US War Department, *Annual Reports of the War Department for the Fiscal Year Ended June 30, 1898, Report of the Major General Commanding the Army*, 177.

Chapter VIII
Epilogue and Conclusions

The United States and Spain ended their hostilities with a protocol in August 1898. Fittingly, both the opening and closing battles of the war were fought in the environs of Manila Bay. Buoyed by Dewey's victory on 1 May, Filipino rebels, who had renewed their drive for freedom in 1896, encircled the Spanish garrison around Manila. Though not strong enough to mount a decisive attack, the Philippine army was sufficiently powerful to keep Spanish forces contained in the city. An uneasy stalemate settled over much of Luzon as both the Asiatic squadron and Philippine insurgents awaited the arrival of US Army expeditions from San Francisco.

Forces from the Department of the Pacific began to arrive at Cavite in summer 1898. BG Thomas Anderson's first expedition reached Manila on 30 June. BG Francis V. Greene's second expedition joined Anderson's men on 17 July. Transports of the Army's third expedition, led by BG Arthur MacArthur, began to anchor in Manila Bay on 25 July. MG Wesley Merritt arrived in the Philippines with the third expedition. By then designated the US Army VIII Corps, Merritt's command consisted of nearly 11,000 Regulars and Volunteers. (See appendix B.)

Merritt would note that by the time of his arrival, Philippine insurgents "held military possession of many points in the islands other than those in the vicinity of Manila."[1] While General Emilio Aguinaldo, commander, Philippine army, and his forces had begun operations around the archipelago's Spanish capital several weeks after Dewey's victory, Filipino resistance challenged the Spanish military elsewhere in Luzon. Insurgents also attacked Spanish outposts in other parts of the Philippines, including Mindoro, the Visayas, and Mindanao.[2]

Merritt and Dewey conferred about Manila. In the short term, both viewed the city's capture to be important to American negotiators who would terminate the war with Spain. The two officers were aware that the president wanted flexibility to determine America's relationship with the Philippines after the conflict ended. That condition meant that an attack on Manila should be conducted unilaterally to minimize any concessions to the Filipinos for their participation in a final offensive. Additionally, the US military feared that Filipinos would exact a bloody revenge upon the Spanish for the revolution if they joined the assault on the capital.

Seeking to secure American objectives without going into battle, Dewey attempted to enduce Manila's Spanish garrison to surrender. He worked through intermediaries, particularly the Belgian consul in Manila,

ADMIRAL DEWEY AND GENERAL MERRITT IN ADMIRAL DEWEY'S CABIN ON THE FLAG-SHIP *OLYMPIA*
DRAWN BY T. DE THULSTRUP, FROM A PHOTOGRAPH BY F. D. MILLET

Figure 103.

Edward Andre. Using Andre to deliver messages, Dewey negotiated with the recently appointed Spanish governor general, Don Fermin Jaudenes y Alvarez. Jaudenes refused to capitulate; however, he did specify that his Manila batteries would not fire on Dewey's vessels if American ships did not bombard the city. Both the Spanish and American commanders were concerned about indirect fire raining down on a city that numerous noncombatants still occupied. Jaudenes also specified how he would indicate surrender if he decided to yield after an American attack on his defenses.[3] Nevertheless, he refused to concede without putting up a fight.

In joint messages to Jaudenes a week before the attack, Merritt and Dewey could not inspire Jaudenes to change his mind and give in.[4] The two American commanders, however, persuaded Aguinaldo to allow the Americans to seize Manila. VIII Corps troops gradually replaced many of the Filipino soldiers in the trenches that surrounded the city. On 13 August, the Americans attacked, unaware of the protocol signed earlier. Supported by the guns of Dewey's squadron, Merritt's command overwhelmed the Spanish garrison. At day's end, the United States controlled Manila. Spanish troops stationed at various posts throughout the archipelago subsequently surrendered and were repatriated.

Figure 104.

American forces, however, did not redeploy to the United States. While the president wrestled with his options concerning the fate of the Philippines, MG Merritt established a military government in a proclamation to Filipinos on 14 August 1898.[5] MG Elwell S. Otis, who replaced Merritt as commander, Department of the Pacific, and military governor in the islands on 30 August 1898, soon confronted indigenous opposition to American hegemony. President McKinley would subsequently decide to annex the islands. Not long after this decision, Aguinaldo, supported by many of his countrymen on Luzon, established the Republic of the Philippines. The United States refused to recognize the new government. Incidents, some violent, escalated between Filipinos and Americans. On 4 February 1899, the two former uneasy coalition partners went to war against each other.

Between February and November 1899, both belligerents fought in a conventional, Western style. They fielded large units, performed extensive maneuvers, and waged major battles. Whenever the two armies clashed, however, Otis' VIII Corps always prevailed. By November, Aguinaldo decided that his forces could not achieve independence by conducting orthodox military operations against the US military.

Aguinaldo reorganized his army into small, decentralized guerrilla units. He made them responsible for attacking and eroding the Americans' will to remain in the Philippines. For a while, these tactics prolonged the war. Aguinaldo, however, could not break the United States' resolve to retain the Philippines. The war continued into 1902 when most of the organized Filipino resistance dissolved. President Theodore Roosevelt declared the war over in July 1902.

America's involvement in Philippine affairs that began after Dewey's victory continued into the 1990s. Over nine decades, the United States established a political, economic, social, and military presence in the archipelago that extended well beyond the islands into the Pacific and parts of Asia. For almost a century, the US military took station at Luzon. From there it campaigned against a host of belligerents, indigenous and foreign, that threatened American hegemony and later Philippine independence.

For the US Army, challenges associated with establishing and sustaining a lengthy presence in the archipelago developed quickly. By virtue of this endeavor and the great bureaucratic machine that had to be created to command, control, clothe, equip, and train an overseas force, the War Department embarked upon a transformation. Starting in May 1898, the Army converted from a frontier constabulary that picketed the Great Plains of North America to a combat expeditionary force that engaged in operations 7,000 miles west of San Francisco. A fundamental component of this transformation matured at the Golden Gate. From various locations in San Francisco, the US Army developed a process to receive, stage, and deploy troops to the Philippines that began with Dewey's victory and lasted through the Cold War.

From a study of the process that evolved in 1898, several impressions emerge. The speed of the Army's response warrants recognition. The president issued a call for 125,000 Volunteers in late April 1898. On 4 May, he directed that troops converge at the Golden Gate to prepare for duty in Manila. On 25 May, the American Army deployed the first of seven expeditions to the Philippines. Composed of 158 officers and 2,386 men, the initial flotilla included Regular infantry troops moved from Alaska and state Volunteers organized in California and Oregon. In less than 21 days the Army had initiated a process to assemble, screen, organize, outfit, and dispatch a body of men to exploit Dewey's success at Manila Bay.

The National Guard made significant contributions in the effort to identify Volunteers and gather forces around San Francisco. Adjutant General BG Henry C. Corbin's calculations on the average number of militiamen in a Volunteer company were interesting but stopped well short of capturing the influence the National Guard exerted in mobilizing manpower. Except for Kansas, states that dispatched forces to Merritt used the National Guard organization as a foundation upon which to create units for deployment abroad. While the Army's AG may have dwelled on raw numbers, the National Guard institution worked effectively to process veterans, guardsmen, ex-guardsmen, and citizens for muster into federal service. One of the reasons San Francisco was so attractive as a port of embarkation was that the California National Guard maintained an infantry regiment in the city. The Army therefore had the authority to muster the 1st California at the port of embarkation and assign the regiment to the first expedition.

The effective use of railroads during the mobilization deserves acknowledgment. No "on-the-shelf" contingency plan or military transport system existed to facilitate the assembly of forces from various states or territories at the Golden Gate. Nevertheless, the Army's Quartermaster General, working with departmental quartermasters, quickly secured the requisite rail transportation to move Regulars and Volunteers to San Francisco. COL Charles Bird, in charge of the Army's transportation division, maintained that only one Volunteer regiment was unable to board trains when ready. This situation developed because the Army was unwilling to pay the rate the particular railroad company demanded. Otherwise, to Bird's knowledge, rail transportation awaited all units after their muster into federal service.[6]

These same quartermaster officials were largely responsible for creating an oceanic transport fleet to move units overseas. When the president decided to send land forces to Manila, the Army had neither plans nor means to get them there. The Navy secured the first vessel, the *City of Peking*, but thereafter Major Oscar Long and COL Frank Hecker worked to charter or purchase passenger and freight vessels. Eventually, the Army developed the US Transport Service, an organization that controlled a small flotilla of ships used to convey forces to and from various Pacific outposts.

The senior commanders of the Department of the Pacific gave the VIII Corps its organization and substance. Unlike the president and War

Department officials who viewed the Philippine expedition as an occupation force, MG Merritt comprehended the need to bolster his command's ability to fight an armed opponent as well as to garrison an overseas outpost. He argued for additional Regular infantry, artillery, and engineers. While he and MG Nelson A. Miles disagreed over the purpose of the expedition, Merritt recognized that the president chose not to identify clear political objectives for his command. Merritt, not unlike naval officers who made policy assumptions to create prewar contingency plans, believed that his force could be directed to seize the islands. Should the president and Congress decide to annex the Philippines (as they subsequently did), the VIII Corps would be in a stronger position to achieve that objective with the forces that Merritt wanted added to his department.

MG Otis commanded the VIII Corps' Independent Division. While Merritt fought his battles with Washington, Otis worked through his subordinates to organize, train, quarter, and equip the division's Regular and Volunteer forces at San Francisco. He knew where to focus his efforts so as to complement his commander. Before Merritt arrived at the Golden Gate, Otis dispatched clear, concise summary reports to the War Department that identified the command's actions and needs. He worked with local quartermasters to secure ordnance and transportation for his men. Once he relocated to Camp Merritt from the Phelan Building, he systematically prepared the troops for duty overseas. In this regard, he tapped into Presidio resources and depot or arsenal assets managed by local quartermaster, ordnance, subsistence, and medical officers. Merritt's command, however, could not depend exclusively on military assistance in tending to expeditionary forces. In that regard, the Department of the Pacific did not need to look far for much-needed support.

The San Francisco community assumed an invaluable role in caring for Army troops who gathered at the Golden Gate. Many citizens were swept up in a spirit of volunteerism. They acted individually or collectively to support those who assembled for duty overseas. Years before the United Service Organizations evolved to sustain the military during World War II, associations and leagues in San Francisco offered their assistance without larger national societies prodding them into action.

Area hospitals, church groups, school children, and business people collaborated to produce medical assistance, personal items, welcoming festivities, and financial support for the military. These citizens and institutions frequently acted through or in support of the Red Cross Society or Patriotic Home Helpers to generate relief efforts on behalf of the troops or, in some cases, their families. Well before the American Red Cross asked

Californians to assist, Bay Area residents initiated support activities. Led by women who served on the Board of Directors at Children's Hospital, the community sponsored both a local Red Cross Society and state association before the end of May.

While some residents joined or supported relief societies that nurtured the sick or destitute, others labored on behalf of community religious organizations having ties to national associations. As was the case with the Red Cross, these groups did not need prompting from parent affiliates to look after troops in a variety of ways. The YMCA, Christian Endeavorers, and Catholic Truth Society (CTS) focused on the spiritual welfare of all men in uniform. While each group pursued goals that were appropriate to the faiths they represented, all labored to fortify souls against temptations that could be encountered locally or abroad. The three organizations prioritized their spiritual ministries in the camps. Nevertheless, all ensured that part of that ministry was devoted to the material and physical well-being of all men who used their services.

Almost a century after Merritt's command prepared troops for duty overseas, the US Army Chief of Staff observed, "The Army's new operations doctrine emphasizes readiness for rapid deployment. It calls for being able to project three divisions as far as 7,500 nautical miles from U.S. shores within thirty days."[7] Over time, the need to project combat power into a complex environment is likely to require even greater speed. If this should be the case, then certainly the roots of this endeavor can be traced to the US Army's efforts to mobilize and deploy expeditionary forces from San Francisco to the Philippines in 1898.

Notes

1. US War Department, *Annual Reports of the War Department for the Fiscal Year Ended June 30, 1898, Report of the Major-General Commanding the Army*, Report of General Wesley Merritt (Washington, DC: US Government Printing Office [GPO], 1898), 40.

2. David F. Trask, *The War With Spain in 1898* (New York: Macmillan Publishing Co., 1981), 406.

3. Thomas M. Anderson, "Our Rule in the Philippines," *The North American Review*, volume 170, February 1900, 277-78; George Dewey, *Autobiography of George Dewey, Admiral of the Navy*, (New York: Charles Scribner's Sons, 1913) 272-78; Trask, 414-22; Statement of Admiral George Dewey, USN, in US Senate, *Affairs in the Philippine Islands, Hearings Before the Committee on the Philippines of the United States Senate*, volume 3 (Washington, DC: GPO, 1902), 2943-47; US Navy Department, *Annual Reports of the Navy Department for the Year 1898, Appendix to the Report of the Chief of the Bureau of Navigation*, (Washington, DC: GPO, 1898), 125-26; Brother V. Edmund McDevitt, *The First California's Chaplain* (Fresno, CA: Academy Library Guild, 1956), 92-99.

4. US War Department, *Annual Reports of the War Department for the Fiscal Year Ended June 30, 1898, Report of the Secretary of War, Miscellaneous Reports*, 54-55.

5. US War Department, *Annual Reports of the War Department for the Fiscal Year Ended June 30, 1898, Report of the Major General Commanding the Army*, 49-50.

6. Testimony of Col. Charles Bird, 2 December 1898, in *Report of the Commission Appointed by the President to Investigate the Conduct of the War Department in the War With Spain*, volume 6, *Testimony* (Washington, DC: GPO, 1900), 2616.

7. *The Leavenworth Times*, 15 September 1993, B8.

About the Author

Dr. Stephen D. Coats is a professor of joint military operations and history at the US Army Command and General Staff College (CGSC), Fort Leavenworth, Kansas. A graduate of the US Military Academy with a Bachelor of Science degree, he earned a master's degree in history from the University of Wisconsin—Madison and a Ph.D. in history from the University of Kansas. He was commissioned in the US Army and served in several infantry assignments. He is the author of articles and reviews on joint operations and military history. Dr. Coats has been a member of the Department of Joint and Multinational Operations faculty at CGSC since January 1994.

Glossary

AG	adjutant general
BG	brigadier general
btries	batteries
CE	Christian Endeavorers
CGSC	US Army Command and General Staff College
COL	colonel
cos	companies
CPT	captain
CTS	Catholic Truth Society
detach	detachment
DJMO	Department of Joint and Multinational Operations
1LT	first lieutenant
GGNRA	Golden Gate National Recreation Area
GPO	US Government Printing Office
ID	identification
IG	inspector general
LTC	lieutenant colonel
MG	major general
NPS	National Park Service
PHH	Patriotic Home Helpers
USO	United Service Organizations
YMCA	Young Men's Christian Association

Bibliography

I. Newspapers
Army and Navy Journal
San Francisco Call
San Francisco Chronicle
San Francisco Daily Report
The Examiner (San Francisco)
The Leavenworth Times
The Monitor (San Francisco)

II. Periodicals
Journal of the Military Service Institution of the United States
Overland Monthly

III. Letters, Diaries, Manuscripts at the US Army Military History Institute, Carlisle Barracks, Pennsylvania
Hugh E. Clapp, 1st Nebraska Infantry
William S. Christner, 10th Pennsylvania Infantry
A.G. Baker, 1st Colorado Infantry, Colorado Volunteers
Karl Kraemer, 51st Iowa Infantry
William Henry Barrett, 2d Oregon Infantry

IV. US Government Record Groups at the National Archives, Washington, DC

Record Group 92. Textual Records of the Office of the Quartermaster General. Entry 1496, Register of Transportation of Troops and Their Equipment, 1898-1900.

Record Group 92. Office of the Quartermaster General. Document File 1800-1914.

Record Group 94. Office of the Adjutant General. Checklist Entry 182, Muster in War With Spain. 1st Call.

Record Group 94. Office of the Adjutant General Document File.

Record Group 395. Preliminary Inventory of the Records of US Army Overseas Operations and Commands, 1898-1942. Entry 887, Independent Division, July-December 1898. Letters Received June-September 1898.

V. US Government Documents

Department of Defense. Joint Publication 4-05. *Joint Mobilization Planning*. Final Coordinating Draft. 28 April 2005.

US Army. Department of the Pacific and Eighth Army Corps. Adjutant General's Office. Index to General Orders and Circulars: Philippine Islands Expeditionary Forces, 1898.

US Army. Field Manual 100-7. *Mobilization, Deployment, Redeployment, Demobilization*. Washington, DC: US Government Printing Office (GPO), 28 October 1992.

US Navy Department. *Annual Reports of the Navy Department for the Year 1898*. Washington, DC: GPO, 1898.

US Senate. *Affairs in the Philippine Islands. Hearings Before the Committee on* the Philippines of the United States Senate. 3 vols. Washington, DC: GPO, 1902.

US Senate. *Report of the Commission Appointed by the President to Investigate the Conduct of the War Department in the War With Spain.* 8 vols. Washington, DC: GPO, 1900.

US War Department. Adjutant General's Office. *Correspondence Relating to the War With Spain and Conditions Growing Out of the Same, Including the Insurrection in the Philippine Islands and the China Relief Expedition, Between the Adjutant-General of the Army and Military Commanders in the United States, Cuba, Porto Rico, China, and the Philippine Islands, From April 15, 1898, to July 30, 1902.* 2 vols. Washington, DC: GPO, 1902.

US War Department. Adjutant General's Office. *The Organized Militia of the United States. Statement of the Condition and Efficiency for Service of the Organized Militia. From Regular Annual Reports, and Other Sources, Covering the Year 1897.* Washington, DC: GPO, 1898.

US War Department. Adjutant General's Office. *The Organized Militia of the United States. Statement of the Condition and Efficiency for Service of the Organized Militia. From Special Reports Received From the Adjutants-General of the Several States, Territories, and the District of Columbia.* Washington, DC: GPO, 1900.

US War Department. *Annual Reports of the War Department for the Fiscal Year Ended June 30, 1897.* Washington, DC: GPO, 1897.

US War Department. *Annual Reports of the War Department for the Fiscal Year Ended June 30, 1898.* Washington, DC: GPO, 1898.

US War Department. *Annual Reports of the War Department for the Fiscal Year Ended June 30, 1899.* Washington, DC: GPO, 1899.

US War Department. *Drill Regulations for Cavalry, United States Army.* Washington, DC: GPO, 1896.

US War Department. *Drill Regulations for Light Artillery, United States Army.* Washington, DC: GPO, 1896.

US War Department. *Infantry Drill Regulations, United States Army.* New York: D. Appleton and Co., 1898.

US War Department. *Regulations for the Army of the United States, 1895, With Appendixes No. 1 and 2.* Washington, DC: GPO, 1900.

VI. State Adjutant General Reports

California. *Biennial Report of the Adjutant-General of the State of California for the Two Years Ending June 30, 1900.* Sacramento: A.J. Johnston, Superintendent State Printing, 1900.

California. *Extracts From Biennial Report of the Adjutant-General of the State of California June 30, 1896 to June 30, 1898.* Sacramento: W. Shannon, Superintendent State Printing, 1910.

Colorado. *The Biennial Report of the Adjutant General of Colorado from December 1, 1896 to November 30, 1898, Inclusive.* Denver: Smith-Brooks Printing Co., State Printers, 1898.

Colorado. *The Biennial Report of the Adjutant General of Colorado From December 1, 1898 to November 30, 1900, Inclusive.* Denver: Smith-Brooks Printing Co., State Printers, 1901.

Iowa. *Report of the Adjutant-General to the Governor of the State of Iowa for Biennial Period Ending November 30, 1899.* Des Moines: F.R. Conaway, State Printer, 1900.

Kansas. *Eleventh Biennial Report of the Adjutant General of the State of Kansas, 1897-1898.* Topeka: J.S. Parks, State Printer, 1899.

Kansas. *Twelfth Biennial Report of the Adjutant General of the State of Kansas, 1899-1900.* Topeka: W.Y. Morgan, State Printer, 1900.

Montana. *Report of the Adjutant-General of the State of Montana for the Years 1897-98.* Helena, MT: Independent Publishing Co., State Printers and Binders, 1899.

Montana. *Report of the Adjutant-General of the State of Montana, December 1, 1900.* Helena, MT: State Publishing Co., State Stationers, Printers, and Binders, 1901.

New York. *Annual Report of the Adjutant-General of the State of New York For the Year 1898.* New York: Wynkoop Hallenbeck Crawford Co., State Printers, 1899.

North Dakota. *Biennial Report of the Adjutant General to the Governor of North Dakota for the Term Ending November 30, 1898.* Bismarck, ND: Tribune, State Printers and Binders, 1898.

Oregon. *Seventh Biennial Report of the Adjutant-General of the State of Oregon, 1899-1900.* Salem, OR: W.H. Leeds, State Printer, 1900.

Oregon. *Sixth Biennial Report of the Adjutant-General of the Oregon National Guard, 1899.* Salem, OR: W.H. Leeds, State Printer, 1898.

Pennsylvania. *Annual Report of the Adjutant General of Pennsylvania for the Year 1898.* Harrisburg, PA: Wm. Stanley Ray, State Printer of Pennsylvania, 1900.

VII. Unit Histories

Bowe, John. *With the 13th Minnesota in the Philippines.* Minneapolis: A.B. Farnham Printing and Stationery Co., 1905.

Camp, Private James. *Official History of the Operations of the First Idaho Infantry, U.S.V. in the Campaign in the Philippine Islands.* n.p., n.d.

Chastaine, Captain Ben H. *History of the 18th U.S. Infantry, First Division, 1812-1919.* n.p., n.d.

Detrick, Charles R. *History of the Operations of the First Regiment, California U.S. Volunteer Infantry in the Campaign in the Philippine Islands.* n.p., n.d.

Gantenbein, Brigadier General C.U. *The Official Records of the Oregon Volunteers in the Spanish War and Philippine Insurrection.* 2d edition. Salem, OR: J.R. Whitney, State Printer, 1903.

History of the Operations of the First Nebraska Infantry, U.S.V. in the Campaign in the Philippine Islands. n.p., n.d.

History of the 10th Pennsylvania Volunteer Infantry: Its Forebearers and Successors in the Spanish-American War, World War I, World War II, and the Korean Emergency. n.p., n.d.

Laist, Lieutenant Alexander. *Official History of the Operations of the First Montana Infantry, U.S.V. in the Campaign in the Philippine Islands*. n.p., n.d.

Luhn, Adjutant William. *Official History of the Operations of the First Washington Infantry, U.S.V. in the Campaign in the Philippine Islands*. n.p., n.d.

Markey, Joseph I. *From Iowa to the Philippines: A History of Company M, Fifty-First Iowa Infantry Volunteers*. Red Oak, IA: Thos. D. Murphy Co., 1900.

Maybe, Charles R. *The Utah Batteries: A History*. Salt Lake City: Daily Reporter Co., 1900.

Maybe, Sergeant Chas. R. *History of the Operations of the Utah Light Artillery, U.S.V. in the Campaign in the Philippine Islands*. n.p., n.d.

McDonald, Allan L. *The Historical Record of the First Tennessee Infantry, U.S.V. in the Spanish War and Filipino Insurrection*. n.p., n.d.

Medbery, Captain Frank W. *Official History of the Operations of the First South Dakota Infantry, U.S.V. in the Campaign in the Philippine Islands*. n.p., n.d.

Nankivell, Captain John H. *The History of the Twenty-Fifth Regiment, United States Infantry, 1869-1926*. Fort Collins, CO: Old Army Press, 1972.

Shortt, First Sergeant Phil. H. *Official History of the Operations of the First North Dakota Infantry, U.S.V. in the Campaign in the Philippine Islands*. n.p., n.d.

Snure, Private John. *Official History of the Operations of the Fifty-First Iowa Infantry, U.S.V. in the Campaign in the Philippine Islands*. n.p., n.d.

Sorley, Captain L.S. *History of the Fourteenth United States Infantry: From January 1898 to December 1908*. Chicago: Privately Printed, 1909.

Steele, Private John M. *Official History of the Operations of the Twentieth Kansas Infantry, U.S.V. in the Campaign in the Philippine Islands*. n.p., n.d.

Stoneman, Madison U. *Official History of the Operations of the First Battalion Wyoming Infantry, U.S.V. in the Campaign in the Philippine Islands*. n.p., n.d.

Tew, Lieutenant Martin. *Official History of the Operations of the 13th Minnesota Infantry, U.S.V., in the Campaign in the Philippines*. n.p., n.d.

US Army. *The Twenty-Third United States Infantry, 1812-1945*. n.p., n.d.

VIII.   General

Alberts, Donald E. *Brandy Station to Manila Bay: A Biography of General Wesley Merritt*. Austin, TX: Presidial Press, 1980.

Alger, R.A. *The Spanish-American War*. New York: Harper & Brothers, 1901.

American Council of Learned Societies. *Dictionary of American Biography*. New York: Charles Scribner's Sons, 1943.

Anderson, Thomas M. "Our Rule in the Philippines," *North American Review*, February 1900.

Ashburn, Percy Moreau. *A History of the Medical Department of the United States Army, 1872-1929*. Boston: Houghton Mifflin Company, 1929.

Atherton, Gertrude. *Golden Gate Country*. New York: Duell, Sloan, & Pearce, 1945.

Baker, Major Chauncey B. *Transportation of Troops and Materiel*. Kansas City, MO: Franklin Hudson Publishing Co., 1905.

Bagwell, Beth. *Oakland: The Story of a City*. Navato, CA: Presidio Press, 1982.

Barton, Clara. *A Story of the Red Cross: Glimpses of Field Work*. New York: D. Appleton and Co., 1928.

———. *The Red Cross in Peace and War*. Washington, DC: American Historical Press, 1899.

Bell, William G., et al. *American Military History*. Washington, DC: Center of Military History, 1989.

Biographical Directory of the American Congress. Alexandria, VA: CQ Staff Directories, 1997.

Block, Eugene B. *The Immortal San Franciscans for Whom the Streets Were Named*. San Francisco: Chronicle Books, 1971.

Bond, Reverend James. *Christian Endeavorers in the School and Army*. New York: American Missionary Association.

Broderick, Robert C. *The Catholic Concise Encyclopedia*. St. Paul, MN: Catechetical Guild Educational Society, 1957.

Burdett, Thomas F. "A New Evaluation of General Otis' Leadership in the Philippines," *Military Review* (January 1975): 79-87.

California State Red Cross. *A Record of the Red Cross Work on the Pacific Slope, Including California, Nevada, Oregon, Washington, and Idaho With their Auxiliaries; also Reports from Nebraska, Tennessee, and Far-Away Japan*. Oakland: Pacific Press Publishing Co., 1902.

Cantor, Louis. "The Creation of the Modern National Guard: The Dick Militia Act of 1903." Ph.D. dissertation. Durham, NC: Duke University, 1963.

Carlisle, Henry C. *San Francisco Street Names: Sketches of the Lives of Pioneers for Whom San Francisco Streets are Named*. San Francisco: American Trust Co., 1954.

Catholic Almanac. Huntington, IN: Our Sunday Visitor, Inc., 1979.

The Catholic Encyclopedia. New York: Robert Appleton Co., 1912.

"Catholic Truth," *The Tablet*, 28 August 1993.

Clark, Rev. Francis E. *Christian Endeavor for all Races*. New York: American Missionary Association. n.d.

Clark, F.E. *Young People's Society of Christian Endeavor. . . . What It Is and How It Works*. Boston: United Society of Christian Endeavor, 1894.

Coffman, Edward M. *The Hilt of the Sword: The Career of Peyton C. March*. Madison: University of Wisconsin Press, 1966.

———. *The Old Army: A Portrait of the American Army in Peacetime, 1784-1898*. New York: Oxford University Press, 1986.

Cole, David C. Organization, Clothing, and Equipment of the Army of the United States in the War With Spain. n.p., n.d.

Cole, Tom. *A Short History of San Francisco*. San Francisco: Don't Call It Frisco Press, 1981.

Collingwood, Cuthbert. "The Catholic Truth Society." *Clergy Review*, November 1952.

Cooper, Jerry. *The Militia and the National Guard in America Since Colonial Times: A Research Guide*. Westport, CT: Greenwood Press, 1993.

Cosmas, Graham A. *An Army for Empire: The United States Army in the Spanish-American War*. Columbia, MO: University of Missouri Press, 1971.

Crocker's Guide Map of the City of San Francisco, Compiled From the Official Surveys and for the Crocker-Langley San Francisco Directory, 1896.

Cross, Robert D. *The Emergence of Liberal Catholicism in America*. London: Oxford University Press, 1958.

Crouch, Thomas W. *A Leader of Volunteers: Frederick Funston and the 20th Kansas in the Philippines, 1898-1899*. Lawrence, KS: Coronado Press, 1984.

deFord, Miriam Allen. *They Were San Franciscans*. Caldwell, ID: The Caxton Printers, Ltd., 1947.

Dewey, George. *Autobiography of George Dewey, Admiral of the Navy*. New York: Charles Scribner's Sons, 1913.

Doxey, William. *Doxey's Guide to San Francisco and the Pleasure Resorts of California*. San Francisco: Doxey Press, 1897.

Drury, Clifford M. *San Francisco YMCA: 100 Years by the Golden Gate, 1853-1953*. Glendale, CA: Arthur H. Clark Co., 1963.

Dulles, Foster Rhea. *The American Red Cross: A History*. New York: Harper & Brothers, 1950.

Eckart, Nelson A. "The Water Supply System of San Francisco," *Journal of the American Water Works Association*, May 1940.

The Elite Directory for San Francisco and Oakland. San Francisco: The Argonaut Publishing Co., 1879.

Encyclopedia of Catholicism. San Francisco: Harper Collins, 1995.

Farrow, Edward S. *A Dictionary of Military Terms*. New York: Thomas Y. Crowell Co., 1918.

_____. *Farrow's Military Encyclopedia: A Dictionary of Military Knowledge*. 3 vols. New York: Published by the author, 1885.

Faust, Karl Irving. *Campaigning in the Philippines*. San Francisco: Hicks-Judd Co. Publishers, 1899.

Freeman, N.N. *A Soldier in the Philippines*. New York: F. Tennyson Neely Co, 1901.

Funston, Frederick. *Memories of Two Wars: Cuban and Philippine Experiences*. New York: Charles Scribner's Sons, 1911.

Gates, John M. *Schoolbooks and Krags: The United States Army in the Philippines, 1898-1902*. Westport, CT: Greenwood Press, Inc., 1973.

George, Jesse. *Our Army and Navy in the Orient*. Manila: n.p., 1899.

Gilbo, Patrick F. *The American Red Cross: The First Century*. New York: Harper & Row, 1981.

Gillett, Mary C. *The Army Medical Department 1865-1917*. Army Historical Series. Washington, DC: Center of Military History, 1995.

Gilliam, Harold. *San Francisco Bay*. Garden City, NY: Doubleday & Co., Inc., 1957.

Ginn, Richard V.N. *The History of the US Army Medical Service Corps*. Washington, DC: Office of the Surgeon General and Center of Military History, 1997.

Goodrich, Mary. *The Palace Hotel*. San Francisco: n.p., 1930.

Greenleaf, Charles R. "An Object Lesson in Military Sanitation," *Boston Medical and Surgical Journal*, volume 141, 1899.

H.S. Crocker Company. *Crocker-Langley San Francisco Directory for Year Commencing April 1896*. San Francisco: H.S. Crocker Co., 1896.

_____. *Crocker-Langley San Francisco Directory for Year Commencing May 1899*. San Francisco: H.S. Crocker Co., 1899.

Hansen, Gladys. *San Francisco Almanac: Everything You Want to Know About the City*. San Francisco: Chronicle Books, 1975.

Harper's Pictorial History of the War With Spain. New York: Harper and Brothers Publishers, 1899.

Healy, David. *US Expansionism: The Imperialist Urge in the 1890s*. Madison: University of Wisconsin Press, 1970.

Heitman, Francis B. *Historical Register and Dictionary of the United States Army, From its Organization, September 29, 1789, to March 2, 1903*. 2 vols. Washington, DC: GPO, 1903.

Hendrickson, Kenneth E. Jr., *The Spanish-American War*. Westport, CT: Greenwood Press, 2003.

Hill, Jim Dan. *The Minute Man in Peace and War: A History of the National Guard*. Harrisburg, PA: The Stackpole Co., 1964.

Hopkins, C. Howard. *History of the Y.M.C.A. in North America*. New York: Association Press, 1951.

House, Jonathan M. *Toward Combined Arms Warfare: A Survey of 20th-Century Tactics, Doctrine, and Organization*. Research Survey No. 2. Fort Leavenworth, KS: Combat Studies Institute, August 1984.

Howard, General Oliver Otis. *Fighting for Humanity or Camp and Quarter-Deck*. London: F. Tennyson Neely, 1898.

Hurd, Charles. *The Compact History of the American Red Cross*. New York: Hawthorn Books, 1959.

Huston, James A. *The Sinews of War: Army Logistics, 1775-1953*. Washington, DC: Office of the Chief of Military History, 1966.

Hutchinson, John F. *Champions of Charity: War and the Rise of the Red Cross*. Boulder, CO: Westview Press, 1996.

Jamieson, Perry D. *Crossing the Deadly Ground: United States Army Tactics, 1865-1899*. Tuscaloosa, AL: University of Alabama Press, 1994.

Jenness, C.K. *The Charities of San Francisco: A Directory of the Benevolent and Correctional Agencies, Together With a Digest of Those Laws Most Directly Affecting Their Work*. San Francisco: Book Room Print, 1894.

Karsten, Peter, ed. *The Military in America: From the Colonial Era to the Present*. New York: Free Press, 1980.

King, Charles. *Campaigning With Crook.* Norman: University of Oklahoma Press, 1964.

———. "Memories of a Busy Life." *Wisconsin Magazine of History*, vol. V, numbers 3 and 4 and vol. VI, numbers 1 and 2.

Kreidberg, Marvin A. and Merton G. Henry, *History of Military Mobilization in the United States Army, 1775-1945.* Department of the Army Pamphlet No. 20-212. Washington, DC: GPO, November 1955.

Lancaster, Richard C. *Serving the U.S. Armed Forces, 1861-1986: The Story of the YMCA's Ministry to Military Personnel for 125 Years.* Schaumburg, IL: Armed Services YMCA of the USA, 1987.

Langellier, John Phillip. "Bastion by the Bay: A History of the Presidio of San Francisco, 1776-1906." Unpublished dissertation, Manhattan, KS: Kansas State University, 1982.

Leffler, John Joseph. "From the Shadows Into the Sun: Americans in the Spanish-American War." Ph.D. dissertation, Austin, TX: University of Texas at Austin, 1991.

Linderman, Gerald F. *The Mirror of War: American Society and the Spanish-American War.* Ann Arbor: University of Michigan Press, 1974.

Linn, Brian McAllister. *The Philippine War, 1899-1902.* Lawrence, KS: University Press of Kansas, 2000.

Mahon, John K. *History of the Militia and the National Guard.* New York: Macmillan Publishing Co., 1983.

Mahon, John K. and Romana Danysh. *Infantry, Part I: Regular Army.* Washington, DC: Office of the Chief of Military History, 1972.

Map, Crocker's Guide Map of the City of San Francisco, 1896

Map, Presidio of San Francisco, California, 1897-1909. Post Engineer.

Markoe, William F. "The Catholic Truth Society." *Catholic World*, January 1891.

Marolda, Edward J., ed. *Theodore Roosevelt, the U.S. Navy, and the Spanish-American War.* New York: Palgrave, 2001.

Martini, John A. *Fort Point: Sentry at the Golden Gate.* San Francisco: Golden Gate National Park Association, 1991.

———. *Fortress Alcatraz: Guardian of the Golden Gate.* Kailua, HI: Pacific Monograph, 1990.

Matloff, Maurice, et al. *American Military History.* Washington, DC: GPO, 1989.

May, Ernest R. *Imperial Democracy: The Emergence of America as a Great Power.* New York: Harper & Row, 1961.

McDevitt, Brother V. Edmund. *The First California's Chaplain.* Fresno, CA: Academy Library Guild, 1956.

McGloin, John Bernard. *San Francisco: The Story of a City.* San Rafael, CA: Presidio Press, 1978.

McKenney, Janice E. *Field Artillery: Regular Army and Army Reserve.* Washington, DC: GPO, 1985.

Mechanics' Institute of San Francisco. *100 Years of Mechanics' Institute of San*

Francisco, 1855-1955. San Francisco: Mechanics' Institute of San Francisco, 1955.

Merritt, Wesley, et al. *The Armies of To-Day: A Description of the Armies of the Leading Nations at the Present Time*. London: James R. Osgood, McIlvaine & Co., 1893.

Millett, Allan R. and Peter Maslowski. *For the Common Defense: A Military History of the United States of America*. New York: Free Press, 1984.

Morse, Richard C. *History of the North American Young Men's Christian Associations*. New York: Association Press, 1913.

Musicant, Ivan. *Empire by Default: The Spanish American War and the Dawn of the American Century*. New York: Henry Holt and Co., 1998.

Muscatine, Doris. *Old San Francisco: The Biography of a City From Early Days to the Earthquake*. New York: G.P. Putnam's Sons, 1975.

The National Cyclopaedia of American Biography. New York and New Jersey: James T. White & Co., 1984.

New Catholic Encyclopedia. Washington, DC: Catholic University of America, 1967.

Nofi, Albert A. *The Spanish-American War, 1898*. Conshohocken, PA: Combined Books, 1996.

O'Brien, Robert. *This is San Francisco*. New York: McGraw-Hill Book Co., 1948.

O'Toole, G.J.A. *The Spanish War: An American Epic, 1898*. New York: W.W. Norton & Co., 1984.

Paterson, Thomas G., J. Garry Clifford, and Kenneth J. Hagan. *American Foreign Relations: A History Since 1895*. 4th edition. Lexington, MA: D.C. Heath & Co., 1995.

Prucha, Francis Paul. *A Guide to the Military Posts of the United States, 1789-1895*. Madison, WI: State Historical Society of Wisconsin, 1964.

Purdy, Helen Throop. *San Francisco: As It Was, As It Is, and How to See It*. San Francisco: Paul Elder and Co., 1912.

Riesenberg, Felix, Jr. *Golden Gate: The Story of San Francisco Harbor*. New York: Alfred A. Knopf, 1940.

Risch, Erna. *Quartermaster Support of the Army: A History of the Corps, 1775-1939*. Washington, DC: Office of the Quartermaster General, 1962.

Roberts, Robert B. *Encyclopedia of Historic Forts: The Military, Pioneer, and Trading Posts of the United States*. New York: Macmillan Publishing Co., 1988.

Russell, Don. *Campaigning With King: Charles King, Chronicler of the Old Army*. Lincoln: University of Nebraska Press, 1991.

San Francisco: Its Builders Past and Present. 2 vols. Chicago-San Francisco: S.J. Clarke Publishing Co., 1913.

Schussler, Hermann. "The Water Supply of San Francisco, California." Spring Valley Water Co., 23 July 1906.

Sexton, William Thaddeus. *Soldiers in the Sun: An Adventure in Imperialism*. Freeport, NY: Books for Libraries Press, 1939.

Sinclair, Mick. *Fodor's Exploring San Francisco*. New York: Fodor's Travel Publications, 1995.

Spector, Ronald. *Admiral of the New Empire: The Life and Career of George Dewey*. Baton Rouge: Louisiana University Press, 1974.

Stewart, Robert E., Jr. and Mary Frances Stewart. *Adolph Sutro: A Biography*. Berkeley, CA: Howell-North Books, 1962.

Stubbs, Mary Lee and Stanley Russell Connor. *Armor-Cavalry, Part I: Regular Army and Army Reserve*. Washington, DC: GPO, 1969.

Taft, William H., et al. *Service With Fighting Men: An Account of the Work of the American Young Men's Christian Associations in the World War*. New York: Association Press, 1922.

Thompson, Erwin N. *Defender of the Gate: The Presidio of San Francisco, A History From 1846 to 1995*. 2 vols. Golden Gate National Recreation Area, CA: National Park Service, 1997.

Trask, David F. *The War With Spain in 1898*. New York: Macmillan Publishing Co., 1981.

Turner, James H., et al. *History of Public Transit in San Francisco, 1850-1948*. San Francisco: City and County of San Francisco, 1948.

Twentieth Century Encyclopedia of Religious Knowledge. Grand Rapids, MI: Baker Book House, 1955.

United Society of Christian Endeavor. *Christian Endeavor Topics*. Fredonia, NY: Society Topics Publishing Co., 1899.

Welch, Richard E., Jr. *Response to Imperialism: The United States and the Philippine-American War, 1899-1902*. Chapel Hill, NC: University of North Carolina Press, 1979.

Whiting, J.S. and Richard J. Whiting. *Forts of the State of California*. Longview, WA: Daily News Press, 1960.

Who Was Who in America. Chicago: Marquis-Who's Who, 1943.

Wilcox, Marrion, ed. *Harper's History of the War in the Philippines*. New York: Harper & Brothers, 1900.

Wirmel, Sister Mary Magdalen. "Sisterhoods in the Spanish American War." *Catholic Historical Records and Studies*, vol. 32, 1941.

Wood, John H. *Seventy-Five Years of History of the Mechanics' Institute of San Francisco*. San Francisco: Mechanics' Institute of San Francisco, 1930.

Wooley, Richard W. "A Short History of Identification Tags." *Quartermaster Professional Bulletin*, December 1988.

Workers of the Writers' Program of the Work Projects Administration in Northern California. *The Army at the Golden Gate: A Guide to Army Posts in the San Francisco Bay Area*. n.p., n.d.

Young, Kenneth Ray. *The General's General: The Life and Times of Arthur MacArthur*. Boulder, CO: Westview Press, 1994.

Appendix A
Units Assembling in/Deploying From San Francisco, 1 May-12 August 1898

Unit	Arrived San Francisco	Date Deployed	Philippine Expedition
1st California Infantry	Present	25 May	first
3d US Artillery (4 btries)	Present	27/29 June	third
7th California Infantry	7 May		
6th California Infantry	8/9 May		
California Heavy Artillery	9 May	25 May (detach)	first
14th US Infantry	9 May	25 May (5 cos)	first
		15 July (5 cos)	fourth
2d Oregon Infantry	13 May	25 May	first
1st Washington Infantry	14 May		
1st Nebraska Infantry	19 May	15 June	second
20th Kansas Infantry	20 May		
1st Wyoming Infantry	21 May	27/29 June	third
13th Minnesota Infantry	21 May	27/29 June	third
1st Colorado Infantry	21 May	15 June	second
1st Idaho Infantry	22 May	27/29 June	third
Utah Light Artillery	22 May	15 June (2 btries)	second
10th Pennsylvania Infantry	25 May	15 June	second
Utah Cavalry	26 May		
1st Montana Infantry	28 May	19 July	fifth
18th US Infantry	29 May	15 June (4 cos)	second
		27/29 June (4 cos)	third
23d US Infantry	29 May	15 June (4 cos)	second
		27/29 June (4 cos)	third
US Engineer Company	29 May	15 June (detach)	second
		27/29 June (1 co)	third
1st North Dakota Infantry	31 May	27/29 June	third
1st South Dakota Infantry	1 June	23 July (8 cos)	sixth
		29 July (4 cos)	seventh
4th US Cavalry	5 June	15 July (6 troops)	fourth
Signal Corps Detachment	8 June	27/29 June	third
51st Iowa Infantry	10 June		
Nevada Cavalry	15 June		
1st Tennessee Infantry	17 June		
Astor Battery	20 June	27/29 June	third
6th US Arty (2 btries)	27 June	15 July (2 btries)	fourth
Wyoming Battery	28 June		
1st New York Infantry	13 July	6 August (5 cos)	Hawaii
		10 August (2 cos)	Hawaii

btries	batteries
cos	companies
detach	detachment

Appendix B
Department of the Pacific and
VIII Army Corps Leadership, June 1898

MG Wesley Merritt, Commander,
Department of the Pacific and VIII Army Corps

MG Elwell S. Otis, Commander,
Independent Division, VIII Army Corps

BG Thomas M. Anderson, Commander, First Expedition

BG Francis V. Greene, Commander, Second Expedition

BG Arthur MacArthur, Commander, Third Expedition

References for Figures

Figure 1	*Harper's History of the War in the Philippines*, 45.
Figure 2	*San Francisco Call*, 19 May 1898, 1.
Figure 3	*Harper's Pictorial History of the War With Spain*, 242.
Figure 4	*The Examiner*, 5 June 1898, 10.
Figure 5	*Harper's Pictorial History of the War With Spain*, 154.
Figure 6	*Harper's Pictorial History of the War With Spain*, 125.
Figure 7	*Harper's Pictorial History of the War With Spain*, 169.
Figure 8	*History of Military Mobilization in the United States Army, 1775-1945*, 151
Figure 9	*Harper's Pictorial History of the War With Spain*, 265.
Figure 10	*Harper's Pictorial History of the War With Spain*, 152.
Figure 11	*San Francisco Call*, 14 July 1898, 8.
Figure 12	*San Francisco Chronicle*, 5 May 1898, 9.
Figure 13	*The Examiner*, 21 May 1898, 1.
Figure 14	*The Examiner*, 21 May 1898, 3.
Figure 15	*The Examiner*, 21 May 1898, 3.
Figure 16	Presidio Army Museum Photo Collection, Golden Gate National Recreation Area (GGNRA), National Park Service (NPS), GOGA-1766.0020, PAM Photo Box II.
Figure 17	TASC Photo Collection, GGNRA, NPS, GOGA-2266, TASC Box 25.
Figure 18	*Record of the Red Cross Work on the Pacific Slope*, 16.
Figure 19	*San Francisco Call*, 21 May 1898, 5
Figure 20	*San Francisco Chronicle*, 11 June 1898, 9
Figure 21	*San Francisco Chronicle*, 21 May 1898, 9
Figure 22	*San Francisco Chronicle*, 20 May 1898, 12.
Figure 23	Crocker's Guide Map of the City of San Francisco, 1896.
Figure 24	NPS, GOGA, Presidio Army Records Center.
Figure 25	*San Francisco Call*, 18 May 1898, 5.
Figure 26	*San Francisco Chronicle*, 9 May 1898, 5.
Figure 27	TASC Photo Collection, GGNRA, NPS, GOGA-2266, TASC Box 26.
Figure 28	Crocker's Guide Map of the City of San Francisco, 1896.
Figure 29	*The Examiner*, 31 May 1898, 3.
Figure 30	*San Francisco Call*, 30 May 1898, 5.
Figure 31	Presidio Army Museum Photo Collection, GGNRA, NPS, GOGA-1766.0001, Pam Neg Box 8.
Figure 32	*The Examiner*, 17 May 1898, 1.
Figure 33	*The Examiner*, 18 May 1898, 2.
Figure 34	*The Examiner*, 27 May 1898, 14.
Figure 35	*San Francisco Call*, 5 May 1898, 2.
Figure 36	*San Francisco Chronicle*, 29 May 1898, 13.
Figure 37	*San Francisco Chronicle*, 29 May 1898, 13.
Figure 38	*San Francisco Call*, 13 June 1898, 5.
Figure 39	*San Francisco Chronicle*, 16 August 1898, 14.

Figure 40   *The Examiner*, 28 May 1898, 3.
Figure 41   *The Examiner*, 31 May 1898, 3.
Figure 42   *San Francisco Call*, 3 June 1898, 1.
Figure 43   *The Examiner*, 3 June 1898, 3.
Figure 44   *San Francisco Chronicle*, 6 June 1898, 5.
Figure 45   *San Francisco Chronicle*, 17 May 1898, 3.
Figure 46   *The Examiner*, 11 May 1898, 3.
Figure 47   *San Francisco Call*, 29 May 1898, 7.
Figure 48   *The Examiner*, 4 June 1898, 3.
Figure 49   *San Francisco Chronicle*, 7 July 1898, 9.
Figure 50   *San Francisco Chronicle*, 28 May 1898, 9.
Figure 51   Presidio Army Museum Photo Collection, GGNRA, NPS, GOGA-1766.0020, Pam Photo Box II, File E, Pam Neg Box 8.
Figure 52   *San Francisco Chronicle*, 3 June 1898, 12.
Figure 53   *San Francisco Chronicle*, 10 June 1898, 7.
Figure 54   *The Examiner*, 11 May 1898, 3.
Figure 55   *San Francisco Chronicle*, 20 June 1898, 5.
Figure 56   *San Francisco Chronicle*, 5 July 1898, 10.
Figure 57   *The Examiner*, 8 June 1898, 4.
Figure 58   *San Francisco Chronicle*, 14 June 1898, 3.
Figure 59   *San Francisco Chronicle*, 10 July 1898, 23.
Figure 60   *San Francisco Call*, 7 June 1898, 7.
Figure 61   *San Francisco Chronicle*, 9 June 1898, 3.
Figure 62   *Record of the Red Cross Work on the Pacific Slope*, 92.
Figure 63   TASC Photo Collection, GGNRA, NPS, GOGA-2266, TASC Box 26.
Figure 64   *Record of the Red Cross Work on the Pacific Slope*, 54.
Figure 65   Presidio Army Museum Photo Collection, GGNRA, NPS, GOGA-1766.0001, Pam Neg Box 8.
Figure 66   *The Examiner*, 1 July 1898, 12.
Figure 67   *Record of the Red Cross Work on the Pacific Slope*, 8.
Figure 68   *Record of the Red Cross Work on the Pacific Slope*, 72.
Figure 69   *Record of the Red Cross Work on the Pacific Slope*, 83.
Figure 70   *San Francisco Call*, 25 May 1898, 3.
Figure 71   *San Francisco Call*, 18 June 1898, 14.
Figure 72   *San Francisco Call*, 19 May 1898, 8.
Figure 73   *Record of the Red Cross Work on the Pacific Slope*, 98.
Figure 74   *Record of the Red Cross Work on the Pacific Slope*, 100.
Figure 75   *Record of the Red Cross Work on the Pacific Slope*, 122.
Figure 76   *Record of the Red Cross Work on the Pacific Slope*, 100.
Figure 77   *San Francisco Call*, 22 May 1898, 7.
Figure 78   *Record of the Red Cross Work on the Pacific Slope*, 180.
Figure 79   *San Francisco Call*, 13 June 1898, 5.
Figure 80   *San Francisco Chronicle*, 14 July 1898, 12.
Figure 81   *The Examiner*, 4 June 1898, 3.
Figure 82   *Record of the Red Cross Work on the Pacific Slope*, 190.

Figure 83   *San Francisco Call*, 9 July 1898, 14.
Figure 84   *San Francisco Chronicle*, 13 June 1898, 5.
Figure 85   *San Francisco Chronicle*, 30 May 1898, 3.
Figure 86   *San Francisco Chronicle*, 25 June 1898, 9.
Figure 87   *San Francisco Call*, 8 July 1898, 6.
Figure 88   *San Francisco Chronicle*, 5 May 1898, 9.
Figure 89   *Harper's Pictorial History of the War With Spain*, 146.
Figure 90   *The Examiner*, 4 August 1898, 4.
Figure 91   *San Francisco Call*, 29 May 1898, 8.
Figure 92   *San Francisco Chronicle*, 18 May 1898, 3.
Figure 93   *The Examiner*, 13 June 1898, 3.
Figure 94   *San Francisco Call*, 19 June 1898, 22.
Figure 95   *The Examiner*, 15 June 1898, 2.
Figure 96   *The Examiner*, 26 May 1898, 1.
Figure 97   *San Francisco Chronicle*, 13 June 1898, 5.
Figure 98   *San Francisco Call*, 24 May 1898, 2.
Figure 99   TASC Photo Collection, GGNRA, NPS, GOGA-2266, TASC Box 26.
Figure 100 *San Francisco Chronicle*, 30 June 1898, 3.
Figure 101 *San Francisco Chronicle*, 16 July 1898, 9.
Figure 102 *The Examiner*, 19 May 1898, 2.
Figure 103 *Harper's Pictorial History of the War With Spain*, 409
Figure 104 *Harper's Pictorial History of the War With Spain*, 233.

Appendix B
BG Thomas M. Anderson   *Harper's Pictorial History of the War With Spain*, 265.
BG Francis V. Greene   *Harper's History of the War in the Philippines*, 57.
BG Arthur MacArthur   *Harper's Pictorial History of the War With Spain*, 411.
MG Wesley Merritt, USA   *Harper's Pictorial History of the War With Spain*, 169.
MG Elwell S. Otis   *Harper's Pictorial History of the War With Spain*, 457.

Index

Aguinaldo, Emilio, 257, 259, 260
Alameda County Union, contributor to Christian Endeavorers (CE), 197
Alameda, CA, 143, 190, 191
Alaska, 15, 16, 19, 67, 68, 260
Alcatraz Island, 55
Alexander, Arthur P., representative, CE, 196
Alger, Russell A., Secretary of War, 11, 16, 17, 23, 24, 26, 27, 30, 54, 68, 69, 70, 71, 74, 86, 88, 90, 140, 222, 236, 240, 243, 245, 246
Allison, W.B., US senator, Iowa, 26
Alvira, river steamer, 156
American Union Fish Company, 149
Anderson, Thomas M., BG, 15, 16, 68, 86, 87, 88, 257
Andre, Edward, Belgium Consul in Manila, 258
Angel Island, 56, 57, 240
Army and Navy Christian Commission, 180, 181, 182, 187, 189, 190, 191
Asiatic Squadron, 15, 165, 257
Associated Charities, San Francisco, 167
Astor Battery, 20, 44, 48, 49, 54, 232
Astor, John Jacob, 20, 21, 46, 48
Australia, oceanic transport, 155, 225, 230
awkward squads, 97

B Street, 192, 193, 197
Babbitt, L.S., COL, commanding officer, Benicia Arsenal, 118
Baer, John Willis, General Secretary, United Society of CE, 195
Baker, A.G., Private, 1st Colorado, 47, 152
Baldwin Theater, 146
Baldwin, William H., COL, Purchasing Commissary, 119
bandages, 148, 159, 163, 165, 203
bands, 48, 51, 116, 237
Baptist, 161, 182, 188, 194
Barber, Thomas H., COL, 25, 244, 245
Barrett, William H., Private, 2d Oregon, 104
Barton, Clara, founder and president, American Red Cross, 139, 140
baseball, 117, 146
basketball, 117, 184
battle of Manila Bay, 16, 218
Bay District Racetrack, 43, 63, 64, 65, 66, 69, 71, 92, 109, 157, 238, 242
Belgic, oceanic transport, 224
Belmont School, 149
Benicia Arsenal, 29, 118
Berkeley, CA, 143
Bermingham, John H., Captain, Supervising Inspector of Hulls and Boilers, 225

287

Berry, John R., COL, commanding officer, 7th California, 60, 115
Berry, Miss Mindora L., State Superintendent of Missions, CE, 190, 194, 195, 196
Bert, Eugene F., president, Pacific Coast Baseball League, 117
Bibles, 184, 185, 187
Big Tent, CTS, 202, 203
Bird, Charles, COL, oceanic transportation, 220, 226, 261
Birkhimer, W.E., CPT, 3d US Infantry, 227
blouses, 121
Board of Health, San Francisco, 161, 243
Board of Medical Officers, 122, 123
Boots, mascot, 10th Pennsylvania, 55
Bovard, Freeman D., pastor, 1st Methodist-Episcopal Church, 182, 183
Brainard, David L., LTC, Chief of Commissary, 73, 74
brigade hospital, 122, 156
Britten, James, Catholic Truth Society, 197
bronchitis, 122, 158
Brooke, John R., MG, 19
Brooks, D., Miss, CE, 194
Budd, James H., governor, CA, 140
Burlingame, CA, 92
Bush Street, 117

California and Pacific Coast Jockey Clubs, 146
California Avenue, 66
California Heavy Artillery, 110, 160, 241
California Hotel, 141
California Red Cross Society, 141, 142, 144, 145, 149, 156, 164
California State Christian Endeavor Union, 190, 194
California State Red Cross Association, 142, 144, 162, 164
California Street Cable Railroad, 152
calisthenics, 106, 107
Camp Barrett, Oakland, CA, 182, 184
Camp McKinley, IA, 26
Camp Merriam, CA, 124
Camp Merritt, CA, 65, 66, 67, 71, 73, 74, 85, 88, 89, 91, 92, 93, 94, 95, 96, 101,
    104, 106, 107, 109, 111, 112, 113, 114, 116, 119, 122, 123, 124, 149, 152,
    157, 160, 161, 181, 182, 183, 185, 190, 193, 195, 196, 197, 199, 200, 202,
    203, 204, 232, 237, 238, 242, 243, 244, 245, 246, 262
Camp Miller, CA, 67, 200
Camp Richmond, CA, 117
Camp, James, Private, 1st Idaho, 45, 102, 104
Canadian Pacific Railway Company, 221
Caribbean, 2, 3, 5, 6, 12, 14, 15, 16, 17, 18, 20, 25, 30, 86, 119
Carrington, Frank de L. CPT, USA, attached to CA Army National Guard, 31, 57, 62
Carsey, Zeke, mascot, 1st Tennessee, 55

Catholic Ladies' Aid Society, 200, 201, 205
Catholic Truth Society (CTS), 90, 161, 179, 197, 198, 199, 200, 201, 202, 203, 204, 205, 206, 263
Cavalry Society, contributor to CE, 197
Centennial, oceanic transport, 224, 225
Central Methodist Episcopal, contributor to CE, 197
cerebrospinal meningitis, 122
Chaffee, Adna R., COL, USA, 86
chaplains, 180, 182, 185, 186, 198, 205
Chautauqua Assembly, 188
Cherington, F.B., Reverend, CE, 193
Chickamauga Park, GA, 19, 20, 23, 30
chief commissary, 73, 119
Children's Hospital, 164, 263
China, 218
China, oceanic transport, 225, 228
Christian Commission, 180, 181, 182, 183, 184, 185, 186, 187, 189, 190, 191, 192, 195, 196
Christian Endeavor Society, 188, 189, 196, 197
Christian Endeavorer's (CE) Golden Gate Union, 190, 192
Christner, William S., Private, 10th Pennsylvania, 28, 47, 151
City of Para, oceanic transport, 163, 186
City of Peking, oceanic transport, 154, 165, 218, 225, 227, 230, 261
City of Sydney, oceanic transport, 155, 225, 230
Clapp, Hugh E., Corporal, 1st Nebraska, 107, 118
Clark, Alfred S., Chaplain, 7th California, 180
Clark, Francis E., CE, 189, 190
Claus Sprekels Building, San Francisco, 51
Clement Grammar School, 146
Cleveland, oceanic transport, 224
Cleveland, Grover, President, 1, 2
Colby College, ME, 67
Colon, oceanic transport, 225, 228
comfort bags, 148, 149, 162, 192, 194, 195, 197, 203, 204
commissary, 31, 119
commissary separtment, CTS, 203
Conemaugh, oceanic transport, 222, 224
congregation, 188
Congregationalists, 188
Consumers' Ice Company, contributor, CTS, 205
contracts, 120, 121, 168, 222
Corbin, Henry C. BG, Adjutant General, USA, 12, 14, 15, 16, 17, 18, 19, 20, 23, 24, 26, 27, 28, 29, 62, 68, 72, 73, 85, 118, 220, 221, 222, 235, 236, 245, 261
Corps, VIII, 11, 21, 123, 257, 259, 260, 261, 262
cots, 203

Council Bluffs, IA, 32
Court Marin, Foresters of America No. 73, Patriotic Home Helpers (PHH), 169
courts-martial, 110, 111
Craig, Hugh, president, SF Chamber of Commerce, 245
Crittenden, M.P., evangelist, 185,
Crocker Estate Company, 65
Cuba, 1, 2, 3, 4, 5, 6, 23, 30, 86, 139, 165

Davis, George W., COL, USA, 86
Davis, Grace, Miss, soloist, 189
de Young, M.H., editor/proprietor, *SF Chronicle*, 90
Del Monte Milling Company, contributor, CTS, 205
delicacies, 158, 163, 185, 201
Denman School, contributor to CE, 197
Department of California, 12, 20, 50, 68, 74, 87, 89, 121, 238, 240, 242, 245
Department of Colorado, 69
Department of the Columbia, 20, 67, 68, 69, 74
Department of Dakota, 21
Department of the East, 22, 24, 25, 72, 74, 235
Department of the Gulf, 14, 19
Department of the Pacific, 6, 7, 73, 74, 87, 89, 95, 121, 123, 124, 218, 221, 233, 240, 246, 257, 259, 261, 262
Detrick, Charles R., Private, 1st California, 62, 231, 237, 241
Devol, C.A., CPT, acting quartermaster, Otis staff, 88
Dewey, George, 1, 4, 5, 6, 11, 12, 13, 22, 54, 70, 164, 165, 217, 218, 257, 258, 259, 260, 261
diarrhea, 122, 123
Dille, E.R., Dr., Reverend, Methodist Church, 183, 191
disease, 121, 122, 139
ditty bag, CE, 194
division hospital, 66, 121, 122, 157, 246
doctors, 202
Doxey's Guide, 116
drill, 7, 25, 28, 29, 31, 57, 60, 61, 92, 96, 97, 98, 99, 100, 101, 102, 103, 104, 105, 106, 107, 108, 109, 111, 112, 116, 118, 146, 147, 159, 188, 189, 205, 234, 243, 244, 246
DuBoce, Victor D., LTC, 1st California, 57, 108
dummy rifle practice, 104
Dunbar, L.L., Mrs., secretary, CA Red Cross, 144, 157

VIII Corps, 11, 21, 123, 257, 259, 260, 261, 262
Easton, Wendell, Mrs., Chair, Committee of Nurses, Red Cross Society, 164
Ellis Street, 184
English Lutherans, 188
Epworth League, 191

evangelists, 184, 185
exercise, 7, 96, 97, 100, 103, 104, 105, 106, 107, 108, 147
expedition, first, 16, 71, 93, 95, 99, 109, 118, 154, 162, 163, 164, 166, 203, 220, 225, 227, 230, 232, 235, 237, 238, 239, 257, 261
expedition, second, 91, 104, 105, 116, 155, 162, 165, 166, 169, 195, 203, 225, 226, 228, 231, 232, 234, 235, 236, 237, 239, 257
expedition, third, 105, 155, 165, 166, 169, 186, 195, 196, 203, 226, 227, 232, 239, 244, 257
expedition, fourth, 155, 162, 232, 236, 240
expedition, seventh, 236
extended order, 97, 98, 99, 100, 101, 102, 103, 108, 189

Fair, James G., "Bonanza King", 144
Ferry Building, 43, 45, 46, 47, 48, 49, 51, 52, 149, 150, 151, 152, 153, 156
Fifth Avenue, 183, 190
First Baptist Church, San Francisco, 194
First Presbyterian Church, San Francisco, 154, 196, 197
Flood Building, 204
Fontana warehouse (Fontana Barracks), 43, 57, 58, 62, 63, 65, 67, 74, 91, 160, 190, 238, 242
Fontana, Mark J., part owner, Fontana warehouse, 63
food baskets, 201
football, 117, 118
Fort Leavenworth, 70, 87, 103
Fort Mason, 55, 56, 57, 58, 62
Fort Point, 55, 182
Fort Winfield Scott, 55, 56
4th Avenue, 93
French Hospital, San Francisco, 157, 158, 183, 202
Froam, George, mascot, 23d US Infantry, 54
Fuller Desk Company, 148
Fulton Street, 63, 93, 199, 202
fundraising, 108, 144, 147, 168, 187, 188, 196, 204, 205
Funston, Frederick, COL, 20th Kansas, 113, 115, 189, 234

G.M. Joselyn and Company, 149
garbage, 123
Garretson, George A., COL, 86
Geary Street, 51
General Depot, 31, 119
General Orders Number 1, 109
General Orders Number 8, 57
German Hospital, San Francisco, 158
Gerstie, Lewis, contributor to PHH, 169
Girls Mission High School, 146

Glunz, Charles A., representative, YMCA Christian Commission, 186, 187, 189, 196
Golden Gate, 7, 15, 22, 28, 29, 43, 46, 49, 50, 51, 54, 55, 56, 66, 68, 69, 70, 72, 74, 86, 88, 90, 93, 108, 112, 116, 117, 118, 120, 122, 124, 139, 140, 169, 179, 180, 182, 184, 185, 190, 192, 194, 205, 217, 230, 232, 236, 237, 238, 240, 243, 246, 260, 261, 262
Golden Gate Park, 93, 102, 116, 243
Golden Gate Primary School, 146
gonorrhea, 122
Grace Church, 149, 155
Grant Avenue, 115
Greenbaum, Weil, and Michaels, importers, 148
Greene, Francis V., BG, v, vi, 86, 88, 96, 257
groggeries, 114, 191, 243
guard mount, 98, 102, 108, 109, 112, 147, 189

Haist, Alexander, Lieutenant, 1st Montana, 102
Harbor View Gardens, 117
Harland, Hester A., Mrs., secretary, PHH, 166
Harrington, Mrs., Williard B., president, CA State Red Cross Association, 141, 142, 144, 157, 163, 164, 165
Hastings, Daniel H., governor, PA, 28
Hawaii, 96, 163, 187, 224, 235, 236, 245
Hawkins, Alexander L., COL, 10th Pennsylvania, 28, 111
Hearst Building, 143, 144
Hearst, Phoebe A., 143, 148, 188
Hearst, William Randolph, 143
heavy guard duty, 99
heavy marching order, 107, 233
Hecker, Frank, COL, Volunteers, 221, 222, 261
Heffner, Mrs., C.A., contributor to CE, 196
Heney, Miss, Spanish class teacher, 203
Henshaw, Park, COL, 8th California, 243
Hicks-Judd Company, publishers, 148
Hong Kong, 218
Honolulu, Hawaii, 187, 217, 245
Hooper, William B., Major, PHH, 166, 167, 169
Hopkins, William E., Dr., Surgeon General, California National Guard, 144
hospital, 56, 66, 88, 121, 122, 124, 140, 149, 156, 157, 158, 159, 161, 164, 165, 169, 179, 185, 194, 198, 200, 201, 202, 231, 246, 262
Hospital for Children and Training School for Nurses, 157, 164
Hotchkiss guns, 19, 228
Howard, Mrs., Spanish class teacher, 203
Howard, Oliver O., national delegate, YMCA, 187, 188
Hubbard, Louis, quartermaster Sergeant, 1st South Dakota, 107

hucksters, 123
Hughes, Robert P., COL, Inspector General (IG), Department of the Pacific, 74, 232, 233, 234
Hull Bill, 5, 21
Humbolt School, 146

identification (ID) badges, 155, 160
Independent Division, 71, 73, 74, 85, 88, 89, 93, 94, 96, 98, 100, 104, 109, 124, 202, 238, 239, 240, 262
Infantry Drill Regulations, 105
inspections, 70, 98, 224, 232
intoxicants, 243

J.R. Gates and Company, contributor to CE, 197
Jacks, David, contributor to YMCA, 188
Jackson, Frank A., representative, YMCA Christian Commission, 186, 187, 189, 196
Jackson, G.H.T., contributor to CE, 197
Japanese Bank, 147
Japanese Society, 147
Jaudenes, Don Fermin y Alvarez, Spanish Governor General, Philippines, 258, 259
John Monahan and Company, 148
Johnson, Major, contributor to CE, 197
Jordan, James Clark, SF real estate, 66
Jordan Tract, 43, 64, 66, 92, 242

Kessler, Harry C., COL, 1st Montana, 113
King, Charles, BG, 87
King's Daughters, contributors to CE, 196
Knights Templar, 47
Kraemer, Karl, Private, 51st Iowa, 87, 104, 105, 107, 111, 112, 189, 233

Laist, Alexander, Lieutenant, 1st Montana, 111
Lake Merritt, 107
Lakme, oceanic transport to Hawaii, 187
Larkin Street, 117
League of the Cross, 198, 199, 205
Lee, Fitzhugh, MG, 23
Leedy, John W., governor, KS, 26, 27
letters, 89, 104, 163, 183, 187, 193, 194, 202
Levi Strauss and Company, contributor to PHH, 169
Lewis, A. Parker, Red Cross Nurse (male), 164, 169
Lewis, H.R., secretary, Portland, OR, Chamber of Commerce, 30
libraries, 116, 183
Lime Point Military Reservation, CA, 55, 149
Lippincott, Henry, LTC, Chief Surgeon, Department of the Pacific and VIII Army Corps, 89

literary department, CTS, 203
Little, Edward C., LTC, 20th Kansas, 112
Lockett, James, CPT, 4th Cavalry, 50
Lombard Street, 51, 57, 60, 61
Long, John, Secretary of Navy, 217, 218
Long, Mrs., Oscar Fitzallen, 168
Long, Oscar F., Major, depot quartermaster, 74, 119, 120, 121, 162, 165, 168, 185, 224, 225, 226, 233, 234, 261
loose women, 113
Lopez, Lieutenant, 224
Lord, William P., governor, Oregon, 26
Los Angeles Times, 87
Los Angeles, CA, 142, 143, 188
Lowell High School, contributor to CE, 197
Ludington, Marshall I., BG, Quartermaster General, 220
Luhn, William L., adjutant, 1st Washington, 242
Lurline Salt Water Baths, San Francisco, 117

MacArthur, Arthur, BG, 87, 88, 239, 257
mailing department, 202
Maine, US ship, 3
Mallory, John S., CPT, acting IG, Otis staff, 88, 93, 232, 233
Manila, v, vi, 4, 6, 11, 12, 13, 18, 20, 23, 94, 95, 101, 120, 144, 149, 153, 162, 163, 164, 165, 166, 185, 187, 188, 189, 195, 196, 199, 217, 221, 228, 234, 238, 257, 258, 259, 260, 261
manuals, 103, 105
Maple Street, 66
March, Peyton C., CPT, Astor Battery, 21, 48, 49
Marin County, 55, 143, 169
Marin, CA, 56
Marine Hospital, US Treasury Department, 56, 121, 156
Market Street, 51, 88, 93, 143, 148
Markey, Joseph I., Private, 51st Iowa, 49
marksmanship, 104, 105, 107
Mason Street, 184
Matthews, W.S.H, Major, 51st Iowa, 244
McAllister-Street Line, cable car service, 93
McBride, George W., chairman, Committee on Coast Defenses, 30
McClosky, Miss Ella, host, musical for CTS, 205
McClosky, Miss Eva, host, musical for CTS, 205
McCorkle, Nathan, Private, 51st Iowa, 201
McCoy, Henry J., secretary, San Francisco YMCA, 180, 181, 182, 184, 185, 186, 187, 188, 191, 192
McCreery, A.B., contributor to Red Cross, 146
McKinley, William, US President, vi, 2, 3, 4, 5, 6, 7, 11, 12, 15, 16, 17, 18, 22, 23,

294

24, 27, 30, 56, 73, 87, 120, 139, 180,195, 217, 219, 243, 245, 259
McReeve, C., COL, 13th Minnesota, 163
measles, 122, 156, 159, 201, 235
Mechanics' Pavilion, San Francisco, 50, 92, 108, 112, 146, 147, 188
Medbery, Frank W., CPT, 1st South Dakota, 102, 103
media, 24
medical department, 85, 121, 194, 197
Meiklejohn, George de Rue, Assistant Secretary of War, 185, 219, 220, 222, 236
Memorial Day, 107
meningitis, 122, 158
Menlo Park, CA, 92
Merchants' Association, 151
Merriam, Henry C., MG, 12, 19, 20, 50, 51, 52, 56, 57, 63, 67, 68, 69, 72, 74, 89, 122, 124, 157, 238, 240, 242, 245, 246
Merrill, Mrs. John F., 142, 144, 148, 153, 155, 157
Merritt, Wesley, 6, 12, 13, 16, 17, 18, 19, 20, 21, 22, 23, 24, 25, 28, 71, 72, 73, 74, 85, 86, 87, 88, 89, 90, 91, 92, 93, 95, 96, 109, 114, 117, 118, 121, 122, 124, 147, 156, 157, 159, 164, 165, 179, 180, 185, 193, 195, 196, 205, 217, 220, 221, 222, 224, 225, 226, 230, 232, 233, 234, 235, 236, 239, 240, 244, 246, 257, 259, 261, 262, 263
Methodist Episcopalians, 188
Michian Street, 66
Miles, Nelson A., MG, 11, 12, 13, 16, 17, 20, 22, 55, 68, 185, 262
Mill Valley, CA, 146
Miller, Marcus P., BG, 87, 99, 100, 117, 240
Mills' College Red Cross, contributor to CE, 197
Minton, H.C., Dr., Presbyterian Church; president, Army and Navy Christian Commission of CA, 182, 184
Mission Parlor Hall, 205
Mission Woolen Mills, 57
Mobile, Alabama, 17, 30
Mogan, Joseph A., Fish and Game Warden, 149
Monarch, tugboat, 155
Monroe School, 146
Monterey, US ship, 45
Monterey, CA, 92, 188
Montgomery Street, 89
Moody, D.L., chair, YMCA International Committee, Evangelistic Department, 184, 185
Moore, Francis, Major, quartermaster, Otis staff, 88, 93
Morgan City, oceanic transport, 225
Morgan, W.P., Mrs., CA Red Cross Society Finance Chair, 145
Morris, J.J., chorus director, 189
Morris, Louis T., LTC, Presidio, 50, 56, 57, 60, 63, 180, 181
Morrow, W.W., US Circuit Judge, PHH, 166

Morse, Richard C., general secretary, YMCA International Committee, 184, 187, 188
Mothers' Christian Commission, YMCA, 185
Mothers' Christian Endeavor Club, 190, 192, 195, 196
Mothers' Club, 190, 192, 193, 194, 195, 197
Mount Gretna, PA, 28
mumps, 122
museum, 116, 117

National Guard, 5, 6, 21, 22, 26, 27, 28, 29, 31, 50, 62, 89, 140, 144, 180, 233, 235
National Guard Association, 21
National Red Cross, 139, 140
Native Daughters of the Red Cross, 148
Navy Department, 5, 226
Neall, John M., 1LT, 4th Cavalry, 57, 60, 69
Needham, A.T., Reverend, Oakland Methodist Church, 182
Needlework Guild, 148
Nelson, oceanic transport, 187
Nevada Cavalry, 117
New Montgomery Street, 89, 143
New Orleans, LA, 15, 16, 30, 54, 68
New York Association of San Francisco, 50
Newport, oceanic transport, 96, 222
North Pacific Coast Railroad, 152
nurses, 141, 156, 164, 165, 166

Oakland, 43, 44, 45, 47, 107, 143, 150, 155, 161, 165, 182, 185, 186, 188, 190, 191, 193, 196, 197, 200, 243, 244, 245
Oakland mole, 43
Oakland Race Track, 146
Oakland Red Cross, 159
Occidental Hotel, 166
O'Farrell Street, 88, 92
Olympia, US ship, 1
Ordnance Department, US Army, 118
Oregon Red Cross, 148
Orpheum Theater, San Francisco, 92
O'Ryan, Philip, Father, St. Mary's Cathedral, 198, 199
Otis, Elwell S., MG, 66, 69, 70, 71, 72, 73, 74, 85, 86, 87, 88, 89, 91, 93, 94, 95, 96, 98, 99, 100, 101, 104, 107, 109, 110, 111, 112, 115, 123, 124, 147, 217, 220, 222, 224, 225, 226, 230, 231, 232, 233, 234, 235, 236, 238, 239, 240, 242, 244, 245, 246, 259, 260, 262
Otis, Harrison Gray, BG, 87, 113
Ovenshine, Samuel, COL, 23d Infantry, 100
Owen, W.O., Major, chief surgeon, 88, 122, 157

Pacific Coast Baseball League, 117

Pacific Coast Women's Press Association, 184
Pacific Mail Steamship Company, 218, 222
Pacific Pine Lumber Company, 149
Pacific-Union Club, San Francisco, 91, 92
Palace Hotel, San Francisco, 92
parades, 98, 107
Parkhill, Clayton H., Major, brigade surgeon, 157
Paterson, Van R., former Supreme Court Justice, PHH, 166
Patriotic Home Helpers, 139, 166, 167, 168, 169, 179, 187, 262
Patterson, William, contributor to CE, 197
Pepper, S.F., Private, 20th Kansas, 116
Phelan Building, San Francisco, 88, 89, 92, 93, 94, 95, 143, 245, 262
Phelan, James D., Mayor, San Francisco, 47, 48, 91, 92, 146, 150, 166, 205, 243
Philippine Islands Expeditionary Forces, 71
Philippines, iii, v, 6, 8, 11, 12, 13, 14, 16, 19, 20, 22, 24, 29, 30, 68, 70, 71, 72, 73, 85, 86, 89, 90, 91, 92, 93, 97, 99, 104, 111, 116, 119, 142, 154, 160, 163, 164, 165, 166, 169, 182, 186, 187, 189, 191, 194, 195, 196, 203, 217, 219, 220, 222, 224, 228, 234, 236, 240, 245, 257, 259, 260, 262, 263
physical exercise drill, 106
physicians, 202
Piedmont, passenger ferry, 44
Pittsburgh, PA, 28
pneumonia, 122, 123, 158, 159, 161, 202
Point Lobos Avenue, 63, 66, 157
Point Lobos Avenue Improvement Club, 114
Police Commission, 114
Pope, James W., LTC, depot quartermaster, 74
Portland, ME, 189
Portland, OR, 26, 30, 120
Post Hospital, Presidio, 121
Post Street, 144, 149
postcards, 155
Postal Telegraph Company, 148
Presbyterian Christian Endeavor Society, 188
Presbyterians, 188
Presidio Athletic Grounds, 117
Presidio of San Francisco, 15, 56, 59, 121
press, 95, 96, 184
Proctor, Redfield, US senator, VT, 3
Puerto Rico, 30, 86

quarantine, 122
Quartermaster Department, 119, 220, 221

railroad, 15, 30, 31, 43, 44, 55, 150, 261
Rathbone, Major, 92

rations, 118, 119
Recreation Park, San Francisco, 117, 146
recruits, 28, 97, 99, 100, 103, 105, 106, 109, 119, 153, 160, 161, 231, 236
Red Cross, 43, 46, 47, 48, 49, 50, 51, 90, 92, 107, 108, 117, 124, 139, 140, 141, 142, 143, 144, 146, 147, 148, 149, 150, 151, 152, 153, 154, 155, 156, 157, 158, 159, 160, 161, 162, 163, 164, 165, 166, 168, 169, 179, 184, 187, 188, 195, 196, 197, 201, 202, 238, 242, 245, 262, 263
Red Cross Society, 43, 46, 47, 48, 108, 141, 142, 143, 144, 145, 146, 147, 149, 150, 156, 158, 160, 161, 163, 164, 205, 237, 262, 263
Red Cross Society of California, 47, 141, 144, 145, 149, 156, 164
Red Oak, IA, 32
Redington and Company, importers, 148
Regulars, 5, 7, 12, 13, 21, 31, 50, 53, 55, 56, 57, 60, 65, 67, 73, 85, 93, 98, 106, 109, 112, 155, 160, 164, 165, 180, 184, 192, 193, 202, 205, 217, 230, 239, 243, 246, 257, 261
Reliance, tugboat, 155
Renton-Holmes Lumber Company, contributor to CE, 197
reporters, 49, 89, 90, 91, 95, 217, 246
Requa, Mrs. Mark, 49
Retail Liquor Dealers, 147
retreat, 98, 109
reveille, 98, 109
Richmond District, 57, 101, 181, 185, 242, 243
Risdon Iron Works, 148
Rix, Alice, reporter, *The Examiner*, 90
Roanoke, oceanic transport, 224
Robe, Charles, Major, 14th Infantry, 99
Roosevelt, Theodore, US President, 260
Ruhlen, George, CPT, acting quartermaster, Otis staff, 88

St. Luke's Episcopal, 155, 158
Sacramento YMCA, 188
Sacramento, CA, 143, 189
saloons, 115, 183, 199, 242, 243
Salvation Army, 47, 150
San Diego, CA, 188
San Francisco, iii, v, vi, vii, 6, 7, 15, 16, 17, 19, 21, 22, 23, 24, 25, 28, 29, 30, 31, 32, 33, 43, 44, 45, 46, 47, 49, 50, 51, 52, 56, 57, 62, 63, 66, 67, 68, 70, 71, 72, 73, 74, 85, 86, 87, 88, 89, 90, 92, 93, 94, 96, 97, 104, 105, 107, 108, 109, 116, 117, 118, 119, 120, 121, 123, 124, 139, 140, 142, 143, 144, 145, 146, 147, 149, 150, 153, 154, 155, 156, 157, 158, 160, 161, 162, 163, 165, 166, 169, 180, 181, 183, 184, 185, 188, 189, 190, 192, 193, 194, 195, 196, 197, 198, 205, 206, 217, 218, 220, 222, 224, 226, 228, 230, 231, 232, 233, 234, 236, 237, 239, 240, 242, 243, 244, 245, 246, 257, 260, 261, 262
San Francisco Bar Association, 148

San Francisco Baseball Club, 117, 146
San Francisco Bay, 44, 56, 140
San Francisco Call, 24, 44, 47, 48, 49, 52, 53, 57, 63, 69, 74, 95, 102, 106, 112, 113, 117, 122, 144, 150, 153, 155, 156, 158, 159, 165, 167, 191, 193, 194, 196, 202, 220, 225, 233, 243, 244
San Francisco Chronicle, 45, 53, 54, 60, 61, 90, 95, 106, 109, 113, 115, 116, 117, 119, 120, 166, 167, 182, 188, 190, 191, 193, 200, 201, 203, 222, 233, 236, 242, 243
San Francisco Daily Report, 47, 49, 50, 51, 52, 95, 96, 106, 108, 109, 113, 115, 116, 144, 148, 161, 162, 163, 165, 166, 167, 183, 185, 201, 227, 234, 235, 242, 243, 244
San Francisco Fire Department, 145
San Francisco News Company, 194
San Francisco Press Club, 146
San Francisco Produce Exchange, 145
San Francisco YMCA, 179, 180, 182, 184, 186, 191, 192
San Joaquin, CA, 143
San Jose, CA, 189
San Rafael, CA, 190
Sanborn, F.G., Mrs., chair, Subscription Committee, CA Red Cross Society, 144
Sanitary Commission, 140, 225
Sanitary Corps, 159
sanitation, 139, 242
Santa Clara, CA, 143
Scandia, hospital ship, San Francisco to Philippines, 165
Scheel, Fritz, Mr., symphony conductor, 146
School of Application for Cavalry and Infantry, 70
school of the soldier, 101
Schussler, Hermann, chief engineer, Spring Valley Water Works, 60
Scott and McCord, contributor to CE, 197
Scott, Henry T., president and treasurer, Union Iron Works, 92
Scott, Mrs. A.W., contributor to CE, 197
Secretary of the Navy, 4
Secretary of War, 11, 12, 13, 18, 19, 20, 21, 22, 23, 26, 27, 28, 30, 69, 70, 71, 73, 91, 140, 165, 185, 218, 219, 221, 222, 236, 240, 243, 245
Sehon, John L., CPT, aide-de-camp, MG Otis, 88
Senator, oceanic transport, 225, 237
setting up exercises, 96, 105, 106, 108
17th Street, 205
sewing department, CTS, 202
SF Post Office branch, Red Cross Society, contributor to CTS, 147, 205
Shafter, William, BG, 68, 86
sham battle, 102, 107, 189
Shaw, L.M., governor, Iowa, 26
Sherith Israel Congregation, San Francisco, 155

Sherman, John, Secretary of State, 139
Sherman, William T., MG, 70
shirts, 121
shoes, 55, 121, 160
Shortt, Phil H., First Sergeant, 1st North Dakota, 29, 237
Showalter, J.B., Congressman, PA, 23, 236
Shreve & Co, cutlery importers, contributors to PHH, 169
6th Avenue, 63
skirmishers, 104
Sladen, Fred W., 1LT, aide-de-camp, MG Otis, 88
Sloane and Company, 148
Smith, James F., COL, 1st California, 57, 60, 98, 109, 112
Smith, Robert R., governor, Montana, 201
Smith, William C., COL, 1st Tennessee, 24
Snow, naval constructor, 224
Snure, John, Private, 51st Iowa, 26, 29, 32
Southern Pacific Railroad, 43, 150, 189
Spain, 1, 2, 3, 4, 5, 6, 11, 14, 15, 21, 25, 30, 67, 68, 74, 114, 139, 140, 180, 217, 234, 238, 246, 257
Spanish classes, 203
Sponsler, George M., contributor to CE, 196
Spreckels, Claus, 146, 148, 169
Spreckels, J.D., president, Western Sugar Refining Company, 144, 205
Springfield rifle, 118, 119
St. Luke's Hospital, San Francisco, 158
St. Mary's Cathedral, 198, 202
St. Paul, oceanic transport, 222
stamps, 183, 187, 194, 195, 202, 204
State Board of Trade, 149
Sternberg, George M., BG, Surgeon General, USA, 122
Stetson, James B., Ferry Godfather, 152, 153
Stock and Bond Exchange, 145
stockings, 121
Stockton, CA, 188, 189
Stoneman, Madison U., Private, 1st Wyoming, 32, 104, 113, 116
Strawberry Hill, 116
Subsistence Department, 31, 119
Sumner, Samuel S., COL, USA, 86
surgeons, 121, 122, 140, 156, 159, 200, 201, 202, 225, 244, 245
suspenders, 121
Sutro baths, 116, 117
Sutro Primary School, 146
swimming, 117
syphilis, 122

Tacoma, oceanic transport (freight), 222
Tampa, FL, 30
Taylor, Robert L., governor, TN, 28
telegraph, 30, 50, 68, 89, 94, 226, 235
telephone, 30, 89, 148
Temple Emmanu-El Synagogue, 150, 155
tents, 60, 94, 116, 119, 120, 121, 122, 123, 149, 158, 181, 182, 183, 184, 185, 187, 191, 192, 193, 196, 197, 200, 201, 202, 232
testaments, 32, 184
The Examiner, 24, 47, 49, 53, 92, 94, 96, 102, 107, 120, 143, 167, 168, 187, 191, 193, 194, 196, 241
Thomas Aquinas Reading Circle, 205
Titania, oceanic transport, 222, 224
tonsillitis, 156, 202
Townsend, A.S., Mrs., SF philanthropist, 146, 148, 149
transports, 30, 71, 89, 96, 111, 155, 156, 162, 165, 169, 203, 217, 219, 220, 222, 224, 226, 232, 235, 246, 257
Treasury Secretary, 121
Trinity Church, 149
trousers, 121
typhoid fever, 122, 158

underclothes, 121, 203
undershirts, 121
uniforms, 21, 31, 51, 61, 62, 97, 118, 120, 121, 168
Union Ice Company, 149
Union Lumber Company, contributor to CE, 197
United Christian Endeavor, 190, 191
US Marine Hospital, 56, 121, 156

Valencia Street, 205
Vallejo, CA, 142, 204
Van Ness Avenue, 51, 57
Van Orden, Charles H., soloist, 189
Van Valzah, D.D., COL, 18th Infantry, 99
Vancouver Barracks, 15, 63, 68
Vaughn, Herbert, Bishop, Catholic Truth Society, 197
Virginia City, NV, 204
virus, 121
Visalia, CA, 142
Volunteers, US, 5, 7, 11, 12, 13, 15, 20, 21, 22, 23, 24, 26, 27, 28, 29, 32, 33, 44, 47, 48, 50, 52, 53, 55, 56, 57, 60, 62, 65, 67, 70, 72, 73, 74, 85, 86, 87, 93, 97, 107, 109, 117, 121, 139, 140, 142, 144, 146, 149, 155, 159, 160, 164, 165, 168, 169, 179, 180, 181, 184, 193, 196, 201, 202, 205, 217, 220, 221, 230, 231, 234, 235, 236, 238, 242, 243, 246, 257, 260, 261

Voorsanger, Jacob, Reverend, 150

Waage, C.M., Red Cross nurse (male), 164
Waldeck Hospital, 202
Walker, L.E., Adjutant General, KS, 26, 27,
Wall, M.J., contributor to PHH, 169
War Department, 3, 5, 6, 7, 11, 12, 13, 14, 15, 16, 17, 18, 19, 20, 21, 22, 23, 24, 25, 26, 27, 29, 30, 31, 43, 62, 68, 69, 70, 71, 72, 74, 85, 86, 87, 91, 120, 144, 185, 187, 190, 218, 219, 220, 221, 222, 224, 230, 236, 240, 260, 261, 262
Watt, Rolla V., Christian Endeavorers, 191
Wellesley Hill CE Society, contributor to CE, 196
Wenck, Morris, contributor to YMCA, 188
West Point, 72, 86
Western Union, 148
Wetjen, Cordie, Miss, whistling soloist, 184
Weyler, Valeriano y Nicolau, General, Spain, 2, 139
Wheeler, Joseph, MG, 23
White, Frank, Major, 1st North Dakota, 111
White, Robert H., Major, chief surgeon, US Expeditionary Force, 164
Whitgift, oceanic transport, 224
Widner, W.B., CPT, 51st Iowa, 160
Woods, E.A., Dr., pastor, First Baptist Church, SF, 194
Woods, F.H., contributor to PHH, 169
Wright, C.S., Mrs., chairman, Mothers' Club of California, 154, 195

YMCA "Rushers" basketball, San Francisco YMCA, 184
Yorke, Peter C., Reverend Father, CTS, 198, 199, 203
Young Men's Christian Association (YMCA), 108, 179, 180, 181, 182, 183, 184, 185, 186, 187, 188, 189, 190, 191, 192, 195, 196, 197, 205, 206, 263
Young People's Society of Christian Endeavor, 179, 189, 191
Yups, Sam, Chinatown, 148

Zealandia, oceanic transport, 225, 228

www.ingramcontent.com/pod-product-compliance
Lightning Source LLC
Chambersburg PA
CBHW081846170426
43199CB00018B/2828